HIMAL
D0329914

Other books by Nicholas Luard

Gondar
Kala

N.

HIMALAYA

Nicholas Luard

ARROW

Arrow Books Limited
20 Vauxhall Bridge Road, London SW1V 2SA

An imprint of Random House UK Limited

London Melbourne Sydney Auckland
Johannesburg and agencies throughout
the world

First published in Great Britain by Century in 1992
Arrow edition 1993

1 3 5 7 9 10 8 6 4 2

Printed and bound in Great Britain by
Cox & Wyman Ltd, Reading, Berkshire

ISBN 0 09 968470 5

For Francesca Luard

1

Iona screamed in her sleep.

Waking an instant later, she could still hear her voice echoing through the top of the house. Her hand jerked up to her mouth. As she tried to choke off the sound, she bit on her thumb so hard she almost drew blood.

She lay trembling in the darkness and listened.

There were two fears now. The first, the panic that had come from the nightmare, was already fading. It would come back – it always did. But for the moment the fanged shapes which prowled the darkness had retreated into their lairs. The second fear, the dread of anyone having heard her, was vivid and needle-sharp.

Iona glanced at the bedside clock. The angle of the slim phosphorescent hands told her it was 10 p.m. She closed her eyes in relief. At least her mother wouldn't have heard. Her mother had gone out to a dance and wouldn't be back until well after midnight, maybe much later.

There were still the other people in the house. Cummer, the butler. Hartley, her mother's lady's maid. And Kate, the daughter of one of the tenant farmers at Mainwarden who had accompanied her to London to look after Iona's clothes. The pudding-faced Kate would be asleep. She slept like the dead. Cummer would be in the basement pantry with his bottle of whisky. If Cummer had heard the scream, he would simply have ignored it.

That left only Hartley. Hartley would certainly be awake watching television. Shrewd and acid-tongued, she was also inquisitive and a trouble-maker. If Hartley had heard, she would want to know what had happened, and no matter what Iona said Hartley would tell her mother. All Iona could hope was that the television had drowned out the sound.

Iona began to count. If she reached fifteen without hearing steps on the landing, she was safe. She got to nine, then she froze. There was the unmistakable tap of feet outside. The doorhandle turned and a shaft of light fell across the floor.

'Darling!'

It wasn't Hartley. Sickeningly and bewilderingly, it was her mother's voice. For an instant Iona thought of huddling under the bedclothes and pretending to be asleep. It was too late. Her mother had crossed the room and was standing by the bed.

'What on earth was that, child?'

Mrs Howard sat down. For a few moments she held Iona to her. Then she leant across and switched on the bedside light.

Iona blinked at the sudden glow before her eyes adjusted to the brightness and she saw her mother. Iona gasped. When Mrs Howard was going out, Iona was usually called down from the nursery to kiss her goodnight. That evening she must have been in a hurry, because Iona hadn't been summoned before she left.

Dorelia Howard's appearance always dazzled the child. Tonight, materializing out of the darkness without warning, her beauty was breathtaking. She wore a shimmering gown of deep forest-green that plunged in a deep V between her breasts. Round her neck was a slender choker of emeralds set in antique gold. The incandescent green of the jewels echoed the colour of the dress, while the gold reflected her hair piled high on her head.

Between the two greens and the two golds, fabric and stone, metal and the gathered curls, Mrs Howard's eyes gazed down at her daughter. 'I asked you a question, darling,' she went on. 'What happened?'

Iona stared up at her in silence. She couldn't answer – she *wouldn't* answer.

'It was your silly nightmares again, wasn't it?'

Her mother's voice was irritable and accusing. Mrs Howard waited. Miserably, Iona nodded.

'For goodness' sake, Iona, I don't know what's come over you. You were never like this before. You're here in this big safe house. What on earth is there to be scared of?'

Iona didn't answer her directly. 'I thought you were going out,' she said.

'Of course I am. I'm going to a dance, just like I told you. I remembered at dinner I'd forgotten my keys so I came back to get them while Cummer was still up.'

'Isn't Dad going with you?'

'No, he's busy. He had some work to do. He's gone to his club.'

'Will Sean be at the dance?'

Mrs Howard hesitated briefly. 'Heavens, child, I've no idea. Why do you ask?'

'I like Sean very much.'

Iona didn't like Sean at all. She hated the stocky Irish-American with his rumpled hair and beery smell, but at that moment she knew it was the right thing to say.

'If I see him, I'll tell him that,' her mother smiled. She glanced down at her watch, a tiny shell of silver set with diamonds. 'Darling, I really must go. You are going to be sensible, aren't you? No more silly nightmares, promise?'

Iona nodded.

'That's my good girl –'

As Mrs Howard reached out for her daughter she paused. She studied the child for a moment.

Iona was twelve, almost thirteen. Slim and long-legged with a wiry small-boned body that was much stronger than it looked, she had her mother's cat-like green eyes but her father's hair. In place of Mrs Howard's short golden curls, Iona's hair was long, thick, and raven's-wing black. Or rather it had been long until Iona hacked it off with a pair of scissors at Mainwarden.

That was a few months ago, soon after the nightmares started. It led to the worst quarrel she and Iona had ever had, although Mrs Howard made no connection between the screams in the night and the bizarrely shorn waif she'd been confronted by at breakfast one morning. Iona's hair was growing out now, Dorelia Howard noted with satisfaction. Soon her daughter would once again be, if not an adornment, then at least a presentable accessory in her life.

The nightmares were infuriating, particularly when there were weekend guests at Mainwarden. Here in London they didn't matter so much – apart from the staff, there was no one in the house. The child didn't seem able to explain them but they were triggered, Mrs Howard guessed, by the approach of adolescence. Whatever their cause, she fervently hoped they would soon pass. At times she needed to summon up all her patience to stop herself from slapping the child.

'Sleep well, darling –' She hugged Iona again, then she turned off the bedside light and stood up. At the door she glanced back.

'And remember, there's nothing to be frightened of.'

The door closed and the glow from the landing was cut off. Iona lay in the darkness gazing at the ceiling.

Her mother's scent hung in the air round the bed. It was called Joy and it came in bottles labelled Patou. It was the first smell Iona remembered, hovering over her cradle when she was a baby. It had marked her mother's presence, or at least her passage, ever since.

Iona drew it into her nostrils and tried to hold it inside herself, tried to prevent it from escaping. The scent was safe. While it was there with her, comforting her, she might be safe too. If she lost it, she was in danger again. Her mother was wrong – there was a vast amount for Iona to be afraid of.

The monsters were still lurking among the deepest shadows in the darkness beyond the bed. They came closest to her when she slept, in what her mother irritably described as the silly nonsense of her nightmares. What her mother didn't know was that the monsters didn't go away when she woke. They merely drew back and hid themselves until night returned, then they advanced and encircled her again.

Apart from Iona herself no one knew that. There was no one she could tell. Often, it seemed to Iona, she lived alone in a private world that existed side by side with the world where everyone else lived. She could look across and see everyone bustling about there – the girls she went to school with, her parents and their friends, the farmers at Mainwarden and the staff in London – but she couldn't speak to them. Even if she shouted they remained unhearing, cut off from her by an invisible but impenetrable wall.

Iona had always known she was different, although she didn't know why. Sometimes she thought it was the way she spoke. The girls at school teased her about her accent – a mixture of Boston American from her mother and clipped Oxford English from her father, with the occasional burr of a phrase she'd picked up in Suffolk or on her uncle's estate in Scotland. But some of the other girls, like tubby little Mercedes Allende whose father was the Peruvian ambassador, spoke even more strangely and no one seemed to notice that.

It wasn't the way she looked either, Iona was sure of that too. It could only be something inside her, something she must have been born with. Iona guessed it was the reason she didn't have any friends. She never brought anyone back from school for supper, or had them to stay in the holidays like the other girls did. That was another source of irritation to her mother, although it had never worried Iona. Iona was happier on her own.

She had Misty. As solitary and self-contained as Iona herself, the cat was a much better companion than any of the girls – or she had been until six months ago. Then the monsters invaded Iona's life and everything changed. For the first time Iona felt an almost desperate longing to break through the invisible wall and talk to someone in the world on the other side. It was as impossible as it had ever been.

Before she had been alone in safety. Now she was alone in fear.

One of the strangest and most bewildering things about the monsters was the place they came from. It was quiet and peaceful. The only sounds were birdsongs, the only movements the flicker of a butterfly's wings beyond the glass or a kestrel hovering against the sky above. Iona knew that because she had walked among them there. She had seen their huge bodies and their tranquil eyes. They hadn't been threatening then. They had been grave, almost sorrowful.

Mr Simpson the gardener had shown them to her. He respected them. He thought of them, he once told Iona chuckling, as his silent friends. They had become her friends too. And then suddenly, inexplicably, they had changed. Iona had no idea why – she only knew that something terrible must have happened. As her mother's scent began to fade, Iona frantically tried to bring Mr Simpson's face to mind.

No one in the world beyond the wall was entirely safe, but a few people had a measure of safety, something she could trust. Her mother had her scent. Mr Simpson had his face, old and whiskery and as gnarled as the thorn roots he dug up in the walled garden, but steadfast and reassuring. Mr Simpson might stand between her and the terror into which the creatures had turned themselves.

Iona clung to the little one-eyed teddy bear on the pillow beside her. Lying utterly still she concentrated on the old gardener.

2

'It's a secret,' Mr Simpson said, 'so ye're not to tell anyone.'

Iona crossed her arms over her chest. 'Not even if dark death threatens,' she replied fervently.

Iona couldn't remember where she'd heard the words, but they had impressed her deeply. It was a real oath. Secrets always had to be protected. She didn't know yet what this one was but, with a tingle along her spine, she sensed it truly warranted an oath to guard it.

The old gardener chuckled. 'I won't hold ye that far,' Simpson said with his soft Scottish burr. 'But it was private to your granddad, and I've always been minded to keep it so since the old gentleman passed.'

'Is Misty allowed to come?' Iona asked.

White and blind in one eye, the cat crouched on the ground behind her. Iona had named her Misty – it was short for Mysterious – when she'd been found as an abandoned kitten in the coach-house. As she grew up Misty had taken to following Iona everywhere, almost like a dog. She was watching Iona now through her single pale blue eye.

'If ye don't talk, I doubt Misty will.' Simpson chuckled again. 'Come on the pair of ye.'

The old man set off through the walled garden. With Misty padding in her footsteps, Iona followed him.

It was an early summer evening. Mainwarden was behind them. The rose-red brickwork of the Elizabethan mansion glowed in the late sun. Light flared off the leaded panes of the windows and smoke lifted from the tall chimneys, on one side from the kitchen range and on the other from the fires that had just been lit in the great hall and in the bedrooms above. Beyond lay the rolling wooded Suffolk countryside.

Iona loved Mainwarden. It was far more her home than the tall elegant house in London would ever be, though her mother insisted Mainwarden was just for weekends and the Boltons was where they really lived. Mainwarden belonged to Iona's father, Michael, the younger of her grandfather's two sons. He had inherited the house and estate on his father's death long before Iona was born, even before he had married Dorelia. The family's much larger house and lands in Scotland had gone to his elder brother who had never married, and in due course the Scottish inheritance would come to Michael too. Meanwhile he had Mainwarden.

Dorelia had never liked the house. When she first saw it only a month before her marriage to Michael, it was in an appalling state. Cold, damp and mouldering, it represented everything that Dorelia most disliked about the British countryside. As a wedding present to Michael – and in her own interests – she'd had the house renovated from the cellar to the roof. She didn't like it any more afterwards. Suffolk was dull and remote, and Mainwarden remained lonely and oppressive, weighed down by its age and history.

The house in the Boltons, in the richest, most fashionable area of London, was very different. That had been Dorelia's wedding present to herself. It would never be home – nothing could replace Manhattan where she'd grown up or Martha's Vineyard where she kept a summer house – but the tall elegant building in South Kensington was an adequate substitute.

'Through here.'

At the far end of the garden Mr Simpson opened a door. Beyond was a heavily overgrown path running beneath a copse of dark-leafed kermes oaks. Stamping down the briars and nettles, Simpson walked forward. Avoiding the whippy branches, Iona tramped on in his wake. Finally the old man stopped. At his side Iona stared ahead in astonishment.

She had never before been this far beyond the walled garden into the woods. The path they'd taken ended in a glade, which unlike the path had been neatly cleared. At its centre was an ornate glass-walled pavilion with turrets on the roof. The turrets and the building's wooden frame were painted a deep luminous blue-green. Though chipped and peeling after years of exposure to the weather, the colour was still the strangest and most vivid Iona had ever seen.

The scent of cut grass rose into the air, butterflies fluttered in the shafts of sunlight between the surrounding trees, the air was full of birdsong and a kestrel hung against the sky. With the sun gleaming off the panes the building looked like some abandoned fairy palace.

Mr Simpson glanced at the closely trimmed turf and grunted in satisfaction. 'Promised your grandpa I'd always keep it tidy,' he said.

'What is it?' Iona whispered.

'Ah, sometimes I'd like to know that myself,' Simpson replied. 'Your grandpa's own design, it is. He copied the colour from the garden of some Frenchie painter. That's what he told me. Said it had to be special because of what he was putting inside. He wasna joking either as ye'll see for yourself.'

Simpson crossed the clearing and stopped before the pavilion's door. He produced a heavy key from his pocket and put it into the lock. There was a rusty scraping sound and the door opened. Iona stepped inside and blinked for a moment at the light dazzling through the glass. Then she froze. The hairs on her arms rose and she had to struggle not to scream.

Iona was surrounded by monsters.

They were on every side of her – huge shambling creatures with bodies covered in thick dark hair, cold hard eyes and scowling faces charged with menace. The breeze moved the branches outside, the light and shadow rippled over the creatures, and they seemed to prowl towards her. Iona whirled round, about to run in panic. Then she noticed that Misty was rubbing unconcernedly against her legs and the old gardener was grunting contentedly again.

Somehow she managed to calm herself and, heart pounding, forced herself to look back. The monsters were still gathered round her, but they were keeping their distance. She blinked at them. They hadn't moved and suddenly she realized why – they were stuffed like the animals in the Natural History Museum in Kensington, the place she always called the stuffed zoo.

'Mothballs,' Simpson said. 'Can't beat them for keeping a hide like the good Lord made it.'

Slowly the racing of Iona's heart stilled. 'What are they?' she asked.

They were monsters, of course, anyone could have seen that. But they must have a name.

'Damn great monkeys if you ask me,' Simpson replied. 'But not to your grandfather. Gorillas, he said they were. Shot them somewhere in Africa before the war, he did. Had them stuffed and mounted in London. Then he built this and brought them up here. His pride and joy, it was.'

Slowly Iona walked forward.

In all there were nine or ten gorillas. Some were male, some female, and one, much smaller than the others, must have been shot very young. Close at hand they seemed very different from her first terrifying glimpse of them. Their size and strength were still awesome, but the menace had vanished. Their eyes weren't cold or hard at all. They were gentle and sad.

Iona stopped in front of the largest male. He had massive sloping shoulders, arms like treetrunks and silvery grey hair on his back. She reached out timidly and touched him, letting her hand rest for a moment on his huge chest. From out of his great brooding face the gorilla seemed to gaze back at her, not in threat, but thoughtfully, almost protectively.

In that instant the last of her fear vanished. The creatures were still monsters. Nothing that looked as they did could be anything else. But until then Iona had believed all monsters were bad and dangerous. She'd been wrong – these were friendly monsters. If she needed any confirmation, it came from Misty. The cat sprang from the floor and climbed up the gorilla's arm. She settled down on its shoulder, curled herself into a ball and began to purr.

'Why are they a secret?' Iona asked.

'As a young gentleman he was a mighty hunter, your grandpa,' Simpson answered from behind her. 'Then he changed his ways. Said there were too few beasts left in the world, and those that remained shouldna be harmed. I think mebbe he was a wee bit regretful he'd shot these ones, although they're such ugly brutes I never kenned why. But when he put down his guns, he closed this place up and kept it private to himself –'

He paused. 'Well, if ye've seen enough, I'll need to be locking up. I must be away home for my tea.'

Iona spun round. 'Oh, please can't I stay with them?'

'They don't frighten ye?'

She shook her head vigorously. 'They're beautiful.'

Simpson looked at her in amusement. She was a strange little creature herself, the old gardener thought. The few visitors he'd brought here in her grandfather's time had been scared fit to bust by the sudden appearance of the gorillas under the pavilion's shadowy glass. Most of them couldn't wait to get away. Not Iona. After her initial surprise, the child had wandered among the great apes as fearlessly as if she'd known them all her life.

Perhaps, he reflected, the confidence had come down to the girl from her grandfather. To Simpson the child sometimes looked like a scarecrow turning in the wind, pale and thin and gawky. Her grandfather would have been horrified by the shock of her ragged hair – the Lord knew what had made her cut it off – but he would have recognized her spare sinewy frame and admired the boldness in her glance. The old gentleman always liked a pretty face. When Iona had colour in her cheeks and her great green eyes shone with laughter, she could be the bonniest lassie he'd ever seen.

Simpson felt in his pocket and gave Iona the key. 'Make sure ye lock it for me then. We can't have anyone wandering in here unawares. They might have a heart attack.' He went out.

As the door closed behind him, Iona sat down cross-legged on the floor and stared up at the huge creatures standing frozen on their plinths around her.

A long time later she became aware that distantly someone was calling for her. Iona shook her head as if she were coming out of a trance. She glanced at her watch – it was suppertime. Iona realized guiltily that she and Misty had been there for two hours. Calling for the cat to follow her, she stood up, locked the door and ran back to the house.

That night Iona dreamed of the monsters for the first time. As so often within moments of waking she couldn't remember what happened in the dream, but she knew it was a quiet, happy one. She told no one about the gorillas, not even her mother, but after that she often borrowed the key from Mr Simpson. With Misty behind her she went to the pavilion and sat wondering about the mighty creatures, while the cat slept in the sunlight on the shoulder of the great male.

Iona often dreamed of the gorillas after her visits. She never man aged to remember what the dreams involved, but like the first one they were always happy. In the morning she would wake smiling.

And then one night without warning everything changed. The creatures looked the same as they'd always done, but they were no longer friendly. Something had infected them with anger and menace. They had suddenly turned into ruthless hunters greedy for prey, and the prey they wanted was Iona. When darkness came they watched and stalked her from every side.

It was then that the dreams became nightmares.

3

'No, I will not accept it,' Dorelia Howard snapped.

At her side Charles Lefanu, her lawyer, lifted his head sharply. He tried to keep his surprise at his client's reaction from showing on his face.

'It was only an outline formulation, of course,' Lefanu said. 'But we felt it offered a path forward –'

'I've changed my mind,' Dorelia interrupted. 'Every time I give an inch it's taken to measure a mile. Not any longer! I've had enough.'

Across the table Mr Greenburgh saw his adversary's discomfiture. Greenburgh leant forward.

There were eight people in the vaulted conference room off the Strand. Seated on one side of the long mahogany table were Dorelia Howard, Lefanu and his two assistants. On the other side, representing her husband, were Greenburgh and the two members of his legal team. Michael Howard, distancing himself as always from anything he found distasteful, was leaning back in his chair at the table's far end. His long legs were stretched out casually in front of him, and he yawned repeatedly in simulated boredom.

'Perhaps you'd clarify that, Mrs Howard,' Greenburgh said.

Dorelia opened her mouth to reply. Before she could speak Lefanu recovered from his embarrassment and stood up.

'I think this would be an appropriate moment to take a short break,' he put in quickly.

At the end of the table Michael Howard said something inaudible and gave his languid mocking laugh. Lefanu saw Dorelia's nostrils flare with anger. He quickly took her arm. 'I wish to speak with you in private,' he added firmly.

Lefanu was almost seventy and his hair had long since turned white, but age hadn't taken away his natural authority and he was still strong. Somehow he managed to manoeuvre her out of the room. As the door closed behind them, Michael Howard's laugh rang out again.

'The bastard – !' Dorelia's eyes were narrowed and her voice was chilling in its venom. 'I'm not playing games with that greedy arrogant prig a moment longer. I'm going to tell him to go fuck himself!'

She struggled to get past the lawyer and back into the room. Lefanu barred her way.

'What do you really want?' he demanded. 'Your daughter or to insult your husband?'

Dorelia stared at him. For a moment the hatred surging through her body seemed to be directed at the stooping figure in front of her. Then she swung round and, shaking with fury, walked away. Lefanu followed her.

'Here,' he said.

He stopped beside a door midway along the passage. Waving his two colleagues away, he ushered Dorelia into another, smaller conference room.

'Sit down, my dear,' he said. 'Don't say anything for a moment. Just give yourself a chance to calm down.'

For once Dorelia obeyed him. The old lawyer sat opposite and looked at her across the table.

How long had he known her? If Iona was almost thirteen, it must be a couple of years longer than that, when Dorelia had been barely twenty-two. Her family affairs in America were looked after by attorneys for whom Lefanu's firm acted as London correspondents. She'd come to see him on some small matter within a few weeks of arriving in Britain, and he'd represented her ever since.

As a client she was of considerable value to the firm, perhaps the most valuable private client they had ever had. Even at twenty-two Dorelia Carnethy, as she then was, was immensely rich. A year later when her widowed father died and Dorelia, his only child, inherited his fortune, she became one of the richest young women in international society.

Yet to Lefanu she was much more important than just a client. He knew about her background even before she came to see him. The stormy childhood, the philandering father, the mother who drank and gambled and committed suicide when Dorelia was seven – and the immense wealth on both sides of the family which, if it didn't cause the misery, then certainly supported all the indulgences that accompanied it.

A kindly, tolerant man, Lefanu had been prepared to be sympathetic to her. He hadn't been ready for the way in which his heart seemed to turn over in his chest when she entered his office. He was fifty-five then. He stood up as his secretary opened the door, came round his desk and held out his hand – then stopped in mid-stride.

He knew Dorelia was beautiful. The endless press and gossip-column photographs in his file had told him that, but the photographs didn't begin to do her justice. They didn't show her vulnerability, the wary innocence in her immense eyes, the wonderful sculpted lines of her face and body, the incandescent radiance of the few smiles she gave him as they began to talk.

Often afterwards, Lefanu would wryly acknowledge to himself that he'd fallen in love not once in his life as his entire upbringing dictated he should have done, but twice. The first time with his wife, the second with Dorelia.

After fifteen years of increasing involvement in Dorelia's affairs, he'd learnt much more about her. Most of it, Lefanu candidly but privately admitted, was not to her credit. She was frequently and increasingly arrogant to the point of being imperious. She was wilful. She changed her mind impulsively without regard to anyone else. She had a sharp sarcastic tongue. According to her whim she could be cold, ruthless and cruel, mindlessly, needlessly cruel.

Above all, she was selfish. She had acquired or inherited the habits of her parents, the habits of self-indulgence. Her inheritance allowed her to express them at her own choice and convenience. Whatever Dorelia wanted, Dorelia obtained – and God help the man, animal, or even child who stood in her way.

Lefanu had watched her over the years. He had seen the worst of what had emerged and hardened in her. Strangely, as he sometimes ruefully reflected too, it made no difference to what he felt – in a way he loved her still more deeply. At thirty-seven her beauty was more vibrant and heart-stopping than ever, her body more voluptuous and enticing. Her mind was sharper and her wit, when it was tempered by the occasional flashes of generosity, funnier and more vital.

And now he had to deal with this. Not the divorce. That was part of his business as a lawyer. Lefanu advised on divorces and the issues they raised every week of the year. Dorelia's divorce from

Michael Howard might be immensely bitter, complicated and costly for both sides, but in essence it would still be another severance of a marriage adjudicated by the courts.

The 'this' in the equation was the child named Iona.

Lefanu and his wife were childless. Endless medical tests on both of them had failed to establish where the cause of the problem lay. All Lefanu knew was that, in his heart and his mind, he did have a child. His child was Dorelia Howard's daughter.

If Dorelia had a fault that he found difficult to forgive, it was the way she treated Iona. Her carelessness about the child equalled that of her husband – the only man in Britain, Lefanu sometimes thought, who was also her equal in selfishness. All Iona's life neither of them had paid her any more interest than they'd have given a pet animal.

As far as she'd been brought up at all, Iona had been raised by the family servants Michael Howard had inherited and whose wages Dorelia's wealth paid for. When they decided to divorce, the last matter Lefanu expected to be contentious was their daughter. In fact, Iona had turned out to be the most bitterly divisive issue of all. For reasons Lefanu was far from understanding but which he guessed stemmed from pride and a mutual desire for vengeance, both were single-mindedly determined to gain custody of the child.

An image of Iona flashed across his mind. Late for supper, she was running towards the house across the south lawn at Mainwarden where Lefanu was spending a summer weekend. Lefanu watched her from one of the windows in the great hall. She was barefoot and wearing ragged jeans and an even more tattered T-shirt. Previously, in spite of her thinness, he had thought of her as awkward and ungainly. Never again.

Iona moved with the grace of a young racehorse testing its speed and balance. She hurdled the lavender hedges, swerved gracefully between the cherry trees, straightened her course and raced for the house. Her black hair fanned out in the wind and her face was pale, it was always pale, but her great green eyes – the eyes she had inherited from Dorelia – shone with eagerness and pleasure.

Unaware she was being watched, she reached the terrace and vaulted the stone balustrade, rising above it like a swirling gust of the evening wind. A moment later she was standing beside Lefanu in the great hall. Barely panting, the child gave him a quick smile.

A moment later Michael and Dorelia had come into the room. As they entered, a shutter seemed to come down over the child's face. She kissed her mother politely, mumbled something, and vanished. Lefanu hadn't seen her again before he left.

Lefanu shook his head and gave a rueful private grimace at the memory. One day the girl would be not only a great beauty, but a great heiress. It was not her beauty that concerned him now, but her inheritance. That would come down to her from both her parents but above all from Dorelia.

'Are you thinking now with that fine Yankee brain of yours, or still with your kneecaps?' Lefanu asked.

Dorelia Howard glanced up at him. She smiled. 'Yes,' she said. 'I've simmered down.'

'Good. Let's take what they were saying point by point.' Lefanu raised his hand warningly. 'Don't burst out on me. Just tell me the truth. Who's this Sean Ryan they want to join in the action?'

Dorelia flushed. Then she said, 'He's an American writer, a very good one. He lives in New York and he's a friend of mine.'

Lefanu was silent. He glanced down at the file in front of him.

'This was handed me by your husband's solicitor, Mr Greenburgh,' he said. 'Of course, he's putting on pressure, pushing a point. But it shows photographs of you and Mr Ryan all over the place. Venice, Seville, here in London ten days ago coming out of Annabel's nightclub –'

He paused. 'The impression it would give – to a judge at least – is that Mr Ryan's a very close friend indeed.'

Dorelia's head jerked up. To anyone else she would have snapped an obscenity and told them to mind their own business. Lefanu wasn't anyone else. She gazed at the lawyer, fighting down her anger, then she lowered her eyes and nodded.

'OK,' she said, 'he's my lover. I don't mean that in the silly banal sense. I mean –'. She hesitated, searching for the words. 'I mean he's a very fine man. He loves me, I think.' The enchanting, almost doubtful smile crossed her face. 'Well, whether he does or not, I love him.'

'Several of the stories,' Lefanu added guardedly, 'state that Mr Ryan has convictions for drug possession and assault.'

'Oh, for Christ's sake, Charles!' Dorelia did burst out now. 'That was back in the late sixties. Everyone was into drugs then. A hell of a lot of people, like Sean, were into radical politics too. They clashed with the police. It's over twenty years ago – Sean was just a kid then.'

'And these other charges Mr Ryan faced. Sexual assault and attempted rape. That was only four years ago.'

'Charles, you can't believe that garbage!' she exploded. 'It was a total put-up job. The girl was an actress, a casual friend of Sean's. She asked him to get her a part in a movie someone was making based on one of his books. Sean tried but failed. The bitch didn't believe him. Out of spite she went to the police with this crap about him attacking her –'

Dorelia paused. 'Anyway,' she added triumphantly, 'the case was thrown out of court.'

Lefanu shook his head. 'It didn't *come* to court,' he said. 'In this instance that's rather different. After representations from both sides the district attorney decided to suspend the criminal proceedings. He was persuaded, as I read his report, that Mr Ryan had offered compensation to the girl which had been accepted. The district attorney decided it was a waste of public money to take the matter further. However, he added that the charges would remain on file as a caution against Mr Ryan's future behaviour.'

Dorelia glowered at him. 'So what?'

'I will tell you exactly, Dorelia.' Lefanu crossed his arms over the table. 'The principal issue here is custody. Your husband's lawyers will argue your relationship with Mr Ryan means that if custody were given to you, Mr Ryan would stand in a father's role to Iona. They will produce evidence of his convictions for drug use and violence. They will also say charges remain outstanding for sexual assault and rape –'

Lefanu shook his head. 'Come on, Dorelia. You're a highly intelligent woman. I need hardly tell you the effect all this is likely to have on the judge.'

Dorelia was silent. 'Who the hell's side are you on?' she demanded bitterly.

Lefanu gave a weary reflective smile. 'If every conscientious lawyer had a penny for each time a client asked him that,' he replied, 'we'd all be very rich men. I'm on your side, of course, but not just on yours. I have by implication another interest to represent.'

Dorelia frowned. 'Who?'

'Iona. She stands at the centre of this whole dispute.'

'Are you saying that to get custody of Iona – of my own daughter, let me remind you, Charles – I've got to give up Sean because of some filthy lying crap about his past?'

Lefanu shook his head. 'I wouldn't dream of any such suggestion, my dear,' he said. 'Not least, if I'm frank, because I doubt a judge would accept any sudden disavowal by you of Mr Ryan as your new companion.'

'Then what are you saying?'

Lefanu looked away. He wrinkled his face thoughtfully. When he spoke he chose his words with care.

'Historically the courts have always had a disposition to grant custody to the mother,' Lefanu said. 'I think we can win custody of Iona. It won't be easy. Given your husband's intractable position, and the ammunition Mr Ryan provides him, we'll have to fight every inch of the way. In view of the high public profile of you both, I fear the case will be widely reported on press and television.'

'Providing I beat the bastard in the end, I can live with that.'

'I'm sure you can, Dorelia,' Lefanu said mildly. 'But can Iona?'

'Iona?' Dorelia stared at him, bewildered. 'This is between Michael and me. What's it got to do with her?'

Lefanu hesitated. Sometimes Dorelia's arrogance and insensitivity, her blind refusal to consider anyone's feelings except her own, almost took his breath away.

'Your daughter will be exposed to everything that's reported about you and Michael,' he answered. 'My guess is it will be most unpleasant. It will be read or seen by her schoolfriends, in fact her friends everywhere. Children are notoriously cruel. For Iona it could be a horrific experience.'

'Then, for Christ's sake, I'll send her away until it's over.'

'An excellent idea.' Lefanu rubbed his chin thoughtfully. 'It would have to be a place and with a companion acceptable to your husband.'

'To Michael?' Dorelia snorted derisively. 'Why? What's that bastard got to do with it?'

'Michael, whatever epithet you use about him, is Iona's father. His agreement would at the very least be desirable. At worst, in the current circumstances, he could apply at law to stop Iona going.'

Dorelia stiffened. Without giving her a chance to speak, Lefanu went on.

'Isn't there someone you could propose as a temporary informal custodian of the child?' he asked. 'Someone both of you might accept as being neutral. Someone in a position to remove her from the whole theatre of the legal process and its public consequences. Someone who, I would suggest, had Iona's affection too.'

Dorelia glanced away from him and stared at the table. It was made of mahogany and covered in moroccan leather stamped round the edges with gold blocking. The effect was imposing. It was what a conference table in a famous firm of London solicitors was meant to look like. Somehow its very solidity seemed to diffuse the fury that was already rising in her again.

'The only person I can think of is her godfather, my uncle, Robert Cabot,' she said flatly.

Lefanu's eyebrows arched upwards in interest. 'Mr Cabot, the botanist and writer? I didn't know he was Iona's godfather.'

Dorelia nodded. 'In a way he was a father to me. Making him Iona's godfather was a way of thanking him, I suppose.'

'Does Iona like him?'

Dorelia nodded again. 'He's an old man now and a bit of an eccentric. But children like that, and he's always been wonderful to her.'

'I imagine he lives in Boston. I'm told most of his name do,' Lefanu smiled. 'Could Iona go and stay with him there?'

'Yes, of course –' Dorelia paused. 'Except I think he's going away on one of his plant-hunting expeditions. He wrote to me a few weeks ago saying he was passing through London. I think he's off to Nepal, the Himalayas, somewhere like that.'

'Would he take the child with him?'

Dorelia glanced at Lefanu, startled.

For Iona to go and stay in Boston was one thing. Sending her away to Nepal was a very different matter. Dorelia wasn't even sure exactly where Nepal was, except that it was very remote. For an instant a tremor of anxiety ran through her. Then she dismissed it.

Not only did Robert Cabot adore his goddaughter, he was the most competent and reliable man Dorelia had ever known. Nothing would happen to Iona while she was in his hands.

'I can't see why not,' she answered.

'If it is Nepal he's off to, I can't think of anywhere better,' Lefanu said. 'It would keep Iona well away from any exposure to the dispute. It could also arguably be considered an educational experience. How in your estimation would your husband view it?'

'I don't care a nickel fuck how he views anything –'

Lefanu had begun to raise his hand, but she had already stopped.

Dorelia stared savagely at her lawyer. She was transferring her rage from Michael Howard to him. She knew that. Somehow she managed to rein her feelings in. She stood up, walked to the window and turned back. 'I'm sorry, Charles –'

She trusted Lefanu more than anyone else she had met in her fifteen ill-fated years in Britain. She longed to be out of the country now. The whole episode had been an appalling mistake, a prolonged and wasted interregnum in her life. All she wanted now was to be back in New York, back this time with the powerful, interesting and red-blooded man she loved.

'Funnily enough my husband likes my Uncle Robert,' she went on. 'He's the only one of my friends or relations that he does. I think he'd agree.'

'Excellent.' Lefanu gave her another of his vague and careful smiles. 'I think it's a useful moment to return and continue our discussions with the other party.'

He stood up and opened the door for her. As Dorelia walked out, he added, 'Does Iona have any idea of the conflict that's going on?'

Dorelia paused. 'Absolutely not.' She shook her head adamantly. 'It's the only thing that bastard and I agreed on. We decided we would keep everything from her.'

'Very wise, very wise indeed,' Lefanu agreed. 'Divorce can be deeply disturbing for children.'

'But, my God, once it's through I'm going to tell her about that arrogant sadistic prig she calls her father –' Dorelia's anger surged again as they walked back towards the conference room.

'No doubt, my dear,' Lefanu interrupted her mildly. 'For the moment let's concentrate on getting you the custody that will allow you to do so.'

4

'Darling, I've got a surprise for you.'

Iona said nothing. She stood silently in front of her mother. Dorelia Howard was sitting in her favourite chair in the first-floor drawing room of the house in the Boltons. The room was huge, stretching almost fifty feet from the windows on to the street to the garden at the back. Dorelia had had the whole house decorated by one of her friends from New York.

The drawing room blended hard-angled contemporary furniture in steel and glass with rich and blowsy fabrics and wallpapers from a century earlier. The paintings that crowded the walls echoed the contrast. Eighteenth-century seascapes and flower studies were grouped between canvases slashed with great barbaric bands of colour which Dorelia had bought at the openings of Manhattan shows.

Linking everything were flowers. It had been Dorelia's only instruction to the decorator. 'Do whatever you like,' she said, 'but give me space for flowers everywhere. I just can't live without them.' The decorator had done exactly what she was told. Every angle and corner and wall division had been given a table or a plinth for a vase. Even on a late February afternoon with the sky dark beyond the windows and an icy rain drumming against the panes, the room glowed and smelt of summer.

Iona knew the room was elegant and beautiful. She would have known it anyway, even if Dorelia hadn't explained so often what a triumph Devon, the decorator, had achieved and exactly how she'd created it. Iona had inherited her mother's love of flowers, and normally her visits to the scented drawing room were a heady, almost intoxicating delight.

Not today. She was wary and suspicious even before she came in. As soon as she saw her mother's face the suspicion hardened into a cold certainty. Dorelia was wearing her warmest, her most open and affectionate smile. It meant, Iona knew from long experience, that her mother was about to tell her something that wasn't true.

'A really lovely surprise,' Dorelia added.

She paused. Iona remained silent. Her eyes slid cautiously round the room to see if her father was there.

Often, although it happened less of late, her father joined her mother when some decision about Iona's life – a change of school, a holiday visit to New England or her uncle's house in Scotland – had to be taken. Michael Howard never took part in the discussion. He simply sat in an armchair in the background, his long legs stretched out in front of him and a polite, vaguely interested smile on his mouth as he listened silently to his wife..

Today all the armchairs were empty. Michael Howard was absent. He was probably in his study on the floor above. Iona's eyes came back to her mother.

It made little difference that her father wasn't there. It never had done. Her mother always decided what should happen to her. The only time Iona had appealed to him over something she didn't want to do, Michael Howard merely shrugged. 'Your mother is a much better judge than I,' he'd said. 'I'm sure you'd be wise to listen to her advice.' He'd picked up the book by the side of his chair, put on his spectacles and settled down to read. Iona had never appealed to him again.

'Don't you want to know what it is?'

The smile on Dorelia's face began to tighten. She'd sensed it wouldn't be easy, but this was proving even more difficult than she'd expected. Sometimes Iona infuriated her. The child's great elfin eyes seemed to have a chilling capacity to see straight through things to what lay beyond.

Iona shrugged. 'I suppose so.'

Dorelia gazed at her daughter. All she saw was Iona's blank, sullen face. She made a deliberate effort not to lose her temper.

'You're going on a great adventure, darling,' Dorelia said. 'Uncle Robert's making one of his plant-hunting expeditions. This time he's going to the Himalayas. Do you know where they are?'

Iona shook her head.

'They're in Nepal, I think, somewhere like that. Anyway, they're the highest mountains in the world. Uncle Robert's taking porters and tents and everything one needs. And, guess what, you're going with him.'

'Are you and Dad coming too?' Iona asked.

'No, of course not, darling,' Dorelia laughed. 'What on earth would Daddy and I do in the mountains?'

'Then I don't want to go either,' Iona said.

'Why not? You love Uncle Robert, don't you?'

Iona nodded. 'But he's not the same as you and Dad.'

Dorelia caught Iona and held her tight. Every time she felt like slapping Iona in anger, the child would say something that for a moment at least changed everything.

'You are the most enchanting child!' She kissed Iona and ruffled her hair, then pushed her away. 'Listen to me, darling. It's only for a few weeks. You'll have the most wonderful time. And you'll come back with stories that will make Daddy and me green with envy.'

'What about school?'

'Iona, this is much more important than school. Uncle Robert is one of the most famous plant people in the world. For a clever young girl like you, it's the chance of a lifetime. I've spoken to Miss Forbes. She agrees entirely.'

Iona stared at her mother. Miss Forbes was the remote headmistress of her school. Much more important and much closer to Iona was Miss Arnold, her form mistress.

'I bet you haven't spoken to Miss Arnold,' Iona said. 'She says I've got to do a lot of studying at home if I'm to catch up on my history.'

'For heaven's sake, Iona,' Dorelia burst out in exasperation. 'Miss Arnold's only a teacher. She's barely more than a girl herself. It's what Miss Forbes says that matters. Most of all it's what I say.'

'When am I meant to be going?'

'You'll be leaving next week. It's all come about at rather short notice. Uncle Robert made his plans a long time ago. Apparently he has to fit in his expeditions with when the plants flower. As soon as we discovered, we knew it was an opportunity you just couldn't miss.'

'Uncle Robert comes here all the time,' Iona said. 'Why didn't he tell you before?'

'Oh, Iona, please! Don't ask such irritating questions. You're being given a wonderful chance. Just accept it and be grateful.'

'I don't want to go, Mum.'

Dorelia looked at her daughter. She'd told the mutton-headed Kate to bring Iona up to the drawing room as soon as she came back from school. Iona's satchel of books was still hanging over her shoulder. From the moment the child entered the room Dorelia had known there would be problems. Now Iona's face was not so much blank and sullen as mutinous.

Anger rose again in Dorelia. Once more she forced it down and made a last attempt.

'Iona, you love Uncle Robert,' she said. 'Just like him, you love flowers and plants. I've seen seen you so often looking after them at Mainwarden with that wretched old grouch, Simpson. And you love the wilds. I've watched you in the woods there. I've seen you when we've taken vacations at Uncle Harry's house in Scotland. You love mountains too. You're being given a chance to have them all. And you don't want to go –' Dorelia paused. 'Why not, darling?'

'Because –' Iona stopped. Her eyes swung away from her mother's face and scanned the room.

When she came into the drawing room the half-light of dusk still filled the street. The light had gone now, and behind every vase of flowers, behind each piece of furniture, behind every angle in the walls, there were deep shadows. The shadows were like caves. The monsters lived in caves.

The monsters were in the room with her now. In moments of despair Iona had begun to think they would always be with her. Sometimes when they watched her and she saw the look in their eyes, she believed she had even created them.

So far at least they had kept their distance. Iona sensed it had something to do with the fact that her parents had been near her, which was strange because in every other way her mother and father were as remote as everyone else beyond the invisible wall. Sometimes she didn't see them for weeks on end. Her father in particular had never been more than a shadowy figure in her life. It had always been like that and until now it had never really mattered. Iona had simply got on with her life on her own. They were still her parents and like all parents they were safe – safe enough, even if they were unaware of it, to halt the monsters at the foot of her bed.

In the mountains her parents would be far away. Then nothing would stand between Iona and the creatures. In the mountains they would even be able to climb into her bed.

Iona felt cold and giddy. She started to sway. Frantically she struggled to stay upright, to show nothing.

'Iona!' Her mother's voice was sharp. 'You're shivering. Are you all right, darling?'

Iona stepped back. She recovered her balance and nodded. 'It's nothing, Mum. I just got cold coming back from school.'

'You were going to say something to me. What was it?'

'Nothing, Mum. I'll go away with Uncle Robert.'

Dorelia smiled. 'Oh, darling, you can be so delightful when you want. I'm so glad. You'll have the most wonderful time. Listen, I'll tell you what I'll get you before you leave –'

Dorelia put her arms round Iona again. As her mother talked on, Iona stared past her.

Her mother was describing what she planned to buy Iona for the journey. Iona barely heard her. She was gazing at the window over the garden. Beyond the panes it was dark. At the front there was at least the glow of the street lamps. At the back there was nothing. Only blackness.

Iona knew what was waiting for her in the blackness.

5

‘Can I open them now?’ Iona asked.

‘Not until I tell you.’

Iona screwed her eyes even more tightly shut. She listened to the roar of the plane’s engines, and waited.

The instruction had come from Uncle Robert. Apart from Mr Simpson, if anyone else in the world had told Iona to sit in her seat with her eyes closed as she flew towards the Himalayas, she would have ignored them. Uncle Robert was different from other people – she’d shut her eyes obediently.

His name was Robert Cabot. He wasn’t really her uncle, he was her mother’s uncle, and he came from Boston. He was immensely tall and he walked with a limp, striding along with the help of a stick with a horn handle carved in the shape of a sleeping otter. He had white hair, startlingly blue eyes the colour of Scottish harebells, and a craggy, quizzical face that always seemed to be tilted upwards to examine the sky, the birds flying overhead or the approaching weather. He wore herringbone tweed suits, he smelt vaguely of leaf-fires burning in autumn, and Iona loved him.

She loved the way he looked at her when she asked him a question. He would peer down at her, his forehead creased and his eyes narrowed, and rub his chin with the back of his hand. Then he would answer her in his flat American voice, his face so deadpan that Iona never knew whether he was teasing her or being serious. Normally she hated being teased. With Uncle Robert she didn’t mind at all. Even when he teased her he still treated her as a grown-up. No one else had ever done that.

He loved animals too, all animals – even the little one-eyed Misty. That was another bond between them. Iona’s mother thought Misty was ugly and dirty. Uncle Robert didn’t. ‘Don’t be so goddamn prejudiced, Dorelia,’ he’d snorted on one of his visits when Misty appeared with a dead mouse. ‘Cats don’t smell – they’re the cleanest creatures on God’s Earth. And if this one’s lost an eye, it sure as hell hasn't affected her ability to hunt which is what the Almighty programmed her to do. She's as smart as a leopard.'

His remarks hadn't altered her mother's opinion of Misty, but Iona had never forgotten them. She wouldn't have surrendered to her mother over the trip if she'd been told she was going with anyone else except Uncle Robert. His gruff, comforting presence was a shield that would protect her from almost anything – anything except the monsters.

With her eyes still closed, Iona shivered.

She and Uncle Robert had left London eighteen hours earlier. Saying goodbye to her parents had been one of the worst experiences of her life. Not just the goodbyes – Iona had endured them often before, whenever her parents went away on their extensive travels or holidays. She hated them going away – she always had to bite her lip and fight back the tears that threatened to fill her eyes. This time it was she who was leaving. She hadn't cried, but somehow the goodbyes had been even worse.

In the past all three of them had been together, but that morning her father had been in his study and her mother in the drawing room. She'd gone first to the study and kissed her father, then she'd walked into the drawing room to kiss her mother. When Uncle Robert's car arrived outside and the horn sounded, her mother came down to the street, but her father stayed inside.

Iona longed to call up and ask him to come down too. She couldn't of course, she'd never been able to do that. Guessing he was too busy, Iona gave her mother a final hug and got into the car. As they drove away she glanced back. Her mother had vanished, but the front door was still open and her father was standing on the steps. He wasn't looking in the car's direction. He was staring the other way. As she watched he strode away down the street.

The car turned the corner and her father disappeared. Slowly Iona swung round to face the front. Uncle Robert was speaking to her, but she didn't hear what he was saying. Her father hadn't been busy at all – he couldn't be bothered to wave goodbye, neither could her mother. They'd both waited until the car had pulled out from the pavement, then, having despatched her like a parcel, they'd hurried off their separate ways, on their own business.

Iona sat stiff and silent on her seat as her godfather's voice rumbled on.

Two hours later they'd boarded the plane at London airport. They flew through the night to Delhi. At midnight Iona had fallen asleep, thinking she was safe in the warm humming cocoon of the plane's body. She was wrong – the monsters were still with her. They came out of the darkness and gathered round her as hungrily as they'd done in London.

As the plane dipped down for the landing at Delhi, Iona woke. Instinctively her hand went to her mouth to cut off the scream rising in her throat. She blinked at the cabin lights and glanced round. There was nowhere for the creatures to hide, but she knew they were still there. They had boarded the flight and travelled with her.

Beside her, Uncle Robert was leaning forward and peering into the darkness as the lights of Delhi appeared below. Iona reached out and held his wrist. Robert Cabot turned. He gave her a half-smile and wrinkled his face.

'Cardamom, cow-shit and drains,' he said. 'That's India. I can smell it from cloud level and it always makes me as happy as a Boston clam. How did you sleep, young lady?'

Iona managed a smile. 'Fine.'

'Good. Now for four hours of airport tedium. And then the early morning flight to Kathmandu.'

Iona had only the haziest idea where they were going. Geography had never been one of her favourite subjects at school, and the atlas in which her mother had traced her journey meant nothing. All she knew was that she was flying first to India, and then on to the little mountain kingdom of Nepal to the north. Kathmandu was apparently the name of Nepal's capital.

Although the atlas had been meaningless, maps had always intrigued her. With their pale colours and their enigmatic little symbols, they were like strange abstract pictures that seemed to have been painted in code. The maps of Nepal and the Himalayas were the oddest Iona had ever seen. Instead of the usual greens and yellows, they were coloured slate grey, dark umber brown, and in places almost black.

As she looked at them Iona had felt a shiver of fear. She knew the colours on the maps were so dark because they represented the highest mountains on earth. To Iona they suggested more than that. They seemed to chart the furthest edges of the world. Beyond the grey, the brown and the black, there was nothing – only stars and hollowness and the beginning of time.

The monsters came from where time began.

'Almost ready, young lady –'

Iona heard her uncle's voice. The four hours in Delhi airport had passed and they were due to board the flight to Kathmandu. An hour after they took off for Nepal, Cabot told Iona to close her eyes. Now, according to her godfather, they were somewhere over the plains of northern India.

'I'm going to count you down,' Cabot went on. 'Five, four, three, two, one. Right, open your eyes and look!'

Iona jerked upright and opened her eyes.

Through the porthole window she glimpsed whirling streamers of grey cloud. For an instant that was all. Iona peered out more intently. Still there was nothing but cloud. A sense of puzzled disappointment started to rise in her. Then she saw the mountains, and her breath caught sharply in her throat.

The clouds and the mist parted. Spearing through the greyness came lances of white light. The tips of the lances clashed together, sprang apart, and fused into separate peaks of snow and ice. Behind the peaks the sky was bluer than any sky Iona had ever seen, bluer even than over the Hebridean islands lying in the ocean beyond her uncle's estate in Scotland. Yet it wasn't the sky that held Iona spellbound. It was the mountains themselves.

Mantled in mist like a cape tossed round the hips of a gypsy dancer, they seemed to float between the sky and the earth. They were still far off and there was nothing to measure them by, but Iona knew they were vast – grander and more immense than anything she had ever seen, or that her imagination could have conceived. Above all, it was the brilliance of their whiteness that astonished her. Veined with rose, honeysuckle yellow and ripples of gentian blue, their snow flanks glittered with frozen fire like diamonds.

As the plane flew on she might have been staring at the towering fortifications and battlements of a gigantic castle of ice belonging to the gods of the world's beginnings. The mountains were ageless. They had been there before the world began and they would be there when it ended. Deep inside them, Iona knew with instant and absolute certainty, they held the oldest secrets of all.

She narrowed her eyes and pressed her nose against the glass, willing them to come closer, but as suddenly as before the cloud surged outside the windows again and the mountains were gone.

Stricken with disappointment but still dazed by the awesome ramparts of splendour that had flashed before her, she sank back in her seat.

Half an hour later the plane landed at Kathmandu. By then Iona had been travelling for over eighteen hours, and she could barely keep her eyes open. She glimpsed the wooden-walled airport buildings with their ancient smoked-glass lamps and saw throngs of little scurrying Nepalese with mahogany skins and dark bright eyes.

She stumbled wearily. Uncle Robert called out and someone ran forward, a burly Indian who seemed to have been waiting for them. She heard him shout to a group of porters who hurried to pick up their baggage. Ignoring Iona's protests the Indian lifted her in his arms, and the little procession went outside.

Iona remembered nothing else until she woke in her hotel bedroom next morning.

'This is Roshan,' Robert Cabot said. 'Roshan, I want you to meet my favourite goddaughter, Iona.'

It was the following day. Iona was standing under an awning in the garden of their hotel in the middle of Kathmandu. She shook hands with the man Cabot had just introduced.

He looked about forty. He had the dark Nepali skin of the hotel servants, but he was taller and more muscular. He wore a pair of lightweight boots, faded jeans, an open-necked shirt and a quilted sleeveless jacket embroidered with flowers. His eyes were almost black, and the smile he gave Iona was the warmest and friendliest she had ever seen. Iona liked him instantly.

'Roshan is a sirdar, which you might translate as a leader,' Cabot went on. 'He's run all my expeditions. How many does this one make?'

'Five, sir,' Roshan replied.

'Not only is his English superb, as you'll have noticed, young lady,' Cabot said, 'but it's only one of the languages he speaks. How many in all, Roshan?'

'Nine, sir,' Roshan laughed. 'With all the different tribes we have in the mountains, miss, it is necessary for a sirdar,' he explained to Iona.

'Furthermore,' Cabot continued, 'he's not just a sirdar, and the best goddamn one in the country, but a true Sherpa sirdar. Tell the young lady what that means, Roshan.'

Roshan chuckled again. 'When you become a sirdar, you are called a Sherpa whatever tribe you come from. But true Sherpas are a tribe on their own. They come from Everest. That is where I was born.'

'So much for the formalities,' Cabot said. 'For the next month we're both going to be in Roshan's hands, Iona, and of course his team's. How many have we got, Roshan?'

Roshan made a mental count. 'Fifteen,' he replied. 'Eight general porters. Two kitchen men to assist An Sering with the food. Dirdar and Tek Bahdur as support guides. Then myself and, for the first two weeks, my wife.'

Cabot grunted contentedly.

The porters and kitchen hands were always something of a gamble. They would come from a variety of the different Nepalese tribes and Roshan would have chosen them himself from the trekking labour market. The Sherpa was a shrewd, experienced judge of men, but even he wouldn't be able to guarantee that they were all reliable. An Sering, the cook, and Dirdar and Tek Bahdur, had travelled with Cabot before. Although they weren't true Everest natives, they were classified and paid as Sherpas. Cabot knew all three. He liked and trusted them. He also knew they had the deepest respect for Roshan.

Roshan's wife, Sharma, was a new factor in one of his expeditions. Cabot had never trekked with a woman in the support column before, but over the years he had often met Sharma in Roshan's Kathmandu house. She was a plump smiling woman, as strong and capable and vigorous as her husband. She was coming with them for the first two weeks only so that she could visit the remote village where her grandmother lived.

Cabot smiled. He had as few doubts about Sharma as he did about her husband.

'OK, Roshan,' Cabot said, 'let's sit down and tell the young lady where we're going and what we're going to do.'

There was a table under the awning. The three of them lowered themselves into chairs around it. Cabot spread out a map.

'We're here, Iona,' he said. 'Where we're heading for is here –'

Cabot's hand swung across the map. Iona peered down. Her godfather's finger had come to rest on one of the fierce dark brown belts of graded contours somewhere to the north-east of Kathmandu.

'It's a region called the Helambu,' he went on. 'It runs right up to the Tibetan border and then over on to the great uplands beyond. I've been part of the way there before. I'd have preferred to make the whole journey on foot, like I used to, but this part of the Helambu's a damn sight further out, and I'm getting older. So we're going to cheat a bit – we're going to use a helicopter to get us in. Well, we've already used those infernal machines, haven't we, Roshan?'

Roshan nodded. 'The porters, the supplies, the equipment, they were all flown in over the past week. Dirdar and Tek Bahdur have set up camp. An Sering has made his kitchen. They are waiting for us.'

Cabot peered at the Sherpa over his half-moon glasses. 'And Sharma?'

'She is there too. It will be a very good camp. It will have an excellent good kitchen.' Roshan chuckled.

'Fine. So that's where we head at dawn tomorrow. A couple of days to acclimatize. Afterwards we start to trek –'

Cabot glanced at Iona. 'Orchids. That's what we'll be looking for, or that's what I've told the Smithsonian. What those senile old buffoons on the board don't know is that I'm actually after something else. The *Primula himalayensis*, the mountain primrose, in a mutant form. Not white but a deep rosy-violet. It's only been recorded once, but the sighting was good and the description was specific down to the tones of the sepals. If we can find that, it would really be something.'

Cabot stopped and turned to the sirdar. 'What do you reckon on our chances, Roshan?'

Roshan spread out his hands. He gave the bubbling laugh that made Iona like him more each time she heard it.

'You know what we say on Everest, sir. In the mountains the man with the open eyes will find everything he looks for.'

As Roshan spoke a cloud drifted over the sun.

Until then the hotel garden had been so hot and bright there had been no question of them sitting anywhere except under the awning. Suddenly a gust of chill wind swept down from the mountains that ringed the Kathmandu valley. The hotel servants ran out and began to set up screens round the tables.

Cabot shivered. He picked up his cane and limped away from the table. 'We'll go over the details inside,' he said.

Roshan stood up too. He pulled back Iona's chair and beckoned her to follow her godfather. As she walked towards the door to the hotel lobby, Iona saw dark pools of shadow forming beneath the bushes that ringed the lawn.

She swung her gaze away from them and hurried inside.

6

Iona peered out of the helicopter's scarred glass window.

It was well over an hour since they'd taken off from Kathmandu. Robert Cabot was sitting in front of her beside the pilot, while Roshan was perched on the jump seat behind. Occasionally during the flight one or other of them had pointed out something below and tried to shout out what it was. The noise of the helicopter's blades drowned out their words. Iona could only shrug and smile and gaze down in the direction of their outstretched arms. What she saw bewildered her.

The panorama that unrolled beneath them as soon as they rose out of the Kathmandu valley was the strangest Iona had ever seen. From Mainwarden to the Scottish borders to her holidays in New England, she was used to landscapes which were essentially level. They featured occasional valleys and hills, of course, even a few mountains, but in general the land she had always known was flat.

Here the world seemed to have been stood on its side. The only familiar feature was the valleys. Even they were much narrower and steeper than any she'd seen – sheer and tortuous knife-cuts plunging deep and dark into the earth. Everywhere else, soaring above them, the land seemed to have been sliced and stacked vertically on some long-forgotten bed of rock far below.

Somehow the Nepalese people had found a way of colonizing the towering walls and mountain flanks. Once, the whole area from the base of the valleys up to the tree line high above must have been cloaked in forest. Now, most of the trees had vanished. Only a few scattered copses of green remained and between them, rising tier upon tier, were slender terraces of tiny stone-banked fields.

From the air, Iona thought, the terraces looked like a staircase built by some immeasurably tall giant to climb up to his castle in the clouds – or, rather, his castles. For there wasn't just one set of terraces – there were first a dozen, then a hundred, then a thousand. As the helicopter flew on, there were so many that Iona's mind reeled in the attempt to guess their number.

Like ants, but even stronger and more implacable, the Nepalese had crawled up the mountains. Month by month, year by year, century by century, they had snipped away and scissored off the mountain's green and golden cloak. They had piled up the stones, made their terraces and seeded their gardens in the skies.

'Only now there's almost nothing left –'

Iona glanced round.

It was her godfather's voice. Robert Cabot must have been speaking to her for several minutes. She had only caught his words because of a change in the pitch of the helicopter's blades. They were dropping down to land and the pilot had slowed the engine.

'It's not their fault, the poor bastards,' Cabot went on. 'They live in one of the most inhospitable areas on earth. They have to feed themselves and they've done it superbly. They're brave and versatile, and as inventive as da Vinci. The way they work would give a Trojan a coronary before his first coffee break –'

Cabot squinted down through his glasses as the helicopter hovered over its landing-place. 'But, although they don't know it, they're committing matricide. That, young lady, in case the term is unfamiliar, means killing the mother who gave you birth and nurtures you. Which is exactly what the Nepalese are doing to their country.'

The helicopter's wheels touched the earth. For several moments Iona could see nothing as the still-whirling blades threw up a screen of dust and pine needles. The blades came to a stop. The screen drifted away in the morning breeze. The pilot swung open the door and Iona followed her godfather down on to the ground.

Cabot frowned and cast a critical glance around them. Roshan had dropped to the ground too. His eyes were fixed on Cabot's face and his expression was tense. Iona sensed he was waiting apprehensively for her godfather's judgement. Iona looked round too.

The helicopter had landed in a small depression on a high ridge. In the last half-hour of the flight, they had left behind the intricate patchwork of spiralling terraces on the bare slopes beyond Kathmandu. For twenty or thirty miles they had been flying over the same precipitous landscape, but a landscape that was still mantled with the original forest.

Falling away to the south was a series of winding ravines. Plunging downwards like the root-corridors of some writhen, storm-felled tree, the ravines seemed to lead into a bowl of land below. As the shoulders of the bowl were hazed in mist even at mid-morning, it was impossible to make out the contours of the land beneath. On the other side to the north rose the mountain peaks that marked the border with Tibet. Beyond, each way, were tracts of fir and rhododendron woodland.

Much closer, on the edge of the depression where the helicopter had put down, was a group of tents. The site was so high the tents seemed to be floating like kites in the sky. The three largest were separated from the others by an already blazing fire. Gathered in a circle between the helicopter and the fire were about fifteen people.

Cabot inspected the site. 'OK, Roshan, I think at a pinch it'll do.'

He grunted and stepped forward. A moment later he was greeting the Sherpas and porters he knew from his previous trips, and shaking hands with the new members of the expedition.

Behind her Iona heard Roshan let out his breath in relief. He grinned and set off to join Cabot. Then he stopped and swung round.

'Miss, you must meet these people too,' he smiled. 'While you and the sahib are here, this is going to be your home also.'

He beckoned and Iona walked up to him. Together they joined the excited chattering group that had gathered round her godfather. As the brown hands reached out eagerly to shake hers, Iona felt momentarily giddy.

Little more than a week ago she had been trudging home from school through dank, rain-swept streets. Then virtually without warning she'd been plucked from the chill of the London winter, flown a third of the way round the world, and put down here on a sunlit ridge in the Himalayas. Her mother said it was 'educational' and an opportunity she couldn't afford to miss.

Iona guessed that was only half the truth. She loved her mother but she knew from long experience that nothing was ever quite as Dorelia presented it. There was another reason for Iona's being sent away. She had no idea what it was and in the whirl of the journey she hadn't had time to think about it. Now, surrounded by a throng of strangers talking and shouting incomprehensibly as they surged around her, she suddenly felt confused and frightened.

Iona glanced round frantically. She saw Uncle Robert separated from her by a group of chattering porters. At the same moment he looked across and his eyes caught hers. Leaning on his stick he shouldered his way through the porters to her side.

'We're not supposed to say it any more, but they make as much noise as a pack of goddamn monkeys, don't they?' he said. 'Give me some protection, young lady, before they deafen me, and that's an order!'

He reached down and took her hand in his own. Iona squeezed it gratefully. He must have seen something on her face. Only Uncle Robert, she thought, would have noticed it, and then had the courtesy to pretend that the fear was his, not hers. Feeling calmer, Iona smiled shyly and stood beside him as the Nepalese eddied round them.

'*Amaye!*'

The sound was partly a scream, partly a squeal of fear and partly a bubbling giggle of laughter. Both Iona and Robert Cabot glanced round from the fire.

It was after darkness on their fifth night in the camp on the ridge, the last of what Cabot called their 'acclimatization' nights. The campsite was at 12,000 feet. It was the highest level, he'd explained to Iona, at which normal healthy people could begin to adapt to the demands of the thinner air at mountain altitudes without suffering from altitude sickness – a condition that resulted from oxygen starvation.

Cabot had erred on the side of caution. Throughout the five days he'd allowed Iona to take no more than short walks from the camp, always accompanied by one of the Sherpas. If she had shown any signs of giddiness, Cabot had the manpower to move her instantly several thousand feet lower down the mountains. At the very worst he had his daily radio link with Kathmandu. Given his influence in the capital a helicopter, a rare and expensive commodity to anyone else, would have been with them within ninety minutes.

The precautions were unnecessary. The child, as Cabot had guessed, was as strong as an ox. More accurately, she seemed to have the lungs of a Nepalese mountain water buffalo – or at least the lungs of his most experienced porters. Within hours of their arrival she was capable of going wherever the porters went, while Cabot himself had to stay within the confines of the camp.

Cabot looked back at his goddaughter across the fire.

There were two fires in the camp. Theirs, the 'sahibs' fire, the main, symbolic fire beside the mess tent which guarded his and

Iona's sleeping quarters. Then there was the Sherpas' great blaze of branches which illuminated, warmed and provided the cooking source for the camp. It was from there that the scream and the giggle had come.

'*Amaye!*'

The squeal came again. Iona recognized the voice of Sharma, Roshan's plump little wife. In the light of the flames Iona saw Sharma reach out and smack one of the porters on the face.

'What's happening?' Iona asked. 'Are they quarrelling?'

'I doubt it,' her godfather answered.

Cabot called out in Gurkhali. Sharma shouted back with laughter in her voice and Cabot chuckled. 'It's that little monkey Perem,' he said. 'He's teasing Sharma, trying to frighten her with stories of the yeti. It sounds as if he's succeeding.'

Perem was the youngest of the porters, a skinny sixteen-year-old with a mischievous face.

'What's a yeti?' Iona said.

'Good heavens, young lady, you don't know about the yeti? Well, there's no one better than Roshan to tell you.'

Cabot called out again. Roshan came over and squatted down by their fire. 'Yes, sir?'

'Iona's never heard of the yeti, Roshan,' Cabot said. 'Explain what he is.'

The Sherpa laughed and looked at Iona. 'He's said to be the wild man of the snows, miss. He lives up here where it's high. He kills yaks and water buffalo for food. He comes out only at night. Very few people ever see him, but sometimes they find his footprints in the snow after he has gone.'

Iona frowned. She wasn't sure if Roshan was joking or telling her the truth. From his description the yeti sounded more like the ghosties that her childhood nurse, an old Highland Scot, used to frighten her with.

'Is he real?'

Roshan chuckled again. He shrugged but didn't answer.

'Well, have you ever seen him?' Iona demanded.

Roshan shook his head. 'Never, miss.'

'On the other hand,' Cabot put in, 'your aunt's daughter saw him, didn't she?'

Roshan rocked back on his heels, his shoulders heaving with

laughter. But when he leant forward again and raised his hands to the flames, Iona noticed there was a wariness in his eyes.

'She was just a girl, sir.'

'Tell Iona the story anyway,' Cabot instructed.

Roshan looked up at Iona. His face was amused and cheerful, yet under the Sherpa's unvarying vitality and good humour, Iona sensed for the first time uncertainty. It was like the hesitation in his eyes she'd seen an instant before. He had been ordered by the sahib to speak. As a good sirdar he would obey the order, but he would do so reluctantly.

'This girl,' Roshan said, 'she was sent out by my aunt to gather wood. On Everest where I come from that is normal. It is girl's work. At night she did not return. My aunt was frightened. It was too dark then to look for her, but next day all of us in the village came together to search for her –'

Roshan plucked a smouldering twig from the fire. Frowning he examined its glowing end. 'We went far, but we did not find her,' he went on. 'Some of us who had trekked high into the snow, I was not with them, found tracks. Not the girl's, but maybe a yeti's. Those who saw the tracks returned. Darkness was close, snow had started to fall and they could see nothing. The storm blew all night. Next day there was nothing but whiteness –'

Roshan shrugged. 'We could not search further. We thought the girl had strayed from the path, she had fallen, she was dead. Five days later she walked back into the village. She said to my aunt she had been taken by a yeti –'

The Sherpa paused. He looked at Cabot, at Iona, and then back at Cabot again. For once his face was puckered with embarrassment.

Cabot pushed his spectacles up on his head. 'You're not dealing with one of the blue-rinse puritan harridans you usually take out on trek, Roshan,' he said gruffly. 'The kid grew up in the country. She's seen animals couple. She knows her biology –'

He looked round at Iona. 'Believe it or not, young lady, Nepalese girls sometimes get themselves pregnant without benefit of social or religious sanction,' Cabot said. 'Unlike other young ladies in every other society – where, of course, it never happens – they have an acceptable explanation. They were abducted and inseminated by a yeti –'

Cabot paused. 'What Roshan is saying is that his young cousin's disappearance and return should have been followed nine months later by the birth of her child. Except it wasn't, Roshan, was it?'

Roshan shook his head.

'And furthermore, when the kid did eventually get pregnant, her husband warranted that she was what we in the West would call *virgo intacta*. In other words she hadn't lain with a man. So she wasn't using the normal excuse.'

Still stiff with embarrassment Roshan nodded in agreement.

'But what did the yeti look like?' Iona asked.

'My people say there are two sorts of wild men,' Roshan answered. 'One, which is not often seen, is very tall with dark hair all over his body. Some say his hair is red, some say it is brown. The other is smaller and his hair is more pale. That is the one more usually seen. It was one of those that took my cousin.'

'Where did he keep her?'

'In a cave.'

'And that's all?' Iona said, puzzled.

'Yes, miss.' Roshan glanced at Cabot. 'As you know, sir, it's what the girls always say.'

Cabot nodded. 'OK, Roshan. We'll leave you to get back to your fire, so you can stop young Perem tormenting your wife.'

Iona watched him walk away. She was still bewildered. 'I don't understand,' she said. 'Is it like a fairy story? Or are there really yetis? Even Roshan didn't seem sure.'

'He's not,' Cabot answered. 'Once as a child he probably was. But then he grew up and was lucky enough to get an education. He moved away from Everest, came to Kathmandu and became a sirdar. Now he doesn't know. Nor do I, nor does anyone except perhaps the old mountain people –' Cabot paused. Then he tried to explain to Iona.

He told her about the stories heard by the early explorers when they ventured into Nepal as the British Empire expanded northwards from India. They were told the Himalayas was home to a great ape-like creature, which from the descriptions they were given resembled Neanderthal man. For a long time the stories were attributed to the fantasies of a primitive and superstitious people.

Then, much later, mountaineers drawn to the Himalayan peaks periodically came across strange, human-like footprints in the snow at heights where no humans were known to exist or even travel. 'The most famous were found by a climber named Eric Shipton,' Cabot said. 'Shipton was leading an expedition up Everest. He didn't reach the top, but high up on the way he and a fellow climber found these prints. They photographed them. No one's ever been able to say for sure what made the prints –'

He blinked. 'Do you remember I once showed you some old photographs of fairies from a Victorian book?'

Iona nodded. She must have been only five at the time but she'd never forgotten it.

The fairies glowed like tiny ghosts between the trees and bushes at the foot of some great sweeping garden. She'd been entranced, and believed in them unquestioningly. Afterwards when Uncle Robert explained they were fakes, and showed her how the photographer had used cardboard silhouettes and a cunning manipulation of sunlight to create them, she was shocked. More than that, she'd been bitterly disappointed. She'd longed to believe in the fairies, but she knew her godfather was telling her the truth.

'Shipton and his companion weren't frauds,' Cabot went on. 'They were decent, honest men. Their photographs were genuine – no one doubts that. Trouble is, no one has been able to agree what they show. The prints of a high-climbing bear? A langur monkey? A Tibetan holy man? They're all possible, except none of them quite fit – not even when you've made every allowance for sun and snow-melt and everything else. The feel, the pattern, still isn't right.'

There was silence.

On the other side of the camp, the conversation at the porters' fire had subsided. Iona could no longer see the angular silhouette of young Perem. He must have abandoned his teasing of Sharma, and retired to his blanket under the tiny tent he shared for shelter with three of his companions. Sharma was still there, on her feet and yawning. Roshan was beside her stoking the blaze for the last time against the night.

Only An Sering, the cook, was still clattering his pans and giving impatient instructions to his two assistants in the kitchen compound. An Sering was always thinking ahead. He wanted to be ready for the morning. But even An Sering would soon be on his way to his bed.

Iona looked at her godfather. 'What do you think, Uncle Robert?'
'About the yeti –?'
Cabot took off his glasses. He polished them carefully with the paisley silk handkerchief he kept in the breast pocket of his jacket.
'Have you heard of the Loch Ness monster, young lady?'
Iona nodded. Of course, she'd heard of the Loch Ness monster. Everyone who'd ever been to Scotland had heard of the Loch Ness monster – and she'd spent holidays in Scotland at her uncle's house ever since she could remember. The idea of a huge scaled creature which had somehow managed to survive beneath the dark waters of the loch had always seized her imagination. Like any child she had alternately been fascinated and terrified by it.
'Our century's secular logic sneers at the Loch Ness monster,' Cabot said. 'It's a fantasy from a superstitious pagan past, we say. Or it is for the vast majority. Not, funnily enough, for those of us at the cutting-edge of the investigations that are meant to be leading all of us into the future. In short: the scientists, as we like to call ourselves. We measure possibilities by other criteria –'
Cabot settled his glasses on his nose and peered through them. 'Asked about the Loch Ness monster my friend, Dr Sharon, the professor of zoology at Harvard, had this to say. "Science is not in the business of disproving negatives. On the basis of the reported sightings, and the wealth of details which accompany them, any responsible scientist would have to say it is more likely that the monster exists than it does not."'
Cabot stopped. For a long time Iona was silent. She wasn't quite sure what he meant, but she knew him well enough to make a guess.
'So like the Loch Ness monster, the yeti may be real?' she said eventually.
'As a scientist and an occasional gambler on the horses your mother runs at Belmont, I would not bet against it –' Cabot gave her one of his rare smiles. 'I haven't often lost my investments on your mother's horses.'
'But if the yeti does exist,' Iona persisted, 'it would be a monster like the one in Loch Ness?'
Cabot gazed at her. His eyes had the same quizzical slant – at the same time teasing and serious – she knew so often from the past.
'The science of zoology doesn't admit of monsters,' he replied. 'It deals only with the concept of living creatures that evolved over

millions of years from much more primitive forms of life. Man is just one example. Somewhere in the remote past we had ancestors. The yeti, if it exists, might be one of them –'

He paused. 'Whether it's also a monster depends entirely on what you consider a monster to be. Only you, young lady, can make that judgement. But then, of course, you'd have to encounter one to do so.'

Cabot leant back. He rubbed his hip, picked up his stick, heaved himself to his feet and limped over to his tent.

On the other side of the fire Iona sat staring into the flames. If her mother had been there, she would have made Iona go to bed at the same time she did but Uncle Robert was quite happy for her to stay by the fire all night if she wanted. 'Just remember to keep a sailor's eye on the stars and make a species' count of the owls from their calls,' he usually said before retiring.

Iona smiled. She hugged her knees to her chest and looked up at the sky. The stars overhead were tumbling down in great whirls and spirals of phosphorescence, and owls were hooting everywhere.

She wriggled her toes inside her boots, feeling for the warmth of the coals, and thought of the yeti.

7

That night, for the first time since Iona left London, the monsters returned.

She woke and jerked upright. For a moment she didn't know where she was. She blinked and peered into the darkness. She could hear the roar of wind and the rustle of what sounded like water. She might have been at Mainwarden, where the river that ran through the park passed close beneath her window and the wind from the fens often rattled the panes, but at Mainwarden there was always a flicker of light beyond the curtains. Here there was nothing, only blackness.

Then Iona remembered. She was in her tent on the ridge and she'd had the nightmare again. As it came back to her she trembled. It was different from before – and much more frightening. At home the creatures had always threatened her inside her room. There at least she'd had the island of her bed as a sanctuary against them. Now they were hunting her in daylight and in the open, where there was nowhere for her to hide.

In the new nightmare she'd been walking along a path high in the mountains. On either side of the path were steep rocky banks. As she walked Iona became aware that something was stalking her, something dark and hunched that grunted and snuffled behind her. She stopped, whirled round, and glimpsed its silhouette flickering behind the jagged stones. Iona knew instantly what it was – it was one of the monsters and it was catching up with her.

Iona tried to breathe in. She had to escape and she needed air to run, but her mouth was so dry that her breath caught suffocatingly in her throat. Panting and choking, she stumbled away. She moved very slowly. Great weights held back her legs. She dragged them after her, heaving them one by one over the rocks. She tripped and fell, struggled to her feet and glanced back.

There wasn't only one monster behind her now, there were a dozen. They gathered in a pack, the domed shapes of their skulls gleaming against the skyline. The pack spread out. The creatures were heavy, but they moved swiftly. They formed themselves into a horseshoe and trailing their arms along the ground they began to close on her. They were dark and hungry, and they were running as fast as the cloud shadows that raced across the mountain flanks.

Iona ran too but she tripped again. As she plunged forward on to her face she could smell the creatures' breath. She screamed.

Iona knew she must have woken then.

In spite of the icy chill in the air, her skin was glistening with sweat. She remembered screaming but for some reason no one seemed to have heard her. She couldn't understand why. Uncle Robert was in his own tent only a few yards away, and the Sherpas and porters in theirs just beyond. In a panic she fumbled for her torch, switched it on and shone it round. The canvas on one side was bulging like an inflating balloon.

Iona listened.

The wind was howling round the camp with a noise like the roar of cascading water. That was what had made her think she was at Mainwarden. A storm had broken over the ridge and the tumult must have drowned out the sound of her scream. Iona started to relax, then tensed again. In the torch beam she could see a dark shape crawling along the canvas at the foot of her bed. It vanished with the storm's next buffet, but a moment later it was back.

Iona stared at it in horror. Part of her mind told her it was only a shadow moulded on the canvas by the gale. Everything else inside her shouted a warning that it was one of the monsters. In the nightmare that had just ended they'd been closer and more menacing than ever. Now they were prowling out of the realm of sleep into the real world.

The wind changed direction and the canvas rippled again. Now there wasn't just one creature, but two. They seemed to be grunting at each other, then they turned and began shambling towards her along the side of the bed. Iona shone the torch at them. The light must have dazzled them, because momentarily they vanished.

Iona sat motionless. They were still there, she was certain of that. They would be lurking very near her, perhaps even beneath the bed itself, but at any second they would reappear. She knew she had to get out of the tent. Keeping the torch beam fixed on the place where the silhouettes had disappeared, Iona wriggled out of the sleeping-bag and swung herself on to the ground.

She knew exactly what she was going to do. She would go to Uncle Robert's tent. She couldn't tell him why. The monsters were an evil that had been visited on her alone, they were her responsibility and no one else's. She would have to make up a story to explain why she had come, but at least with her godfather she would be safe until morning. After the sun rose the creatures would retreat until night came again, and from her watch Iona that knew daylight was close.

She pulled on her heavy linen mountain trousers with the waterproof pouch of survival equipment that Uncle Robert insisted she carried buckled to the belt, laced up her lightweight boots and draped her quilted jacket over her shoulders. Then she turned towards the entrance, paused and glanced back.

Lying on her pillow as it did wherever she slept was her little ragged bear with its missing eye. The bear had no name. It had been with Iona all her life, and it had never been known as anything but Bear. Bear could do nothing about the monsters, but against every other danger it was her talisman and her safety. She picked it up and slipped it into the pouch, then she bent down and backed outside.

As she emerged into the darkness Iona reeled and staggered. Nothing she'd heard inside the tent had prepared her for the storm's violence. The force of it struck her with the savagery of a brutal blow in the face. The night air was thick with snow and the gale almost blew her off her feet. She clutched the tent's guy rope and regained her balance, but a moment later an even fiercer gust of wind plucked the torch from her hand and knocked her down. Iona lost her hold on the guy rope and tumbled backwards.

She rolled over and over. Finally she managed to scramble to her hands and knees. She searched for the torch and spotted its beam but by the time she had crawled towards it the glow had vanished, buried beneath the snow. She scrabbled desperately in the drifts, but the light was gone. Iona lifted her head and scanned the darkness, looking now for the outline of her godfather's tent.

The Sherpas had pitched Uncle Robert's tent less than ten yards from her own, but she couldn't see it. The churning snow had reduced everything to an impenetrable stinging screen of cold and greyness. Round her the wind snapped and roared and howled. Iona brushed the flakes from her eyes and began to crawl in what she thought was the right direction. A few minutes later she stopped. There was no sign of the tent, only the same icy curtain driven over the ridge by the storm.

She must have chosen the wrong angle. She turned and tried to retrace her footsteps.

It was useless. The snow had obliterated the tracks she'd left only moments before. Hunched and bowed down by the wind's onslaught, she began to cast from side to side. If she couldn't find Uncle Robert's tent, she must come across one of the Sherpas' – their tents had been pitched only a few yards further on.

Ten minutes later Iona had found nothing.

Her teeth were chattering and the bitter air had blinded her eyes with tears. Her face was raw and her feet dragged in the snow that was deepening every instant. She felt more alone than she had ever felt in her life. The entire physical world, the world of rocks and trees, sunlight, earth, stars and people, had been wrenched away from her. In its place was only this icy maelstrom of murderous howling chaos.

She paused. She was lost, but she made a last grim effort not to give up. The campsite had to be within yards of where she was kneeling. If she tried once more, she was bound to find it. Exhausted and sobbing but with her mouth clenched in determination, she set off again.

Seconds afterwards Iona's feet slipped from under her. She twisted, fell on her back and began to slide. She never really knew what happened next. She was plummeting downwards. There was snow above her and beneath her and all around her. The wind howled in her ears, half-buried branches of bushes lashed her skin, rocks buffeted and bruised her. A boulder caught the side of her head. Stunned and sickened with pain, Iona knew she was losing consciousness.

Seconds before she passed out, she sensed in a terror of bewilderment that she must have strayed to the edge of the ridge and tumbled down the great precipitous wall that dropped to the hidden, mist-laden bowl in the mountains beneath. As she plunged through the snow and the darkness Iona knew, in a momentary flash of lucidity, that she was falling over the edge of the world.

Afterwards there was only blackness.

8

Manu came to a halt. Swinging his head slowly from left to right, he sifted the air through his nostrils.

Manu had been doing the same every few minutes for the past eighteen hours. He did it instinctively, without thinking, whenever he travelled more than a hundred paces from the island. Manu's vision was acute, but his sense of smell was sharper still. His nostrils functioned like the eyes of a hunting falcon.

Just as a falcon could scan huge areas of the landscape far beneath it, drawing up into sharp focus a single scrap of ground thousands of yards away, so Manu's nostrils could pick up and decode scent spores carried on the air from distant places hidden from his eyes by the mountain folds. That morning in the aftermath of the storm the wind was light. It made no difference to Manu's ability to read the airstream drifting past.

A cluster of Himalayan primroses had opened in the sun. The flowers were in a sheltered gully at least a mile away, but from the fragments of pollen that reached him Manu could even identify their colour – they were the violet, not the blue variety. A pair of muntjac deer were grazing somewhere out of sight in the scrub. He could smell the secretion from the glands on the deers' haunches. A group of vultures, also hidden, were feeding off a piece of carrion. Manu sniffed. From the tang of the uric acid at the base of the birds' primary feathers, they were griffons. He flared his nostrils again. The carrion stench came from the carcass of a young male boar.

Much more information reached him on the wind. Constantly changing, the messages had come to him all night and throughout the morning. Manu read them all. Everything the air currents brought was normal for the day and the season.

Manu lowered his head and glanced round.

When he'd stopped the leopard had been trotting at his heels. Now she should have been crouching on the turf behind him, but she'd vanished. Manu searched the landscape but there was no sign of her. That didn't surprise him. Although the leopard was bred to the snows, when she was hunting she could blend invisibly into the valley's grasses. Normally Manu would have let her hunt. Today was different. Today they had to hurry on.

'Babilla!' he called, making an urgent growl of her name.

He repeated the call twice. Babilla appeared between the low bushes, her tail erect and her ears pricked. She came up and twined herself round him, rubbing her face against his thighs. Manu ruffled the creamy rose-patterned fur on her back. 'Come, Babilla, we must go on,' he said.

Unconsciously Manu switched the main mode of his awareness from his nose to his eyes. He strode forward, following the winding course of the river. It was important that he reached the island as quickly as possible. It had been a long journey and he was anxious to reach its end.

Manu was young and close to the peak of his strength. The concept of fatigue had never entered his mind. He considered himself tireless. Yet for the first time in his life he knew he was weary – his muscles ached and once or twice he stumbled. It wasn't so much the length of the journey as its unrelenting pace and the route he had been forced to take.

He often travelled between the grounds of the two clans. The outward journey from the valley to the crests involved a long, taxing climb, but it was one he always enjoyed, particularly in the summer's warmth. It was constantly exhilarating. He loved the challenge, the demands on his body, the strength and cunning needed among the clefts and rock faces, the sounds and scents of the new year's life surging round him at every step. He loved the crispness of the mountain air as he climbed higher, and the piercing clarity of the stars when darkness came.

Above all Manu loved the return trip to the grounds of the holding, as the valley clan was known. Not just because he was travelling downwards, but because he was returning to what had become much more his true shelter, his home, than the birth shelter he was leaving behind.

This time had been different. There was the reason for the journey first, the dark, troubling reason which had made old Yerto send him up to the crests. Manu had some of the answers now. They would have cast a shadow over his return anyway, but the angry response from the other clan, the ranging, wasn't all Manu was bringing back. There were new questions that neither old Yerto nor Gaggau, the ranging's leader, knew anything about – although it was Gaggau who had unwittingly raised them.

Old Yerto said it was impossible that all the prey animals had vanished from the ranging's hunting grounds in a single season. That was the message Manu had taken to the crests. Privately Manu thought it was true, although it was not for him to say so. Gaggau, on the other hand, was adamant his fellow patriarch in the valley below was wrong.

Gaggau had instructed Manu not to return to the holding by the ordinary route – the direct descent into the valley that would have taken him only the daylight hours – but to circle the crests to the west and search for the tracks of prey. Gaggau hadn't said how far west Manu should go before he turned down. He left that to Manu's judgement – and above all to what Manu found as he travelled.

Gaggau doubted he'd find anything. The old male was angry, bitter and pessimistic. In telling Manu to search to the west he was making a point: if Manu couldn't find prey, and Gaggau was certain he'd fail, the animals had truly gone. Manu hadn't found the animals. He'd found something else, something he hadn't been looking for.

He had gone much further round the crests than he'd intended. Just as he was about to break away from the ridge and head down, the storm had broken. In a driving Himalayan blizzard neither Manu's eyes nor his nose were of any use to him, so he'd sheltered in the lee of a rock and waited for the storm to pass.

The blizzard lasted for perhaps an hour. When it rolled away towards the northern peaks Manu stood up. On an impulse that had nothing to do with either sight or smell – snowflakes were still clouding the air and the scent spores had been chilled to numbness by the cold – Manu decided to make a final sweep of the knifeback ridge.

He came across the tracks half an hour later. They were very recent, although they had been almost buried by the last snow scurries before the storm moved on. No member of the holding would have noticed them. The holding had become Manu's home, but he had been born in the ranging and however long he had been away he remained a hunter with all a hunter's instincts. He spotted the faint ridges beneath the snow canopy, and knelt down. Using his spatulate fingers as delicately as if he were lifting tiny eggs from a bird's nest, he scooped away the flakes and uncovered the prints.

Manu knelt for a long time, frowning as he studied them. Then he stood up. He swung away from the crests, and headed down the nearest cleft that led to the valley. With the leopard leaping from boulder to boulder at his back, he made the descent to the valley floor at breathtaking speed, then strode out for the island.

His face was intent and clouded. The reply from the crests was bad enough on its own, a burden he'd longed to transfer to Yerto from the moment he was given it and left the caves. What he'd found on the ridge was infinitely stranger and more threatening. Briefly the knowledge of that belonged to him alone. It bore down on him, slowing his steps and making his shoulders ache as if he were single-handedly hauling a bear's carcass back to the island.

Manu didn't believe anything more fearful and bewildering could happen to him in the space of a single journey. He was wrong – in the valley something much worse awaited him.

He was crossing a water meadow close to the river when he stopped abruptly and his head jerked up. There was something close in front of him, something alien that shouldn't have been there. His eyes swept the landscape. He saw the bowl of the valley with the river flowing through its centre, the almost vertical hill flanks that walled the valley in, the rim of the snow-covered ridges high above. Everything in the range of his eyes was safe and familiar. His nostrils took over and scanned the air. The wind currents gave back the same message.

Nothing.

Manu hesitated. For an instant he thought he might have been dreaming. Then he realized the hairs on his wrists and shoulders were standing up and quivering as alertly as the antennae of the day-flying Himalayan moths. His skin was reacting to something neither his eyes nor his nose had been able to pick up. Puzzled, Manu moved on.

He spotted the object an instant later. It was lying in a sprawled huddle on a sloping bank above the river shallows to his right. Manu stared across the water. The object had the hunched, limp shape of a drowned animal, although it wasn't one Manu had ever seen in the valley or up on the crests. If it was an animal that had drowned, however recently, Manu's nostrils were so sensitive he should have smelt the changes already taking place in its body, but there was no trace of the death smell in the air drifting across the water.

Manu's face creased in puzzlement. Warily he stepped into the river and waded forward. He reached the far bank and looked down. For several long minutes he stood there, amazed, as the water lapped round his ankles. Finally he forced himself to accept what he was gazing at. It was a young shumbi.

In the language of Manu's people a shumbi was a human.

Manu recognized the creature only by description. Like most of his people he had never seen one before, yet he knew unquestionably what it was. Bemused, he reached down and touched it, running his finger-pads over the shumbi's skin. Then he lifted his head and studied the surrounding landscape, this time reading it keenly with eyes and nose. Afterwards his gaze returned to the shumbi.

Manu's mind had been flooded with uncertainty from the moment his skin prickled. When he recognized the shape on the bank, more questions surged up to perplex him. Now he had worked out the answers to most of them. Adult shumbi, particularly the males, gave off a hot sickly smell, midway between the stench of carrion and the vibrating charge that ran before a thunderstorm. Their smell could be detected from miles away. That was why they could always be avoided.

Young shumbi, like the young of most creatures, gave off virtually no smell, least of all young females. The field of scent spores from female shumbi children was weaker than a bird's. This shumbi was a child and a female, which was why Manu hadn't registered her until he'd stood over her. He knew, too, where she had come from. Her pelt, as he thought of her clothes, was sodden. There were no tracks on the bank around her, but there had been shumbi tracks high up on the crests above.

It was the discovery of those tracks which had so disturbed Manu when he came across them after the snowstorm. He had only spotted adult prints, but this child must have been with the group whose heavier spoor had concealed hers. She must have been swept off the ridge by the storm and somehow fallen into the river at the point where it emerged from the mountains midway down the almost vertical wall of the valley. The waters had swept her down here to the valley floor.

Manu knew why no decay was lifting from her – he'd discovered that when he examined her body. As his hands travelled over her, a pulse had flickered beneath the creature's skin. The shumbi was alive.

Manu squatted and crouched above her. The shumbi child stirred and coughed, spewing out the river's peat-brown water. Then she opened her eyes and stared up at him.

Iona screamed.

As the shriek of terror erupted out of her, torn from the deepest depths of her being, Iona realized she wasn't dreaming.

There was sun on her skin and she could smell peat and flowers. Her body felt bruised and aching and she could taste blood in her mouth from a cut on the inside of her lip. Her clothes were wet, and clouds, real clouds, raced overhead.

None of that happened in the nightmares. She was alive and awake and there was wind on her face. And yet the two worlds, the world of darkness and dreaming and the world of light, had melted together, the boundary between them dissolved. The creatures of the blackness had prowled into the morning.

She was gazing up at a monster.

Iona twisted on to her front and heaved herself on to her hands and knees. She had no idea where she was, no idea how she came to be there. She knew nothing at all – except that she was on a river bank with mud oozing round her and a monster in front of her.

In blind panic she tried to get to her feet to run. It was useless – she was too weak even to stand. Her knees buckled and she slipped back into the mud. She opened her mouth to scream again, then stopped before any sound emerged. Her mind was dizzy with fear, but a thought struggled through the confusion – if she screamed, she might provoke the creature. She bit her lips and silenced herself. She was trembling, and waves of sickness rippled over her stomach. Tiny, vulnerable and gulping for air, she stared across the water.

The creature had retreated into the river when she screamed. It stood there, thigh-deep, watching her. Gradually Iona began to take in its appearance. It was very tall, covered all over in dark brown hair that shone with the gloss of autumn chestnuts. Although she couldn't see its lower legs, she guessed it was at least as tall as her Uncle Robert – well over six foot and perhaps even taller. The creature's shoulders were broad and sloping, and its arms immensely long. Its face was coarse and rugged with a backward-sloping forehead, splayed nostrils and sunken eyes.

It was a vast monkey – an ape, as Uncle Robert preferred to call them. At first sight it could have been a living version of one of the mounted gorillas at Mainwarden. Though numb with terror, Iona knew it was different from the gorillas. It was as powerful as them, but its frame was lighter. The gorillas were stiff and bulky, but outlined against the sun shining off the water, this animal looked lean and supple, with muscles that seemed to stir and ripple beneath its hide.

The most vivid difference was in its eyes. Set deep in the animal's face, they were examining her with a penetrating intensity. Golden-yellow in colour, they ranged up and down her body with the fixed, unblinking stare of a night-hunting owl. Finally they came to rest on her face. The creature's eyes were wild and feral, but at the same time there was something almost human in the curiosity with which they studied her.

Iona stared back at them, transfixed. Behind the eyes was an intelligence that was neither an animal's nor a man's, but rather one that seemed different from either, hovering midway between the two.

The creature parted its lips. 'Shumbi,' it grunted. Its teeth showed long and yellow-white, like the fangs of a wolf or a great dog baboon.

Iona shuddered and shrank back against the bank. The sound wasn't that of an animal. It was closer to a word in human speech. She had no idea what it meant, but as it rang across the water and echoed inside Iona's head everything suddenly came back to her.

Her godfather. The camp high up in the mountains. The talk at the fire with Roshan squatting smiling beside the flames as Uncle Robert questioned him. The storm, the crawling shadows on the billowing canvas of her tent, the roaring wind and the snow in the darkness outside as she struggled to escape from the creatures hunting her. She didn't know what had happened afterwards, but she knew what this animal was.

It was what the Sherpas called a yeti. Somehow she had fallen into the hands of one of the monsters which haunted the Himalayan mountains. As she realized it, the creature began to wade forward.

Behind it something else caught Iona's eye. She glanced over the creature's shoulder.

Crouching on a mound was a leopard. The leopard had thick, almost white fur. As she looked at it, it tossed its head, opened its mouth and snarled. Switching its tail from side to side it began to crawl towards her.

Iona slid sideways into the river and fainted.

9

Manu splashed through the shallows and set off across the meadow. The island was still some distance ahead. With the shumbi lying draped across his shoulders, he hurried towards it.

When Manu lifted her she had become limp again. Apart from the fact that shumbi were dangerous, which was why they were so carefully avoided, Manu knew nothing about their habits or behaviour. He had sometimes seen the smaller animals of the valley freeze in shock when they were threatened until they looked as if they were dead. Perhaps it happened to small shumbi too. Manu didn't know. He only knew that he had to take her back to the holding as quickly as possible. Her appearance was even more momentous than the tracks he'd found on the crests, or the grievous news he was bringing back from the ranging. Manu's mind had been troubled before. Now it was in turmoil.

No shumbi had entered the valley within the memory of the holding's oldest member. The child's arrival would have been extraordinary in normal times, but the times were not normal. They were dark with problems and hazards and dissension that even old Tonemetapu, the holding's guide and seer who was thought to be older than the tree that sheltered him, had no experience of.

In such times the bedraggled little creature washed up on the river's bank could only be a portent, adding a new and bewildering dimension to the burdens they all had to share. Manu had been sent up to the ranging as a messenger, but also as a mediator. Everyone, above all old Yerto, clung to a thread of hope that he would return with at least the beginnings of a solution. Manu brought none.

What he brought back to them was an infinitely graver problem than any he had set out with. His heavy brow creased in worry, Manu strode on.

Draped across his shoulders like an antelope on the back of a returning hunter, Iona opened her eyes.

Manu had been partly right in guessing what had happened when he picked her up – Iona had fainted. The chief reason was the terror that swept over the child as he bent down towards her, but what he hadn't realized was the weakening effect of Iona's exhaustion. He'd assumed her clothes were a pelt which, like his, had insulated her against the chill of the spring water.

Soaked and clinging to her after she came to rest on the bank, Iona's clothes kept the sun from her skin. When she saw the young male yeti, it wasn't only fear but the ordeal of her icy journey down the river which had thrown her back into unconsciousness. Now, two hours later, her clothes had almost dried out and her body had begun to warm again.

Iona blinked and lifted her head. For several moments she was as confused as before. She had no idea where she was or what had happened to her. Before she could take anything in, she felt something rough prickling her thighs and her arms and glanced down. She saw dark brown hair. Below the hair the ground tilted rhythmically as someone strode across it – someone who was carrying her on his shoulders.

For the second time everything returned. The last thing Iona remembered was the leopard approaching her across the water. She must have fainted. Now the creature was carrying her somewhere.

Panic surged up in her throat so violently that she thought she would vomit. She managed to swallow but her mouth went dry and her head spun. She fought the panic down. She was too weak to try to escape so she had to remain calm and try to think. Her head bumping on the creature's shoulder, she peered out across the ground.

The creature was carrying Iona across the floor of a great rolling valley. The undulations in its surface rose and fell gently on every side. Above the ground hung mist, immense banners of soft, grey-white haze that coiled away into the distance. Higher still, everywhere she looked Iona could see snow-flanked crests and peaks glittering in the sunlight.

One of the mountains, its twin peaks shaped like a fishtail, looked vaguely familiar, so for some reason did the waves of mist. Then her bewilderment turned to understanding – she'd seen the mountain from a different angle at the camp on the ridge. The mist round her now was the greyness that had been swirling in the valley far below. Somehow she must have been taken from the ridge and carried down to the valley thousands of feet beneath.

She peered at the skyline. Up there somewhere were Uncle Robert, Roshan, the tents, the other Sherpas and porters, and the campfire. She searched for a column of smoke, a flash of light on the Sherpas' mountain glasses, the silhouette of a figure. It was too far, there was nothing – only the chill, brooding presence of the icy peaks and the immensity of the sky beyond.

Iona lowered her head despairingly. Her eyes filled with tears, but she knew she couldn't give way to crying in case she disturbed the huge shambling creature beneath her. She bit on her tongue and forced herself to concentrate again.

By now Uncle Robert would have found out she'd vanished. He, Roshan and the others would already be searching for her. They'd quickly discover she wasn't anywhere on the ridge and the only other place she could be was below them in the valley. They would climb down and find her.

The sun rose higher, the air warmed and the mist began to drift away. Beneath her the creature strode on with a steady, almost hypnotic rhythm to its steps. Iona's eyelids closed. Exhausted, she started to doze, but just before she fell asleep a question darted uneasily through her mind. From the campsite on the ridge the walls plunging down into the valley had looked not only vertical, but unclimbable. She had somehow made the descent but that, it suddenly occurred to her, could only have been because she'd been carried down by the yeti. Her godfather and the Sherpas would have to find another route down – and from what she'd glimpsed of the valley from its floor, the same sheer, plunging rock faces enclosed it everywhere. It might be days, even weeks before they reached her.

Iona was too tired, too shocked and too frightened to dwell on the possibility. Unconsciously the child surrendered to her body's own defences. She slept.

Iona was woken by the sound of water. She raised her head cautiously and peered round.

She was stiff and aching, and she was still lying across the creature's shoulders. It seemed an eternity since she'd found herself there. In reality, Iona guessed as she studied the position of the sun in the sky, it was probably five hours. She'd been taught to use the sun as a rough-and-ready clock by old Duncan, her Uncle Harry's stalker in Scotland.

'Think of it as an hour hand curving across the sky,' he used to say when he took her up on to the moors. 'It travels east to west. Ye'll have to know when dawn comes one end and darkness the other. But at the sun's highest point it'll always be midday. With a wee bit of practice and mebbe some guesswork, it will tell ye the time.'

The sun had just cleared the crests when she'd first seen the yeti. That happened, Iona noticed in camp, at about 7 a.m. Now it was clearly at its peak. Five hours. At a steady walking pace, old Duncan had also taught her, a man could cover four miles in an hour. The yeti's loping stride was much faster than Duncan's – they must have covered at least twenty miles.

All the while they'd been following the river as it wound through the valley. At the start the stream had been narrow and fast-running. Later it broadened out and the flow of the water slowed. In the intervals between her fitful rocking sleeps Iona had seen nothing except grass, reeds, occasional clumps of trees, and once or twice glimpses of the distant crests. Now at midday the creature was moving with his swift effortless stride down the river bank and into the water. He waded out into the shallows and began to swim, breasting the flow of the current with his head held high and his arms paddling quickly and strongly.

Iona heard a splash behind them. She glanced back. The leopard had entered the river too and was swimming in the yeti's wake. Iona stared at the animal.

Whenever she'd woken on the journey, the first thing she'd seen was the leopard padding behind after her. It frightened her almost more than the yeti. The yeti was so strange, so alien and unknown, it belonged to the borderland between reality and nightmare. Leopards were different – Iona knew about them.

Leopards were immense cats, among the most efficient and elusive hunters in the world. They seldom attacked man unprovoked, but if they were cornered they could be more ferocious and deadly than lions. This one must be a member of the group called snow leopards, which she knew from Uncle Robert were the rarest of all the leopard species.

The animal shadowing her had pale fur the colour of winter ermine scattered all over with the roseate print of leopards everywhere. It moved silently and swiftly, its tail switching from side to side and its muscles rippling under its hide. Occasionally when it yawned Iona saw its rows of yellow teeth, teeth set in jaws so powerful they could tear an elephant to pieces.

Most of all she was mesmerized by the animal's eyes. Cold and unblinking, they gleamed in its face like ovals of green-specked agate. They were terrifying and yet, bewilderingly, they were also familiar. It was only now, when the yeti entered the water and the leopard followed, that Iona realized why. The creature's eyes were exactly the same as Misty's, although Misty had only one. Its behaviour was similar, too – it followed the yeti step by step just as Misty followed her.

To Iona the realization was extraordinary. In an instant the leopard changed from a menacing presence at her back into nothing more than a larger version of her own cat. At the same moment something else occurred to her – the leopard wasn't tracking her, let alone hunting her. It was simply following the yeti.

Cats, she had learnt from Uncle Robert, were the first animals to adapt their existence and become parasites on man. They would follow only a human master or mistress. The leopard wasn't following her but the yeti.

The river rose and lapped round Iona's legs and the chill of the water made her wince. She turned her head and looked forward. A little earlier the river had divided into two streams which curved round the sides of what appeared to be a large, low-lying island. The yeti was fast approaching the island and as she gazed ahead Iona felt his feet touch its shore.

Over the past five hours the sun had dried out her clothes and, tired as she was, Iona's body had warmed enough for her to remain at least intermittently awake. Now, her clothes sodden again, she felt her skin and then her body begin to chill once more. She heaved herself up on the creature's shoulders, trying to lift herself above the icy flow.

Beyond the grass and reeds at the river's edge she saw a shelving bank, split by a path that led up to a clearing at the top. Gathered in the clearing and spilling out down the path were thirty or forty more of the creatures. Although their hair was lighter in colour than the hide of the yeti beneath her, they obviously belonged to the same race. They were watching her closely and Iona recoiled. The expression on their faces was hostile and threatening.

Iona turned away. She tried to hide her head behind the yeti as the creature stepped out on to the shore. She saw the leopard spring up on to the bank, its yellow eyes cold and blank and its mouth flecked with the river's foam. She heard the leopard growl, there was a low murmur from the assembled yeti, from somewhere owls hooted in the sun.

Iona's head spun. She clung to the yeti's neck but her hands seemed to have lost all their strength. Chill, exhausted and terrified, the child drifted into unconsciousness again.

10

Manu waded ashore and shook the water from his pelt.

At his side the leopard did the same. As spray rose from them both, Manu felt the weight of the shumbi on his shoulders. Compared with the deer Manu brought back on his hunting trips with the ranging when he visited the crests, she was so light that for a moment he had almost forgotten she was there.

Manu reached up and lifted her down. He held her in his arms and looked up. From above him came the hiss of indrawn breath.

Every member of the holding had assembled in the clearing. They would have been aware of his approach for the past hour or more, scenting him just as Manu had scented them as he came closer. He could see them all staring down at the shumbi. They stood in little groups whose order corresponded to the clan's hierarchy.

At the front was old Ryena, the patriarch's greying but still graceful mate, and her tall powerful son Wengen with his cunning inscrutable face and his strangely pale eyes. Close to them stood the clan's elders, the males and females beyond breeding age, and behind them the mated couples with the adolescents and the young right down to the crawling infants. At the rear were the single males and the mature but unseeded or unmated females – the slender Kekua with her sightless eyes, the pregnant Churinga beside her, Bitta, Canena and the others.

Their faces had been apprehensive even before he came into sight. Because the shumbi gave off no scent they hadn't registered her presence any more than Manu had until he stood over her, but their skins had warned them of something strange. When Manu waded out of the water and the older members of the holding identified the creature lying across his shoulders, their apprehension turned to bewilderment. Like Manu none of them had seen a shumbi before, but all of them recognized what he was carrying.

The bewilderment gave place to fear, which spread contagiously. Within moments of Manu and the leopard shaking themselves dry, even the smallest of the holding's young was whimpering. To the infant yeti a shumbi had no meaning, yet even they knew something was fearfully wrong.

Manu stood on the shore. He could see the anxious frowns on every face, the questions forming in every mouth. There was nothing he could do to answer them until Yerto came forward. Several minutes passed before the tall grasses parted and the patriarch appeared. Yerto was old. His fur had paled to silvery whiteness and he moved stiffly. Most of the time he could still walk upright, but occasionally, when he was tired, he dropped forward and used his arms as well as his legs to support his great wasted body.

Yerto was tired now. He came down the bank on all fours, his eyes thoughtful and his face grave. The old one has been lying in his shelter, Manu thought. He would not have been sleeping. With the passage of the winters, Yerto slept less and less. He lay down now only to rest and he had to do so more and more often. Yet Yerto remained the patriarch, responsible for the holding. Until he had greeted Manu there could be no communication between Manu and the others.

As Yerto came to a halt, Manu placed the shumbi on the ground. 'Guard!' he grunted over his shoulder to the leopard.

The leopard dropped to a crouch with her head resting on her outstretched front paws. She watched Iona's motionless body through narrowed eyes.

As Manu stood up he realized that it was the first time he had ever given the leopard a guard instruction over a creature that wasn't dead. The leopard guarded fallen prey against other predators. There were no other predators here, only the gathered members of the holding. Manu tried to puzzle out why he'd done it.

Across his mind flashed an image of the shumbi when he'd first spotted her. She had been alien, almost frightening, but as he came closer she looked stricken and vulnerable too. The huddled, half-drowned shape on the bank reminded him of a fledgling bird he'd found as a child at the water's edge the first summer he'd spent on the island. He should have plucked the bird and eaten it – it was what any other member of the holding would have done. Manu didn't. He picked the fledgling up, dried it with his hands and carried it to his shelter. He fed it with pounded grass-seed kernels and insects he caught in his cupped hands. The bird survived. One day when he took it out into the sun, it rose from his hands and flew away. He laughed as he saw it vanish over the trees. He never saw the bird again but he didn't mind – it lived because he had protected it. Unaccountably he had felt the same sense of protection towards the shumbi child – Manu wanted her to live too.

He came face to face with Yerto. For the moment he dismissed the shumbi, the bedraggled bird, from his mind and concentrated on the old patriarch.

Yerto heaved himself up on to his haunches. Manu leant forward and dropped down. Using his stiffened arms and his bunched hands to support himself as the patriarch had done, he advanced and halted before the old one. His head still lowered, he reached out and scratched Yerto's nose. Yerto grunted and scratched Manu's nose in return. Afterwards they both stood up, Manu helping Yerto to his feet.

Yerto looked down and studied the shumbi for a long time, then reached down stiffly to touch her face. The leopard bared its teeth and snarled.

'Hold!' Manu instructed. At his command the animal sank back to the ground. Its tail continued to switch warily from side to side.

Yerto ran his fingers over the child's skin. Painfully he heaved himself upright. 'Where did you find this?' he asked.

'By the river as I returned,' Manu answered.

Yerto scratched his jaw. 'So Gaggau does not know?'

'No, it was long after I left him.'

'And yet you bring word from him?'

Manu nodded.

There was silence. Manu knew what was going through the patriarch's mind. There had to be a connection between the appearance of the shumbi, Gaggau's claims that the prey animals had vanished, and Manu's mission to the crests. The events were so extraordinary it was impossible they weren't linked, yet the patriarch clearly had no more idea than Manu what the link could be.

'We will go to the shelter.' Yerto turned and began to climb the bank. 'I must know everything. Above all I must know about the shumbi child. Never before has one come to the valley.'

Manu picked up the shumbi and walked behind the silver-backed patriarch, the gathered yeti parting in front of them. When they reached the circle of shelters round the much larger clearing at the island's centre, Manu placed the child on the ground.

The child lay very still. Her dark head hair straggled damply across her face, and her pale hide had the bruised grey-blue colour of the stomach of a dying animal. She was close to death herself. Only the shallow movement of her breast showed she was still alive. Manu's face creased with anxiety.

'Leave her to me!'

He glanced up. It was the blind Kekua. As she spoke Kekua knelt down beside the child. Manu knew that in Kekua's hands she would be as safe as the bird had been in his.

He turned and followed Yerto into the shelter.

11

'Start!' Yerto instructed. The old yeti gazed at the much younger dark-pelted figure before him.

They were facing each other in the shadowy light of Yerto's shelter. The patriarch was propped up on the thick bed of dry reeds and grass where he rested. Manu squatted on the earth. He shrugged his heavy shoulders. Where should he start? There was so much to tell, so much that was unprecedented and unresolved. Somehow he would have to find a way to report it all, but his mind churned with uncertainty about where to begin. Instinctively he raised his hands.

Although he had lived on the island from childhood, in moments of difficulty and stress Manu still reverted to the ways of his birth clan, the ranging. Calls and words were the island-dwellers' main means of communication, and over the years speech had become second nature to him. The clan on the crests used speech too, but to Manu it could never be as subtle and expressive as the gestures of the ranging.

Gesture was the first language he had learnt and, like his hunting skills, Manu had never lost it. Using his hands and his fingers, he could pass on virtually any information across almost any distance. Over short distances the drumming of his thumb against his index finger could reproduce the call of a pheasant. It could also draw the prey bird to a given tree, and tell his fellow hunters where the bird had perched. At longer range his palms – cupped and swivelled to flash back the sun or the starlight – could transmit messages across vast areas.

Once as a child Manu had run away from the ranging. The whole clan was hungry and so was he. For a week the hunters had failed to find and kill. Manu was convinced they were stupid, he knew he was better than any of them, he knew he could find prey on his own. Above all, he was starving and he wanted to live.

Two sunrises later, far from the ranging's home grounds, Manu spotted a musk deer above the snow line. The buck was still plump but it was lost. Manu could easily have tracked it down and killed it for himself. He did not. He climbed to the crest above where the disorientated buck was wandering. Then he began to call to it, using his palms to make the quick hollow bark of the deer's mating call.

Manu repeated his calls all day, retreating step by step as he drew the buck towards the ranging's territory. When he'd placed the animal where he wanted, he turned. It was evening. Using his hands as reflectors now to catch the setting sun, Manu started to signal towards where he'd last seen the hunters. One of them spotted the distant flashes and read their message. The hunters set out towards him. Next day in the pre-dawn twilight they came on the buck and killed it. Manu helped them carry the meat back to the ranging's caves.

Within the ranging the story of Manu and the musk deer entered legend. The child had signalled the animal's presence across seven peaks. The feat was examined in cloud-time. The cloud-time discussions confirmed what all the ranging knew, and by then the holding too. Not even the best and most experienced of the ranging's adult hunters could have done what the child had. It marked him apart.

Manu listened to the cloud-time debates in silence. He realized long afterwards that in not killing the buck for himself he was merely responding to the tie of the bonds, which held both the clans in thrall. The bonds were essential and inescapable, Manu accepted that, but they had changed his life in a way he had never wanted.

When the cloud-time decision was taken for the exchange between the holding and the ranging, it was inevitable that Manu should be chosen to be sent down to the valley. His sharing of the deer uniquely exemplified what the bonds meant.

Manu had lived with the holding ever since. Yet even today, years later, his hands sometimes seemed to acquire a life of their own. They rose and began to speak for him. Already halfway to his chest, they were doing it now. Unconsciously they made patterns in the air, gathering the dim light of the shelter, cupping it in their palms, pouring it out and talking with it – every shift of luminescence across the fingers and through the skin conveying a different message. It was how his people, the hunters of the ranging, had always spoken to each other.

Manu clenched his fists. He extinguished the light as if he were crushing a handful of fireflies. He was not among his own people. He was with the holding. Yerto would understand his voice much better than his hands.

'The young female shumbi,' he replied. 'As I have said, I found her by the river a short distance below the crests.'

He described how he came across the limp, huddled shape on the bank. He told Yerto that she'd given off no smell and it was only by accident that he had chanced on her.

The old yeti nodded. It was always so with the children of the shumbi. Yerto had been told so himself long ago.

'There was no other shumbi with her?' Yerto asked. 'No spoor to show that they might have left her there?'

'No spoor in the valley.' Manu paused. Then he added, 'But on the crests there was spoor. There were many prints.'

Slowly, carefully, Manu retraced his own thought processes after he'd found the shumbi, and the line of deduction that led him back to the point on the crests where he'd cut down into the valley. As he finished Yerto grunted in agreement.

The old yeti belonged to the holding and Manu to the ranging. The holding gathered, while the ranging hunted. Yet the skills of the two clans overlapped, and even as a lifelong gatherer Yerto could read and interpret the prints left by other creatures on the landscape. In spite of his years, Yerto knew he would always be a novice compared with Manu.

Manu was no ordinary hunter. Seasons ago when Manu was still little more than a child, Yerto remembered, it was already being said in cloud-time that he was among the best hunters the crests had ever reared. It wasn't surprising for, like Gaggau, he was Burra's son. It was sometimes difficult to believe that the two, the ranging's patriarch and the young dark-pelted figure in front of Yerto now, were brothers. An entire breeding generation separated them, but their mother had always been a law unto herself – taking her seeding mates as and when she chose.

No female had done that before, but then there had never been a female like Burra in either of the clans. Long since dead, Burra had been the greatest hunter of all. Manu could barely have known his mother, but his skills came from her. In the matter of animals, and the shumbi was an animal, Manu could see things the island patriarch would never have seen even in his prime. Given the faintest mark on the earth, Manu could not merely tell what had made it – he would know when, what sex and age the animal was, what condition it was in. Where it had come from, where it was going, and where it was now.

'So there are shumbi on the crests,' Yerto said. 'Many of them, and this young one was with them. Somehow she has been given to us.'

Manu nodded. 'I think she fell and the river carried her down.'

Yerto was silent for a time. 'You may be right,' he said eventually. 'But you think as a hunter, Manu. You treat her as a deer and you work out what might have happened to bring the deer to where you found it. The shumbi is an animal but she is not a deer. There may be other reasons for her being there –' The patriarch paused. 'You must have noticed she is not as other shumbi.'

Manu frowned. He had no idea what the old yeti meant. Manu had never seen any shumbi before, but the small creature conformed in every way to all the descriptions of them he had ever heard. Yerto himself, at first glance, had accepted her as a shumbi child.

'Surely there are just shumbi. Apart from age and sex they are all the same –'

'No,' Yerto interrupted him. 'Beneath their pelts the skin of shumbi is dark. It has the colour of tree bark in winter. This shumbi's skin is as pale as the snow in spring.'

Manu's head jerked up. It hadn't occurred to him until then that from the moment he'd found her he had concentrated on the shape and texture of the child, on what might have cast her up on the bank, on the impelling need to carry her back to the holding. He hadn't even considered her skin colour. Yet now that Manu thought about it, Yerto was right – all the descriptions of the shumbi spoke of them as being dark-skinned. But not this one. As Yerto had pointed out, the child's skin was almost white.

'Then what sort of shumbi is she?' Manu asked in bewilderment.

'I do not know,' Yerto answered. 'That will be for Tonemetapu to decide. What I can guess even before Tonemetapu pronounces is that she is part of everything else. I have seen her with my own eyes and you have told me about the spoor on the crests. You have not yet told me about the ranging. That, after all, was the reason for your journey –'

The patriarch paused. 'Gaggau sent word to the valley that he must speak urgently with us because, so he said, the prey animals had gone from the crests. I sent you to him to find out more. Not just because you are his brother and come from the ranging yourself, but because I trust you to bring me back the truth.'

Manu looked back at the earth. Old Yerto was right again. The extraordinary events of the past hours had almost made Manu forget the reason for his journey – why he had been sent up to the ranging and the messages he had been entrusted to bring back. Now he was forced to remember.

'The ranging cannot feed itself,' he said. 'The animals are not there.'

'There have been seasons like this before. They pass. The animals return.'

'Gaggau says there has never been such a season. There are no animals anywhere.'

Yerto grunted derisively. 'Gaggau is lame. He always has been. Now he is getting old and can only hunt close to the caves. Well, the great hunter must swallow his pride and let the young hunters do the work for him. Perhaps for a while they must range further than before. The animals will come back. Who knows? Before he sleeps finally in cloud-time, maybe even Gaggau himself will hunt and kill again.' Yerto chuckled.

Manu hesitated before answering. He knew there was no love lost between the two patriarchs, the one in the valley and the other on the crests. He knew of the ancient rivalries and jealousies between the old of both the clans, and even within the clans. Manu sensed this was different – and it mattered nothing that Gaggau was his brother.

Outside the vast bowl of the valley and the battlements of the crests which guarded it, something was happening. He had seen it himself with a shock. There had never been as little spoor in his lifetime as he had found on his travels to and from the crests. He had spoken long to the younger hunters of the ranging. Uneasy and confused, but adamant, they confirmed it – the animals were retreating.

'I think this is truly different,' Manu ventured. 'The ranging's prey may return but perhaps not for a long while. Until then Gaggau foresees famine beyond what the ranging can endure.'

'Then what does he propose?' Yerto demanded.

Manu swallowed. It was the question he knew the old yeti would sooner or later put to him, and the one above all that he did not want to answer. Now he had no choice.

He stiffened his facial muscles and replied, 'He wants to share in the gathering.'

'In what we gather here in the holding –?' Yerto stared at him. He shook his head in anger and disbelief. 'Gaggau cannot be serious. His mind is growing as useless as his foot. The holding can scarcely gather enough for itself.'

'Gaggau says he will send his hunters down to help,' Manu said flatly.

'His hunters?' The old yeti gave a harsh, deep-throated laugh. 'What do the ranging's hunters know of gathering? What did you know until you came here? Nothing! You came eighteen seasons ago. Yes, you are starting to learn now. But compared with the youngest of the holding's females, even with the children, how would you consider yourself?'

Manu didn't answer. There was nothing he could say. Eighteen seasons after his arrival in the valley, he still lacked the skills of any but the smallest of the island gatherers.

'Even that is not important,' Yerto continued. 'Were Gaggau's hunters the most skilful gatherers too, it would make no difference. However it is cropped, the valley's harvest is not large enough for us all. It can support the holding. It cannot sustain the ranging as well.'

Yerto's voice had been rising as he spoke. Painfully he pushed himself upright on the bed of grass and reeds until he was gazing down into Manu's eyes.

'You come from the ranging,' he said fiercely. 'You must go back there. You must talk again to your brother, Gaggau. You must tell him what he says is madness. His hunters must range further, maybe, than they have ever done. They must find the animals and their own salvation. There is no room for them in the valley.'

Manu looked back at the patriarch then and drew in his breath. He had saved the worst for the last. To the very end he had hoped to avoid it. No longer. It had been a vain, stupid wish and Manu cursed himself for ever entertaining it.

'Gaggau's hunters have gone far,' he said quietly. 'Nine days ago on the southern crest one of them found a stray water buffalo. He killed it. He called for his companions. Before they arrived and as he was butchering the animal, an oduna appeared –' Manu drew his hands across his face, trying to pluck out the torment of what he had to say. It was useless. The pain, the obscenity, the wound, remained unhealed.

'Gaggau's hunters and the oduna fought over the buffalo's carcass,' Manu went on. 'The oduna was slain.'

Yerto stood silent, in shock. 'You are telling me we have killed one of the half-bloods?' he asked disbelievingly.

Manu nodded. The pain on his own face was as nothing compared with that on the old patriarch's.

The oduna, or half-bloods as they were sometimes known, lived outside the confines of the valley, no one knew exactly where. Like the shumbi the oduna were acknowledged but almost never seen. Fifty seasons could pass without a glimpse of one. Unlike the shumbi – who were a mystery, a race apart – everyone knew who the oduna were and where they came from. They were the outcasts. Former members of either the ranging or the holding, they had suffered the yeti's ultimate sanction – exile from the valley. No one, not even Tonemetapu, could say when the first oduna was expelled. Whenever it happened and for whatever reason, the first exile had been joined by others.

Across the generations since then, it was said, the oduna had occasionally made shelter with bands of wandering shumbi. They had hunted and gathered with them, and occasionally, it was suggested in the darkest of the cloud-time stories, the oduna and the shumbi had even bred together. Whether that were true or not, the oduna had become aliens, shameful and degraded shadows of the people. If the stories of the interbreeding were true, they had degenerated into mongrels. They were smaller and their pelts were paler than the true yeti. Yet they were still in their essence, in the very centre of their being, of the seed and rootstock of the two clans.

They were yeti.

Of all the rules and taboos that governed the life of the ranging and the holding, only one could never be broken, only one was inviolable. No yeti, not even an oduna, must be slain.

'We shall visit Tonemetapu,' Yerto said quietly. 'If the animals have truly retreated from the crests and the ranging have killed a half-blood, the two are also joined –'

He paused. 'In all my long seasons there have never been matters such as these. The shumbi child you have found must be at the heart of them all. Tonemetapu will say what must be done with her.'

Grim and harrowed, the old patriarch raised himself up and limped out of the shelter.

12

Kekua was still kneeling beside the little shumbi where Manu had left her in the clearing outside.

The blind yeti had wrapped the child in a deer hide, and placed a bed of dry grass beneath her. Manu and Yerto had been in the shelter for several hours. While they'd been talking the sun had curved over the island. It was setting now but the combination of the hide, the grass and the afternoon's warmth had removed the blue-grey pallor from the shumbi's skin. The child was still unconscious, but her breathing was stronger.

The entire holding was gathered in a circle watching her. Manu had never before seen them so intent and absorbed. Even the young were silent. The shumbi's arrival was the most extraordinary event in the holding's history, and the young had caught the mood of their parents. Not even the smallest infant made a sound. Standing or squatting, everyone gazed down in fear and bewilderment at the tiny alien creature which had been washed by the river into the valley like a portent from the crests.

The patriarch beckoned and Manu stooped. He picked up the shumbi and settled her in his arms. She felt as light as one of the drowned birds the holding occasionally scavenged from the river after the spring rainstorms. Yerto turned and Manu followed him towards the head of the island. As they went the eyes of the holding followed them. The holding knew where they were going, and their gazes were filled with anxiety and foreboding.

It was almost dark. Normally it was the time of day Manu liked best. They all did. The gathering or the hunting was over until the sun rose again. The valley's smells were still sharp, but at dusk they could be sifted and considered without the need for action, their messages stored for the morning. Dawn meant a new beginning, but dusk was for rest, for peace. Dusk was satisfaction. Muscles uncoiling. Laughter and tales and touching. Teasing and playing and reflecting. Dusk was when the expenditure of energy ended, and its rewards came.

Not tonight. For everyone dusk tonight meant only the fragile and fearsome burden in Manu's arms that Tonemetapu alone could explain.

'It is I, Yerto,' the old patriarch said several minutes later when they had reached the head of the island. 'I come with Manu. He brings a shumbi.'

In front of them rose an immensely old juniper tree. Its roots ran deep into the earth at the point where, like the prow of a ship, the twin arms of the river came together after circling the island, and fell in a single flow towards the south. The tree was dark against the evening sky. Even darker was the bowl of shadow at the base of its trunk.

Yerto rested his weight on a broken branch which he'd used as a crutch as they walked. He waited. Behind him Manu waited too, the passive body of the shumbi seeming to float in his arms.

'Lay her down.'

The instruction came out of the darkness in front of them. Manu placed the little shumbi on a patch of starlit ground before the tree, then stepped back. He couldn't see Tonemetapu, but the scent field surrounding the oldest of all the yeti fixed his presence at the base of the trunk just as clearly as if it had been full daylight. There had been no need to warn Tonemetapu they were coming – he would have sensed their approach in the same way.

'How and where did you find her?'

Tonemetapu's voice was as hoarse and frail as the first bark of a new-born sambur deer. He couldn't have known what they were bringing him because the child gave off no scent, but there was no surprise in his question.

Manu told him about the storm on the crests, his journey down into the valley and his discovery on the river bank.

'There is more, is there not?'

Manu looked startled. Then he realized what Tonemetapu meant. He was referring to Manu's mission to the ranging, and the grievous news he had returned with from the snows.

'Yes,' Manu said. He recounted the death of the oduna, the disappearance of the prey from the crests and Gaggau's demand to share the harvest of the gathering.

When he had finished there was silence. The last of the twilight drained away and the glow of the still hidden but rising moon began to flood the distant ridges. Stars glittered and owl-calls filled the air. Moths churred round their faces. Once a far-off leopard growled as it marked its territory on the slopes. The sound was no more than a remote whisper in the night. Ordinarily it would have drifted in and out of Manu's consciousness almost without registering, but tonight every sound and scent was significant. As Manu heard the leopard's growl, every hair on his skin rose and bristled as if in sympathy with the stiffening fur on Babilla's hide. Babilla was a nocturnal hunter, while for Manu darkness meant rest. Tonight he and the leopard were one.

'Tonemetapu –'

It was Yerto who eventually broke the silence. He swung himself impatiently forward on his crutch and peered into the shadows where Tonemetapu was sitting. 'She is at the heart of it all, is she not?' he demanded.

The silence beneath the tree continued. Finally Tonemetapu spoke. 'The troubles?' he answered. 'Yes. She floats upon them as she floated on the river which brought her here. She may be their cause, or she may be their healing.'

'How do we find out?' Yerto demanded. 'What do we do with her?'

The confusion in his face reflected the torment in his words. The pain was so evident, so acute, that Manu tore his eyes away from where they had been focused on the scent pattern in the darkness, and he gazed instead at the patriarch.

Tonemetapu might be the link between the holding and its beginnings, between all the yeti and their beginnings. He might control and interpret cloud-time for both the clans. He might be the ultimate authority for everyone. But Yerto was the holding's patriarch. Yerto dealt with practicalities. In the old silverback's hands lay the clan's immediate destiny, the way in which it foraged, fed, defended its grounds, bred and reared its young.

The holding's safety was at hazard. The vanishing prey, Gaggau's demands, the killing of the oduna, the arrival of the shumbi child – each one on its own was perilous. Together, Yerto knew, they combined to threaten the holding as it had never been threatened. Tormented and bewildered, the island patriarch was asking what he had to do to safeguard his people.

'In the shumbi we shall find the answer,' Tonemetapu replied from the darkness. 'She may look as weak as the fledgling hawk

Manu thinks he has been carrying in his arms. In truth she is as strong as the branch which can move great rocks and find the honey beneath –'

Tonemetapu paused. At Yerto's side Manu's eyes widened in surprise. Twice he had thought of the shumbi, so frail and so weightless in his hands, as a bird. He hadn't seen her as a hawk then. Now he remembered her eyes – green and steady and flecked with gold – and he knew the seer was right. The child had a hawk's colouring. She had wept when she saw him but there was a hawk's boldness, too, in the gaze behind the tears.

The branches the yeti used to lever away the boulders beneath which the Himalayan bees made their hives and honeycombs came from the hardest of all the mountain trees. If the child was as strong as them, she was the strongest creature in the valley.

'We will succour and feed her,' Tonemetapu went on. 'We will teach her to talk with us. When she can do that, I will speak with her. From her answers, I will decide.'

'Talk?' Yerto said. 'How shall a shumbi learn to talk?'

'Give her to Kekua. Let Kekua be her teacher.'

'Kekua?' Yerto looked astonished. 'Kekua cannot even see.'

'From behind the darkness of her eyes, Kekua sees further than any of the holding,' Tonemetapu replied. 'Churinga can be Kekua's sight. Between them they will teach the shumbi child. When they have taught her, bring her back to me –' He broke off again.

Manu couldn't see what he was doing, but he sensed that Tonemetapu was examining the child on the ground beneath him. In the silence Manu considered what the seer had said. The idea of a shumbi speaking the language of the people was almost inconceivable. But if it was necessary, the more Manu thought about Tonemetapu's instructions, the wiser they seemed.

In the world of the holding the blind female yeti, Kekua, was an enigma. The few yeti who were born blind as she had been invariably died young but for some reason Kekua survived. Slim, graceful, and the same age as Manu, she had grown to become one of the clan's best gatherers. Her lack of sight was more than compensated for by an extraordinary ability to find harvesting areas that the rest of the holding had overlooked by smell alone. Her blindness meant that she was unseeded and unmated – none of the males would ever breed with a female of her disability – but her skills had won her the respect of the entire clan. Churinga, on the other hand, was large, strong and good-natured. Churinga had been created for breeding. She was unmated, but she had been seeded and soon she would bear her child. Churinga would be the perfect companion to Kekua in instructing the little shumbi.

'She is a gift from the snows,' Tonemetapu went on at last. 'Such a gift has never been made to us before. Whether the gift comes filled with the cobra's venom or the sun's warmth, only the river and the star without a name can tell us. The river cannot talk, but the star will speak through the child when she can speak. Meanwhile care for her well – on the shumbi may depend whether the entire people live or die.'

Something shone briefly in the blackness beneath the tree. Manu realized it was the flash of light off Tonemetapu's wrist as he indicated the child should be removed. Manu bent down and picked her up. As he turned and headed back for the clearing, he struggled to take in the implications of what the old seer had said. If Tonemetapu was right, Manu was carrying in his arms the undecided future of both the clans.

With Yerto tramping stiffly and painfully behind him, Manu strode on. He held the child as carefully and delicately as if she were the egg of a mountain hawk.

13

Iona opened her eyes.

She was lying on her back. Overhead she could see the sky. It was still and blue and cloudless. Iona found that puzzling. Her last vague memory was of a black vault lashed with icy banners of whiteness. Something else was strange too. Above her face was what looked for a moment like the branch of a tree.

Iona blinked at it. It wasn't a branch – it was an arm, an arm covered in thick brown hair. Everything came back to her then. She was in a valley and she had been captured by a monster – by a yeti.

Iona was too exhausted even to try to scream now. Numb with terror she lay motionless on the ground. The arm moved and vanished, then a vast bristling spider descended on her face. Iona's skin crawled and she struggled desperately not to faint again. As the sweat poured off her she closed her eyes. The spider crawled over her skin, its feet probing and pressing as it scuttled backwards and forwards.

Almost choking, Iona held her breath. Strangely, there was something familiar about the spider's movements. Iona saw it wasn't a spider at all, it was the yeti's hand. The monster was examining her face with its fingers.

The fingers moved away. For a long time Iona continued to lie without moving. The creature was still there – she could hear it breathing somewhere close to her – but it didn't touch her again. Her stomach churning, Iona began to inch her head round. Eventually the creature came into sight.

The first thing she realized was that this was a different monster. The one which had picked her up was taller, larger and had much darker fur. It was also unquestionably a male. This one was smaller, its fur was much lighter in colour, and just as unmistakably it was a female. Iona could see its breasts and the V between its legs.

The second thing she noticed was that the creature was blind. The eyes of the first yeti had been keen and alert. Golden-brown in colour, they had studied her, she remembered, with the searching, unblinking intensity of an owl. This one's eyes were milky-white and opaque. The new female yeti was sitting on her haunches a few feet away, gazing sightlessly ahead and scratching her armpits.

Iona frowned, trying to work out what the creature had been doing. Then she understood. It had been examining her by touch. Briefly Iona closed her eyes. Inexplicably, for the first time since the nightmares of the darkness had spilt out into the daylight, she felt a quick, uncertain stab of comfort. Her Great-aunt Flora, her Uncle Harry's mother in Scotland, was blind too and Iona had often seen her exploring people's faces with her fingers in exactly the same way. Iona liked her great-aunt. She laughed a lot and kept toffees in the pocket of her skirt and she had a nice smell.

Iona hesitated, then cautiously she pushed herself upright.

She had barely begun to move before the creature's head swung round towards her. Iona knew the yeti was blind, but the blank milky eyes seemed to be staring not so much at her but deep inside her, as if the yeti could sense each of Iona's movements even before she made them. Iona froze. The creature stood up, came over to Iona and squatted beside her. It reached out and gently scratched Iona's nose. Then it took her hand, raised the hand to its nose and paused expectantly. Trembling and bewildered, Iona knew she had to respond. For an instant she couldn't think what to do. Then it came to her – she uncoiled her fingers and scratched the yeti's nose in return.

The creature grunted.

Iona knew animals, had lived with them all her life. There was Misty of course, there were the cows and sheep at Mainwarden, the dogs and ponies in Scotland, the horses her mother's friends kept at their farms in Maine and Massachusetts. Iona knew the sounds they made and what they signified, hunger, fear or pleasure. The sound the yeti had made was unquestionably a grunt of satisfaction. What happened next took Iona totally by surprise.

The yeti let go of Iona's hand, rocked back on its heels and gazed at Iona through its shuttered eyes. It lifted its hand to its own nose, and its mouth parted.

'Kekua.'

Iona stiffened.

Yetis were animals, Iona knew that. Yet the sound wasn't a grunt or a call or a whistle. It sounded almost like a human word. The creature had spoken, just as Iona remembered how the dark yeti had seemed to speak on the river bank. Transfixed, Iona stared at it.

The creature reached out again, took Iona's hand and placed it against its nose. 'Kekua,' it repeated.

Iona swallowed. Dizzily she tried to take it in. The animal, the yeti, was talking to her. It – she – was telling Iona her name. It had to be, it could only be that. Frantically, Iona tried to think of a response. Her hand was still clasped in the yeti's and touching the creature's nose. She scratched it again.

'Kekua,' Iona said.

Carefully she slid her hand out of the yeti's grasp and, hardly daring to breathe, caught the creature's wrist and pulled its arm towards her own face. 'Iona,' she said, pressing the powerful furred hand against her nose. 'Iona.'

She said her name again very slowly, enunciating all the vowels. The yeti's forehead creased and she opened her mouth. Her tongue flicked out between her teeth, her breathing quickened. Inside herself the creature seemed to be struggling to memorize the sound and reproduce it. Then her lips snapped shut.

Iona's heart sank. For a moment she had seemed to be on the point of making contact with the creature. She'd failed. Her name was beyond the yeti's ability to repeat. Dismally Iona went on staring at the yeti's face.

Minutes passed in a silence that was finally broken by a low rumbling sound. Iona started. For a moment she thought the sound had come from the yeti, that the creature was once more trying to communicate with her. The rumble came again. Iona suddenly realized that the noise was coming not from the yeti, but from her own stomach. At the same time she felt a hollow ache inside her.

Iona gripped her waist. Her insides were churning and she instantly knew why. From the angle of the sun it was almost mid-morning again. She must have slept or been unconscious for a full twenty-four hours since the yeti had found her, and it had been twelve hours earlier still when she'd wandered out into the storm. She hadn't eaten since she'd left the camp, a day and a half ago. Now she was starving – as her stomach was painfully and noisily reminding her. As the rumbles continued, the yeti studied the child through her unseeing eyes, then she shuffled across the space between them and ran her hand unerringly over Iona's midriff.

'Agwan,' the yeti said. Her hand moved briefly to Iona's face, her touch gentle, almost soothing. She stood up and strode away.

Iona remained on her knees. She had no idea what 'Agwan' meant, but somehow she sensed it had to do with food – she fervently hoped so. At that moment she cared about nothing else. Even her fear of the creatures had vanished. She had forgotten her mother, Uncle Robert, Roshan, the camp on the ridge – everything. All she wanted to do was eat.

Trembling and faint with hunger, Iona waited.

14

Some ten minutes later the grass rustled and Kekua, as Iona had already begun to think of the blind female yeti, reappeared.

This time she was accompanied by another female yeti. The second creature was covered in the same pale fur, but she looked younger than Kekua and she clearly wasn't blind. She was also very obviously pregnant. Her distended stomach protruded in front of her and she walked with a careful shuffling stride.

The second yeti's eyes examined Iona keenly as the two of them approached the child. While Kekua waited, her companion squatted in front of Iona and stretched out her hand. Iona glanced down. The yeti was holding a small bulging pouch made out of leaves that had been carefully stitched together with plant fibres. The leaves must have been dampened with water because the pouch glistened wetly in the sunlight. Iona frowned. Something about the pouch was familiar. Then she remembered.

The pouch was the casing of a Nepalese weaver bird's nest. Iona had noticed the nests hanging like fruit from the wayside trees on the second day of the trek. She'd asked Uncle Robert what they were and he'd told her. As Iona stared at it uncertainly, the yeti opened the pouch's neck and held it closer to her, shaking the little bag encouragingly.

Gingerly Iona took it from her and peered inside. It was filled with what appeared to be a thick grey porridge. Iona dipped her finger into the gruel and licked it. The taste was dry and woody and the texture coarse, but the mixture seemed clean and appetizing. She licked her finger again and then a third time. Then ravenously she scooped out the entire contents and ate them from her palm.

The two yeti watched her intently and, when she had finished, Kekua handed her companion something else. The yeti turned and presented it to Iona. It was a dish-shaped piece of tree bark filled with what appeared to be nuts and seeds. The nuts had been husked but the seeds were still encased in their protective shells.

Iona took one of the nuts and nibbled at it. This time the taste was sweet and a ripple of fragrance lifted into the air as her teeth bit into the nut's flesh. She split one of the seeds between her fingers and warily tried that too. The kernel was salty and oily, reminding her somewhat of the sesame seeds on the bagels her mother bought for her when they visited Manhattan on their way to Martha's Vineyard. Iona placed the bark dish on the ground beside her and began to work her way through its contents.

Fifteen minutes later she was sated. The rumbles in her stomach had stopped and her hunger had vanished. Iona pushed the now almost empty bark dish aside and leant back on her ankles. The two yeti were still in front of her, Kekua standing and the other one squatting. As Iona looked at them, Kekua came up to her. She stepped past the second yeti, reached down and felt for Iona's hand, then drew the girl to her feet and led her forward.

They walked through tall waving grass and down a bank until they were standing on the edge of the river. Kekua stopped, scratched Iona's nose again and repeated her name.

'Kekua,' the yeti said.

Iona hesitated. Tentatively she reached out and did the same, saying her own name as she'd done before.

'Iona.' She spoke almost in a whisper.

This time Kekua didn't try to repeat the word. She listened intently, her head on one side and her white fathomless eyes fixed on Iona's face. For several moments the yeti didn't move. Then she turned, waded into the river and stood with the water surging round her waist.

Kekua's back was towards Iona, but over the churning of the current Iona could hear the murmur of the yeti's voice. Kekua was speaking to herself. Tossed up and down by the river's flow, the murmuring continued for a long time before it abruptly ended. Kekua waded ashore and stood in front of Iona.

Three times the yeti opened her mouth and her tongue flickered between her lips without any sound emerging. Then she spoke. 'Iona,' she said very clearly.

Iona looked at her, astounded. A short time earlier her name seemed to be beyond the yeti's ability to pronounce. Somehow the creature had memorized the sound in the river. Now she'd reproduced it almost perfectly.

For the first time in thirty-six hours Iona managed to smile. 'Iona,' the child repeated in confirmation.

Kekua took Iona's hand and lifted it to the other yeti's nose. 'Churinga,' Kekua said.

Iona scratched the second creature's nose. 'Churinga,' she repeated.

Churinga scratched Iona's nose in return. Afterwards, like Kekua, she stepped into the waters. She too stood for a long time murmuring to herself. Finally she climbed back on to the bank.

'Iona,' Churinga said. The sound she made was nothing like as clear as Kekua's, but Iona could still just recognize it as her name. Hesitantly Iona smiled again. Churinga smiled back.

'Iona!' Kekua was speaking to her again.

Iona turned. The blind yeti was staring at her. Kekua made a circling gesture round Iona's body, then lifted her hand. She touched her own ears and lips, and pointed at herself. Then she swung round to face Churinga. She pointed at Churinga and her fingertips brushed Churinga's eyes. Afterwards her hand circled Iona again.

It took several minutes for Iona to understand what Kekua meant. Slowly it dawned on her – she was going to be taught. Kekua was going to be her teacher, her eyes and voice and intelligence. Churinga was going to be her ears. Between them Iona was going to learn the ways of the yeti.

The realization taxed Iona's will and imagination to their limits. She had fallen among monsters. She had been captured by them. That was the only certainty. As far as she was capable of thought, Iona had been certain they would kill her first and perhaps eat her afterwards. That was what monsters did, her nightmares had brutally taught her that.

Kekua was a monster. Even if she had a name, she *had* to be a monster – Iona had only to look at her to know that. So was her companion, the heavily pregnant Churinga. So was the big dark-haired male who had crouched above her on the river bank, and whom she hadn't seen since. They were all creatures of the darkness that Iona knew so well. Only now there was a difference – the monsters hadn't just prowled out of the night into the daylight. They were taking her back into the night with them.

Beyond the stars and the darkness, they had their own life, their own ways, their own language. They were going to make Iona part of it. She was going to be taught the speech of animals.

The idea was so awesome that Iona felt dizzy as she tried to absorb it. The tumult and confusion of the time between her disappearance from the camp and her presence now in front of the two creatures on the island had disorientated her utterly and she didn't know what had really happened to her. She yearned for Uncle Robert. She clung to the belief, as much as she'd been able to hope or believe in anything, that he would rescue her. The idea that she might be able to escape herself hadn't occurred to her.

When the blind yeti beckoned to her, Iona stepped forward obediently. Churinga came round and stood on her other side. The two yeti took her hands. Towering above the child, they led her away through the grass.

Iona was trembling but her hunger had gone. Her stomach was full, and in the company of the two females she felt precariously safe. For the moment all that mattered was that she survived.

15

'Sir! Sir!'

Robert Cabot's head jerked up.

The call came from somewhere ahead and above him. He quickly scanned the ridges, his eyes watering in the morning sunlight dazzling off the snow. All he could see were dark belts of trees and the precipitous flanks of the soaring mountain landscape outlined against the brilliant cloak of whiteness which canopied the ground on every side.

'Here, sir!'

The call came again. In spite of its faintness the shout was unmistakably urgent. Cabot peered upwards, frantically searching for its source. He spotted a tiny figure standing thigh-deep in snow in a gap between the trees. The figure was waving. It could only be Roshan.

Cabot threw himself forward. He was old and lame. Wielding his stick like a crutch, he forced himself to run for the first time in years. Stumbling, lurching from side to side, dragging his arthritic leg behind him, he headed for the little plateau where he'd glimpsed the Sherpa. Cabot didn't care what Roshan had discovered. Anything would be better than the not knowing.

Cabot covered two hundred yards, then tripped and fell painfully. Brushing the snow from his face, he managed to climb back to his feet. He stared up again. Roshan had been running towards him too and Cabot could see the Sherpa clearly now. He caught sight of another figure, moving more slowly some way behind. His heart beating wildly, Cabot shifted his gaze.

A moment later a wave of despair swept over him. The second silhouette against the whiteness was much too tall to be Iona's. It could only be another man. Panting and grim-faced, Cabot waited.

The last two days had been the worst of Cabot's life. On the morning after the storm he'd been woken as usual by An Sering, the cook, with a bowl of hot water. When An Sering put his head into the tent, Cabot had seen Roshan standing behind him, a puzzled expression on his face.

'Is Miss Iona with you, sir?' the Sherpa asked.

'No, of course not,' Cabot answered. 'She'll be in her own tent –' The first cold needles of anxiety pricked him and he paused. 'She is there, isn't she?'

Roshan shook his head. 'No, sir. Her tent is empty.'

Cabot pulled on a sweater and ran outside. He hurried the few yards to Iona's tent and peered in through the open flap. Roshan was right – Iona wasn't there. Cabot withdrew his head and glanced round.

The spring storm that had raged across the ridge during the night had woken Cabot several times. It was one of the fiercest and noisiest he could remember in the more than thirty years of his Himalayan trips. Some time well before dawn it had blown away. He knew that because the last time he woke his own tent had stopped bucketing and shaking as if the wind was about to tear it loose from its deep-hammered anchor pegs.

The storm had left the ridge covered with five inches of snow. Inside the campsite the porters' feet had already flattened out lanes round the fire and between the tents. Apart from sets of footprints to the latrine areas and the woodpile, the surface on every side as far as Cabot could see was unbroken.

'I have already looked, sir.' Roshan confirmed what Cabot was thinking before he could speak. 'There are no tracks. No one has left the camp since the snow settled.'

'What about the camp itself?' Cabot demanded. 'Have you searched it?'

'Yes, sir. Everywhere. She is not here. There is nowhere she could be.'

For a moment Cabot stood in silence. He was utterly bewildered.

Roshan was right. There was nowhere for Iona to hide inside the camp – not that Cabot believed for a moment she would try to hide. The child had no reason to. If she'd wandered away, the lack of tracks in the snow meant she must have done so before the storm started or while the snow was still falling.

That made no sense either. Cabot had taught her about the unpredictability of the Himalayan weather and Iona was much too careful and responsible to have ignored him, he was certain of that. Even if she'd walked out in her sleep, the gale and the icy swirling snowflakes would have woken her at the tent mouth as quickly and brutally as a hard slap on the face. Then she'd simply have ducked back inside again.

She couldn't even have been making for the lavatory. She'd had her own pot in the tent from the start and had never been shy about using it before, even on the calmest nights – let alone when the blizzard was howling round them. It would barely have been possible to stand up in the roaring ferocity of the gale.

Perhaps the child had been so terrified by the uproar she'd been prepared to brave the onslaught of the snow and wind to try to reach his own tent. Even that wasn't likely. Cabot had known Iona all her life. Her mother, Dorelia, claimed she could be 'difficult' but Cabot had never seen that. What he had seen over the years was that in facing the natural world, the child had less fear than anyone he had ever met. If Iona had been frightened, it would have taken something infinitely more menacing than a storm to alarm her.

'Roshan!' Cabot swung round. 'I want everyone out searching. Split them into pairs. Start with a circle close to the camp. Then make other circles further and further away. The child may be lying somewhere half buried in snow. Maybe there'll be tracks further out on rocks where the snow has partly blown away. I don't know. I just want her found. For Christ's sake, tell everyone to shift their butts!' As he finished, Cabot was shouting.

Roshan nodded. 'Yes, sir!' He started to bellow instructions to the porters. Cabot limped back to Iona's tent, went inside and looked round more carefully.

Iona's sleeping-bag had been half unzipped and the flap tossed casually back. Iona, Cabot had noticed, was remarkably tidy for a child of her age. It was one of the many things that made her such a good companion in camp, and so popular among the Sherpas. The state of the sleeping-bag indicated she'd only meant to leave it briefly. If she'd been going out for longer, she'd have zipped up the flap and smoothed down the bag.

That was Cabot's first impression. The second immediately contradicted it. The canvas stool by her bed where she put her clothes was bare. Cabot wrinkled his face, trying to remember what she'd been wearing for supper. It came back to him. The temperature – reflecting the approach of the storm – had been unusually cold. Iona was dressed in jeans, a shirt, two sweaters and her goosedown duvet jacket. She'd even been wearing an oiled-wool Tibetan cap on her head. All those garments had vanished, as had her boots. That wasn't all. Coming closer to the bed Cabot saw that the two tie tapes on the tent wall above the stool were dangling down unfastened. Iona used the tapes to hold the canvas survival belt and pouch Cabot had given her. The belt and pouch had gone too.

Iona couldn't have been searching for his tent in terror of the storm. She would only have taken her survival equipment if she'd been setting out on an expedition.

Cabot closed his eyes. It was a nightmare. Nothing made any sense. All he knew, he realized suddenly with a chilling ache, was that he loved his goddaughter – far more than her wilful and imperious mother, his niece Dorelia. He loved Iona's courage. He loved her serenity. He loved her elusive child's beauty, her perceptiveness, the way she understood his dry jokes, the way she sometimes laughed at him and teased him back. Above all he loved the dyed-in-the-bone streak of hickory toughness in the child. She would lock her hand round her chosen stars and it would take portents to unloose the grip. Cabot knew where that came from – not from her mother or her languid father – it came from him.

His eyes bright with tears but his mouth set in a grimly determined line beneath his shaggy grey eyebrows, Cabot leant on his stick, swung his hips round and limped out of the tent. He didn't know how he was going to do it, but if he had to walk barefoot on ice through hell he was going to find the child.

Cabot waited anxiously for Roshan and the man, probably a Himalayan tribesman, hurrying behind him.

16

The yeti lived on an island.

That was Iona's first realization as she walked behind blind Kekua and the pregnant Churinga. Somewhere in the deep recesses of her memory she seemed to know it already. She cast back into her mind and discovered why. Her last memory of the journey on the male yeti's shoulders was of water lapping at her waist as the creature waded into the river.

There had been water all round her then. There was water all round her now. She could hear it gurgling and rustling and lapping on every side. The island it surrounded was about half a mile long and half as wide. Iona knew that because old Mr Simpson had taught her how to measure land in the great walled garden at Mainwarden.

'Good seed doesn't come cheap,' he used to say. 'Buy more than ye need and what ye can't use goes to waste. So measure the area you're planting.'

Mr Simpson could calculate the size of a piece of ground at a single glance. His skill came of long experience. He'd shown Iona how to acquire it in the way he'd learnt himself long ago – by pacing out the land with his feet. Although Iona had no chance to pace the island that day, she simply used her eye as the old gardener would have done, and later, when she did get the opportunity to count her steps, she found that her first guess was almost exactly right.

Half a mile by a quarter, the island floated on the river like a low raft of rippling grass with a humpbacked ridge rising at its centre. Sometimes the water on either side ran still and black and deep. Little whorls of golden peat fragments turned in the current and turquoise dragonflies skimmed the surface. At other times, after rain or when snow-melt swept down from the crests, the twin arms of the streams rippled and surged. The stillness and the dancing veins of golden peat vanished, and rough brown foam covered the flow.

Yet whether the river ran slow and quiet or whether its waters churned, the island always looked the same. Nothing, it seemed, inhabited the low sleepy mound apart from a few darting birds.

This impression, Iona soon realized, was false. The island teemed and throbbed with life. There were the birds, of course – and infinitely more of them, she quickly discovered, than those she saw on the first day. Hawks, owls, kites, kingfishers, crows, ravens and dozens of other species had made the island their home. There were bees and butterflies, moths and insects. There were throngs of animals from tiny ever-present voles to the occasional wandering deer which swam across to feed. There were bats and otters and snakes. Above all there was the overwhelming presence of the holding.

The holding. After Kekua's and Churinga's names, it was the first word she learnt in the language of the yeti. It took her a long time to find a satisfactory equivalent in her own tongue for the sound the two female yeti made again and again that day as they pointed.

'Mirja,' they said. 'Mirja.' Their arms swept out. They pointed and mimed sleeping and eating, then they smiled. There was a particular warmth in their smiles. 'Mirja', it dawned on Iona, was very important to them. Gradually she began to understand.

Mirja was their home. It embraced not only the area of earth their gestures spanned, but the other yeti there too. More than that, it was a space they had won and held.

Mainwarden belonged to her father. His ancestors had won it. It provided him and his family with shelter. It was a place to grow food, a place of safety and sanctuary – it was his holding. The island was the yeti's holding.

The yeti lived below the small ridge at the island's centre. There, hidden in a clearing surrounded by the waving grass, was a number of what Iona could only think of as huts. They weren't like any huts she had ever seen. At their highest point the roofs were less than four feet from the ground. Each roof sloped back in a low tunnel from a single hooped branch, sharpened at both ends and planted like a bow in the earth. Covered in woven grass and reeds, the huts looked like nothing so much as great birds' nests loosely anchored to the ground. No higher than the surrounding grasses, the shelters were invisible from more than a few yards beyond the perimeter of the holding. It would be easy, Iona thought, to cross the entire island and be unaware that the yeti were there.

The twin streams of dark river water. The raft of waving grass between them. The almost unseen birds' nests of the yeti's shelters clustered at the island's heart beneath the humpbacked ridge that rose above them. That was Iona's initial impression of the holding. For several minutes after Churinga and the blind Kekua led her into the clearing, the shelters seemed to be deserted. Then Iona's eyes began to spot other yeti. She shivered. She had been captured by one monster and now she was standing between two more, but there were others, many others.

It was mid-morning. The sun was high and the air drowsy and hot. The creatures were resting. Once, in a world that seemed so remote it might have belonged to another life, Iona had seen on television a film of lions in Africa's Kalahari Desert. The lions, too, rested in the day's heat, the tawny golden-brown of their hide so like the summer-dry Kalahari bush that only when the camera closed in on them was it possible to tell the animals from their surroundings.

It was the same with the yeti. The pale yellow-ochre of their fur blended with the island's grasses. Iona blinked. She made out one silhouette asleep in a patch of shade, then another, then more. She began to count. In all, there were maybe twenty-five or thirty within her sight. Some were males, some females, and a number were young – the young ones betrayed themselves more readily than the adults by twitching restlessly and occasionally scampering from place to place, chattering as they moved.

Kekua and Churinga walked forward to the clearing's centre. At their approach the young yeti fell silent and scuttled fearfully back to their parents. All the others, even those who had been sleeping a moment before, sat up and stared at Iona. Apprehensively Iona looked back at them, her gaze travelling round her in a circle.

When she had glimpsed them from the river, the yeti's faces had looked hostile and threatening. Now they were expressionless, but their eyes seemed to be filled with a combination of fear and curiosity. As Iona stared at them, two thoughts occurred to her. She was probably, she guessed, the first human they had ever seen – that explained the curiosity. The fear had another cause, of which she was totally ignorant. Whatever it was, the creatures were as frightened of her as she was of them.

'Manu!' Kekua called out.

The grass rustled and a male yeti came into sight.

Iona recognized him immediately. Her stomach contracted and her heart raced. He was the monster who had found her, the tall young yeti accompanied by the leopard who had picked her up on the river bank and carried her to the island. As Iona watched him walk towards them, she held her breath. Slowly her heart stopped beating wildly and the tension drained out of her. The set of the creature's features was thoughtful, almost kindly, and in spite of his massive physical presence there was nothing threatening in his attitude.

As Iona studied him, a lesson from her godfather flashed through her mind. 'To a stamp collector every piece of paper the goddamn mail makes us buy is different, young lady,' Cabot had said. 'People make fortunes from spotting the differences. Creatures are even more different than stamps. Look at them carefully. The differences between them, if you can spot them, won't make you a fortune, but they're more important still.'

Although the young male was evidently just as much a yeti as the others, he seemed to belong to a different type. As she'd noticed before, his fur was thicker and darker, a deep red-brown like the old mahogany furniture at Mainwarden instead of the tawny walnut colour of the island yeti's hides. His body was different too. The yeti around her were heavily built, some of them almost portly. He was leaner and more muscular, and he moved with a long loping stride. The eyes of the island yeti were a pale stone-grey, his were larger and golden-brown. If the holding's eyes, Iona thought, reflected the colour of the dawn sky above the valley, then his took their hue from somewhere else – perhaps from the peat-covered fissures and clefts that lanced up towards the crests.

The male yeti stopped in front of them. He reached out and scratched Iona's nose in what she knew now must be some form of yeti greeting. She steeled herself not to back away as his fingers ran over her nostrils.

'Iona,' he said quietly.

Iona stared at him, dumbfounded, even more astonished than when Kekua had uttered her name. At least she'd repeated it to Kekua again and again. She hadn't even spoken to the male yeti. She could only imagine that Kekua had managed to teach him what she was called.

'Manu,' the yeti added. He took Iona's hand and drew it slowly over his face and across his chest. 'Manu,' he repeated.

He let her hand drop. Iona hesitated. The creature seemed to be waiting expectantly. Trembling, she lifted her arm and scratched his nose. 'Manu,' she said in an uncertain voice.

The yeti smiled. A surge of relief swept over Iona. The yeti's name was Manu and she'd made the right response in returning his greeting.

Before she had time to take in anything else, the blind Kekua started speaking to Manu. It was the first time Iona had heard the yeti speak in anything but the few single slowly delivered words they'd addressed to her. The words had been strange and unknown but, once she'd worked out their meaning, they were understandable as some form of language.

In conversation the sounds that came out of Kekua's mouth were not so much like language, even an unknown foreign language, as a bubbling stream of clicks and grunts and fluting whistles. If Kekua had been speaking Chinese or Bulgarian, Iona would have recognized it as a human tongue, but the flow of sounds from the blind female was different in kind from any language she had ever heard. Echoing off the grass, bouncing across the clearing in the sunlight, mingling with the noise of the flowing river, the ropes of words Kekua wove together sounded like an infinitely complicated tapestry of birdcalls and animal cries.

Kekua stopped. Manu, the male yeti, nodded. Kekua turned and smiled at Iona. 'Mirja,' she said.

Manu was already walking away. Kekua took Iona's hand and set off behind him. Together they crossed the clearing and came to the ring of shelters.

For a time Manu searched around between the shelters. He strode backwards and forwards, testing the ground with his foot. Once he knelt and smelt the earth. Finally he settled on a small flat shelf slightly higher than the other dwellings. He cleared the tall waving grass that covered it and piled the stems to one side. Then he vanished, reappearing some minutes later with an armful of fresh-cut saplings, and a bundle of long, broad foliage from the water plants Iona had noticed growing on the river bank. He dropped his load on the earth, then produced what looked like a bone knife and set to work. It took Iona only a few moments to realize what he was doing – Manu was building a shelter.

The yeti worked with extraordinary speed and skill. He sharpened the ends of one of the saplings, bent it into a bow-shape, and drove the ends into the earth to form the shelter's entrance. He took half a dozen of the other, longer saplings, lashed them to the top of the bow with green withies and ran them back to the ground behind to form the roof support. Then he covered the structure with the water-plant leaves, weaving them expertly in and out through the frame.

As he worked, the yeti occasionally glanced across at Iona, indicating what he was doing, or trying, it appeared, to point out why. Iona was bewildered. She could see he was skilful, but the reason why he placed a withy in a certain position or angled one of the roofing leaves in a particular way eluded her.

Finally he rolled the stacked grass inside and spread it across the floor. There wasn't enough to satisfy him, so he cut some more, building up the bed on the floor until it was thick and springy and comfortable. He stood back and examined it critically, then he looked at Iona and smiled.

'Mirja,' he said.

He beckoned her forward to inspect it. His face was eager, almost proud. He touched her arm with his massive hand and this time Iona didn't flinch. She glanced up and gave him a hesitant smile. Then she peered inside.

The little shelter was as warm and clean and, from what she could judge of the roof, as waterproof as any tent she had ever slept in. It had taken Manu less than two hours to construct. At Iona's side Kekua laughed. The blind yeti ran her fingers over Manu's face and said something to him. Churinga laughed too, clutching her belly as the laughter rippled over her. Then Kekua put her arm round Iona's shoulder. 'Mirja,' Iona heard the word again.

Kekua pointed at herself, then at Iona, and then at the shelter. Iona frowned a moment before she understood. The shelter hadn't been built for her alone, she was going to share it with Kekua. She had already been made part of the holding.

Kekua took Iona's hand. Squatting down, the yeti drew the child in through the entrance. Iona crawled behind her.

Iona had been given her home.

17

'Batal!' Kekua called out to Churinga.

Iona watched.

A week had passed and Iona, the blind Kekua, and Churinga were standing together on the island. To Iona, the island had come to seem more than ever like a raft floating in the water. That morning they were at its stern, where the river divided into the two streams that flowed by it on either side.

Every year the spring snow-melt carried down a layer of silt from the mountains above. The silt had built up into a rich and dark canopy along the river banks and along the island's marshy shore. Over the centuries the moist fertile soil had been colonized by a tapestry of plants, reeds and grasses. Kekua had instructed Churinga to bring her one of them. Churinga waded into the marsh and returned with her legs stained black with mud. She gave the stem to Kekua and waited.

The stem was a whippy frond studded at intervals with apple-green leaves and ending in a cluster of yellowing berries. Kekua raised it to her nose. Forming a V with her finger and thumb, she stripped off the leaves and put the frond's base between her lips and chewed it. Then she broke off one of the berries, peeled away its leathery pod and placed the berry's kernel in her mouth. She turned her face towards Iona. 'Batal,' she said, repeating the sound she had made to Churinga.

Kekua handed Iona the frond. At her side Churinga mimed instructions for Iona to copy Kekua and chew the frond's stem. Iona put it in her mouth and cautiously shredded the woody fibres between her teeth. The taste was chalky and slightly sweet.

Iona swallowed. 'Batal,' she said hesitantly to Kekua, but the sound she made didn't sound like the one which Kekua had uttered.

'Batal,' Kekua repeated.

Iona tried again. This time she was closer. Both the yeti raised their hands and scratched their nostrils. Instinctively Iona knew it was a gesture of approval.

Kekua reached out, her hand hovering close to Iona's as she searched for the frond. She found it, broke off another of the berries and unpeeled it. 'Orindi,' she said, holding out the berry towards Iona.

Iona crushed the kernel in her mouth. The taste was as sour as the skin of an unripened lemon. She opened her lips to spit the fruit out, then stopped herself and went on chewing. The sourness vanished. It was replaced by a strong dry flavour that wasn't unpleasant. It reminded her of the early unripened brambles she used to gather in Scotland.

'Orindi,' Iona said.

By accident she must have reproduced the new sound almost perfectly. The yeti scratched their nostrils again, then the set of their faces changed. Until now the features of the two creatures had seemed immobile, frozen in the intense, wary gaze of hunting animals.

Now, like Misty when Iona stroked her, their faces relaxed. They appeared to be smiling. Kekua stretched out her arm. She found Iona's face and stroked her nose. Out of the yeti's body came a small satisfied rumble of what Iona knew could only be pleasure.

Iona took a deep breath. 'Batal,' she said. 'And Orindi.' She didn't know what either of the words meant, but they were obviously the names of a grass and its fruit. The yeti understood her. She was starting to communicate with them.

Tentatively Iona smiled back.

Language.

The word ran insistently through Iona's mind. It was night. She was lying in the shelter Manu had built with Kekua asleep beside her. Earlier, holding little one-eyed Bear for comfort, Iona had wept.

By day all that week she had been kept too busy to cry. Kekua woke her before the sun rose and in the fading darkness of dawn they ate a handful of berries with Churinga whose shelter was next to theirs. All round them in the clearing the other yeti were doing the same. By the time the first of the cold Himalayan daylight seeped over the island, the three of them had left the clearing.

With Kekua walking ahead, they methodically combed the island. Patiently for hour after hour the two yeti, the one blind and the other carrying her swollen pregnant belly before her, instructed Iona. As dusk began to fall they returned to the clearing and ate again. Afterwards, exhausted, Iona crept into the shelter and lay down on the bed of dry grass and reeds Manu had gathered for her.

It was then that Iona cried. Every night, choking back her sobs into silence for fear of provoking the yeti, the tears flooded down her face on to the rustling stems beneath her. At first she wept for her mother. Iona loved her father but he had always been a remote and shadowy presence at the edges of her life. Her mother stood at its centre. In her earliest and deepest misery Iona convinced herself that only her mother could take her away from where she was imprisoned. She longed to smell the dizzying fragrance of her scent, longed for the flaring colours of her dresses, and the brilliance of her jewels. Achingly Iona longed for the strength and safety of her mother's arms around her.

Her mother scorned monsters. She didn't believe they existed. Her mother was wrong, but that didn't matter. In the face of her scorn and anger, even these ones – living monsters, not the ghostly, prowling creatures of Iona's nightmares – would retreat and scurry away like the shapes who haunted the darkness. Her mother would pluck her out of the valley and carry her back to Iona's own bed.

To her mother, Iona's bed was in the house in London. To Iona it was at Mainwarden. In her loneliness Iona wept for Mainwarden, too, for gruff Mr Simpson, for her cat Misty, for the house and the tall plumes of smoke above the chimneys, for the walled garden and the path that led to the pavilion in the woods where the other, frozen monsters stood.

Lonely, cold and frightened, Iona cried again at the thought of Mainwarden.

Then as the days passed and she began to think more rationally, Iona wept instead for Uncle Robert. Her mother wouldn't save her. She was almost half the world away, and in any event she would have been lost in the wild mountain landscape. Uncle Robert, on the other hand, was still no more than thirty or forty miles from her. He was at home in the Himalayan wilderness, he had Roshan and the other Sherpas with him and, most important of all, he'd be doing everything in his power to find her. Iona was so sure of that that on the seventh night she stopped crying. She propped herself up on her elbow and wiped the tears from her cheeks.

In a way, it suddenly occurred to her, her godfather loved her more than her mother did, and now she came to think of it, she trusted him more than she trusted her mother. Her mother came and went, drifting in and out of her life with her jewels and her clouds of scent in the darkness. With his stick and his compasses, his knowledge of plants and animals, his caustic observations and his dry jokes, Uncle Robert was there in the daylight.

Daylight would save her, not the darkness which belonged to the monsters, and it was in daylight that Uncle Robert lived. She could depend on him rather than her mother.

It was a startling, almost a shocking realization, but a wave of hope ran over Iona's body. As it did she sniffed. Angrily. The anger was directed at herself. Her face was pale and she was shivering, but her mouth was suddenly tight and determined. Uncle Robert would expect her to play her part in her rescue, and crying would achieve nothing. For the moment she was alone, and the only person who could save her was herself.

Fear dropped away from her like a worn-out skin cast off by a wintering snake as it emerges into the summer sun. In the darkness of the shelter Iona wrinkled her face. Language. It came back to her again and again. If she could speak, she could change everything. She could talk her way back into the world she came from. She could escape.

Iona glanced at the sleeping Kekua. The blind yeti was still a monster. She was tall and bizarre and her skin was covered in thick bristling hair, the colour of oak leaves before they fell in autumn. Kekua would grunt and scratch herself. Often she would lie down and doze without any sign of tiredness. And she was blind. The sightless eyes, opaque and clotted with marble veins of whiteness, stared out of her face more chillingly than any of the monsters which had prowled Iona's dreams.

Kekua was an animal and yet Kekua could speak.

Language.

Iona remembered Uncle Robert talking to her once. It was long before she came with him to the mountains and she had been much younger then. Uncle Robert had used a word she didn't understand. She asked him what it meant and afterwards what words themselves meant, where they came from and how people knew how to use them.

'Gestures were probably our first real means of communication,' he told her. 'We still use our faces, hands and bodies to talk. Danger, be silent, stay away, come closer, take this and eat. We can say all those things and much more without speaking. So can the animals. But just like them we gradually discovered it wasn't enough. A gesture's no use unless you can see it being made. Often you can't. You need something else. That's where sound comes in –' The tall grey-haired figure paused as he and Iona walked through the park at Mainwarden.

'The animals developed calls. Calls can bridge distances, keep you in contact and pass information when you're out of sight. They're more flexible and subtle than gestures. They convey more precisely what you want to say. Owls and wolves, frogs and deer, everyone in the animal kingdom uses them. So do we. But we can put our calls together. We named the calls words and invented speech. Using it, we can create whole pyramids of ideas and pass them to others. No other animal can do that. It's what sets humans apart from the rest of the animal kingdom.

'There's something else strange about human language,' Uncle Robert finished. 'For centuries people thought we learnt it as babies by copying our parents, but today scientists believe differently. They've studied babies of different races in different parts of the world and they found that as babies start to speak they use words in the same basic patterns everywhere. It may be that speech isn't learnt. Instead we may be born with the ability to use it. If that's so, then anyone who can speak is by definition a human.'

Kekua wasn't human, she was clearly an animal. Yet equally obviously she could speak. Like everything else about the yeti it was both bewildering and frightening. So was the fact that for some reason Kekua was determined that Iona should learn the yeti's language.

Iona didn't know why but it no longer mattered. Throughout that first week Iona mouthed the sounds Kekua taught her. She didn't even think about them. Between her tears and the lessons, she might have been sleepwalking. She remembered the words only to survive. But now it was different – now Iona wanted to learn as much as Kekua wanted to teach her.

Iona learnt quickly. Her mother's world was cosmopolitan and from the moment Iona started school Dorelia Howard had insisted she learnt French and Spanish. Iona had a natural ear for languages. Even as a small child they intrigued her – they were rather like the puzzles where one had to join up an apparently random series of dots until they made a picture.

By the time she was twelve Iona was fluent in both French and Spanish. The language of the yeti was very different. It was at once much simpler and infinitely more complicated. The simple part was the structure. Iona grasped that with little difficulty. The problems came with the vocabulary.

The frond of grass Kekua told Churinga to collect that day was an example. To Iona grass was grass. There was just one word for it, and Iona knew it in three different languages. In the yeti's tongue there seemed to be twenty, fifty, even a hundred different words for grass. Iona soon realized why. When she looked at a meadow, she simply saw a mantle of green. Looking at the same meadow the yeti saw every individual plant of every different species. They had names for each one.

And not only for each grass. They had names for each plant at every stage of its growth. As a young shoot, when it was full-grown, when it carried seed, when it turned yellow at the summer's end, even for the root that was left as winter approached. Kekua was determined Iona knew every one.

'And what is this?' Kekua asked her. She was holding up a tuber Churinga had dug from the river's silt and brought back to the island. Iona studied it.

Only three more days had passed, but Iona no longer had to puzzle out the meaning of each sound, each word Kekua spoke. They were beginning to join together and make sentences Iona could understand. Now she could recognize a question and concentrate on the answer. She examined the tuber. It was plump and pear-shaped and had the dark purple colour of a beetroot with a wrinkled, mud-coated skin. Iona rubbed off the mud, peeled back the skin and nibbled. The flesh was waxy and sweet.

Iona frowned. 'Amadan?' she suggested uncertainly.

Kekua shook her head. 'It is amadan when it starts to wake after the snows have gone, when it is small and dry. This is full and ready for the leaves to shoot. Now we call it –'

'Pota!' Iona interrupted her. The name had suddenly come back to her. 'Pota!'

Kekua nodded. 'And what do we do with it?'

'You gather it. Some is eaten fresh, but most is dried to keep for the snows.'

The tuber, Iona remembered, was one of the first plants Kekua and Churinga had taught her about. To the yeti it was also one of the most prized, both for its taste and for its ability to be dried and stored as a winter food.

'Very good,' Kekua smiled. 'As a reward you may keep it. Let us see what else we can find.' With Churinga following she set off along the bank. Iona walked behind them. A week ago she wouldn't have known what a pota was, let alone how to find the glutinous, mud-caked object. Now she peeled away the rest of the skin and gnawed hungrily at the purple root inside.

As she walked Iona glanced back. In the far distance and high above her she could just make out the circle of rocky ridges, plunging gorges and snow-flanked crests that by now she'd worked out enclosed the valley and the island at its centre. Somewhere on one of the ridges would be Uncle Robert. In her mind Iona saw his tall angular body poised awkwardly over his stick, his eyes narrowed behind his half-moon glasses, his face angled down over the great bowl of the valley below.

Roshan, the dark-skinned smiling Sherpa from the slopes of Everest, would be with him. Both of them would be trying to search the valley's rolling floor, half concealed as always beneath the veils of mist. Tears blurred Iona's sight. She longed to call out, to scream, to leap and wave to show that she was there so close to them. She bit back the cries in her throat.

It would be useless and Uncle Robert would not expect her, as he might have put it, to make a 'monkey' of herself – though pointing out that monkeys, in fact, were invariably dignified, composed and sensible. Monkeys lived in wild landscapes and survived. Her godfather would expect her to do the same.

Gritting her teeth Iona walked on.

'Now!' Kekua said. 'Am I not right?'

Iona glanced away from the distant crests. She looked at the blind yeti in astonishment. 'Yes,' she answered. 'It happened just as you spoke. How do you know, Kekua?'

It was early evening and a week later still. The two of them were standing on the ridge above the island. Kekua had been telling Iona about the second of the two yeti clans, the ranging. Iona asked where they lived and Kekua had taken her up to the ridge to point out the crests. The sun was setting when they reached the ridge's top, and the blind yeti said she would tell Iona the exact moment it disappeared.

'I can feel it on my skin,' Kekua smiled. 'My skin tells me much. Sometimes too much.'

The smile faded from her face. She reached out and took Iona's hand. 'If you have seen enough, let us go back to the holding,' she went on.

Iona guided her back down the ridge. Kekua was perfectly capable of negotiating the descent on her own. Over the course of her life she must have made the journey dozens of times alone. But when there was help available, friendly comforting help, Kekua liked, as Iona had come to realize, to make use of it.

Together they walked back side by side to the cluster of shelters below. 'The height of the season is past,' Kekua said. 'Today we lost the sun ten owl's wing-beats earlier than yesterday. So it will go on.'

'Ten owl's wing-beats?' Iona said puzzled.

'It is one of my ways of measuring,' Kekua replied. 'Here, I will show you.'

They stopped and stood together in the gathering twilight. Kekua took Iona's hand and pressed the girl's fingers round her wrist so that Iona could feel Kekua's pulse beating beneath her fingertips. Ten minutes or more passed. Iona shifted restlessly from foot to foot.

'Be patient,' Kekua said quietly. 'It is his time. He will come soon. I can tell that by my skin too.'

The owl drifted overhead almost before she had finished speaking.

Iona, almost without realizing it, had seen the bird often before. She looked up now and watched it plane down the wind over the river. At the head of the island it circled and headed back. On its downward journey it had simply been floating on the current of air funnelled down from the mountains. Returning, it had to use its wings to propel itself forward.

'Can you hear it?' Kekua asked.

Iona shook her head. She had never thought of 'hearing' an owl except when it hooted. This one was flying silently.

'Wait until it is close,' Kekua said. 'Then listen carefully. I will tell you.'

The owl drifted away from them over one of the arms of the river and circled the water. Then it turned back on a course that would take it over their heads again.

'Now!' Kekua whispered. 'Count from beat to beat!'

Iona strained her ears. Somewhere above her head, somewhere between the stars and the water, she identified a tiny clicking sound from all the other myriad noises of the approaching night. It might have been a frog's croak, the rustle of a grass stem, the rub of a summer-dried fruit against its still unfallen leaf. It was none of those things. With Kekua's guidance, Iona knew the whisper of sound was the revolution of the owl's wing-bone in the socket that held it to the bird's body.

Iona heard it and began to count. She counted slowly to five, then the sound came again. Under her finger she could feel the pulse of Kekua's blood. The second time she counted, she found the passage of time her mind measured out exactly matched Kekua's pulse. She did it for a third time and then the owl was gone.

The bird was absent for only a few moments. It turned somewhere upstream, floated back across the island, then began to beat its way over the river again. As it passed overhead once more, Iona resumed the count. The result was the same – five pulses of Kekua's blood marked exactly one sweep of the owl's wings. Fifty pulses spanned ten sweeps.

'Is it not so?' Kekua said. 'Eyes are not needed. Practise and you too will be able to measure by blood-beat and owl's wings.' She smiled at Iona.

As they reached the edge of the clearing, Churinga came out to meet them. She saw Iona smiling back at the blind yeti and asked what the two of them had been doing. When Kekua told her, Churinga laughed and asked something else. Iona missed the question, but she understood Kekua's reply.

'No, she is not ready yet,' Kekua said. 'But the shumbi is beginning to learn. Soon she can be taken to Tonemetapu.'

18

'The shumbi is beginning to learn. Soon she can be taken to Tonemetapu.'

Kekua's phrases echoed through Iona's mind as she lay in the shelter that night.

The shumbi was herself, Iona knew that. It was the name the yeti gave to humans. The second sentence meant nothing to her – she had no idea who or what Tonemetapu was. For all the child knew it might be either a place or another yeti. Whatever it was, the words filled her with disquiet.

Cautiously and uncertainly Iona was beginning to trust Kekua. She trusted Churinga too, but that was much easier. From the moment Iona first saw the young female with her simple open face and her heavily pregnant stomach, Iona knew there was nothing to fear in Churinga.

Kekua was different. She was gentle and graceful, much more graceful than Churinga who could often be blunt and clumsy in a way that had nothing to do with her pregnancy. Kekua was the leader. She took charge of everything from what they ate when they rose to the choice of their journeys across the island, to the plants and animals Iona was instructed to learn about. Churinga, as Iona had realized at the start, was little more than Kekua's hands and eyes. The blind yeti made the decisions.

She made them, Iona sensed, for a reason. Iona didn't know what the reason was, but increasingly it worried her and the fear she had cast off returned to haunt her. The yeti might be able to speak, but they were still monsters – unknown and unpredictable monsters. Iona's only safety lay in doing exactly what they wanted. To protect herself she had to lock everything inside her and allow nothing to show – not the fear or the tears, which still returned, or the aching sense of loss for everything she'd been cut off from when she wandered out into the snowstorm.

Yet Iona was doing what she'd determined to do – she was learning to talk. She clung to the task fiercely and stubbornly, memorizing every word, repeating the sounds to herself again and again, starting when she woke in the dawn darkness and ending only at night when she lay down beside Kekua on the bed of grass and reeds inside the shelter. She even whispered them to Bear when she knew Kekua was asleep.

Although Iona didn't yet know how it would happen, she had an iron conviction that speech would be her means of escape.

It was making a difference already, a huge difference. Iona still walked with a lowered head. She still smiled eagerly and obediently, and averted her eyes when she came across other groups of the island's yeti. But now she was beginning to absorb what was going on around her. In learning the yeti's language, Iona was beginning to understand the holding.

She also watched and listened to the rhythms of the yeti's lives.

When darkness filled the valley the yeti retired to their shelters, lay down on their beds of dried moss and lichens and fell asleep almost instantly. All her life Iona had done the same. The difference was that until the nightmares came, Iona had slept without break for eight hours or more.

The yeti didn't. They slept for a couple of hours, then woke and went outside. There they scratched each other, talked quietly, or simply squatted in the starlight. Occasionally one of them would climb up to the ridge and stand for a long time sniffing the night air. Afterwards they returned to their shelters and slept again. Two hours or so later the cycle would be repeated.

Even in her own sleep Iona was aware of the traffic in the darkness. She would wake and listen to the movements. As the days passed, she found it increasingly harder to slip back into sleep herself. One night, after tossing restlessly for a while, she opened her eyes and sat up. Kekua's bed of moss and grass was empty.

Iona crawled outside. There was no moon and it was almost impenetrably dark. Iona glanced round the worn-down circle of earth at the centre of the shelters. In the thin starlight she saw the silhouettes of several of the yeti before identifying Kekua's. Iona knew it was Kekua because she turned her head at the child's appearance, and the starlight flashed white off her blind eyes.

Iona went over and knelt beside her. For several moments the child stayed there, upright and puzzled. Then impulsively, without knowing what she was doing, Iona inclined her head and rested her cheek against Kekua's. Kekua breathed out softly and rubbed her own cheek against Iona's.

'Put your head on my knee,' Kekua instructed her.

After a moment she felt Kekua parting her hair and running her fingers over her scalp. Iona had often seen the other yeti do the same thing. She had thought they were scratching each other, but Kekua's movements were too careful and systematic for scratching, and her fingertips barely brushed Iona's skin.

'What are you doing?' Iona asked.

'Is this not done among the shumbi?' Kekua asked in return.

Iona shook her head. Kekua gave out the throaty clicking sound Iona had heard once or twice before when the yeti were puzzled.

'Among the people it is done all the time,' Kekua said. 'We name it the "little gathering" or sometimes the "home gathering". We take from each other the small creatures that crawl from the meadows to settle and feed on us, as the beetles do on carrion. It is important we do so. If not, the creatures breed and become many. Then they cause irritation and sometimes sickness.'

Kekua found something on Iona's scalp. Iona felt a quick tingling sensation as the yeti plucked it off. Kekua passed her fingers across her nostrils to scent what it was. She placed it in her mouth and swallowed noisily. Then she went back to combing through Iona's hair.

Iona realized what she was doing. She even remembered Uncle Robert teaching her the proper word for it – not scratching, but grooming. It was what animals did as they cleansed each other of fleas, lice and ticks. 'It's a social activity,' he'd said. 'It requires cooperation. It happens most often among the higher mammals – and that includes both the chimpanzees and ourselves.'

Iona lay still in the darkness as Kekua's fingers went on exploring her hair. Later, Iona had no idea how much later, she and Kekua went back to the shelter where Iona fell asleep quickly and easily. Afterwards, whenever she woke at night, Iona went out into the darkness like the yeti. Sometimes Kekua was there, sometimes Churinga.

There was a difference now in her relationship with the two yeti. Her knowledge of their language had developed beyond the mere exchange of words to an ability to communicate at a deeper, more complex level. The difference was intangible, but immense.

*

That was the night.

The day had a different pattern. The midday hours, the hours of mountain heat, were spent inside the holding. The yeti either slept again or occupied themselves with the many tasks involved in the holding's life. But every morning and evening they left the island to feed.

The feeding ritual never changed. It was always directed by the old patriarch, Yerto.

'Tell me –' Iona began.

Churinga laughed and cut Iona off before she could go on.

'Tell me, tell me, tell me!' Churinga said. 'Is that all you have learnt to say? For certain it is what you say most often, little shumbi. I think we must name you Iona-tell-me!'

Iona flushed. It was true. Since discovering that she could talk to the yeti rather than merely mimicking them, '*Akarn-j*', tell me or explain to me, had become her favourite phrase. There was so much to discover, and she wanted to know it all.

Churinga relented. 'What is it that "tell me" must know this time?'

'Yerto,' Iona said. 'Who is he? Why is he so important? Why does he direct the gathering?'

The questions Iona had started to ask Kekua had done more than shatter the barrier between her and the blind yeti, and Churinga too. It had opened the whole life and world of the holding to her. When she crossed the clearing between the shelters the fragments of the yeti's talk no longer consisted of incomprehensible sounds – they had a pattern and meaning that Iona could understand. She could interpret the calls of the children, the grumbles of the elderly, the long, earnest discussions of the younger adults.

Iona was perceptive and aware. Simply by keeping her eyes and ears open she'd learnt much about the holding, but there still remained areas she knew nothing about. The role of the old grey-furred yeti, Yerto, was one of them.

Each morning everyone gathered by the river and waited for him to appear. Although Iona wasn't yet allowed to cross the river into the feeding grounds with the others – her food was brought back to her – Kekua and Churinga always took her down to the water's edge. Sooner or later the old patriarch came down the bank. His movements were stiff. On good days, the dry days when he could flex the joints of his limbs, Yerto walked upright, but more often he dropped forward and supported his weight on his bunched fists.

When he reached the bank Yerto consulted the out-searchers first – young male yeti who travelled far beyond where the holding would go. Their task was to bring back news about the extent and ripeness of the plants and fruit which were the holding's principal diet. When he had spoken to them, Yerto would turn to a group of the older female yeti.

'You have heard the out-searchers,' he would say. 'The suval is budding beyond the low hill. The trigem is shooting near the crest path. The lomas is in fruit where the moon's shadow passes –'

Yerto always paused as he came to the end of the information the out-searchers had given him. 'So where do we forage today?' he finished.

The female yeti conferred, then gave Yerto their advice. Yerto almost always took it, but not invariably. Sometimes for no apparent reason he chose a quite different site, and when he did, no one questioned his decision. The choice was his alone.

'Yerto?' Churinga said in answer to Iona's question. 'He is the holding's strength. With Tonemetapu to guide him, he is also our safety – he knows where we should go in danger. Have you not seen his grey hairs? They tell of the seasons he has passed and the knowledge he has gathered. That is why he directs the gathering.'

Iona thought for a moment in silence. In many ways Yerto was like the great silver-backed males in the films she'd seen of the mountain gorillas. They too led their family groups. Yet Yerto's role wasn't the same as theirs. The silverbacks owed their position to their physical strength. When they lost that, they lost their dominance too.

Yerto must once have been strong. Now he was virtually a cripple. It didn't seem to matter – he still led the holding and everyone continued to defer to the wisdom he had acquired over the years. Then there was Tonemetapu, whose name she heard mentioned for the second time. Although she couldn't be sure, it seemed to refer to another yeti. She was about to question Churinga, but suddenly felt apprehensive. Tonemetapu, she sensed, belonged to a part of the yeti's world she hadn't even glimpsed yet – a darker hidden part. Instinctively, Iona shied away from it.

Instead she said to Churinga, 'And Ryena is Yerto's mate?'

Apart from the blind Kekua, Churinga and the dark-furred Manu, the identities of most of the members of the holding were still blurred and shadowy. Iona could recognize old Yerto – he was unmistakable. So in a different way was the yeti Iona guessed was his mate, Ryena, whose name she'd heard called out on several occasions. Once she must have been handsome and well built like Churinga. Now she was old and stooped, her breasts had shrivelled and her pelt was tinged with grey, not the deep shining silver of Yerto's but smudged and pale at the hairs' ends. She stood close to him at the consultations on the bank, and her shelter was the nearest to his.

Yerto's lined face was always grave. Often when he frowned, Iona thought, it was filled with sadness. Ryena's features were much calmer. Yerto never smiled, while Ryena did often – an infant yeti had only to run and tumble in front of her for Ryena to laugh affectionately as she stooped to pick it up. Yet underneath the laughter and the composure, Iona felt Ryena was sometimes troubled too. If so, she was much more successful at concealing her worry than the patriarch.

Churinga nodded. 'That is so. Ryena is with Yerto.'

'Do they have children?' Iona asked.

'They have one. They have the male named Wengen.'

Iona wondered again. If Yerto didn't owe his position as the holding's leader to his strength, maybe he had inherited it from his father, in which case perhaps his son Wengen would succeed him.

Iona asked Churinga. 'So when Yerto dies, does that mean Wengen will lead the holding?'

Churinga laughed. 'Tell me, tell me, tell me!'

Afterwards, when Iona thought back, she realized there was something forced and uncomfortable in Churinga's laugh, but at the time she didn't notice it. Anxious to learn all she could, she pressed impetuously on.

'Please tell me, Churinga.'

The yeti was silent. Then, 'Maybe,' Churinga said.

Iona looked at her, puzzled. Churinga's face was blank. 'Well, which one is Wengen, anyway?'

'Over there.' Churinga pointed across the clearing.

A male yeti was lounging in the shadowed entrance of one of the shelters. Iona hadn't noticed him before. She narrowed her eyes and peered through the morning sunlight.

The yeti was a mature adult. Even lying down Iona could see that he was taller and more powerful than most of his companions. His fur was sleeker too. It gleamed as if it had been groomed not occasionally like the other creatures, but constantly and carefully. For several moments Iona couldn't make out his face. It was hidden in the well of shadow.

Then the yeti casually elbowed himself forward across the earth and Iona started. His eyes were fixed on hers and she realized he had been watching her too. She saw his face and tensed. Apart from its heaviness the face itself was unremarkable, with plump jowls, a broad pug nose and hooded eyelids. It was the expression on the yeti's face that startled her. Directed deliberately across the space of earth that separated them, it was charged with malevolence. Iona shrank back. She put her arm round Churinga and scratched the female's nose. Across the clearing Wengen continued to gaze at her with what on a human's face, Iona knew, could only have been implacable hatred.

Iona felt a surge of panic ripple across her stomach. She thought she had got rid of her fear, but she hadn't. It had returned with Kekua's mention of the enigmatic Tonemetapu, and now it sharpened as she stared back at Wengen. Iona tore her glance away and looked down. Her heart was pumping.

She had been found and captured by a clan of great apes, of monsters, as she still thought of them. Though immensely strange and alien, the yeti's world had begun to appear orderly and composed, a world of animals untouched by any of the human emotions of anger, ambition, bitterness and resentment. Uncle Robert would have expected her to react to it just as he would have done – calmly and dispassionately.

Iona had done her best. She had observed the creatures, watched their behaviour, fitted herself into the rhythms and patterns of their life. With her acute ear she was well on the way to understanding and speaking the sounds and calls that made up their language. Iona had been certain that this achievement would somehow provide her best means of escape.

Suddenly she realized she was wrong. The yeti's world wasn't as it seemed. Shadows lay over the calm surface of their existence, and beneath that surface, beneath the shadows, dark and violent currents were churning.

Kekua's almost obsessive desire for Iona to speak their tongue – the blind yeti prompted and instructed her from before dawn until long after darkness had fallen. Churinga's uneasy laugh and the enigmatic references to Tonemetapu. The sadness in the faces of the patriarch, Yerto, and his mate Ryena. The fury and bitterness in Wengen's eyes a moment ago. They were all part of it.

The valley was living through its own nightmare. She, Iona suspected with dread, was the key to its resolution.

That night, despite her fears, Iona didn't weep. She didn't think of her mother, or of Mainwarden, or even of Uncle Robert. Instead, she found herself concentrating on the tall, dark-pelted yeti who had found her on the river's bank. The yeti, Manu, was the only one of the creatures who hadn't studied her with fear or demanded anything of her. Manu had simply built Iona her shelter – and smiled at her.

Clutching Bear, Iona eventually fell asleep with the memory of Manu's smile warming her mind.

19

Wengen heaved himself to his feet.

He walked away from the clearing and climbed to the top of the low ridge that ran the length of the island like a knobbly spine. There he squatted on his haunches and gazed out over the river. His eyes were unusually pale for the valley yeti, a chill grey-white like the stones beneath the water at the river's edge rather than the deeper slate-blue of the other members of the holding. Wengen narrowed them against the glare from the water. Below him on the bank he could see Manu's leopard, Babilla, asleep in the shade.

Wengen waited.

Sometimes he seemed to have been waiting all his life. Certainly he had been waiting every day for the past three weeks, ever since Manu had swum across the encircling waters with the shumbi across his broad shoulders and the agate-eyed killing animal paddling in his wake.

Although he never let it show – Wengen never let anything show – the leopard infuriated him. It had no business to be there. It belonged to the crests and the snows, not to the valley. Wengen disliked and distrusted the creature, as dangerous and alien, and he knew the leopard disliked him too. He felt its hostility whenever they came close to each other. The leopard's hairs would bristle, its black-tipped tail would switch like a snake's, and it growled menacingly until Manu calmed it.

Above all, Wengen resented the way it was tolerated by the rest of the island yeti. Although he was Yerto's son and his successor as leader of the holding, Wengen himself could never have brought the animal to the island. No one would have accepted its presence. Manu, it appeared, could get away with anything he wanted. Even Wengen's own mother, Ryena, didn't seem to groom him as often as she attended to Manu – and that was the surest of all the signs of favouritism.

He, Wengen, only son of the holding's patriarch, heir to the decision-maker of the gatherings and the councils of cloud-time, had somehow been shouldered aside by a stranger from the crests. Manu the interloper from the ranging had the pick of the females, and the best of the gathering. Most bitter of all, the younger members of the holding seemed to see the intruder as their natural future leader.

Wengen let out a low growl. He rocked backwards and forwards on his heels. Then, with the cold unyielding self-control he'd used for as long as he could remember, he calmed himself.

He was different from the others. He couldn't explain why or how, not to his mother, least of all to Yerto. But he sensed it deep inside himself, had known from his earliest childhood that he was set apart from the rest. He saw further than they did, he was stronger in will and mind than any of them. He was physically stronger, too, at least if he chose to be.

Manu's muscles might be harder for the moment. That was only because the mountain yeti stupidly chose to exercise himself by taking part in the daily gatherings. Wengen was content to stay on the island, to leave the work to the gatherers, and enjoy what they brought back to the holding. As Yerto's son, it was his privilege. But when the time came he knew that his strength would be greater even than Manu's.

When the time came – it wouldn't be long now. Everything in the valley was changing. The shumbi's extraordinary arrival could only be part of a pattern that included the disappearance of the prey from the crests. Inevitably it was Manu who found the child – Wengen had transferred his resentment for that to Iona. She was unknown and threatening – but now his hostility was tinged with fascination.

Wengen didn't yet know what the discovery of the shumbi meant, but nothing in the holding would ever be the same again. He somehow sensed the child would provide him with the opportunity he needed, and Wengen was never slow to take advantage of an opportunity. Licking his lips, he remembered the last time he'd been given one.

The year before, young Churinga had been gathering a crop of spelt at the end of the summer season. Wengen had decided to go out with the gatherers that day. Churinga had been promised to Manu in the cloud-time, but Manu was away on one of his missions to the crests. Drawn by the rippling seeds on the far edge of the valley, Churinga had wandered away from the others. Wengen had followed her.

He'd waited until she was far out of sight and earshot of the rest of the holding. Then he struck. He took her from behind, clamping his hand over her face so that she couldn't scream and pulling her head back until he felt the blood pounding in her temples. He forced his way brutally into her, unlocking his fingers briefly to hear her moan with pain as he drove at her again and again.

Afterwards there had been blood on the grass – and over the fat ears of the ripe spelt. Wengen bared his teeth at the memory. He had been the first male to mount her – that was the best part, the real triumph, the blood shining in splatters on the meadow. Before he left he licked some of it up. The taste was salty and good. Wengen had walked away, leaving Churinga crumpled and sobbing on the ground behind him.

He knew she would be too frightened to tell anyone what had happened. Manu had mounted her since then. He would know she'd already been penetrated, but he wouldn't know who by. And now Churinga was big with child. It would be born any day now. Wengen bared his teeth again in a grin. Manu wouldn't know whose child Churinga was carrying. Some day when the time was right Wengen would tell him. Meanwhile he would leave the dark-skinned mountain yeti to torment himself with wondering.

As Wengen swayed backwards and forwards on his heels, the glitter of a splash caught his eye in the river below. The lowering sun was almost directly in his face now. Wengen raised his hands to his forehead to screen out the fierce light.

It was the shumbi. She had removed her rainbow-coloured hide, the hide that unlike the yeti's fur she could put on or take off at will. She was wading into the shallows to bathe herself.

Transfixed, Wengen watched the tiny naked silhouette below him.

Standing waist-deep in the river Iona splashed her face with the cold mountain water and rubbed it quickly over her body.

Her skin tingled. She plunged her head beneath the surface and came up gasping. Shivering, she headed back for the shore. Breaking off a twig from a willow branch, she peeled away the bark and dipped the end in a patch of clean white sand shot through with veins of silver. Kneeling at the water's edge she began to brush her teeth.

As she did, a deep-throated growl sounded somewhere above her and to her left. Iona's head jerked up. Her eyes searched the bank.

Babilla was lying thirty feet above her under a mountain alder. The leopard yawned and growled again. There was nothing menacing in the sound, only Babilla's acknowledgement of the coming evening and Iona's splashing in the river below.

'Babilla!' Iona called out softly. 'Are you going to come and join me?'

It was the end of her third week in the holding. Almost from the start the leopard had chosen to join Iona in her daily washings in the river. It paddled into the water beside the child and cleansed itself with the same deliberate fastidiousness of any domestic cat.

'Come on, Babilla.' Iona patted the water, raising little fans of spray. 'It's almost warm today.'

The leopard gazed at her through alert half-closed eyelids. It growled again, then its head dropped back on its paws. The animal was quite happy where it was in the evening sunlight. It wasn't going to move.

Iona laughed. She might have been talking to Misty. Stubborn and private, Misty went her own way too. Babilla was no different. Iona picked up the twig. As she went on brushing her teeth she heard a rustle above her and glanced up again. One of the yeti was watching her, she was certain of that. Her gaze travelled along the ridge, hesitated, and swung back. There was something half hidden in a clump of waving grass. Iona peered intently at the shadowy shape.

It was Wengen.

Ever since Churinga had pointed Wengen out, Iona had been aware that the yeti's pale eyes never left her. She remembered the terrible malevolence in them as he'd stared at her across the clearing that morning. There was the same look in them now, but there was something else too – greed. As Iona stared at him she saw his tongue emerge and flicker round his mouth.

Suddenly the hairs prickled on the back of her neck. She thrust the twig into its place in the cleft of a willow alongside the handful of moss she used as a sponge. Then she ran up the ridge at an angle away from the silent brooding presence above her to find Kekua and Churinga.

As she ran, Iona thought of the pregnant yeti. The previous day Churinga had placed Iona's hand on her belly so that she could feel the movement of the baby inside. Churinga made rocking movements with her arms and began to laugh, but at that moment Wengen had ambled across the clearing. Churinga had stopped laughing and shrunk back with a sudden flash of fear in her eyes.

Iona asked her what the matter was, but Churinga simply shook her head and turned away without answering. Now Iona was determined to learn the truth. It wasn't only Churinga who was frightened of the yeti – Iona felt threatened too.

As Wengen watched the shumbi run away, he shifted on his haunches and his eyes shone briefly under their lowered lids. Not yet, but soon. He licked his lips again, tasting the blood on the spelt.

Kekua was squatting beside Churinga. They were both husking grain in a circle of the holding's females and young.

Iona came up behind them and stopped uncertainly. She couldn't speak to Kekua now. She would have to wait until they were alone together. As she hesitated, Kekua must have sensed her presence. The blind yeti broke off and glanced over her shoulder.

'The seeds must be cleaned,' she said. 'Then they can be dried and stored for the weeks that follow the next snow-melt. If they are left in the sheaf, the water will cover them and they will rot. Come and help us. Churinga will teach you.' She beckoned and Iona knelt down.

The fingers of the yeti, even the children's, moved with astonishing speed and skill. They stripped away the spiny leaves and stems, plucked out each plump ear of grain, and flicked it into the slowly but steadily growing mound in front of them. Iona tried to copy them. Her own fingers were slow and clumsy, and her skin began to bleed from the lacerations of the razor-sharp grass. She licked away the blood, gritted her teeth and set to work again.

They finished an hour later. One of the females fetched a length of hollow branch sealed at one end with dry mud. The grain was shovelled inside, and the other end sealed too. The branch was carried away and the yeti drifted back to their shelters. Churinga vanished on some errand of her own, and Iona was left alone with Kekua.

'What do you want to know?' Kekua said.

Iona's eyes widened. She had said nothing, but even without speaking the blind yeti knew there was anxiety and questions in Iona's mind.

'Wengen,' she replied. 'Why is Churinga frightened of him? Why does he hate me? He frightens me too.'

There was a long silence. Kekua stared at Iona with her unseeing eyes. 'You will learn from Tonemetapu,' Kekua said.

'Who is Tonemetapu?' Iona asked. 'I keep hearing the name, but I do not know what it means.'

'He will tell you.'

'But when?' Iona demanded insistently. 'I heard you say yourself I would be taken to him when I could speak. How much longer must I wait? I can speak now! I am talking to you!'

'You speak well,' Kekua agreed quietly. 'But there is much you have not done. You have not yet gathered except on the island with Churinga and myself. You have not been to the grounds with the holding.'

'Then let me go with the gatherers. You have taught me the grasses, the fruits, the roots. I know them – I even know their names!' Iona shook her head in frustration.

'It is true. The time has come for you to gather.'

'When? Tomorrow?'

Kekua nodded. 'Yes, it can be tomorrow.'

'And after that, what else must I do?' Iona's voice was still filled with urgency.

The blind yeti smiled at the shumbi child's impatience. 'After that,' she said, 'you must show that you truly belong to the holding.'

The statement shocked Iona into silence. How could she belong to the holding? She wasn't a creature, a yeti, she was a human. Her world was Mainwarden, not this strange island with its birds'-nest shelters floating on the river in the midst of the snow- and ice-walled valley. If she became part of the holding, she would be part of it for ever.

In her fear and confusion every instinct in Iona rose to reject the idea. Panic started to invade her. Once more, as she'd done so often in the past, she fought it down. She wasn't a monster, she'd never become one whatever they made her do. She was herself, and she'd return to the world she came from. Until then, even with Kekua she would have to pretend she was joining the yeti's life.

'How do I do that?' Iona asked quietly.

Kekua's shoulders lifted slightly in a small graceful shrug. She spread out her hands and turned her palms upwards to catch the sunlight.

'When the time comes, you will not have to ask,' Kekua said. 'You will know.'

20

Next morning, when the holding assembled on the river bank at dawn, Iona was there with the other yeti.

She'd been on the bank every day since her arrival, but today was different. For the first time she was being taken out into the feeding grounds to gather. Apprehensive and shivering slightly in the early chill, she waited with the others for the patriarch to appear.

Old Yerto walked painfully down from the clearing. He listened to the reports of the out-searchers, and consulted the senior females. Afterwards he thought for a while, scratching his silver-grey chest and muttering abstractedly to himself. Then he stretched out his arm and gave his instructions.

'Today we go to the meadows between the mound where the sambur stood and the trees where the child of the dark storm struck,' he said.

There were grunts of approval at the news.

Every yard of the gathering grounds, Iona had learnt, was known by name. The area Yerto had chosen was obviously a popular one. The gathering party waded into the river and began to swim to the far side, Kekua and Churinga among them. It hadn't occurred to either of them that Iona might have difficulties with the crossing – every yeti child could swim as soon as it could walk.

Iona hung back on the bank. She eyed the dark, foam-flecked waters uncertainly. She could swim well enough, but the powerful current eddied frighteningly and she lacked the yeti's fur to protect her against the river's icy cold.

Manu, with Babilla behind him, was the last to step in. He took a few strokes and glanced back, saw Iona hesitating, and returned. Laughing, he heaved her up on his back and set out again. A few minutes later Iona was standing on the far shore.

The holding walked for almost an hour. Then they fanned out in a line and began to work their way through the meadow. Iona watched. The yeti were cropping the seed-pods of different grasses.

Each carried a weaver bird's leaf-nest as a gathering basket. When the baskets were full, the gatherers emptied the contents on to the hide of a deer spread out on the ground behind them.

Two weeks earlier Iona wouldn't have known which seed-bearing grasses to look for. Now she could recognize most of them. One looked like young oats, another had the sharp-tongued whiskers of barley, a third resembled wheat. Iona tucked herself in behind Kekua and began gathering too.

Minutes later, as happened the day before when she tried to husk the grain, her fingers were cut and bleeding. Iona stopped and licked her wounds angrily. The blood on her tongue tasted of salt and iodine and for some reason of blackberries. She wrinkled her face, wondering why. Then she remembered. She used to go out with Mr Simpson at Mainwarden collecting blackberries – 'brambles' the old gardener called them.

Simpson used to chide her with being too impatient as she plunged into the bushes, searching eagerly for the bright black fruit. 'Hold ye back,' he would say. 'Be careful and logical. There's a proper way to harvest everything. Think how we gather the grain on the farm.'

On the valley floor Iona did as Mr Simpson had taught her. She made herself slow down and feel carefully for the seedheads instead of grabbing at them. As Kekua and the others moved ahead of her, something caught Iona's eye. She paused and looked up.

The yeti had moved into an area of shorter, thicker meadow. As they advanced they were putting up a number of small furry animals which scuttled away before them. Iona frowned. They were like the rabbits which bolted in front of the harvester at Mainwarden. Old Silas who drove the harvester used to string out nets to trap the rabbits – 'Tastiest meat in the land for a thanksgiving stew,' he would say as he plucked one from the netting and broke its neck with a chop of his flattened hand.

Standing under the Himalayan sun Iona thought of the thyme-scented pie his wife, Margaret, made with them, and her mouth watered. Margaret always picked out a piece of tender saddle fillet for Iona, and made sure the child had a slice of pie-crust well soaked with gravy to go with it. As memories of the harvest suppers in Margaret's kitchen flashed across her mind, Iona realized she'd never once seen meat being eaten in the holding.

Half her mind on the row of reapers ahead and half on the simmering cauldron in the farmhouse, Iona noticed Manu at the end of the line, Babilla padding slowly behind him. Suddenly Babilla dropped to her stomach and froze. Her ears pricked and her black-tipped tail switched slowly from side to side. Babilla waited. One of the small animals that had been running before the reapers turned and bolted back between them.

Thinking it had reached safety the little animal slowed and snuffled through the grass. Babilla sprang. Her body rose from the earth in a pale arc of muscle and claws and shining, rose-patterned hide, and arrowed back to the ground. There was a squeal and a frenzied flurry. Babilla lifted her head. Iona saw flecks of blood on her mask. An instant later the leopard sprang again.

Several more of the small animals had followed the first in running back through the line. They were escaping into a deathtrap. Babilla pounced a third time, a fourth, and then again and again until Iona lost count. Finally the leopard stopped, looked round and snarled defiantly. Then she settled herself on her paws and began to gnaw at her last prey.

Manu strode back. Babilla had finished her hunting only a few paces from where Iona was standing. Manu gathered up the carcasses, punctured their cheeks with a stab of his finger and strung them on a length of plaited fibre round his waist. Then he walked over to a rock and lowered himself against it. Neatly, using his sharp front incisor teeth and a splinter of sharpened bone, he started to skin the animals. He did it exactly as Iona remembered old Margaret skinning rabbits at Mainwarden.

'There's one thing all young women should know, young lady,' the old woman used to say as she expertly gutted and jointed the meat. 'And that's how to catch a man who can catch a rabbit. In *that* order, mind you. For what's the use of a man who can't trap and shoot and snare? None to you, and none to me. So to be sure you catch the man who can catch, learn what to do with what he brings back. Learn how to feed his belly, and how to make him a jacket to keep him warm in the cold when he goes out again.'

Iona remembered, too, that she had thought the rabbit-skinning was just like her mother pulling off her long kid gloves when she came back from one of her dances. At the memory her eyes suddenly flooded with tears.

'Iona –'

Rubbing her face with the back of her hand, Iona glanced up. Manu rose from the rock and walked over to her. He smiled and touched her nose. 'Come with me,' he said.

He took her hand and led her back to the rock. Iona glanced down at his waist. The animals he'd picked up after Babilla's hunting bumped against his hips. Iona didn't know what they were, but they looked like a cross between a large rat and a marmoset.

At the rock Manu squatted again. He had already begun to eat the first animal he'd skinned. Its back and haunches had been stripped away, and its shoulders bore the imprint of his teeth. Beyond him Babilla had finished her meal of what must have been a dozen or more of the little creatures. As they approached, the leopard yawned and started fastidiously to lick herself clean.

Using his bone knife, Manu carefully filleted a long ribbon of meat from the saddle of one of the animals, and held it out to Iona. 'I do not know if the shumbi gather or range. But take this. Eat it. It is good.'

The ribbon of flesh was dark and dripping with blood. She was suddenly ravenously hungry for meat, but she knew she couldn't eat the animal raw as he had done. It needed cooking, and one of her earliest realizations about the yeti was that they didn't use fire. Everything they gathered was eaten raw. They had no knowledge of fire except as a destructive living creature which Kekua taught her they called the dark storm's child, almost certainly, Iona guessed, because when fire struck the valley it came from lightning discharged from a thunderstorm.

As Iona started to shake her head, she remembered something. Among the contents of her survival pouch was a box of waterproof matches. She'd unclipped the pouch from her belt that day and left it in her shelter. Even if the yeti didn't make fires, there was no reason why she shouldn't. When she got back to the holding she'd use the matches, build a good charcoal base like Mr Simpson had taught her, and roast the meat on a spit.

Iona smiled gratefully at Manu and took the strip. She wrapped it in a large leaf and tucked it inside her shirt. Then she reached up and rubbed his nose. Manu nodded gravely. He returned the gesture, called to Babilla and stood up.

As he walked away Iona stared after him. The gatherers had circled behind him. Compared with them, pale-furred, heavily built, and bowed down as they combed the meadow, his dark muscular body looked lean and swift, almost elegant. Without ever tripping or stumbling he leapt from tussock to tussock of the marsh reeds as swiftly and easily as the leopard behind him.

Once he glanced back. He noticed Iona watching him and did something that bewildered her. He raised his hands, cupped them to catch the sunlight, and then seemed to throw the light at her, dipping and lifting his open palms again and again. Manu was too far away by then for her to see his face, but it was almost as if he was sending a signal to her – a signal that in its warmth and brightness could only be a smile of support and encouragement.

Afterwards he turned. Iona glimpsed the silhouette of Babilla bounding in his wake. Then they both disappeared behind one of the folds in the valley's surface.

Iona set off to rejoin the line of reapers. As she caught up with them, she saw Kekua was holding Churinga by the elbow. The younger yeti's belly was tightly distended, her face was drawn, and she was stumbling. Anxiously Iona took her other elbow.

Both she and Kekua were still supporting her when the day's gathering ended, and they headed back for the island.

Iona lay in the grass on the ridge above the holding. Beneath her the dark shapes of the yeti restlessly crossed the clearing. No one was asleep. Churinga had been in labour since they'd returned from the gathering the previous day, and Kekua had never left her side. Manu was a frequent visitor to the shelter and even Yerto had limped in and put his hand on the young female's heaving belly. He shook his head thoughtfully, and went out again.

That morning Wengen had come to the shelter. He stared impassively at Churinga for a long time. Then he turned and left without a word or even the briefest of greetings. Churinga was so exhausted by then she was barely conscious, but she'd registered Wengen's presence. Once again Iona felt the fear it aroused in her.

The day had been the longest Iona had ever spent. To escape Churinga's drawn-out pain and the nervous claustrophobic tension it created in the holding, she'd climbed up to the ridge at what she guessed was three hours ago. It was only a guess – her watch had been one of the casualties of her fall from the camp – but Iona's guesses were becoming more and more accurate.

Without a watch she'd had to find other ways of measuring time. At the start she'd simply used the difference between day and night. Later she'd begun to break down the darkness and light into smaller blocks. Dawn and dusk had their own colours and degrees of radiance. So did pre-dawn and pre-dusk, the midday hours, and the deepest blackness of the night.

Soon the sun and moon became her clock hands, and the peaks her dial. The darkness was intense now and the dew was heavy on the grass. The moon had slid away behind Orion's fishtail, and Iona couldn't see any of the peaks on the crests. If she was right it meant dawn was very close. At that instant the song of a single lark lifted over the valley.

The song grew stronger, pouring out over the reeds and rushes, drowning even the sound of the water. It rose higher and higher into the air. As the song mounted, a faint thin shell of light lifted over the mountains to the east. Morning was coming. Day had been joined with night and the bird was its herald. Next would come the first call of a pheasant.

Iona waited. From the scrub beyond the island came the familiar jarring, rattling bird-sound. She smiled. She would never be as accurate in timing the valley's rhythms as Kekua with her pulse and the beating owl's wings, but she was learning quickly.

A moment later Iona climbed purposefully to her feet, the smile gone from her face.

She had been hiding all night, hiding from the almost tangible stress and fear and misery that enveloped the holding below. What was going on there had nothing to do with her. She was no part of the island clan. She was simply their captive, a creature from a different world who had fallen among them, among monsters. She had only managed to survive by pulling over herself an invisible cloak, a cloak of obedience, at first mute and then haltingly expressed in sounds, to every one of the yeti's wishes.

Today the holding were frightened that Churinga was going to die. They were right to be frightened. Churinga probably would die – certainly her child would. Iona knew why. Her baby was lying back to front in her swollen womb. In its struggles to be born it would kill not only itself, most likely it would rupture Churinga beyond salvation too. Without help, that was, and without the knowledge of what was happening to the mother and child.

The yeti didn't have that knowledge, but Iona did. She knew what was happening and she knew what needed urgently to be done. It required not just knowledge of the mechanics of birth, but small, strong and agile hands. Iona had both.

Churinga was one of Iona's captors. She belonged to a time and place so remote they had left no trace in even the deep-buried middens of pre-history. She was pleasant but simple-minded. If she had been a young pregnant girl Iona had passed in a London street on her way home from school, Iona might have smiled casually at her but that would have been all.

Here on the island in the valley it was different. Churinga had been Kekua's eyes as the blind yeti taught Iona the ways and language of the holding. Iona could not stand by and let her and her child die.

As she walked down to the shelter Iona shivered with apprehension, unsure whether she could do it again, whether she would get it right. She had only done it once, but animals – whether they were cattle, monsters or people – couldn't be so different from each other. She only knew that she had to try.

She tried to remember the last time, almost two years ago. Iona had been not quite twelve. Pudding-faced Kate had got her up at dawn. Just like today there had been a cock pheasant calling beyond the stable yard. Kate took her into the warm straw at the back of the dairy where Morning Star, the gentle-faced Jersey in her first breeding season, had been struggling to give birth.

'I'm sorry, Iona,' Kate's brother Tom, the cowhand, said. 'But it's a breech and the poor creature's towards the end. We need someone with small hands. She's too narrow for the rest of us. You'll have to get deep up inside her and turn the calf. If you can't, she's gone.'

Guided by Tom, Iona fearfully slid her hands up into the exhausted cow's womb until she could feel the soft fur of the calf inside.

'Can you feel the bend of the leg? Now pull it right out so I can get a hold –'

Terrified she might break a bone, Iona tugged. Nothing seemed to happen and she heaved harder, and then harder again.

'You can do her no harm that isn't already done,' Tom muttered reassuringly. 'If you can't straighten it out, push the calf right back and then try again. Here she comes now –'

A tiny transparent hoof appeared in the contracting passage beside Iona's arms. 'Now the other. That's it. Now we have it.'

Suddenly, miraculously, Tom managed to seize the two slender legs and the calf slid out into the dim light of morning. Tom let out a shout of joy. Expertly he scooped the mouth free of obstruction, and tied and cut the umbilical cord. An instant later the calf was struggling to its feet.

Iona scrambled up, her arms streaked with blood and mucus. Her arms were shaking uncontrollably and she was too tired to do anything except give a limp smile. All she knew was that she had saved a life, perhaps two lives.

If she could do it with a pregnant cow, Iona thought as she reached the clearing, she could do it with Churinga. She ducked her head and entered the shelter. Kekua glanced up. Her sightless eyes lacked their usual sheen. They were dull and weary, and her face was haggard. Iona stepped past her. Churinga was still heaving and straining, but her movements grew increasingly feeble with every passing minute.

Iona knew the time had come.

21

Churinga rocked slowly on her heels.

Despair and exhaustion had almost defeated her. The terrible heaving had stopped and she was moaning weakly. Her pelt was matted with sweat and her heavy belly swung from side to side above the blood-soaked hay of the shelter's floor. Murmuring reassurance, Iona persuaded the yeti to lie on her side so that she could try to work her hands into the womb to see if there was any chance of turning the child.

As gently as she could, Iona pushed her fingers between the sweat-soaked swollen lips of the vulva and up into the vagina, until she felt the hard wishbone shape of the pelvic girdle. The muscles of the birth canal were in violent convulsion, churning and heaving as they strained to expel the trapped obstacle. Gradually the spasm passed and Iona could reach in far enough to feel the ball-shaped joint of a tiny knee crushed against what must be the infant's curved backbone.

With a surge of hope she knew it was not too late. Under her probing fingertips she could feel the warmth of blood pumping beneath the soft wet skin. Churinga gave a whimper of pain as Iona's fingers probed deeper. Vaguely she was aware of Kekua's hands soothing and rubbing Churinga's churning belly as Iona pushed her fists upwards into the mouth of the womb. The channel was so slippery with mucus and the fluid from the birth sac that her arms slipped in easily. Carefully she felt round the compressed limbs until she found the hard conical shape of the head. In her mind she heard Tom's quiet voice. 'If you can't straighten it out, push it right back and then try again. You can do her no harm that isn't already done.'

As Iona reached further in and tried to get a firm grip on the slippery invisible body, she felt Kekua's reassuring presence. The blind yeti had realized what Iona was doing. Firmly and gently Kekua manipulated the heaving belly from the outside as Iona pulled and pushed from within. She felt what seemed a formless bag of muscle and bone slowly begin to turn, rolling against the clenched walls of the womb's mouth, until at last the bullet-shaped head was forced round and down into the birth channel.

'Quick, Kekua!' Iona pulled her blood-streaked arms out of Churinga's body. 'When the next spasm comes, help me!'

The pelvic girdle opened wide, and the tip of the infant's head emerged between the lips of the vulva. Carefully the blind yeti felt round the outline of its features, a smile of relief on her face.

The spasm came again, stronger this time, as Churinga felt the birth channel part. Within moments the head and the shoulders appeared, pressed downwards by the heaving muscles. Seconds later the infant yeti was lying in a shaft of dawn sunlight on the floor of the shelter.

Kekua quickly licked the black birth fluid from the infant's mouth and pinched its nostrils to open the breathing channel. She felt for the umbilical cord, nipped it short between her sharp incisor teeth and looped it back on itself to stop the blood flowing. Then the blind yeti put the tiny creature on to Churinga's breast, and, with a grunt of pleasure, rocked back on her heels. The infant searched for the teat, and began to suckle greedily.

Kekua turned her sightless eyes towards Iona, and rubbed her nose in greeting. 'You have saved them both, little shumbi,' she said. 'The holding will remember what you did. Did I not say you would know when the time came? Now you belong to the people.'

Iona stared at her. They were almost the same words that Kekua had used before. Then Iona had rejected them in fright and bewilderment. Now she wasn't sure what she felt. As she hesitated, across her mind flashed an image of Tom when the calf clambered uncertainly to its feet.

'It's a good one that,' he'd said. 'It'll be a fine beast when it grows. I reckon someone will still be breeding from its stock long after all of us are gone.'

Churinga's baby had looked strong and healthy in spite of its troubled birth. Generations from now there might well be yeti living on the island descended from the tiny creature. If there were, it would be due to Iona – without her the infant would have died. It was an awesome thought but, as she considered it, Iona found it appealing. She didn't belong to the holding, she would never belong to the holding, but she no longer minded if the yeti thought she did. The idea had lost its fear.

She gave Kekua a shy smile.

Iona crawled to the shelter's entrance and stood up outside, yawning and stretching in the morning sunshine.

She felt light-headed from tiredness, but above all she was hungry. She hadn't eaten since the onset of Churinga's labour. There was food in the gathering pouches stacked beside the shelter, but she suddenly yearned for something richer and sharper than the grains, roots and nuts they contained. Iona remembered the meat Manu had given her, and instantly her mouth watered.

She glanced round. Most of the island yeti were already clustered round the shelter, making small sounds of pleasure at the news which had just travelled across the clearing. Leaving them behind her, Iona climbed the ridge and scrambled down the bank beyond until she found her favourite spot on the river's edge. She pulled out the piece of meat from her pocket, laid it on a stone and began to gather dry twigs from under the willows as kindling for a cooking fire. Then she felt for the matches in her survival bag.

Iona had counted the matches carefully. There were thirty of them in the box. They weren't ordinary matches, like the matches old Mr Simpson used to light his pipe. Their stems were thicker and stronger, and their bulbous striking heads were coated with wax to make them waterproof.

Iona took one of them out. She was about to strike it when unaccountably something made her hold her hand. She frowned. Tom had been in her thoughts before. Now in her mind she saw the face of Uncle Robert. As craggy and inscrutable as always, he was leaning forward in the darkness over a fire with the light of the flames playing over his white hair. He was telling her something.

It sometimes occurred to Iona that in her entire life she had learnt almost nothing from her parents. Everything she knew had been taught her by other people, the least interesting part by her teachers at school. The rest she had learnt from old Mr Simpson, from Silas, Margaret and Tom at Mainwarden, from Duncan on her uncle's estate in Scotland, even from her mother's cook who had taught Iona how to bake bread. The strangest, most interesting lessons of all came from her godfather.

'Fire,' Cabot had remarked as he poked the glowing embers in front of them. 'Perhaps the most remarkable of all the natural phenomena man has harnessed for his own purposes –' He paused.

Iona remembered the occasion now. Last summer they had been sitting in the darkness before Cabot's large, rambling clapboard summer house on the Massachusetts shore close to the old whaling harbour of Martha's Vineyard. Cabot had built the fire and cooked clam chowder to his own recipe over it.

It was Iona's summer holiday and her parents should have been with them. Her father had promised to come, but at the last moment he said he had to attend a conference in Cambridge. Dorelia Howard had accompanied her daughter across the Atlantic and up to Boston but after a few days in her own house at Martha's Vineyard she'd become bored and flown back to New York.

Iona had been passed on to her godfather, who lived only a few hundred yards away, and she was spending the final few days of her vacation with him. That evening, the last before Iona returned home, they sat together by the fire after dinner, listening to the sound of the breaking waves.

'Did you know fire can create animals, Iona?' Cabot asked.

Iona stared at him. As so often, she didn't know if he was teasing her or being serious. 'Fire doesn't create anything,' she said uncertainly. 'It just burns things up.'

'Sure?'

Less and less sure by the moment, Iona nodded. Uncle Robert's eyes began to twinkle. Then he gave his slow dry chuckle.

'You're right of course, young lady,' he said. 'But so in fact am I. Consider Africa. Africa's almost certainly our birthplace, the cradle where man was first rocked. It's also the place where we discovered how to use fire. We used it to feed ourselves. Or rather we used it to hunt so we could feed ourselves.'

'How can you use fire to hunt?' Iona asked.

'Our ancestors discovered long ago what we all know now, that animals are terrified of fire,' Cabot replied. 'Until then, hunting prey on the African plains had been hard and exhausting, it bushed the hell out of you. Fire changed all that. Using fire intelligently, you could drive the animals where you wanted them to go. The flames did the work. And then, when the flames had herded the animals into the place you'd chosen, you could kill them quickly and efficiently.'

Iona frowned. In her mind she worked through what Uncle Robert had said. It made sense. What it didn't explain was how fire could create animals, rather than guide them to their deaths.

Iona put the question to him. Uncle Robert gave his long slow chuckle again. 'That of course is the paradox,' he said. 'The answer, like the answer to most paradoxes, is simple when you think about it. Animals like grass plains, they don't like trees. Grass plains give them food, trees are out of reach. For every ton of animal life in a forest, there will be a hundred tons on the plain. But if you don't stop the forests encroaching, they'll invade the plains. By using fire we accidentally also rolled back the trees. Fire made the plains bigger, it allowed the animals to feed and breed. Fire created the herds that throng them even today –' He stopped.

Iona watched him keenly. She knew he loved the conundrums he set her. He loved explaining them too, and there'd been a wry, happy smile on his face as he'd resolved this one. Now the smile vanished and his features became grave.

'Never forget that fire is also deadly,' he finished. 'On Africa's plains we used it once in innocence. We've lost that innocence. Now we call fire energy, and we're stripping the planet bare to consume it. Fire no longer creates animals. Every flame we light today destroys them. It destroys plants too – it destroys everything.'

It was the most sombre pronouncement Iona had ever heard her godfather make. A moment later he stood up. Normally he gave Iona an affectionate peck on the cheek before he retired. That evening he simply wished her a curt goodnight and strode away into the darkness.

Iona had glanced round her. The waves were pounding on the shore. On the ground was the big metal stewpot Uncle Robert had used for the chowder, still full of the water in which he'd cooked the clams. Impulsively, Iona picked up the pot and poured the water on to the fire. The flames sizzled and died. She gazed for a while at the steam rising from the embers.

Iona stood up too. As she walked slowly back to the house, her godfather's footprints showed dark and clear in the sand. She stretched out her legs as far as she could and trod neatly in the prints. She had put out one fire. For some reason she felt it was vitally important to put out other fires too.

Now, on the island's bank Iona stared at the match. Her glance switched to the piece of meat lying on the stone. A tiny trickle of blood seeped over the stone and down on to the sand. Manu had eaten the meat raw, but Iona still knew she couldn't do the same. She looked at the pyramid of twigs she'd piled together, and hunger gnawed even more sharply at her stomach. For an instant she felt torn in two.

Then she gave in. She struck the match and touched it to the kindling. The fire flared up, the little flames bouncing and licking at the dry twigs. She broke off a sapling, stripped its end to sharpness on a rock and speared it through the meat so that it was ready for roasting. Then she stood up and searched for some larger branches to raise the heat of the fire before she turned the spit above it.

Iona stopped again.

Someone was watching her – here, now, on the island. She pushed away the after-image of Uncle Robert and set her mind on the present. Her first reaction was that it could only be the sly, pale-eyed Wengen. She scanned the slope of the ridge and then its crest, but there was no sign of the yeti anywhere – he wasn't even in his favourite perch in the clump of willow below the ridge's top. Even Babilla, the only other creature who habitually rested on the west-facing side of the island, was absent.

The entire shelf was empty – yet Iona knew she was being watched. The eyes studying her weren't friendly like the leopard's, nor were they menacing and hostile like those of the big sleek yeti. Ancient and remote and uncritical, they were simply observing her to see what she would do. In their all-seeingness, in their patient neutrality, they were even more frightening than the narrow, angry slits of Wengen's eyes.

Iona hesitated, then suddenly she pushed the pile of burning twigs into the water and threw the skewered piece of meat after the coals that sizzled as they sank. She picked up the matches and thrust them back into her pocket. Then she scrambled back up the path that led over the ridge, and ran down to the clearing. Only when she almost collided with Kekua did she stop running.

'Little shumbi I came to look for you.' Kekua's voice was soothing as she held on to the shaking child. 'I knew you were hungry. Come, I have prepared grain for you. You must eat well. It has been decided – you are ready to go to Tonemetapu.'

22

The path ran along the westward side of the island.

Kekua must have travelled it often because she followed the winding track without hesitation, never pausing once to orientate herself or to ask Iona to act as her eyes as she did Churinga. Finally they emerged into a small open space at what Iona thought of as the island's bows. At the end of the clearing was a writhen juniper tree, its branches hanging out on three sides above the water.

Kekua walked up to the tree, stopped and stooped under the branches. The base of the trunk was deeply shadowed by the leaves. Iona peered forward. As her eyes adjusted to the shadow, she saw a tangle of gnarled roots with an arched hollow above the ground at the centre. She could just make out the shape of what appeared to be a male yeti sitting cross-legged in the hollow.

Kekua knelt and gave the yeti the nose greeting. Then she said, 'I bring you the shumbi named Iona who came from the waters.'

Kekua reached back and felt for Iona's hand. Iona knelt beside her and gave the yeti the greeting too.

'Tonemetapu,' Kekua added, then without another word she got to her feet and disappeared, leaving Iona alone in the pool of shadow.

Iona gazed into the tangled roots. She could see more clearly now. The yeti was the oldest creature she had ever seen. He was very thin and he sat completely still. His fur was silky and almost white, far paler than the grey hide which covered Yerto. The whiteness seemed to be mottled with green and for a moment Iona thought the green was a reflection from the leaves. She started.

It wasn't a reflection, it was moss. Moss grew over his shoulders, down his sunken chest and across his legs. If it hadn't been for his eyes Tonemetapu might have been part of the ancient tree roots that were cloaked in the same soft green mantle. His eyes were ringed and marbled with age, but they still had sight in them. Iona became aware of that as he blinked and examined her.

Then he spoke. 'The holding says the river brought you,' Tonemetapu said.

Iona nodded. Kekua had told her to listen to the old yeti, but not to speak. The talking would be done by Tonemetapu.

'Sometimes in the snow-melt the river flow brings creatures,' Tonemetapu went on. 'There have been eagles washed down from the ranging. Ravens, too, and deer and occasionally the cub of a bear. If the holding decides to keep them, then they must be brought to me to learn the holding's bonds. Ravens I have taught to speak, so they can repeat the bonds. The others not, but they understand –'

He paused. Tonemetapu spoke very slowly. His voice was so frail and husked with age it sounded like frozen winter grass rustling distantly under the night wind.

'There has never been a shumbi before. With other creatures I must repeat the bonds again and again. But you can speak as the ravens without the need to be taught by me. Kekua has done the teaching.'

Iona nodded again.

'I am Tonemetapu,' the old yeti said. 'So listen well. I am neither of the holding nor of the ranging. I am of the clouds between. That is why the cloud-time is mine. Only in cloud-time can you be truly bonded to the holding. Until cloud-time comes, I can only tell you how it was that the clouds and the people were made, and of the bonds between them. Listen well again.'

The old yeti's voice had sunk to an almost hypnotic whisper. Spellbound, Iona leant forward.

'In the beginning before the people there was only snow,' Tonemetapu said. 'The snow covered everything, even the sky. In the sky there were ice-stars. Every star but one had a name. The raven-star and the deer-star, the bear-star, the vulture-star, and many more. Because of the snow the stars grew hungry and were about to die. The star without a name knew he would die first because even if food came he would be unnoticed and forgotten. All he had was dreams. He dreamed of the sun, his dream was strong, the sun came, the ice melted and the stars fell down the wind to feed on the greenness the sun made –'

With difficulty Tonemetapu lifted his hand from his knee, and gestured round the shadows. Iona knew the old yeti was indicating more than the space beneath the tree. The shaking fingers encompassed the island, the valley, and the mountains beyond.

'For a while the stars grew fat,' Tonemetapu continued. 'All of them – except the star without a name. He had dreamed the sun, it had melted the ice, it had saved his companions, but it had not saved him. Without a name he could find nothing. Then the greenness failed and the other stars weakened. They became so weak they could not climb back up into the sky. The nameless star was the weakest of all for he had not fed, but he made himself dream again. This time he dreamed of clouds.' Tonemetapu nodded distractedly to himself.

Watching him and the pain that suddenly filmed his cavernous eyes, Iona knew he was reliving the story he was telling. Inside himself the ancient yeti felt the star's anguish and hunger.

'The clouds came but not quickly,' Tonemetapu went on. 'The dream of the unnamed star was not as strong now, he was too close to death. The clouds came over the mountains and tormented him. They rolled forward. When they were close, they retreated and hung above the crests. The star made a last effort and dreamed harder than he had ever done. This time he drew the clouds to him. He pulled them over himself and held them there until they emptied themselves. When he opened his arms and let them go, the snow had been chased away and the land had flowered again –' Tonemetapu stopped.

Iona had promised Kekua she wouldn't speak, but as the old yeti talked, she had to struggle several times not to interrupt. Now she couldn't restrain herself.

The star without a name had dreamed down the sun and cleared the land of ice, Iona could understand that. Then he'd dreamed rain and made the land green again. All that was clear too. But what had happened to the starving nameless star then?

'Did the star eat at last?' she demanded.

Tonemetapu shook his head. 'Without a name he still could not eat. The other stars fed, they regained their strength, they climbed back up the wind into the sky. The nameless star remained.'

'What happened to him?'

'The clouds ran away when the star let them go,' Tonemetapu answered. 'One cloud, the smallest, didn't run fast enough. The star caught her and with the last of his strength he dreamed his third dream. The dream became the river. The little cloud thought she could escape while he dreamed, but because he was cunning the star kept hold of her. When he woke he was in the river's waters and his arms were still round the cloud. The star mounted her in the water and seeded her. The seed was named the people.'

'Who named it the people?'

'The river. The waters told the star their name, and he became one with his seed. All the people since are named by the waters. He was and so are they.'

Iona frowned and thought back. Weeks ago now – she had no clear idea how long – Iona had told Kekua her name. The blind yeti had walked down to the water's edge. In the river she had repeated the word *Iona* again and again, listening to the rustle of the surging, leaf-strewn current over the stones every time she voiced it. Finally the river had answered her, echoing the sound she was making, and Kekua had turned, smiling and satisfied. The waters had accepted Iona. They had given the sound back to her. The name of the shumbi child was as she claimed. She was Iona.

'What happened then?' Iona asked. She had entirely forgotten her promise to Kekua now. Tonemetapu had told her of the ice in the sky, of the star without a name who dreamed the sun and came to earth. Of the clouds, the rain, the river, and how the people came to be.

There was more. There *had* to be more. Iona was filled with longing to know.

'For many seasons the people lived as one,' Tonemetapu replied. 'The little cloud watched them and became angry. They were her children. The star had stolen them from her, and taken their name so that he could eat. The little cloud asked the other clouds to withhold the rain so that the people would desert the star and return to her. The clouds did as she asked. In the valley the grasses and the fruits failed, the animals fled to the crests, the people began to starve. The star tried to dream again, but no dreams came to him –'

A fork-tailed kite planed down the morning air and settled with beating wings on a branch at the top of the juniper tree. The bird started to preen itself, oiling the brilliance of its coppery flight feathers. Tonemetapu's eyes flickered up. The bird stopped its preening. It seemed to gaze down at the ancient yeti. Then it flapped away into the sky.

'The hunger grew worse and the people started to die,' Tonemetapu went on. 'Then one of them stood up, a female named Burra. Many since have been named after her but she was the first Burra. Burra said: "There is food here, but only for half of us. Let us divide ourselves in two clans. Some of us are more skilled in gathering, some in hunting. Let the gatherers stay here to harvest the valley. Let the hunters come with me to the crests, where the animals have gone." The people agreed. Burra led half of them away. They went up to the crests. They became the ranging.'

The ranging.

Iona had heard the word several times – Tonemetapu had used it himself when he first spoke to her. Somehow she'd always disregarded it, as she did the names of some of the rarer plants Kekua taught her about, names Iona knew she'd never be able to remember. Now in her eagerness she concentrated keenly on the word.

The ranging. The ranging was part of the yeti's world, but it was different from the holding. Suddenly something occurred to her. 'Does Manu come from the ranging?' she asked.

Tonemetapu nodded in the shadow.

So that was why Manu was different from the valley yeti, why he had dark fur and golden eyes, why he and his leopard, Babilla, hunted the small animals of the valley when they went out with the gatherers.

'But why does Manu live with the holding?'

'Before Burra led the hunters away,' Tonemetapu said, 'the people decided that one child from each of the clans should always grow up with the other clan. It was to keep the bonds between the holding and the ranging.'

Iona frowned. 'The bonds?'

'The people became the holding and the ranging, but they are still one people. In the end they live or die together. The bonds remind them that if the worst comes, they must share once again as they did when they divided the crests from the valley. The little cloud could not make the other clouds withhold the rain for ever. The snows came. The other clouds became impatient. When the season returned, the clouds released the rain again. The people survived.'

'What happened to the star without a name?' Iona demanded. 'Did he stay with the holding, or did he go to the ranging?'

For a long time Tonemetapu didn't reply. He sat as still as if he were waiting for the slow growth of the roots to invade him and embed him in the tree. Finally his eyes swung round and searched for the child's face.

'I am the unnamed star,' he said. 'Do you not understand my name that is not a name, little shumbi?'

Iona's eyes widened. Tonemetapu. Of course. She had heard the word spoken quickly with the yeti's clicks and cadences. She hadn't listened to what it meant – she'd simply assumed it was a name like Kekua or Yerto. It wasn't. In the yeti tongue it was a sentence which meant the star without a name.

Angry at her own stupidity, Iona leant forward again. 'But you can't be the unnamed star itself?' she insisted.

Tonemetapu gave a small dismissive shake of his head. 'Like those named after Burra, there have been many before me,' he answered. 'When Burra took the hunters to the crests, the star without a name came here to this tree –'

Tonemetapu gestured at the branches. Caught in the light between the leaves, his skin was as translucent as the membrane on the throat of a newly hatched bird.

'He thought of the holding and the ranging. He thought of the valley and the crests. Most of all he thought of the little cloud he had seeded. He wished to make peace with her so that the rain would not be withheld again. He dreamed again. This time he dreamed the cloud down to him. The cloud came but she was angry. He caught her in his arms, he held her hand, he walked the plains and peaks with her, he stilled her. He spoke of the children he had seeded on her. He and the little cloud were quiet together. They made peace –' Tonemetapu paused. His voice was becoming huskier and fainter.

'In their peace they agreed to share the children, just as the people shared the valley and the crests,' Tonemetapu struggled on. 'For the spring and summer the people would belong to the star. But when the snows fell, he would give them back to the cloud. Then they would be hers. Then the star would stand only to speak between the people and the cloud.'

'And that is what you mean by cloud-time?'

The old yeti gave his small weary nod again.

Iona started to understand then. The distant beginnings of the yeti race. The importance in their world of the river which had given them birth and given them their name. The anger and jealousy of the little cloud. The long-ago failure of the rains and the division of the people into the two clans to save themselves from starvation. The bonds that still held them together, that required Manu the hunter to be brought up among the holding.

And then the pact the nameless star had made with the cloud. The pact had led to cloud-time, which came when the snows began to fall, when the icy winter winds swept the crests and froze the valley. Iona had learned that. Mysterious and unfathomable, it joined the yeti of the holding and the ranging, and held together the world they both inhabited.

The secrets of cloud-time were the secrets of the yeti.

'Will I go to cloud-time?'

For an instant Iona forgot everything. She forgot the monsters. She forgot her terror. She forgot her careful plan that she'd followed so stubbornly in the lonely places of her mind, the plan to learn the yeti's language and somehow use it to escape. She even forgot the idea of escape itself. Gripped by the story of the nameless star, the river and the people, she thought only of the snows falling and the yeti meeting in cloud-time.

She had seen the towering peaks on the flight to Kathmandu, and had known immediately that within their citadels of ice they held the first and last secrets of the world. She had fallen among the only creatures who shared those secrets with the mountains. She wanted desperately to be with the yeti when they gathered.

Cloud-time remained a mystery, but Iona was certain it was then and only then that the secrets would be revealed.

'You – ?'

Tonemetapu was too old to laugh. Laughter would have torn the twig-like ribs from his body and sent them tumbling away through the air. All he could do was tremble slightly and expel his breath through his nostrils, but when he spoke again a brief flicker of amusement sparked in his eyes.

'Little shumbi,' Tonemetapu's voice was gentle, 'you have much to learn before it is decided whether you go with us to cloud-time. You are a shumbi. Your people cannot dream, but they are strong. They can call down the dark storm's child, and make it obey them. We see it flickering in their holdings in the night. We see them using it to destroy the green hide where we gather and hunt –' The old yeti paused.

'Where your people go, starvation and death follow. They do not have cloud-time and they cannot learn – that is why we avoid them. Now they have destroyed so much they are coming closer to the valley. The river carried you here ahead of them. I do not yet know whether you were sent to bring life or death. You saved Churinga's child, but you also carry the sticks that summon the dark storm. I have seen them in your mind –'

Briefly Tonemetapu's voice grew stronger and he leant forward. For the first time Iona saw his eyes clearly. She recognized them, and tensed. They were the eyes that had watched her when she'd been about to light the fire on the river bank.

'What I do know is that you were not sent to the holding alone. The people are one, they cannot be divided. Whether you have come to protect or destroy us, you must be shared with the ranging. Only when you have gone to the crests will it be known whether you should come with us to cloud-time, or be cast back to the waters so that the river may return you to where you came from. On you, little shumbi, the people's lives depend.' Tonemetapu paused again. 'I have spoken. It is finished.'

'Who will decide?' Tonemetapu's voice was fading every second, but Iona implored him to go on.

'The star without a name will decide,' Tonemetapu whispered. 'I will speak for the star. If you stay, then you will stay with us for ever.' The old yeti's head fell on his chest and he was silent.

Iona knelt in front of him, dazed. Her mind was in turmoil, and she felt as if she had been paralysed. All she could hear, echoing repeatedly through her brain, were Tonemetapu's last words: 'If you stay, then you will stay with us for ever.' Somehow she managed to stand, then, trembling and white-faced, she backed away from the well of shadow.

In the sunlight outside she whirled round and started to run. She had barely taken three steps when she met Kekua. Tears had started to stream down Iona's face, and through her blurred eyes she hadn't even seen the yeti standing behind her. She rocked back, then threw herself weeping into Kekua's arms.

'Quiet, little shumbi, quiet,' Kekua said soothingly. She stroked Iona's hair, her gaze focused sightlessly over the child's shoulder. As Iona recovered, Kekua took her hand and led her back along the path.

'Where are we going?' Iona asked.

'Back to the holding,' Kekua answered. 'You will spend the darkness there. Then tomorrow you will leave –' She paused. 'Manu will take you to the crests. You are not ours alone. As Tonemetapu said, you must be shared with the ranging.'

Kekua's voice was more commanding than Iona had ever heard it. As she listened, she was overwhelmed with dread.

She knew nothing about the crests, but something inside her told her they were chill, dark and dangerous – infinitely more dangerous than the island lying at the river's heart in the valley's sunlight. The island yeti gathered. The yeti of the ranging were hunters. Hunters, as Iona knew well, killed.

Dry-eyed but cold and shivering, she walked beside Kekua with her head lowered.

23

'Mrs Howard, I must put this to you again. Your friend Mr Ryan has admitted to the court that he has convictions for –'

The man in the black gown with the yellowing wig on his head paused and glanced at his notes. From the witness box Dorelia Howard stared down at him. Her cheeks were white and a pulse was throbbing at the side of her neck.

The man's name was Welieb. He was short and plump with a scarlet face, a quiet chuckling voice and small friendly eyes that blinked out from behind gold-framed glasses. Welieb had been briefed as leading counsel for her husband, Michael. Dorelia's own solicitor, Charles Lefanu, had warned her about him before the hearing started.

'Don't be taken in by the smiles and the jovial Dickensian appearance,' Lefanu said. 'Welieb's got the soul of a barrow-boy, and the instincts of a killer shark. Providing you don't forget that and answer his questions exactly as I've told you, you'll be all right.'

Dorelia had barely heard what Lefanu was saying. She had her own image of courtroom advocates. They were tall lean men with aggressive hard-jawed faces. They probed, dissected and challenged. They were difficult and provocative, but above all they were masculine. They were the sort of men she'd handled superbly and confidently all her life.

Not this one. Everything Dorelia believed and assumed had dissolved into an empty, frightening nothingness within minutes of the start of Welieb's cross-examination over an hour ago. Dorelia was used to manipulating people. During the past hour, quietly but ruthlessly, she'd been manipulated herself. Every answer she'd given had been torn to ribbons, and the ribbons themselves held up to amuse the judge.

Now she felt helpless. Even as Welieb consulted his notes, he was exploiting and harrying her. Welieb knew exactly what Sean had said to the court. So did she and everyone else. Welieb was using the silence to remind the judge of its gravity.

'Yes, yes, I have it here.' Welieb peered at the judge and smiled apologetically. 'I'm sorry, my lord, the catalogue is long and unusual. I needed to refresh my memory of its contents. Perhaps a summary will suffice?'

Dorelia glanced at where the judge was sitting. Grey-haired and impassive-faced, he nodded without comment.

'Convicted of possession of cocaine,' Welieb read out. 'Convicted of common assault. Convicted of possession of cocaine again, coupled with a conviction for assaulting a police officer. Convicted of domestic violence in an attack on his then wife, the attack being carried out with a knife. Finally, another conviction for an assault on a police officer –'

Welieb broke off. He looked back at the judge again. 'Other charges involving allegations of sexual assault lie on file, my lord. The charges are grave and perhaps relevant given the nature of this hearing and the central matter at issue. However, as they have not thus far been proceeded with under the jurisdiction where they were lodged, at this moment your lordship may prefer to leave them aside.'

Welieb's voice had slowed and hardened as he came to the words 'thus far'. The judge nodded again and Dorelia shivered.

Welieb knew that the allegations about Sean and the young woman who'd been their source were unproven and inadmissible. They were nothing more than poisonous lies. Wickedly but skilfully he'd managed to inject the poison into the hearing and at the same time distance himself from the falsehoods. As the little gowned figure turned back to her, she looked at him with hatred.

'Mrs Howard, are you really going to tell the court you knew nothing about Mr Ryan's convictions when you took him as a companion for yourself and your daughter?'

'Mr Ryan is not my companion, whatever that means,' Dorelia snapped back.

'Indeed,' Welieb smiled. 'Then how would you describe him?'

'A friend.'

'A close friend?'

'Yes.'

'A friend in the habit of spending nights at your house?'

Dorelia hesitated. She knew what she was being drawn into. Welieb had simply substituted one word for another. Next he would use a third word. She knew it – and she knew there was nothing she could do.

'Yes.'

'While your daughter is there?'

'She isn't always there.' Dorelia shook her head. 'Sometimes she spends nights with her friends from school.'

'But she's normally there, isn't she? Your husband has said she's a very home-loving little girl.'

'Yes, I think she loves her home. I think she loves being with me.'

'And there's nothing at home to frighten her, to make her want to be somewhere else?'

'No, of course not –' For the first time Dorelia knew she was on firm ground. She could speak with complete confidence.

Iona loved her home, the house in the Boltons was the centre of her life. Iona liked Mainwarden, too, but that was only a passing phase. As a child, animals and the company of people like Mainwarden's absurd old Scottish gardener were bound to appeal to her, but as soon as she grew up everything would change. Then, just like any teenager, she would want shops, clothes, nightclubs, the bright lights of the city. She would want London – and after London, New York, Paris and Madrid.

Dorelia could give her daughter all that. She would need it very soon. Iona certainly had nothing to be frightened about. Her absurd nightmares were irritating but, in Dorelia's view they were merely a signal of the arrival of adolescence, of the chemical changes happening in her body. Chopping off her hair, though infuriating too, was part of the same process. It made the wretched child look like one of those bizarre scarecrows which peopled the late-night horror movies. For a while Dorelia had been so embarrassed by the child's appearance she'd despatched her every weekend to Mainwarden. Then, as Iona's hair began to grow back, one of Dorelia's friends had told her about pheromones.

Pheromones were totally convincing. They explained everything from puberty to sex, from war to art, from anger to love. Iona, Dorelia realized gratefully, was enveloped in clouds of adolescent pheromones. The pheromones would drift away, the child's hair would grow back, and Iona would emerge like a butterfly from a chrysalis as an enchanting, long-legged teenage beauty Dorelia could take anywhere.

'She's a very happy child. With me, she always has been,' Dorelia finished.

'With you,' Welieb continued smoothly almost as if she hadn't spoken. 'And, of course, with her father, your husband.'

Dorelia hesitated. 'Iona's never been particularly close to her father. Daughters seldom are. It's their mother who matters.'

'So a father isn't important?'

'I didn't say that.' Dorelia knew her answer was being twisted as Welieb had twisted it so often before. 'It's just that a mother means more to a child. Of course, a father's important in a different way.'

'As a role model of what a man should be?'

'Yes.'

'Which he shows by his presence around the house? His behaviour? His values and his record as a male human being?'

Welieb's voice was suddenly fierce and insistent. All the jocular mildness in the little man had vanished. It was as if he had suddenly caught her face in a brutally dazzling spotlight. Dorelia flinched. She looked away and nodded helplessly.

'I suppose so, yes.'

'I see –'

Welieb turned from her. For an instant Dorelia felt relief that his eyes were no longer boring into her. Then, as he started to address the judge, she froze.

'My lord, I suggest Mrs Howard has made her position more than clear in her own words. She accepts the co-primacy of a father in a child's upbringing. The court has heard nothing – even from my learned friend – to suggest that my own client, the child's natural father, has not discharged his parental obligations in an exemplary manner. On the other hand, your lordship has heard much evidence about Mrs Howard's most recent and perhaps permanent companion for the future –'

Welieb put his hands to his face. In a gesture of apparent puzzlement and regret, he frowned and pushed up his glasses. 'Mr Ryan has convictions over many years ranging from drug abuse to persistent violence. Yet this is the man who could well become the surrogate father to and male role model for Iona –' He paused.

'I do not lightly use terms that are often considered emotive, but I think it not inappropriate to employ one here. In an enlightened society such as I think the court would consider ours to be, a man of Mr Ryan's record would not suggest himself as an ideal putative father-figure. Indeed to a young and impressionable child suddenly faced with a sundered family – and we all acknowledge the child's interests are paramount – he might well appear as a monster.'

Welieb sat down abruptly. Almost before he reached his seat, Dorelia's own counsel leapt up to protest.

'My lord, I must object strongly to my learned friend's choice of language –'

His voice went on. Dorelia barely heard him. Sickened and stunned she stood absolutely still in the witness box. The suggestion of Iona seeing Sean as a monster was so false, so inconceivable, a lie so cruel and brazen it left her dazed. Iona loved Sean – she'd said so often. There were no monsters in her life. The only person who merited the description was the child's father, Michael, but Iona wouldn't be able to understand that until she grew up.

Dorelia closed her eyes in silent gratitude to Charles Lefanu. His suggestion of sending the child away during the hearing was the best advice she'd ever been given. In her godfather's hands, Iona was shielded and safe. Briefly Dorelia wondered where at that moment Cabot and her daughter were.

Her barrister finished his submission, Welieb stood up, and she forced herself to concentrate again on the venomous little man's questions.

24

'Why?' Iona demanded.

Churinga was kneeling opposite her, her face creased and unhappy. 'Because Tonemetapu says it should be so,' Churinga began. 'Because –'

Her voice trailed away into silence, and her fingers plucked distractedly at the earth. Her child, Tumba, was lying on a mound of soft grass at her side. Iona glanced at the baby and her eyes filled with tears.

Kekua was squatting on her haunches just outside the entrance to the shelter, staring intently into the distance, as Iona had noticed she often did when she was thinking carefully about something. The blind yeti turned and entered the shelter. Because of the low roof she bent forward and supported the upper part of her body on her arms.

In the shadowy tunnel beneath the reed thatch she was for an instant no longer Kekua, the almost human creature Iona had started to know and trust. Ambling forward on her hands she resembled one of the great apes – reminding Iona of old grey-backed Yerto as he came down the bank to the morning assemblies of the gatherers. The child shivered. Then the blind yeti spoke and she became Kekua once more.

'Iona, little shumbi,' she said. 'You must be brave.' She fixed her unseeing eyes on the child, and rubbed Iona's nose.

'Why must I go, Kekua?' Iona demanded.

Her cheeks were pale, her hands shook and she was close to tears. She had virtually lost track of time. She no longer knew when she had tumbled off the ridge, fallen into the river and been swept down to the valley to be found by the yeti. She had learnt that in their own language they called themselves the people, but at moments like this they became monsters again.

All the precarious trust Iona had managed to build up was suddenly and bewilderingly shattered. She had slept night after night with Kekua, she had foraged with the holding, she had obediently done whatever was asked of her. She had done it out of a stubborn and unquenchable urge to survive. If she lost herself in the landscape of their life and world, they might forget she was there – they might let her live.

Iona had failed. Inexplicably she was to be sent away from the holding. She glanced at little Tumba and another wave of misery engulfed her. She had tried to keep her distance from the yeti, to see them as creatures different and apart, reasoning that too would help her survive. But then she'd delivered the breech-born child, and somehow it had made the baby almost as much hers as Churinga's. She couldn't leave the infant.

'Why, Kekua?' Iona repeated, shaking Kekua's wrist in a frenzy of anxiety.

'Listen carefully –' Kekua's face was anguished but firm. 'You heard what Tonemetapu said. You are a shumbi who was washed down from the crests. There has never been a shumbi in the valley before. You are a gift from the snows, but the gift cannot belong to the holding alone – it must be shared with the ranging for we cannot divide ourselves from them. However different we are, we are all still the people and we must share as we have always done. This season, for the first time in all the long memories of the past – memories that go back to the star without a name – we do not know how we should share. There are quarrels and disputes –' Kekua paused. Her blind eyes seemed to bore into Iona.

'Tonemetapu tells us you may have been sent to heal them or you may have come as a warning like the birds which fly before the storm or the grass which yellows and curls down before the snows. Until you have been given to the ranging too, neither Tonemetapu nor any of us will know. Without the ranging's knowledge of you, we cannot speak together in cloud-time. Do you understand?'

Iona stared back at Kekua. No, she did not understand. The reason Kekua had given her wasn't important, it was trivial. Briefly Iona had been enthralled by Tonemetapu's story of the yeti's beginnings, but the magic conjured up by the old seer's whispering voice had vanished abruptly when she discovered where the story led to. All that mattered to Iona was that she had found a fragile measure of safety in the holding's world on the island, and that safety was to be seized from her.

'I don't want to go,' she said bitterly. 'I'm not going to go!'

She wept. She felt Kekua's hand reach out and touch her cheek, then the strong arms of the yeti went round her, and she felt herself being rocked just as she herself had taken to rocking little Tumba when Churinga was late in returning to suckle her.

'Hsst, little shumbi. What will strong Manu say when he comes for you? What will Babilla do when she sees these wet cheeks?'

'I trust Manu. He won't let anyone take me away!'

As her voice rose to a shout of fury, Iona tore herself from Kekua's arms. She ran out of the shelter, climbed the ridge and plunged down the slope to the water's edge. She threw herself on the ground and beat her fists on the earth until she felt blood running from her knuckles.

Above her on the ridge, Wengen crouched immobile. His pale eyes had narrowed to gleaming slits under his heavy brows.

Wengen had seen Kekua lead Iona to the head of the island. Like all the yeti he knew where the child was going. There could be no secrets about an event as extraordinary as the arrival of a shumbi in the valley, or what happened to her afterwards. Iona was to be questioned by Tonemetapu. Within an hour of her return Wengen also knew, like everyone else, what Tonemetapu had decided.

The child was to be sent to the ranging.

Wengen had retired to the ridge to consider what this might mean when he saw Iona run down the bank below him and hurl herself sobbing on the ground. For several minutes he watched her, then silently he rose to his feet. He set off back for the clearing in search of his father, Yerto.

Wengen found the old patriarch sharing a pouch of grain with Ryena, Wengen's mother and Yerto's favourite female. Yerto had to be approached with the proper degree of respect, even by his own son and natural heir. It had always enraged Wengen that he had no preferential treatment, that he had to wait, back half turned, head tucked down between his shoulders in the required gesture of submission, until the greyback acknowledged him, gave the greeting signal and permitted himself to be addressed.

From a distance a handful of the other young males – Babu, the half-brother to squint-eyed Kalu, the restless Momuru and the burly

Naku – had sensed the tension in the air. They settled down to watch, out of earshot but well within sight. Wengen waited too. The patriarch was in no hurry. The sun had travelled the full arc of the sky before the old leader gave his son the sign that he was prepared to listen.

Raging against the humiliation of being made to stay outside the shelter in full view of the holding, Wengen managed to swallow his anger. He bent his head as required by the bonds, watching his father warily out of the corner of his eye as he entered the shelter. Yerto might be old, but he was still strong and his authority over the holding could not be challenged. If he lost his temper and attacked his son, Wengen was not permitted to resist him.

'I am told Tonemetapu has said the young shumbi is to be sent to the ranging,' Wengen said. 'Tonemetapu is wise. We must share the snows' gift with those of the crests. But it is also only right that I, Wengen, should deliver her into the care of Gaggau the cripple so that the ranging can join its decision to your own.'

The old silverback looked deeply and thoughtfully at his son. He was silent for a long while. When he spoke at last his voice was both angry and sorrowful.

'Do not think I do not know your secrets,' he said. 'Do not think I do not know who fathered Churinga's child, or the manner of the seeding of her. You strain the bonds to breaking point, Wengen. Churinga was promised to Manu in the cloud-time. It is as well for you and for the peace of the holding that Manu is of the ranging and cannot read the thoughts of the holding –' Yerto paused. 'Nevertheless,' he went on slowly. 'I will let you go with the young shumbi to the ranging. It will do honour to my brother Gaggau that you go. It will help him judge her more carefully still. But –'

Yerto held up his hand. 'You will not go alone. Manu will lead the shumbi child to the mountains. He knows the path to the crests as you never will. He will also be guardian for the shumbi's safety. Manu can be trusted. You will follow behind them, and make your shelter at a distance from theirs.'

As Yerto finished, Wengen's head jerked up. His face flushed dark with anger, but Yerto had nothing more to say. The old silverback turned and set about grooming Ryena.

Wengen backed away. Outwardly he was calm again, but behind the surface of his bland, impassive face he was seething with murderous rage. The blood pumped and throbbed in his veins. He felt cold and dizzy.

The shumbi, the gift from the snows, should have been entrusted to him alone. Manu was more than a stranger, an interloper. He was a usurper, a worm gnawing at the heart of Wengen's world, destroying that world as remorselessly as the worms that ate out the core of the alders and junipers which lined the river's banks, leaving the trees as dead husks.

Manu was seducing the young of the holding. At the gatherings he was useless, but he had bold bright eyes and he knew tricks. He and his poisonous creature, the leopard, could catch the animals of the valley. The leopard hunted them, Manu snared them in traps. The holding had always supplemented their diet with small birds and animals on the rare occasions they fell into the island yeti's hands. Manu's way was different – he was creating an entirely new way of living. Catching prey was becoming a habit and the younger males of the holding were greedy for it. It was more demanding than gathering, asking for different skills. It was also more challenging and exciting – and the protein it yielded was just as rich as any that came from the gatherer's slowly harvested birds'-nest baskets of grain and fruit.

The holding's males not only loved Manu's skills, they seemed transfixed by the dark-pelted mountain yeti himself. He had bold open features and an easy smile. He could run faster than any of them, but he would often hold himself back so that the pack could keep up with him. As a teacher of the ways of hunting he was endlessly patient. Among the shelters on the island he patiently and good-humouredly shared the burden of carrying out work that still, after many seasons, remained unfamiliar and unnatural to him.

Resentful and jealous – he knew he had none of Manu's talents and even less of his appeal to the other members of the holding – Wengen returned to the ridge. He squatted down and brooded. Until now, Manu had been the only target of his hatred. Now there was another, the shumbi child the mountain yeti had found.

On the river's bank, Iona had stopped sobbing.

Now she was staring into the water, bleakly turning over in her mind the events of the day, which had begun with the birth of Churinga's baby and ended with Tonemetapu's story of the ancient beginnings of the yeti people. The star who dreamed the sun, but had let it go. The first clouds which had brought rain and growth to the valley. The fear of all the yeti of the encroaching shumbi race, and of their command of what Iona had learnt they called the dark storm's child – of fire.

Iona glanced up sharply. Fire. The shumbi – Iona had already begun to see herself as the yeti saw her – were not afraid of fire. She, the little shumbi who had been washed down from the crests, had what Tonemetapu called the sticks which made fire. It was the only power she had over the yeti. She had been loyal to them, but they had betrayed her – even Kekua and Churinga.

Distraught and frightened, Iona realized suddenly that she had a way to defeat them. She would make fire – not a little cooking fire like the one she'd pushed into the water in panic when she sensed unseen eyes were watching her, eyes that for once didn't belong to the sly Wengen but to the old seer. This would be a real fire, a fire that would show all the yeti, including Tonemetapu, her power. She would frighten them even more than they had frightened her. Then they could not send her away to the crests. They would have to let her stay on the island.

Iona's troubled face calmed. She threw a pebble into the churning pool and watched the rings it made. Rings and rings and rings, until the wavelets lapped the mossy stones at the edge of the water and glittered in the golden afternoon light.

Triumphantly Iona reached into her pocket for the matches.

Manu slipped into the river. With Babilla behind him, he struck out for the island.

He and the leopard had been hunting all day. It was something Manu rarely did. When he went out with the gatherers of the holding, he would occasionally break away from them if Babilla found prey and join the leopard in the chase. He couldn't help himself. Something older and stronger than his bond to the holding spoke to him, and he was unable to resist its urgent call.

At other times, when the harvest was sparse, he would leave the gatherers, and plait and set snares as the ranging did on the crests. Manu did that out of boredom. For him to hunt alone, alone apart from Babilla, was different. He had done it only occasionally since he had come to the holding as a child, each time when he'd been deeply worried. Hunting was the only way he knew of healing the hurt, of burying it in physical effort.

Manu had slept little during the night. He rose long before dawn and called softly for Babilla. Together they crossed the river into the feeding grounds.

They had caught little. That was unimportant. The chafing tensions between the holding and the ranging had vanished from his mind in the solitary pleasures of the chase. They would return as soon as he stepped ashore, but for a while at least he'd been free of them. Now, refreshed, he was nearly home again. Home – he wondered what it meant. Often he felt confused about where his home was. After all the years he'd spent with the holding, the island seemed to belong to him more than the crests.

Then, whenever he'd begun to think that, he'd return to the crests on one of his visits to the ranging. He'd smell the high clean air of the snows and lie at night not on the soft straw and grass of the valley, but on the springy mountain heather the upland clan collected for their beds. He'd watch the stars through an opening in a towering vault of rock. He'd rise with the hunters. All day he'd scour the chill, wind-riven slopes in search of spoor.

Occasionally Manu might close with the others to make a kill. He never minded if they failed to find prey. He could exist for days on end without eating. What mattered was the search, the pursuit, the chase. For that and the exhilaration of the icy winds across the crests, he would trade everything. The winds touched his heart.

There were few winds below the mountains, and all of them were warm and soft. What there was on the valley's plain around the island was plenty for the gatherers.

Manu swam steadily and powerfully. In the middle of the stream the dark brown foam-flecked water was running with the speed of a tidal race. Manu barely noticed it. He headed undeviatingly for the far bank as if he were crossing one of the small still lakes in the mountains. At his side Babilla swam with the same rippling strength.

The two of them, the yeti and the leopard, reached the bank and climbed out. They shook themselves dry and set off up the slope. Manu glanced round the clearing. Most of the holding were out harvesting in the gathering grounds. Apart from a few of the oldest yeti and some children, Manu could see only Kekua and Churinga squatting outside their shelters, the new-born infant suckling at Churinga's breast.

Manu walked towards them. Smiling he scratched the infant's tiny nostrils, his touch as light as a butterfly's on the soft and still hairless skin. He glanced round. 'Where is Iona?' he asked, puzzled. The shumbi child seldom left Kekua's side, but there was no sign of her.

'She was taken to Tonemetapu,' Kekua replied. 'Tonemetapu spoke with her long. He says she must go to the crests to be shared with the ranging. You are to take her there. Iona defies it all. She does not want to leave the holding. She has run to the river in anger and grief.'

'Then she cannot understand,' Manu replied, perplexed. 'I will find her and explain.'

He swung round to head for the river. As he moved, Kekua rose and caught his arm. 'Leave her to be alone, Manu,' she said. 'You are right. She does not understand. The child will learn, but she must learn on her own.'

At the head of the island a small lizard, its viridescent sides pumping with the warmth of the evening sun, ran up the trunk of the juniper tree and scuttled over Tonemetapu's shoulders.

The old yeti sat so still that the lizard noticed no difference between the trunk it had climbed and Tonemetapu's body. It found a shaft of light and settled down to bask in the green moss on the yeti's back. A small black and white flycatcher, its crop bulging with the evening's trawl of insects, alighted on Tonemetapu's knee. Like the lizard it made no distinction between the old yeti and the tree. For an instant the bird eyed the lizard warily, then it began to digest its meal.

Tonemetapu took no more notice of the two creatures than they did of him. Tonemetapu dreamed.

He dreamed of Manu and the leopard swimming back to the island. He dreamed of the troubles that had driven Manu out to empty his mind in hunting. He dreamed of the threat from the ranging yeti that they would come down to the feeding grounds below the crests, and claim their right to raid the valley's larder. He dreamed of the tormented patriarch, Yerto, tossing restlessly in his shelter and the patient worried Ryena watching at his side.

The shaft of light moved. The lizard stirred. It flicked its long jewelled tail and crawled after the fading heat funnelled down from the darkening sky. The flycatcher had ground up the insects pouched in its crop. Now delicately perched on Tonemetapu's leg, it began to pick at a small cache of lice in the long hair at the yeti's knees.

Tonemetapu dreamed.

He dreamed the shumbi child and the firesticks hidden in the fold in her pelt. He had seen them before. He saw them more vividly now. He dreamed the child's thoughts and saw what was in her heart. Flames snarled and gnawed at the shelters round the clearing. Kekua stumbled in the smoke. Churinga with little Tumba clasped close to her breast screamed as she ran to the water. The other yeti howled and scattered before the choking wall of flames.

The shumbi child was dreaming too. In her dream she was calling down the dark storm's child.

Tonemetapu's body was shaken like a dying thornbush tugged backwards and forwards by a gale from the crests.

The lizard felt the sudden convulsive movements, and the scales of its spine flared erect in terror. It leapt from Tonemetapu's back, raced down the twisted roots of the juniper and hid itself in the grass. Equally alarmed the flycatcher rose from the yeti's knee. It circled twice beneath the branches, its wings beating frantically, then spotted a gap in the leaf canopy and hurled itself upwards towards the sky.

The trembling passed and Tonemetapu dreamed on.

This time he dreamed of his long-ago ancestor, the nameless star whose own dreams had conjured first the sun, then the clouds, and finally the river which had at last given him a name and given birth, too, to the people. The star's last dream had also returned rain to the valley.

In the juniper's shadow Tonemetapu dreamed rain.

Darkness was falling over the valley and the island.

Iona crouched in a thicket of the shoulder-high grass on the river's bank. She reached out and plucked a handful of stems. It was midsummer and the grass came away easily from the earth. The plants had already passed the brief life of their flowering. They had formed their fruit, seen the sun dry it, and cast the seeds back to the earth. Now they were dying.

Iona crushed the stems between her fingers. She tapped out one of the matches and held its fat waxed head close to the rough ignition strip. She glanced up.

At that first hour of the evening the sky was always bright with stars. Iona had never seen it so clear and brilliant before. It dazzled her eyes. The constellations poured down in plumes and catherine wheels of luminescence like a vast, constantly changing kaleidoscope of fireworks. Owls and bats fished the air, blacking out the incandescence in their tracks only to let it pour back even more brightly than before.

Iona blinked. The scents of the evening were sweet and warm with the late flower smells and the fragrance of ripening fruits. The wind was blowing from off the crests, but the ridge curled the tangle of odours back into her face. When she set fire to the grass, the flames would sweep down towards the river on the western side. The wind would slip under the flames somewhere between the ridge and the shore. It would halt them, turn them, and bring them searing back towards the clearing.

Then the fire would devour the shelters.

Iona clenched her teeth. She didn't want to do it. She hated doing it, but the island yeti had broken faith with her. She had done everything asked of her, Iona repeated to herself again. She had even struggled to learn their language. In her fury and misery Iona forgot that the decision to do that had been her own, that she believed it held the key to escaping from the valley. All she remembered was the yeti's decision to abandon her and toss her to the unknown ranging – 'a gift', as old Tonemetapu had said, 'which must be shared'. She was no one's gift. She was herself. And she had the power to make them understand that.

Iona struck a match. As it ignited, the flare dazzled her eyes. She smelt the acrid scent of sulphur, and screwed up her face. The flame crept down the match's stem. She should have touched it to the grass stems, but, seemingly paralysed, she waited until the flame reached her fingers. Then she winced with pain and hurled the matchstick into the water.

As Iona sucked at the scorch marks on her skin, she realized for the second time that day that unseen eyes were watching her. Now she knew who the eyes belonged to, not Wengen but Tonemetapu. From the hollow in the gnarled juniper tree, far beyond Iona's sight and hidden from the river bank by the swell of the ridge and the dense thickets of the island's scrub, the old yeti was gazing at her.

A small cloud drifted across the sky from the direction of the crests, briefly blotting out the stars. From the darkness of the cloud and its swollen belly, Iona knew it was carrying rain. The cloud passed on and the constellations reappeared above her. Iona knew why – there was no need for rain. The match had burnt out, the dark storm's child had died before it ever came to birth, and the threat of fire had passed from the island.

Iona burst into tears. Weeping in frustration and loneliness she made her way back to the shelter. As she reached the entrance, she pushed Kekua away and threw herself down sobbing on her bed of grass and reeds.

In the darkness Tonemetapu's head slumped forward on to his chest.

The black and white flycatcher had long since swooped off to a safer perch. The emerald-eyed lizard had flicked its tail and scuttled away to spend the night in the sheltering grass. Now only owls visited the juniper tree. They perched briefly in the upper branches, before launching themselves at prey in their own night feeding grounds below.

Tonemetapu was unaware of the owls' hunting calls. He slept. This time he did not dream.

As dawn approached, Iona didn't stir when Kekua rose from the bed of grass beside her and moved out into the clearing, nor was she aware of Manu's approach until he reached down and started to lift her. As he picked her up Iona woke and her eyes cleared. She shook her head, realized what Manu was doing, and screamed. If any of the yeti could be trusted, if any one of them should have saved her, it was the tall dark-skinned yeti who had rescued her from the river, built her the shelter and given her the meat.

Instead Manu had turned on her like the others. He had done worse than fail her – he had betrayed her. In bitterness and shock she bit at his wrist, but his hide was too strong for her teeth to penetrate. He heaved her up on to his shoulders, and strode down towards the river.

Lying across his back Iona sobbed again.

25

Geraint Hughes stood in the darkness looking out to the west.

At 14,000 feet on the Helambu Ridge the temperature was well below freezing. Hoar frost coated Hughes's hair and the night wind, cutting like a sword blade along the crests, stung his eyes. Hughes barely noticed it. He'd long since become almost impervious to the cold. Somewhere below him was the vast bowl of the Helambu valley, but for the moment the sky was overcast and the valley was hidden.

Hughes waited.

The clouds were sweeping over from the north, from the direction of the Tibetan border. In the distance far behind them a few stars were emerging. It might be half an hour before the sky cleared. When it did he would be able to see what he was looking for. Half an hour. Only a madman would stand for half an hour on the Helambu Ridge unprotected against the icy night air. But then of course that's exactly what he was – a madman. Hughes chuckled at the thought.

He wasn't mad all the time. The madness came and went. Sometimes he'd be sane for weeks on end, or at least as he saw it. Then without warning the madness would overwhelm him in a surging red tide. When that happened it was unmistakable. Those occasions never troubled Hughes. He exulted in them. The madness gave him back his former strength, even doubled it. It allowed him to see things with a vivid penetrating clarity, let him take the risks he thought in his periods of sanity he would never dare take again.

Above all, it swept away the years. When the madness was on him Hughes became, paradoxically, what he'd been before it first attacked him. He knew, too, exactly what caused it and the place that had visited it on him. He was waiting to look at the place now, just as he'd stared at it almost every night for the past forty years – every night, that is, when the Himalayan sky had been clear.

The clouds rolled away and the moon appeared, a magnificent full summer moon thronged on every side with stars. The ice-white, ice-bright peaks of the great western range suddenly materialized against the blackness. They seemed to be soaring towards the heavens. One towered above the rest, the one on which Hughes's shuttered and streaming eyes focused with the same spellbound intensity as when he saw it first.

The mountain had many names. On most maps it bore the name of its first European surveyor. To the Britons who first attempted to climb it, it was 'the cathedral of the snows'. In his mind Hughes had privately christened it with a much more modest but to him even more chilling name. The mountain which had almost destroyed him, which had driven him mad, which had haunted and obsessed him ever since, wasn't a cathedral.

Everest was a Welsh chapel.

He could have been the first man to scale it – he *should* have been the first. Hughes had known that by the age of eight in the Welsh valley where he'd been born.

Not the Rhondda valley, which was the only valley in Wales anyone from outside the principality had ever heard of. Hughes's valley was much smaller. It lay in North Wales not far from the foot of Mount Snowdon. He had few memories of his father, but he recalled a walk they'd taken one winter's day when Hughes was four years old. They'd walked until they could see Snowdon's peak against the chill grey sky.

'That's the second highest bloody mountain in all bloody Britain,' his father said with pride in his voice. 'Conceived at its foot you were, boy. There's not many as got their start that way. Don't you ever forget it.'

A year later his father was dead. A forester on one of the great local estates, he'd tripped in the path of a falling tree and was crushed by its trunk. His widow and Geraint, the only child, were left destitute.

It was the early thirties. The economic depression was biting savagely all over the Western world, and no more so than in Wales. Hughes remembered the gaunt, hollow-cheeked men from Merioneth gathering to set out on the hunger marches towards the remote parliament in Westminster. Much more vividly he remembered hunger itself. On good days there was a bowl of barley and root gruel. On bad days there were crusts from a begged oatmeal loaf, *bara Ceirch* in the Welsh language, and the occasional watery stew of a trapped or limed wild bird – often a sinewy, rancid-tasting crow.

On the worst days there was nothing.

His mother was a determined and resourceful woman with a child to support. She detested charity, but Geraint needed food. She scoured the Snowdonia valleys for paid work, and eventually she was taken on as kitchen maid at an inn. The inn was five miles walk from her home, but an important perk of the job was that they could both feed for free off the leavings from the inn's restaurant. Each day she took Geraint with her, making him walk part of the way, carrying him on her hip when he grew tired. The name of the inn was Pen-y-guraig.

'If the noble and hazardous sport of high-altitude mountaineering has a true genesis,' a historian of climbing once wrote, 'it is at Pen-y-guraig. Wherever in the world men aspire to the ultimate heights and set out to conquer them, whether they know it or not, their spiritual starting point lies at the foot of Mount Snowdon. There mountaineering began. The route to the peak of Everest starts in a tavern in a Welsh valley.'

It was in the valley, but most of all at the inn of Pen-y-guraig, that Geraint Hughes learnt to be a mountaineer.

'All right, bach, you can carry the packs up to the sled.' The burly red-faced man gave way at last to Geraint's entreaties.

'Thank you, Mr Davies, thank you.'

Geraint hurried away before Mr Davies could change his mind. He picked up one of the packs. It was so heavy his knees almost buckled under its weight. He managed to heave it over his shoulders, then, swaying and stumbling, he headed upwards into the darkness.

It was almost midnight and the snow lay thick on the ground. The mountain rescue team, formed only a year earlier and the pioneer for many others which would spring up all over Britain in the years ahead, had been called out an hour before. A climber had been reported missing on Snowdon and the team assembled at Pen-y-guraig. Its leader was Huw Davies, an upland forester who'd been a friend of Geraint's father.

By then Mrs Hughes had been given a tiny attic bedroom at Pen-y-guraig where she and Geraint could sleep during the week.

The boy was asleep when the cars began to arrive at the inn but the sound of their engines and the headlamp beams criss-crossing the ceiling had woken him. He'd pulled on his winter school clothes and run downstairs.

'Good lad.' Mr Davies tapped him approvingly on the head as Geraint lowered the pack beside the sled. 'Learn to use the crampons and the ice axe properly, and it won't be long before you're up there on the slopes with the rest of us.'

Geraint grinned as the sled and the seven-man team swished away into the night. He'd loaded all their packs. The effort had left him breathless and panting, but it had been worth it. Mr Davies wouldn't forget what he'd done. Next time, well, over the next few years at least, Geraint wouldn't be left at Pen-y-guraig while the rescue squad climbed into the sleet-thick air of the Welsh December darkness.

Geraint watched them until the pilot torches on the sled vanished in the whirling snow. Then he turned and climbed back up the stairs to bed. When he fell asleep again Geraint dreamed of the mountain, and the day when he would be climbing its gullies and rock faces beside Mr Davies.

It happened much sooner than Geraint had dared believe.

During that winter the rescue team was called out a dozen times. Each time Geraint helped load the sled. When the team returned, Geraint took charge of their boots and climbing equipment. He dried and waxed the leather, he cleaned and sharpened the ice axes, he hammered straight the bent metal teeth on the crampons that fitted over the boots' soles, he greased the sled's runners and learnt how to splice the frayed climbing ropes.

'You should have cut this out,' Davies said reprovingly, pointing to a worn length of jute fibre as he inspected one of Geraint's rope repairs when the winter ended. 'But it's not a bad job you've done, bach. Maybe it's time to get you up on the hill.'

Davies's praise was given rarely and grudgingly. Geraint's face flushed with pride.

Davies was as good as his word. A few weekends later he passed by Pen-y-guraig, and called for Geraint.

'Get your boots on, bach,' Davies said. 'There's a gentleman from London as claims to have found a new route up the Bwyelli face. I want to take a look at it. You can come with me.'

Geraint raced upstairs to collect his boots.

Davies took him to the foot of Bwyelli on Snowdon's western flank. He spent a bare half-hour instructing the boy. He showed him how to place pitons, the steel spikes that could be hammered into cracks in the rock to hold a rope and help the climber upwards. He explained how a climber should move with three 'points' always anchored, and only the third, a hand or a foot, searching for a new hold or a new purchase. He taught him how to travel roped together with a partner, each one taking turns to lead as they inched their way upwards.

Then Davies scrambled on to the boulders at Bwyelli's base, and launched himself up the face. Geraint paid out the rope and waited. When Davies called down for him to follow, Geraint set off behind him. The moment his hand found the first spur and his foot the first knife-thin ledge, Geraint felt at home in a way he'd never felt before.

Like a child tossed into a river who knew instinctively how to swim, Geraint knew how to climb. It came to him as instantly and easily as breathing. The route was steep and technically difficult and had Davies known how challenging it was, he would never have considered taking the boy with him. Often he had to pause and search for a way to tackle the next section. Sometimes he had to climb down and try a new approach.

Geraint never faltered or hesitated. Once, glancing round anxiously at the child after a particularly difficult passage up an outward-slanting corridor, Davies saw that Geraint's gaze was fixed not on him but on a point somewhere above his head.

'If you traverse left, Mr Davies,' Geraint said eagerly, 'there's a sloping shelf beyond the outcrop with a few holds we can maybe use.'

The boy's eyes glittered with the cold pale brilliance of the peregrine falcons that had swept round the mountain as they climbed.

Davies glanced upwards to his left. The shelf was in shadow and he had trouble in picking it out. When he did, he saw Geraint was right. It had a few precarious handholds that even the English gentleman – a famous climber who had been to the Himalayas – had failed to spot. Davies changed direction and set off again.

An hour later he hauled himself over the ridge at the top of the face. Panting, he turned to pull the boy up behind him. He had no need. His breath scarcely troubled, Geraint scrambled up like a cat and joined him, then, without pausing to rest, he turned and studied the fall below them.

'I don't think that English gentleman has it right, Mr Davies,' he said. 'If we'd traversed before the second fissure and taken that little couloir by the raven's nest, we'd have been here ten minutes ago –'

He paused and glanced at Davies. 'I'm quite sure, sir,' he added earnestly. 'Couldn't we try it again to see?'

Davies stared at the boy. Davies was fit and strong and experienced. He had climbed the mountains of Snowdonia all his adult life. He knew the high landscape of the Cambrians as well, he guessed, as anyone knew any landscape anywhere. And this boy, this child who had never climbed before, was suggesting there was a better, faster way up Bwyelli than either he or the English mountaineer had found.

Davies began to laugh. As he laughed he ran back their ascent through his mind. When he came to the point where they'd encountered the second fissure on the face, he saw the alternative routes. Davies examined them in his mind. He stopped laughing. The boy was right. If they'd traversed as Geraint suggested, they would have reached the summit of the ridge sooner.

Davies looked at the boy. 'Never cheek me again, bach,' he said. 'But I'm begining to think you were born to climb mountains. Now let's go home.'

The thirties passed. Slowly the harrowing depression ended, and more and more English mountaineers came to the inn at Pen-y-guraig to scale Snowdon and practise their skills on the surrounding peaks. Geraint left school at fourteen. Unlike most of his contemporaries, he didn't have to search for work. A job was waiting for him – a job he'd created for himself.

Even at fourteen, a wiry, broad-shouldered boy with heavily muscled hands and narrow Celtic eyes the colour of Snowdon's winter-shadowed snow flanks, he was one of the best and most sought-after mountain guides in Wales. Davies generously recommended him as outstanding on the high hills. Geraint's own skills did the rest.

As the thirties ended the war came, Hitler's war as it was known in the principality. Davies was too old to fight but, when Geraint was ordered to enlist, Davies gave him a letter to take to the recruiting office. As a result of it Geraint was sent not to one of the Welsh infantry regiments, but to train as a commando at Loch Fyne in Scotland.

From there he was posted to Norway. He fought and skied and fought again as the disastrous Norwegian campaign came to an end. Among the last to be evacuated from the fjords, Geraint spent the rest of the war training units of the special forces from a base within a few miles of Pen-y-guraig. When the war ended and he was discharged, Geraint stripped off his uniform and walked the nine miles back to the inn at Snowdon's foot.

There he took up his old job again. Hunger, disease and a violence that was almost worse than the war itself lay like a shroud over post-war Europe. The nightmare encompassed Britain. It did not seem to touch the mountaineers. Almost as if the war had never happened, they returned to Pen-y-guraig in their thick tweed suits with their ice axes, their crampons and their jokes.

By then Geraint's mother was dying of cancer. Geraint looked after her by night and took the mountaineers out by day. When his mother died, Geraint took the morning off to bury her. That afternoon he was back at work, guiding two English bankers up one of the easiest routes to Snowdon's peak. Mist came down as evening approached, giving the men the sense of excitement and adventure they had been looking for.

Geraint brought them back in darkness to Pen-y-guraig. They tipped him handsomely and headed, laughing in exhilaration, for the bar. As Geraint stood in the hall of the inn counting the notes they'd pressed into his hand, the innkeeper came through. He looked contemptuously at the retreating backs of Geraint's charges, then he glanced back at Geraint.

'A message for you, bach,' he said. 'Howe, the gentleman's name is. Very different from your two fancy boys today. Mr Gerry Howe's after Everest. He's bringing some of his boyos here to work them up before they leave for the Himalayas. He's heard your name. He wants you to show them Snowdon.'

The two bankers called and the innkeeper went through to serve them.

In the hall Geraint closed his eyes. He'd never met Howe, but the mountaineering community was small and Geraint had heard his name often. Howe was one of the most experienced high-altitude climbers in Europe. He was also very rich. If anyone had the energy, skills and resources to mount an expedition with a realistic chance of conquering the world's highest and still unclimbed peak, it was Gerry Howe.

Geraint shut out the noise from the bar. He shut out the spring wind that was roaring round Pen-y-guraig. He shut out everything. In his mind he saw a single white and ice-bright peak rising like a spear's head above the clouds. The peak was named Everest.

Geraint hadn't been asked to join the expedition, but he knew he would be. He knew, too, he was going to be the first man to scale the mountain.

'Hughes!'

Geraint turned and peered through his snow goggles. Usually he could see clearly through their dark lenses but for some reason today the glass seemed to be blurred. Geraint took them off, polished them, and stared out again.

The glass was still misty but he could just make out the silhouette of the expedition's lantern-jawed doctor, Robin Carew, outlined against the snow beneath him. Geraint raised his hand and set off down the slope.

It was only five months since Howe and the core team for his assault on Everest had arrived at Pen-y-guraig to complete their final training. Geraint had been a little bemused but not at all surprised by what happened within days of their moving into the inn.

Geraint had taken them out on to the rock faces. He climbed for a week as point, leading them all as he made the traverses, hammered in the pitons and set the ropes. At the end of the week, Howe took him aside.

'Where the hell did you learn how to climb, Geraint?' he asked in his deceptively casual voice.

'I picked it up here and there, sir,' Geraint answered.

'Sounds like measles,' Howe grunted. 'Wherever you got it, I can use it. There's some damn New Zealander who's planning to tackle Everest next year. I want to be up it first. I reckon you'd better come to the Himalayas with the rest of us. No pay. Just your fare, your food, and maybe a bottle of brandy at the end –' He paused. 'Are you on?'

Geraint grinned. 'I won't even need the brandy, Mr Howe.'

Now, as Geraint moved down from Camp Seven towards the doctor, who'd struggled up from Camp Six, the expedition had been on Everest for five weeks.

After setting up a base camp at 11,000 feet, they'd progressively pushed up the mountain until six days ago when Camp Seven had been established. Camp Seven, no more than a pair of small tents already almost buried by snow, was only 4,000 feet below the summit. It was from there, when the weather cleared – there had been blizzards ever since the tents were pitched – that the final assault on the peak would be made.

As Geraint walked, his eyes still strangely blurred, he thought back over the five weeks. Apart from himself all the other climbers with the expedition were amateurs. That didn't mean they weren't good. Like Howe they were all fearless, skilful and infinitely more experienced at high altitudes than Geraint was. What it did mean was that they didn't earn their living from mountains, or spend their lives on the slopes. Geraint did. It had given him a knowledge of rock and ice conditions and, above all, a stamina they lacked.

Geraint hadn't the slightest doubt that Howe had picked him, the one professional among the others, as a reliable work-horse, a white equivalent of the expedition's Sherpa porters. If he was going to be considered for the assault on the summit, Geraint knew he would have to prove himself to be much more than that.

From the moment they trekked into base camp, Geraint single-mindedly set out to show Howe what he was worth. He volunteered to carry loads alongside the Sherpas as the ladder of camps stretched upwards. He offered himself for the tedious reconnaissance sorties to check snow and ice conditions. When the Sherpa cook collapsed with dysentery at Camp Five, Geraint took over the tiny frozen gas ring and fed the others until a replacement hauled himself up from below.

He drove himself until his lungs ached and his muscles felt as if they were sheathed in lead. At night he huddled into his sleeping-bag, placed his boots between his legs to thaw out the ice that coated them, and dozed as fitfully and dizzily as if he'd been drunk. Next morning he was always the first to wake, even before the Sherpas. He crawled out of the tent, gathered handfuls of snow and began to melt it for the dawn tea.

The brutal, unremitting effort paid off. Towards the end of the expedition's fifth week on the mountain, Howe ducked into Geraint's tent at Camp Six.

'You're doing a good job, Geraint,' he said. 'Some of the others are having trouble with the altitude. You seem to be keeping up the pace. How are you feeling?'

'I'm just fine, sir,' Geraint replied.

'Up to taking the Sherpas forward to dig in Camp Seven tomorrow?'

'No problem, Mr Howe.'

Howe nodded. 'Do that and you can bloody well stay there. Because I have a feeling, Hughes, I'm going to leapfrog you up the pecking order, and put you in for the first assault –'

Howe paused and scraped the frost from his beard. 'You'll take a Sherpa with you, of course. It's their damn mountain, and we don't want to offend local sensitivities. But how do you feel about being the first European to stand on the highest place on earth?'

Geraint grinned. 'I think I can handle it, sir.'

'I should bloody well hope so. Because if the weather holds, that's just what you're going to be.'

Howe backed out of the tent into the darkness.

His visit to Camp Seven had taken place forty-eight hours ago. Since then raging winds and snowstorms had blown round the camp and the peak above but today the weather had cleared. According to the three Sherpas who were sharing Camp Seven with Geraint, the window that had opened in the spring tempests would last for several days more.

It was the ideal moment to tackle the peak. As he descended towards the doctor, all that Geraint had to decide was which of the Sherpas would go with him to the highest and loneliest place on earth.

'How many fingers?'

Carew raised his hand as Geraint reached him. Geraint peered through his dark glasses. For some extraordinary reason he couldn't make out how many fingers Carew was holding out before him. The doctor's hand was a blur.

'Two,' Geraint guessed as Carew wavered in and out of focus before him.

'Hughes, take off your glasses, please!'

Carew's voice was urgent and worried. Geraint removed his glasses. The reflected light from the snow dazzled his eyes.

'How many?'

He heard Carew repeat the question. Now Geraint could see nothing, nothing at all apart from a vast, hurtful bowl of whiteness.

'Two,' he said again.

It was a short word but Geraint stumbled over it. He clutched for something to support himself. He found nothing. He swayed forward, groping again for something to hold on to. Then he tumbled face-down in the snow.

Dimly Geraint heard Carew shouting, 'He's got altitude sickness. We've got to get him down. For Christ's sake, someone help me!'

Geraint was aware of feet slushing through the snow. The noise was accompanied by the rancid smell of cured animal hides, a smell which could only have come from the Sherpas. It filled Geraint's nostrils and briefly shocked him back into consciousness. He managed to raise his head from the ground. Blindly he searched for the Sherpas.

'Leave me, leave me!' he shouted. 'Don't take me away! I'm going to climb Everest!'

Geraint spilled out the words in a frenzy. Then darkness overwhelmed the scalding brightness of the snow.

26

They slept.

There were fifteen of them. Eight males, five females, and two half-adult young, both males too. They lay in an untidy circle loosely centred round the fire, but far beyond the range of the flames even when the fire had been blazing high. Now at midnight the fire had burnt down to a few smouldering coals. The embers gave just enough light to outline the man they called Ma-na-kakua, the creature with the pelt of winter flakes. Ma-na-kakua was sleeping too.

They had given him the name when he first appeared from the snows. Unlike them he had no fur. His skins – they considered his own skin and the hides he had wrapped round himself as the same – were congealed with ice. So were his face and hair. His eyes were almost invisible behind the crust of hoar crystals which rimmed his eye sockets. When he learnt their language and discovered what they called him, the man tried to translate the name into his own tongue. The closest equivalent he could come up with was the Snowman. The man chuckled. He liked the idea of being known as the Snowman. He adopted the name for himself.

The man, the Snowman, slept deeply and silently. The others in the darkness beyond him did not. Part of the reason was the fire. The fire was the Snowman's creature and companion. He brought it out and wakened it every night. He'd done so ever since he'd come down to them from the snows and by now they were used to its presence. They knew it was important to the Snowman, he valued it.

That they accepted. The fire itself remained unpredictable and dangerous. Several of them in the early days after the Snowman's arrival had been bitten by it. The fire's teeth were as sharp as the ice-wind on the high peaks, causing the same pain and swellings and seeping of blood as the wind, but much more swiftly and brutally.

The fire's breathing, the spirals of hissing scarlet and yellow stars that lifted into the night, continued to disturb them when they rested. So did the rustles and bone-snaps of its body when it turned on its bed. They had learnt to stay away from it. It was a creature best left to its guardian, the Snowman. The Snowman, although they didn't know it, had another name. He hadn't used it for almost forty years. Sometimes, particularly when the madness was on him, he had to struggle through the mist that seemed to cloud his brain to remember what it was. When it eventually came back to him, he would smile in relief.

As long as he had a name, a name other than the Snowman, he would never be entirely lost. He rolled the two words of his name round his tongue, and spat them out into the Himalayan wind.

He was mad and his eyes were scarlet but he still knew who he was. He was Geraint Hughes.

Geraint woke.

He climbed to his feet and walked up to the ridge again. The sky was still dark and burdened with stars, but dawn was close. He could feel it in the slight warming and thickening of the night air. He gazed out towards the west.

The clouds of morning were beginning to gather round the lower flanks of the distant mountain, but its peak soared defiant and inviolate against the wheeling constellations. Everest, the highest watch-tower on the battlements of the earth, was keeping its lonely vigil above the turning globe. So, on a ridge above the Helambu valley, was its last sentry.

Through his blurred, bloodshot eyes, Geraint feasted his wavering sight on the distant summit. For an instant he held it in focus. The focus dissolved and all he could see was a red rain across his vision. Geraint snorted in anger and swung stiffly round.

He gazed down over his camp. Now that the dazzling flanks of the mountain were at his back, he could see more clearly. The fire was still burning. Round it, beyond the glow cast by the smouldering coals, the oduna were lying huddled in sleep. Two or three of them were snoring, and the heavy rasp of their breathing echoed up the slope.

Geraint stared at them with contempt. In a sudden rage he stooped, plucked a stone from the snow, and hurled it down. The stone bounced off the night sheen of ice on the snow and struck one of the oduna in the ribs. The creature sat up and yelped. It gazed blearily round the campsite. A moment later it was asleep and snoring again.

Geraint swore. He hobbled back to the fire and eased himself under the canopy of skins beneath which he slept. In the darkness round him the oduna stirred and mumbled.

The oduna.

In their own language the word meant the outcasts. It was the first word of theirs he had learnt. How long ago was that now? Often Geraint couldn't remember, but tonight his brain was calm and clear and he could remember without difficulty. He lay awake, thinking back.

Geraint never knew exactly what happened after he collapsed unconscious at Camp Seven. The weeks that followed were lost to him. His first lucid moment came over a month later when he woke in the little hospital in Kathmandu. He was lying in bed and he could hear two voices talking. One of them was Howe's, the other had an American accent.

'What's your prognosis, Doctor?' Geraint heard Howe saying.

'It's not good,' the American answered. 'We don't get many cases of altitude, or mountain, sickness. The Nepali are acclimatized to the heights and don't tend to suffer from it. But of all the cases who've been brought in for treatment, I guess this is much the worst. I'm afraid we could be looking at irreversible brain damage.'

'Is there anything that could be done for him in Europe?'

'I just don't know, Mr Howe. You've nothing to lose in trying. Whatever they've got over there is bound to be more advanced than anything we've got here in Nepal.'

'I'll get him out as soon as possible, with any luck on the flight to Delhi tomorrow –' Howe paused. Geraint sensed he was looking at the bed and kept his eyes closed.

'Poor bastard!' Howe went on. 'He was one of the best men on rock and ice I've ever seen. I'd picked him to go for the peak. Not that it would have made any difference. When those storms set in the day he keeled over, we'd have had to clear the mountain anyway. I just hope to God I didn't push him too hard earlier.'

'I wouldn't blame yourself, Mr Howe,' the American said. 'The condition can hit anyone. And Everest's a law unto itself. That mountain's always been a killer. The only way it's ever going to be cracked is with supplementary oxygen – and even then someone's going to need a bundle of luck.'

Still talking, the two men left the room. Soon afterwards Geraint drifted back into unconsciousness.

When he woke again it was night. Through the window he could see the jagged, shadowy shapes of the mountains surrounding the Kathmandu valley, and the stars above.

For a few moments Geraint lay on his back with his eyes open. Then he swung himself on to the floor. He stood up and cautiously tested his legs. He crossed the room twice. He felt weak and light-headed, but at least he could move. He searched for his clothes and found them neatly folded on a chair with his boots and climbing equipment underneath. In the wallet inside his jacket was the unused bundle of Nepalese rupees he'd been given in exchange for sterling when the expedition reached Kathmandu.

Geraint dressed quickly. He opened the door and walked quietly downstairs to the reception hall where the duty orderly was asleep inside a cubicle. Geraint tiptoed across the hall and stepped out into the street.

Barely ten minutes had passed since he'd opened his eyes. Every word of the conversation between Howe and the American doctor was still ringing vividly through his brain. The doctor's mention of irreversible brain damage meant nothing to Geraint. He didn't believe it, he didn't accept it, and it wasn't true. The proof was in the decision he'd just taken.

Everest was still unconquered and Howe was flying him back to Europe tomorrow. Geraint wasn't going back to Europe. If he did, he knew he would never return. He had been given the chance to scale the peak, and the chance had been seized from him. He felt cheated. He felt bitterness and rage that flooded through him in hot pulsing tides. He didn't accept what had happened – he rejected it violently and savagely.

The storms Howe spoke of wouldn't have driven him back. His nerve wouldn't have failed as the expedition leader's nerve had failed. Geraint would have gone on. He would have fought his way through the snow and the blizzards, and placed his foot on the summit. In the childhood of Judas, he had been told once, Jesus was betrayed. In his own childhood in the valley beneath Snowdon, Everest had been climbed.

The mountain was still there. He would find a way to scale it.

Geraint vanished into the Kathmandu night.

In the fifties the little mountain kingdom of Nepal was still officially closed by royal decree to foreigners and the outside world.

In practice, beyond Kathmandu the king's law was at best vaguely enforced and more often ignored. Along the country's northern border with Tibet, the law was simply unknown. Geraint headed north. He didn't speak Gurkhali or any of Nepal's many tribal languages, but like any high-altitude mountaineer he was capable and resourceful. He had his clothes, his boots, his equipment, and a stock of rupees that by the subsistence standards of the local peasant economy made him virtually a millionaire.

It took him seven weeks to trek across country to the foothills of Everest. He followed one of the many paths upwards until he reached one of the high Sherpa villages that stood at 10,000 feet. There he took lodgings in the upper room of a teahouse. A week later he hired two young Sherpas as porters, and began to climb.

There was no question of going for the mountain's peak that year. The clear weather of the summer was already almost at an end, and storms – like the freak storms which had ended Howe's expedition – had begun to sweep Everest's flanks. Geraint only wanted to reconnoitre the upper slopes so that he would know what route to follow when spring came again. He remembered Howe speaking of the New Zealander. Geraint was determined to make his own assault well before the New Zealander's expedition even reached the foothills.

The first day passed without problem. Climbing slowly and carefully, taking note of every gradient above them, Geraint and the two Sherpas reached 14,000 feet and made a bivouac for the night. When he rose the next morning, the sky was a cloudless blue and the early sun was incandescent with warmth as it flared off the high shelves of ice. Geraint glanced round him and laughed aloud with pleasure.

As the Sherpas lit a fire and began to brew the breakfast tea, Geraint set off for a knoll just above the camp. He took three steps. Suddenly the mountain vanished. A dark red cloak came down over his eyes. Bewildered, he tried to take another step. Inexplicably, he couldn't lift his foot from the snow. He tugged at it. Dimly he realized that his heart was racing and his lungs felt as if they were about to explode.

Geraint collapsed.

If he hadn't been mad before, Geraint became mad then.

He knew it, and the Sherpas, who carried him back down to the village, knew it too. Geraint woke five days later. His eyes, filmed with blood now, had barely opened before he lurched off the birch-filled pallet in the smoky room above the teahouse. He dressed clumsily, trying to put his boots on the wrong feet before he managed to work out which one was meant to go where.

He stumbled downstairs, kicked open the teahouse door and set off up the track that led upwards to the mountain. The two Sherpas had been paid only half the money he'd promised them. While Geraint had been unconscious, they had waited in the room below for him to recover. As he staggered past them, they jumped up and ran after him.

They caught up with him a hundred yards above the village and tried to pull him back, pleading that he hadn't recovered. Geraint turned on them in a frenzy of anger. He screamed and kicked and lashed out with his hands, gouging at their eyes. Terrified, the Sherpas retreated. Geraint stared at them in triumph. He opened his mouth to curse them – and fainted again.

It was the last time he fainted. When he regained consciousness – he had no idea how much later – he asked hoarsely to be carried further down the mountain. The Sherpas took him to a village 5,000 feet below, and installed him in another teahouse. Geraint paid them off. Then he set about trying to recover.

He knew little about altitude sickness, only that the thinning of oxygen at heights could cause the body's fluids to invade and exert pressure on the brain. The standard defence against it was step-by-step altitude acclimatization. He thought he'd achieved that. Clearly he'd been wrong.

If he'd been wrong once, he wouldn't make the same mistake again. This time he'd move slowly up the heights until he was fully conditioned to whatever they might try to torment him with. Using the teahouse as a base, Geraint started to walk. Each day he tried to stretch himself further. Winter was rapidly closing in. Some days he was able to travel for two or three hours, but on others the storms would drive him back within minutes of leaving the village.

Geraint persevered.

A week came when he couldn't leave the village at all. He waited in frustration until eventually a window appeared in the clouds, by day a weak sun shone, and at night a full glowing moon. Geraint took to the paths that spiralled away from the village. One evening, feeling stronger than he'd done at any time since the sickness struck him, he walked upwards towards the west for three hours.

As he finally slowed down Geraint saw a small bow-shaped ridge above him in the moonlight. He decided to climb the ridge and then return. He trudged up through the snow, peered across the mountain flanks and swung back. He took a dozen steps and stopped. He looked at the ground.

He was retracing the route he'd taken only minutes earlier. Then his footprints had been the only marks in the snow. Now they were overlaid with other prints, prints of bare feet. Far larger than his, almost giant-like in size, the prints belonged neither to a bear or a monkey – they were unmistakably human. The tracks followed his own for a while, then they angled upwards.

Geraint tried to follow them, but the path they took was too steep and after a while he was forced to halt. Panting he gazed up into the night. Sure and unswerving the tracks led towards the remote peak, the summit of Everest, hidden somewhere above him.

In that instant, as he stared at the prints until they disappeared beyond the range of his vision, Geraint knew beyond doubt what had made them – a yeti. He realized too – and the shock of the awareness almost stunned him – what that meant. The American doctor had said Everest would never be climbed without supplementary oxygen. Geraint had tried and mountain sickness had driven him back. He could prepare himself again and again, but unless he could find a way to overcome the oxygen starvation induced by Everest's height, all his efforts would be doomed.

There was a way to conquer the mountain without oxygen. The yeti knew it. If Geraint could find them, if he could learn their secret, he would be able to do it too.

Under his pile of skins high on the Helambu Ridge, Geraint Hughes laughed.

Forty years. In his obsessive search for the yeti, the years had gone by almost without Geraint noticing. He still hadn't found the creature, although he had seen its tracks countless times, but he was closer now than he had ever been. Five years earlier, roaming the Himalayan uplands along their ramparts on the Tibetan border, he'd found the oduna, the outcasts. He'd done more than find them – he'd killed and eaten one of them.

Geraint's mind was still clear and he shook with delight at the memory. It was the best possible way he could have chanced on them. After what he'd done with his gun and then the fire, his authority over them was unassailable.

It had been early spring. The gun, an ancient British flintlock rifle, had been Geraint's first major purchase after he left Everest. He'd been offered the weapon in a Gurung village, together with a crate of ammunition, and it had served him well ever since. He used it to kill deer, wild boar, occasionally bears, and once a snow leopard as he travelled the high slopes.

When he came on the oduna Geraint was walking upwind across a wooded mountain shelf of rhododendron and fir. Ahead of him in a clearing between the trees he spotted a group of animals. His sight was troublesome that day and from a distance he thought they were grazing sambur. Geraint stalked them. A hundred yards away he realized they weren't deer, but some sort of animal he'd never seen before.

Geraint picked out one and killed it with a single shot through the chest. At the sound of the shot, the others scattered and vanished. Geraint walked forward. When he reached the creature, his first thought was that he'd killed a yeti. He looked again and changed his mind.

Although he'd never seen a yeti, over the years Geraint had formed a vivid mental picture of their appearance. They were immensely tall and strong, and covered all over in thick chestnut-brown hair. The animal at his feet was smaller than his image. It was only patchily covered in hair and the hair was pale, the yellowish-grey colour of old straw with a few streaks of grey. Its face, too, was quite different from the yeti of his imagination. It wasn't rugged and strong. Its features were weak and almost humanoid, somewhere between a monkey and a man.

If the animal's original stock had been the yeti, Geraint thought, it had degenerated almost beyond recognition. Most likely, he decided, it was some species of mountain ape he had never come across before. Whatever its origins, the creature was strong and well fleshed, and Geraint was hungry. He butchered it, sliced a pair of steaks from its haunches and lit a fire. He turned the steaks on a spit of mountain ash, and settled down to eat.

He was halfway through his meal when he became aware of several pairs of eyes watching him from the surrounding undergrowth.

He continued to eat. He had never had the slightest fear of wild animals, and least of all when his gun was lying at his feet. The creature he'd shot was obviously a pack animal – he'd seen its companions before he fired. Geraint could think of only one reason why animals would return to a place where one of them had been killed – acute hunger.

Geraint flared his nostrils and sniffed. The wind had dropped and the air was very still. The clearing was full of the scent of roasted meat. On a sudden impulse he picked up the haunch from which he'd carved the steaks, and lobbed it towards the trees. Instantly the eyes vanished. Minutes later they returned. After a long, silent interval, one of the creatures padded cautiously out from the undergrowth, seized the haunch and scuttled back into the shadows.

Geraint reached for another part of the carcass and threw it in the same direction. A second creature came forward to take it. Geraint had butchered the entire carcass, intending to dry and store its flesh. Instead he tossed the meat piece by piece across the clearing. Soon fifteen of the creatures, no longer bothering to hide, were feeding on the grass.

When they'd eaten everything they disappeared again. Geraint slept that night with his rifle between his legs. When he woke at dawn and continued on his way, he knew the animals were following him. Two days later he killed a mountain boar. He carved off his own portion and grilled it over a fire, then, leaving the rest of the boar in the glade where he'd shot it, he walked up to a ridge and settled down to watch.

This time the animals didn't hesitate. They appeared from the trees and stripped the carcass bare. When they'd finished, all but one of them vanished again. A female, he saw, and judging by her withered breasts and deeply wrinkled face, an old one. For a long while she stared up at Geraint. Then she approached him. Normally, he had noticed, the creatures walked upright. The old female came towards him on all fours, propping her upper body on her bunched fists and extended arms.

She stopped in front of him. 'Oduna,' she said, tapping her chest. She gestured at him. 'Shumbi,' she added.

She glanced down at the rifle and then back at Geraint's face. She reached out and touched his nose. Then she lowered her head to the earth.

Geraint stared at her.

While the many Nepalese he had questioned over the years had different views on the appearance of the yeti, they were all agreed on one thing. The creatures could speak. Geraint hadn't understood the sounds the animal had made, but he knew she had spoken to him.

27

Geraint learnt a modicum of the creatures' language within a few weeks.

It wasn't difficult. The language was primitive, and for the most part he needed only a handful of words and phrases. They were mainly commands. The oduna had identified him as a source of food. With his mysterious smoking branch Geraint could kill prey more often and more easily than they could through hunting. They attached themselves to him like a pack of hungry and obedient dogs, and he treated them as such.

The oduna were equally useful to Geraint. He no longer had to find and track game himself, particularly on the bad days when his eyes flooded with blood. The creatures did it for him, learning quickly to bring him within shooting range of his prey. They were strong and tireless, and they carried his possessions. He taught them a few simple skills like how to fetch water in stoppered bark hollows, to build a shelter for him, to gather dry wood for his nightly fire – although they never fully overcame their terror of fire itself.

That suited Geraint too. Apart from his gun, fire was the other weapon that allowed him to dominate them. Fire was his secret. He could call it down from the skies and terrorize them with it, as he could terrorize any other animal of the mountains.

But there was another, more important reason for Geraint's adoption of the oduna. They were not yeti – but they were descended from the yeti. Somehow, he sensed, they would lead him to the true yeti.

Mentally he'd translated their word for themselves, oduna, as outcasts. They weren't outcasts themselves – they were descended from creatures who seemed to have been expelled from what they called 'the people'. How or why their ancestors had become outcasts none of them knew, only that it had happened an immensely long time ago. Once their ancestors had lived in a fertile valley and on the crests above. Since their expulsion the oduna had roamed the mountains scavenging and foraging for whatever they could find.

Over the centuries they had reproduced themselves, not just from their own kind, but occasionally by mating with young girls they seized and carried off from the settlements of what they called 'the hairless ones'. Sometimes, if the girl survived the birth and suckling, they would return her to the outskirts of the village from where they had stolen her. After giving birth, the girl was simply a burden on their resources. All they wanted was the child.

In the forty years of his wanderings, Geraint had often heard tales of young women abducted from tribal villages by the unknown creatures of the mountains. He had always treated the stories as superstitious fantasy. No longer. He looked at the oduna's almost human features and the patchy hair on their bodies, and realized that the stories were true – throughout their long exile, the outcasts had bred with man.

They had also learnt how to raid his stores. In winter they haunted the outskirts of villages, plundering barns and killing yak or water buffaloes penned against the snow. Sometimes they chanced on stores left behind by mountaineers after an expedition to the peaks, and occasionally they were bold enough to thieve from the larder of a base camp when an expedition was in progress.

Bold and cunning, but fearful if challenged, they scavenged everywhere. Once they must have been hunters and gatherers. Their skills were still considerable, but blunted. They had become parasites, Geraint realized, who had anchored themselves to humanity for survival. He was a mere host off which they could feed. In the past, there had been many more of them, but the growth in the Nepalese population and the cutting down of the mountain forest had reduced both their feeding territory and their numbers.

It had also turned them into nomads. When Geraint came across them he was at the extreme north-western corner of Nepal. For a year and a half afterwards he and the oduna worked their way in a long slow arc eastwards.

Geraint was obsessed by the valley from where their yeti ancestors had come. If the yeti had lived there once, they might be there still. As far as he could tell, the valley lay somewhere to the east high up in the mountains near the Tibetan border. Its location seemed to be embedded like a sacred icon in the oduna's memory, but to Geraint's frustration they became frightened and dull-witted when he tried to force them to take him there. Their halting speech slowed and their eyes glazed over with confusion. They glanced away from him with what might almost have been shame in their lowered heads. Geraint swore. He kicked them, he fired the gun over their heads, he threatened them with brands of fire. Nothing made any difference. They scampered away muttering and yelping. Hours, sometimes days later, they returned as mute and blank-featured as before.

Geraint gave up.

The oduna knew where he wanted to go. Reluctantly and fearfully, they were leading him there, but he had to travel at their own pace and in their own way. Every morning and evening Geraint checked their direction by the position of the sun and stars. They were still heading east, although their progress was infuriatingly slow.

Then early one evening the withered old female who'd approached him first came up to Geraint. He and the oduna had hunted the mountain flanks all day without finding a prey animal. None of them had eaten for more than seventy-two hours and they were all, Geraint and the creatures, tired and hungry. Finally they had climbed up to the top of a narrow ridge.

The old female caught his arm. She led Geraint through the trees where they'd stopped, and pointed down. 'Mirja,' she said.

Geraint stared at her, puzzled. The ridge must have been much higher than where they usually travelled. His head throbbed in the thin air and he could feel his eyes start to blur as they filled with blood from the ruptured veins.

He turned and peered down. Through a wavering scarlet haze he could just make out the great bowl of a grassy plain spread out beneath him. On every side the mountains sheered up in towering walls of rock to the icy crests above. Geraint gazed at the bowl. He blinked, and altitude blindness came down like a dark curtain over his sight.

Rubbing his face he swung away. The oduna word 'mirja', Geraint had learnt, meant home. The oduna had at last brought him to the valley from which they came.

As Geraint stood there some of the blood drained from his eyes and a small window of vision opened. He made out the silhouette of another of the creatures approaching him. It was a male, one of the leaders of the pack. The oduna gestured at his own mouth before pointing first at the old female and then at the rifle, which Geraint was holding in his hands.

There was no need for Geraint to work out what he meant. Unhesitatingly the old female knelt in front of him. Her bony face shadowed but calm, she took the rifle's barrel and guided it until the muzzle was resting against her throat. She looked up at him and smiled. It was the first smile Geraint had seen on an oduna's face. He squeezed the trigger.

Later, after butchering the old female, he and the rest of the oduna fed off her. The oduna ate her flesh raw. Geraint lit a fire and roasted her ribs for himself. When the meal ended, the oduna settled down to sleep, but Geraint couldn't rest. He stood up and stared down into the darkness.

Most of his sight had returned, but in spite of the brilliant light from the night stars the valley below was lost in mist. The mist meant the valley held water – marshes certainly and probably a river. Water meant grass and trees. They in turn meant fruit, berries and prey animals. From all Geraint knew about them, the yeti were true hunters and gatherers like the oduna had once been.

The great misty bowl of the valley must have been both a cornucopia for the yeti and a sanctuary from the encroaching human tribes. As he gazed down over it, Geraint became certain it still was. When his eyes began to ache, he lay down by the fire again. He still couldn't sleep. He tossed restlessly, his mind churning with excitement about what he might discover below the ridge.

Finally he got back to his feet and, leaving the sleeping oduna behind him, set off alone along the ridge to see if he could find a way down to use in the morning.

Geraint left the camp at nine o'clock that night. He walked steadily for five hours. The moon had risen and by its light and the radiance of the stars the narrow track along the ridge's top, trodden out by generations of musk deer, was easy to follow. The track seemed to come to an end when the ridge dropped into a saddle, but it appeared again when Geraint crossed the saddle and climbed to another ridge on the far side.

The second ridge gave way to a third, and then a fourth. Geraint walked on. Sometimes he had to balance himself above crumbling walls of scree. Sometimes he moved in a crouch beneath the tangled branches of rhododendron thickets. Sometimes he struggled through late-lying snowdrifts or over ice-coated moraines, cupped in the chill shadow of the peaks above.

At two in the morning, when he was fifteen miles from camp, the storm broke over him. It erupted without warning. One moment the sky was as clear as it had been all night. The next it was blotted out by waves of dark, racing clouds. The wind rose and within minutes the air temperature had plummeted. Then the snow began to fall. It fell not in slow spiralling flakes, but in a raging blizzard of icy whiteness.

Geraint had no time to find a proper shelter from the storm's fury. He could only throw himself into the lee of a rock, and huddle there close to the ground. The wind screamed and the driving snow tormented his face. In spite of the bitter chill he was sweating – his mind a dark, swaying hive of disconnected and contradictory messages. Dimly he knew that in his urgency he had come too high, too fast. Altitude sickness, the oxygen starvation which had almost killed him on Everest, was attacking him again.

When a lull came in the blizzard, he managed to force himself to his feet. The storm hadn't passed yet, but briefly the wind had dropped and for a moment the snow drifted gently across the night air. Geraint reeled away from the rock and set off downwards.

He took twenty steps and stopped.

He was walking with his shoulders hunched and his head lowered. Below him on the newly snow-covered earth were footprints – not one set but two. The first, pressed deeper into the fresh layer of snow and already blurring, were small and ridged with sole marks. They could only have been made by a child wearing boots.

Above the child's prints and crossing them at an angle was the second set. Crisper and harder-edged, they had the shape of naked human feet, although they were much longer and the spread of the toes was far broader than any human foot would have left. The indentations at the edges were sharp and clean. In the hollows where the heel had trodden the ice crystals hadn't yet bonded together. The round depressions gleamed like little bowls of fire.

Geraint lifted his head and listened. The wind was beginning to rise again and the snow was thickening. Below the wind's roar he could just make out a sound he hadn't heard before, the sound of water tumbling over rocks, the sound of a river. From where he was standing the river could only be falling into the valley.

The storm swept over the ridge again. Geraint found a forked treetrunk and hid himself at its base. He was exhausted and shivering, but it no longer mattered. He wasn't concerned about the blizzard – the blizzard would pass. All that mattered was what he'd found. Nepalese children didn't wear cleated boots. Only a European child could have made the first set of prints.

Only a yeti could have left the second – a yeti which had passed by within the last few minutes.

28

As Roshan came closer, he broke into a run, leaving the other man trailing behind him. On the ridge below, Cabot tensed.

'Roshan – !'

Robert Cabot started to shout while the Sherpa was still a hundred yards away.

'For Christ's sake, what have you found?'

Roshan called something back but the mountain wind plucked his words away and Cabot couldn't hear them. In a frenzy of impatience Cabot drove his stick through the snow deep into the earth beneath. He leant on it and glowered impotently upwards.

Cabot felt bruised and sick to his soul.

After two days there was no trace of the child. Not a footprint. Not a track. Not a piece of clothing. Nothing. Iona had simply vanished off the face of the landscape. As he waited for Roshan to reach him, Cabot steeled himself to accept what looked more and more likely to be the only explanation – that she'd wandered away in the storm and fallen from one of ridges.

Roshan came to a halt, panting, and gestured over his shoulder. 'This man, sir, he says he saw tracks, Miss Iona's tracks.'

Cabot's gaze swung away from Roshan up the slope. The second man had started to hurry too. He moved stiffly and awkwardly, as if he were hobbling, but he covered the ground almost as fast as the Sherpa.

Cabot had assumed the stranger would be a local Nepalese tribesman, but as the man stopped in front of them, he saw he was mistaken. To Cabot's astonishment he was a European, and one of the strangest-looking figures the American had ever seen.

He was about sixty. On the lower half of his body he wore Tibetan leggings and felt boots. The upper half was covered by what Cabot guessed was a bearskin coat that hung down to his thighs. He had long yellow-white hair, a trenched and ravaged face and staring red-veined eyes. As they examined Cabot, the eyes seemed to slip in and out of focus, at one moment watching him shrewdly, the next wandering vacantly into the distance. To Cabot the overwhelming impression was of an alcoholic derelict from the Boston waterfront, who'd somehow been transported to the Himalayas.

'Hughes,' the man said before Cabot could speak. 'Geraint Hughes.'

As he held out his hand, the stranger suddenly laughed, the sound exploding from his throat with a hoarse, maniacal loudness. He wrinkled his nose and glanced away. Totally absorbed, he peered at something out of Cabot's sight.

Cabot looked at Roshan, bewildered. The man seemed to be mad. Roshan must have known it, but the Sherpa nodded, silently imploring him to speak.

'Good to meet you, Mr Hughes,' Cabot said. 'My name's Robert Cabot. Roshan says you've seen my goddaughter's tracks –'

'About thirteen, is it?' Hughes interrupted him. 'And maybe five foot three, I'd say, is it?'

The curious rhythmic lilt in the man's voice was dimly familiar. Cabot frowned and it came back to him. Hughes's accent was Welsh.

'That sounds like Iona,' Cabot said eagerly.

'And this is hers too maybe, is it?'

Hughes rummaged inside his bearskin coat. He pulled out what looked like a ball of crumpled, brightly coloured cloth. Cabot seized it and straightened it out. He recognized it immediately. It was Iona's oiled-wool cap.

'Yes –' He glanced up.

Still gazing over Cabot's shoulder, Hughes barked out another ferocious laugh. Cabot's patience snapped. He caught Hughes by the shoulders and shook him furiously.

'For God's sake, man, look at me!' he shouted. 'The child's been lost for two days. What do you know about her? Where the hell is she?'

Cabot was a powerfully built man and almost a foot taller than the little Welshman, but with a strength he was totally unprepared for Hughes wrenched himself away and hurled Cabot back. Hughes dropped to his haunches and spread out his hands, like an animal crouching to spring in attack.

'Dhu, dhu, dhu,' he chuckled between his teeth. 'Not yet, sir, not yet. There is much more than tracks and a hat. There is money, and what I want, not what you want. You have lost her. I know where she is. I can get her back for you. Are we going to do business, is it?'

Cabot and Roshan stared down at the Welshman.

Hughes was squatting beneath them. His body quivered with menace and aggression, but once again his eyes had lost their concentration. They were no longer blazing out, dark and red-veined, at Cabot's face. They had slid away and were studying some remote ridge in the mountains as if neither he nor the Sherpa existed.

Cabot realized he'd been right the first time. The man was insane. From the scarlet tide that had flooded his eyes, he was almost certainly a victim of mountain sickness. In Hughes's case, the oxygen starvation that caused the condition hadn't only ruptured the network of blood vessels in his eyes. It had led to brain damage too.

Cabot clenched his hands. The fingers of his right hand caught against something. Cabot glanced down. He was still holding Iona's cap. He raised his head again and thought, then he spoke to Roshan.

'Bring us some coffee and two chairs, Roshan,' he said. 'Mr Hughes and I are going to sit down here, and talk quietly together.'

'The yeti have her,' Hughes said. 'Do you believe in the yeti, is it?'

He was sitting opposite Cabot with a mug of coffee cupped between his hands.

Cabot glanced up at Roshan. They had been there for almost an hour. Roshan had stayed close to Cabot, hovering like a shadow behind his shoulder. Now he nodded, encouraging Cabot to say yes. Cabot wrinkled his face. He accepted the Sherpa's silent advice.

'Yes,' he said.

'Good, very good,' Hughes replied. 'Some do, some don't. Those who don't are fools. I've been learning about the yeti all my life. They sleep in winter, did you know that? Prolonged hibernation, it is called scientifically.'

Hughes held out his mug. Roshan refilled it. As the little scarlet-eyed Welshman went on talking, Cabot listened.

He'd been listening almost without interruption since they'd sat down. He'd heard Hughes's rambling account of his history – the Everest expedition, his betrayal by the expedition's leader when he was about to go for the summit, the years he'd spent roaming the Himalayan ridges. Cabot had heard the fury, the bitterness and the accusations.

Cabot knew his guess was right – altitude sickness had unhinged the man's brain. Hughes had only become fully lucid a few minutes earlier when he'd finally turned to the matter of the yeti. On the yeti, Hughes was totally convincing. Cabot believed him, and he knew Roshan did too.

'Mr Hughes,' Cabot said as the Welshman paused for a moment, 'you say the yeti have the child. What makes you think that?'

'Tracks, prints, spoor, call them what you will.'

Hughes told Cabot what he'd found when he was searching for a better shelter during the break in the storm. Two sets of prints – the first of a child wearing boots and the second of a yeti.

'It is what they do,' Hughes finished. 'If they find a human girl, they will take her for breeding.'

'Iona is too young to breed,' Cabot said.

'Then they will keep her until she is ready, bach.'

Cabot was silent.

The idea sounded like a demented fantasy – and Hughes was clearly demented. Then Cabot thought of all the stories he had heard about the yeti over the years. He remembered Roshan, the reliable and pragmatic Roshan, telling Iona by the fire on the night before she disappeared what had happened to his cousin on Everest.

Cabot rubbed his face thoughtfully. As a scientist he knew that, however strange, what could not be disproved by scientific law was, on the balance of probability, more likely to be true than false. That was what he'd told Iona. The yeti could not be disproved, nor could the many accounts of their seizing young human females.

'I don't doubt you, Mr Hughes,' Cabot said carefully, 'but is there any way you can prove this?'

Hughes glanced at him shrewdly. His little red-veined eyes blinked. Then he stood up and, without speaking, beckoned. Cabot and Roshan followed him as he set off along the ridge.

A hundred yards from the camp Hughes stopped. Most of the snow had been trampled flat by the feet of the Sherpas and the porters as they passed backwards and forwards in the two days they'd spent searching for Iona. The occasional patch of snow on either side of the track they'd beaten out was still untouched.

Hughes turned towards one of the patches. Gesturing to Cabot and Roshan to stay behind, he took off his bearskin cloak and cast it forward. The skin fanned out and dropped to the ground. Hughes hauled it back to him. He gathered it in with a layer of snow clinging to the hairs, shook the snow away and cast it out again. Ten minutes later, without disturbing the snow beneath, he'd uncovered a circle that reached down four inches below the surrounding surface. Hughes stood back and pointed.

Cabot came forward. Faint and already melting in the sunlight, but still unmistakable, he could see the two sets of prints Hughes had described – the cleated impressions of Iona's boots, and overlaying them the outline of what appeared to be huge naked feet.

No one could have fabricated that. Hughes was speaking the truth – Iona had been seized by the yeti. His heart pumping, Cabot swung round.

'You've convinced me, Mr Hughes,' he said huskily. 'Where have they taken Iona?'

'There.' Hughes lifted his arm.

He pointed down from the ridge to the large valley lying in a bowl far below them. Cabot peered downwards. He had noticed the valley before, but only in the early morning or at evening when its floor was always covered with mist. The sun was starting to set and mist was beginning to fill it now. Vaguely Cabot made out a rolling plain and the glitter of light off a winding river.

Cabot glanced round. Beneath him the rock face fell sheer from the ridge for what must have been 6,000 feet. On every side for as far as he could see he was confronted by the same vertical mountain walls, with the snow-covered crests rising in jagged lines high above.

'How the hell do we get down?' Cabot demanded. Now he knew where Iona was – and any lingering doubt he'd had about Hughes had vanished – his anxiety about the child was rising with every second.

The Welshman gave his maniacal laugh again. He turned and spoke to Roshan. The two talked for a moment in Gurkhali. Then Roshan faced Cabot.

'It is difficult, sir,' Roshan said frowning. 'Somewhere there will be animal tracks down, but they must be sought for. It will take us much time, days, weeks, maybe even months, but that is the smallest problem. The other, the big one, is the yeti themselves. This man says they can smell humans approaching from many miles away. If we try to go near them, they will take Miss Iona and run away and hide. We will not be able to find her –'

Roshan paused. 'What he says is true, sir. I know it, every Sherpa knows it. It is why those who search for the yeti never find them.'

Cabot looked at him in fury and frustration. For the first time in all the years he'd known Roshan, he felt like hitting the Sherpa. He restrained himself. If Roshan said it was true, it had to be true. Tense and tight-lipped, he swung back to the Welshman.

'You said you could get her back, Mr Hughes.' Somehow Cabot managed to keep his voice level. 'You want money. You shall have whatever you ask for, I promise you that. I would just like to know how you can find and approach the yeti when we cannot.'

'I have friends, sir, I have friends.'

Blood swirled through Hughes's eyes as he answered, and he gave his wild hoarse laugh again.

Cabot felt his control snapping. He lifted his stick and swung it over his head. Roshan's fingers caught his elbow and dragged his arm down. He was whispering something. Cabot couldn't hear what it was, but he didn't need to ask. The Sherpa was saying what Cabot knew, too.

The Welshman was mad. He was also their only hope of finding Iona.

As Cabot stared at the contorted, wild-eyed figure in front of him, an agonizing question flashed across his mind. Iona had been abducted. According to Hughes she was in the hands of the yeti. If she was, what were the mysterious creatures doing to the child?

29

Gaggau limped up the rock-strewn hill flank, dragging his club-foot behind him. He had to hurry.

The mountain goat was somewhere out of sight ahead, hidden by the folds in the ground. Raku was pushing it on from the saddle where the sun rose. Very soon the goat would crest the ridge and see the gully beneath it. To the animal the gully would signal danger. It would try to break away along the ridge line.

Penga and Soru would be waiting to turn the goat back. Then the animal would have no choice except to drop down into the gully. If it reached the gully's end, the funnel that opened out into the mountains, it could still get away. The creature would realize that when it got there. That was why Gaggau was hurrying.

He heaved himself over the boulders. The ground between them was covered with slate and shale, and over thousands of years the action of the winter snows had honed many of the stones to razor-like sharpness. Twice Gaggau tripped and fell. Each time when he got up and set off again, he felt blood running down his legs from cuts in his hide. At 17,000 feet the blood coagulated slowly in spite of the hot summer air. Gaggau limped painfully on.

He reached the gully, scrambled down and positioned himself across the deep V-cut mouth. He stooped and held the sides of the deepest wound together with his fingers. Then, heaving and panting and with blood trickling over his hands, he waited for the goat to appear.

Gaggau was too old to hunt, far too old. Every member of the ranging knew that, none more so than Gaggau himself. Like all the yeti Gaggau measured the passage of time by seasons. In human terms he had lived for one hundred and twenty years, almost as long as his fellow patriarch, Yerto, in the valley far below. Cloud-time effectively cut the span in half, yet even allowing for that he was still sixty and sixty was too old for a hunter.

Furthermore, Gaggau had the lifelong handicap of his club-foot.

He limped. His bones were stiff and dry. The hair on his back had turned from silver almost to white. And the younger members of the ranging were good hunters in their own right. Raku, who was harrying the goat up towards the corrie, was a fine tracker. Penga was even better – and he had the mind and cunning to go with it. Soru was simpler than the other two, but his strength was great and he could run for ever.

They were all good, but he was better. That was why, Gaggau reflected as he stood clutching his bleeding leg, he still led them. He was perhaps the best hunter the ranging had ever had – apart, of course, from his mother Burra who had taught him everything. Burra was dead now and joined with the snows. Like her great namesake from the past she had entered the ranging's mythology, but her skills lived on in Gaggau.

This season, when the animals had almost vanished from the crests, it was more important than ever that they did. The goat was the first prey they had found in nearly a week. The ranging depended on him to see it didn't escape.

'Tchk!'

The call came from several hundred paces away. It started as a whistle and ended as a hoarse bark. The sound would have puzzled the Sagat tribesmen who occasionally ventured into the uplands. To them it would have sounded like a cross between the alarm call of a nervous deer and the growl of a hunting leopard. To Gaggau it was unmistakable – Raku had turned the goat at the corrie's head. He was both alerting Gaggau and summoning Penga and Soru to join him in driving the animal down the rocky defile.

Gaggau saw the goat a moment later. It raced towards him, wary and uncertain. Gaggau watched it. The animal moved with an extraordinary sure-footed grace, leaping from boulder to boulder, its nostrils constantly sifting the air ahead. Gaggau saw the delicate blues and umbers of its skin as the morning light swept the creature's flanks. He smelt the gland scents of its body, and saw the fear prickles of the hairs on its back.

When the goat was only ten paces away, Gaggau let go of his bleeding leg. He hurled himself into the air and bellowed.

The goat stopped in mid-stride. It registered the forked creature in front of it. Its eyes and nostrils dilated in terror, then it swerved, turned, and galloped desperately back up the corrie.

Raku, Penga and Soru were waiting for it. As the goat rounded one of the corrie's serpentine bends, they rose from behind the rocks and fell on the animal. A stone club lifted and smashed across its neck. The goat dropped to its knees. An instant later they had rolled the animal on to its back and severed its neck.

Gaggau limped up to join them. The three stood over their prey looking at him exultantly. Gaggau studied the skyline. He had used the corrie as a trap many times before, and he had trained them how to use it too. That day he had left them to work out the hunt on their own. They had done well. They could have done better.

'There.' He pointed at the sky. 'See the cloud's movements.'

Three pairs of eyes glanced up.

'What does it tell you?' he demanded.

There was silence for several moments. Then Raku answered.

'The wind-drift is from the high peaks,' he said. 'Here it will be funnelled upwards –'

Raku paused. He was trying to work out the implications. 'Go on,' Gaggau said gruffly but encouragingly.

'The wind might have caught your scent,' Raku ventured. 'If so, it would have reached the goat at the corrie's head. Then the creature would have bolted straight across the corrie and we would have lost it.'

'And to prevent that, what should you have done?' Gaggau demanded again.

'Moved the hunt line downwards?' Raku suggested. 'Brought the beast into the corrie much lower where the wind-drift wouldn't have mattered.'

The other two thought for a moment. It hadn't occurred to them until now. They bowed their heads in assent.

Gaggau nodded. 'Right. At least today you killed. May you always be so fortunate.' He turned and limped off down the corrie.

In the past he would have helped the hunters bring the quarry back to the ranging. Now the young ones could do it themselves. They needed him still, not for his muscles but for his knowledge.

Gaggau limped into the cave.

'Tana!' he called out.

She appeared from the darkness at the back. The cave was over fifty paces long and it took her several moments to reach him.

Clutching his wounded leg with his hand, Gaggau leant against the great arch of rock at the entrance and watched her.

Tana walked with a slow sinuous grace that made Gaggau catch his breath. It had always been like that. She had had the same effect on him the day she arrived at the ranging as a child. The females of the ranging moved like the males, quickly and purposefully. They had to, of course. Hunters needed strong muscles and a long swift stride, and this applied to the females as much as the males.

Tana was different. Everything about her was different. She came from the valley, from the gatherers of the holding. She had the soft pale brown hair of the island clan. She had their eyes, steady and thoughtful with the delicate grey-blue colour of an autumn sky. She had their shape too, the curving slope-shouldered shape of the holding young.

As a child Tana was 'rosala', the ranging's term which described everything that was desirable from a plump doe to a virgin snowfield on which a quarry's tracks could be read from five thousand paces.

'I see you, Gaggau.'

Tana stopped in front of him. She swept her hand quickly across his forehead. Gaggau extended his hands, palms upwards. She touched them in turn with her fingers.

Tana smiled. In the world of the holding where Tana was born, the acceptance greeting was on the nose. Here among the mountain clan it was twofold. First, it was made to the eyes – her hand drawn across Gaggau's forehead acknowledged the power of his sight. Then, in touching Gaggau's hands, Tana had recognized his ability to signal. As hunters the ranging yeti needed to see and communicate with each other over great distances. Their eyes found their prey, their hands flagged and directed the hunt.

'Here.' Gaggau tapped his thigh.

Tana had already seen the wound. She knelt and licked it clean, then she studied it for an instant. It wasn't a prey wound, a kick from a lashing hoof or a slicing cut in the flesh from the antlers of a cornered deer. Tana had seen many of those since she came to the ranging. A cut from an animal would have left a jagged tear. This one was straight and deep. He had fallen again.

She glanced up at Gaggau. The great silver-haired male was gazing at the darkening sky outside. Vultures were flocking home to roost. Tana knew what Gaggau was doing. He was memorizing the angle of their flight. It was early summer and the vultures were heading back for their nests. In the nests there would be eggs.

Tomorrow Gaggau would lead the young males out on a nest plunder. He would gather there at dawn and ask whether any of them had traced the birds' course against the stars. None of them would have done, of course. Only Gaggau. Chuckling, he would lead them up the mountain slope.

'Lie down on the platform,' Tana instructed.

Gaggau limped across to the stone slab which stood five paces inside the cave's mouth. It had always been there, just as there had always been a stone slab five paces back from the entrance to every one of the ranging's caves. No one had been able to tell Tana why the slabs were positioned thus, or why the dominant males of the ranging – from the silver-backed Gaggau downwards – occupied them.

Finally Tana worked it out for herself. She was alert and observant, and as a valley yeti her cast of mind was different from the ranging's. In the valley there were no large predators. Up here on the crests there were several. During her first winter a bear had come to the caves. Skeletally thin and ravenous, it had either scented the ranging's children, or it was seeking shelter against the snows.

The bear tried to enter one of the satellite caves. The young yeti at the cave's entrance challenged it and there was a terrible fight. The yeti was badly hurt but the bear was killed, and none of the young were harmed. The male yeti occupied the stone shelves, Tana realized afterwards, to guard the weaker members of the ranging.

'Be still!'

Tana's instruction was uttered in a lisp. Pressed between her lips were a row of hook thorns. Gaggau winced as she began to insert the thorns into the sides of the wound and bind them together with ribbons of grass.

He lay there feeling the pricks in his hide. Slowly he forgot about the little stabs of pain as his thoughts turned to the goat. The animal would be shared between all the ranging. It was a big young male, but it would barely satisfy the day's hunger, let alone the week of emptiness before they'd killed it.

Something fearsome and unprecedented was happening on the crests.

30

'She bleeds again,' Jinga said. 'It is over. Now you must send her back.'

Gaggau raised himself on his elbow. For an instant his eyes met Jinga's. Confronted by her implacable stare, by her dark eyes as hot and red and dangerous as a cornered leopard's, Gaggau's gaze slid away.

He was lying at the rear of the cave on the thick pile of skins and hides where he slept. The pile was made up of offerings from the kills of the young hunters. When they hunted with the ranging's leader, the leader was entitled to one quarter of the hide of any animal they killed. When they hunted and killed without him, he was given an eighth. Any hides that weren't used by the leader for hunting thongs, or by his females in the cave, were thrown into the arch at the cave's back for his bed. A strong leader of the ranging needed to rest well. The greater the height of the bed, the greater the leader's prowess as a hunter.

Over the years Gaggau had many times waived his right not only to the eighth-cut skins, but to the full quarters. He had no need of the young hunters' tributes. His sleeping couch was still piled a full knee's height above the stone, higher than the oldest member of the ranging had ever known, higher even than in the stories of cloud-time.

Gaggau closed his eyes. His mother Burra had often frightened him, but Gaggau had never avoided her eyes. Jinga, his mate, not only frightened him. In anger, and Jinga was almost always angry, her gaze was too fierce for Gaggau.

'She is not your daughter,' Gaggau replied. 'She does not tend to you. She warms me. How can you be sure she bleeds?'

The question was tentative, almost desperate. Gaggau knew as soon as he'd spoken that he'd embarked on a defence that was doomed.

Jinga gave a harsh guttural laugh. To Gaggau it sounded like the call of a raven diving on carrion.

'I smelt her blood in the cave.' Jinga tapped her nostril. 'For that she does not need to be my daughter or tend me. Like any female I would smell the blood anywhere. And you do not warm her. You have nothing to warm her with. Have we not tried together? Have you not tried with others? Of course you have! You have tried all your life. And what do you have at the end? You have nothing!'

Jinga's voice rang with bitterness. As she looked at him her eyes narrowed with a resentment that bordered on hatred.

'I have Manu,' Gaggau said.

'Manu is not yours,' she answered. 'He is your mother's. He may be your brother, but seasons separate you. Not the ordinary seasons between brothers, but whole long spans of sun and snow. Manu could be your own child –'

She paused. 'Except he is not. The truth is you have no seed.'

Jinga spat out the breath between her teeth and rocked back on her heels. Humiliating the old patriarch of the holding gave her pleasure – a deserved pleasure.

Gaggau forced himself to ignore the insult. 'Manu is a good hunter,' he said stubbornly. 'All the ranging knows that. He can be a great hunter. With time here, he could lead the ranging.'

'With time?' Jinga sneered. 'There is no time, Gaggau. Time is past. The prey has almost gone. Your brother has been away for seasons. All he knows is the ways of the holding. Even if Manu came back now, there are no animals left for him to learn from. At least Raku, Penga and Soru have had the chance to hunt. Any one of them would be better than Manu.'

Gaggau stared at her. It was not true. Manu was a natural hunter. Like Gaggau himself, Manu was Burra's child, and they had both inherited her skills. The other three, Raku, Penga and Soru, were good only because Gaggau had taught them so long and so carefully. Compared with what Manu could be, they were nothing.

Gaggau knew that, but he could not say it. Confronted by Jinga he was too vulnerable. There was too much she could wield against him, too much he could not argue with. It was true that Manu had been absent for many seasons. True, also, that the prey was vanishing. True above all, as Jinga saw it, that he had not seeded a child.

That, more than anything else, was the source of her bitterness – a bitterness which had crusted into hatred. Gaggau had left her barren. She might have accepted that if he had seeded any other of the ranging's breeding females. Jinga would have adopted the child as her own, as was her right. Gaggau had tried. He had mounted them all, and failed.

Each month they bled as if he had never emptied himself into them. He had failed even with Tana. That was extraordinary. The ranging's females were simply passive vehicles, heavy-shouldered and muscular. Their fur was dark and thick, their eyes a dull yellowy-brown, and they moved with a long rocking stride that while it could tirelessly cover ridge after ridge was awkward and ungainly.

Tana was different. From the moment she arrived at the ranging as a small child in exchange for Manu, Gaggau had been obsessed by her. By her fine silky pelt, by her clear and vivid eyes, by the slow grace of her movements. When she came to adulthood and was ready to breed, Gaggau had mounted her – not out of duty but from desire. He covered her insatiably again and again. The result was the same as with all the rest. Nothing. At each moon change Tana bled with the others. Gaggau might have spent himself in the mountain wind. Jinga taunted him with having no seed. He knew it wasn't so, but he'd long since stopped denying her jeering allegations.

Only one thing would silence her – a swelling in Tana's belly. Passionately, blindly, Gaggau knew he could make it happen. There was little time left to him. He could feel his power retreating like the stilling of the songbirds' calls in the face of winter, yet he still had enough to last him through until the snows fell.

Meanwhile there was the other matter which had goaded Jinga into scorn of his leadership – the disappearance of prey from the ranging's grounds. To the ranging that was far more important than whether or not he sired a child on Tana. Gaggau glanced at the female he had chosen so long ago as his partner. Her face was as hard and malevolent as ever. He decided to humour her.

'I did what you advised,' Gaggau said. 'Manu took back my message to Yerto. We must be allowed to share what the holding gathers.'

'You think Yerto will agree?' Jinga snorted contemptuously. 'Never! Like you he's old, but Yerto has seed. In Ryena he seeded Wengen. Ryena is slow, but she is cunning too. She will take her time. She will unravel what you said as if she is picking apart a weaver bird's nest. Then she will pronounce. The holding, she will say, cannot also feed the ranging – and Yerto and Wengen will support her.'

'They are the people too,' Gaggau answered. 'They cannot say no.'

'And if they do?'

'We must find another way.'

'What other way? To hunt the clouds for prey? To gather from the air? You are a fool, Gaggau!' Jinga stormed at him. 'There is no other way. We either take from the holding, or we starve.'

Once again the brutal intensity of Jinga's stare was too much for him. Gaggau blinked and lowered his head. 'We must wait for Manu to return with Yerto's reply,' he mumbled.

Jinga laughed then. It was a terrible chilling laugh that echoed round the cavern.

'You do not believe me when I say I know already? Then I will show you. Look!'

The force and urgency of Jinga's command was irresistible. Reluctantly, fearfully, Gaggau lifted his eyes from the floor.

Hanging from Jinga's waist on a plaited leather thong was a pouch made from the stomach of a deer. Jinga plunged her hand inside it. She pulled out a young female mountain hare. The hare was alive – Jinga must have trapped it somewhere in the rocks close to the cavern. For a moment she held it up to Gaggau. Its dark liquid eyes glistening in terror, the creature twisted and struggled in her grasp.

Jinga let Gaggau register its frantic efforts to escape. Suddenly she whirled her hand over and left the animal dangling on its back. She lowered her head, opened her mouth and sank her teeth into the hare's throat. The hare screamed once, and the sound gurgled away into silence. Jinga gnawed and tugged at the animal's neck tendons until they parted from its body, then she spat the tendons out and threw the hare to the ground.

Systematically, using her heel as a hammer and treading in a circle round the carcass, she broke all its bones. When she had finished, all that was left untouched was the hare's belly. Jinga put her thumb inside the animal's vaginal passage and tore the flesh apart. She plucked out its womb and stomach, and ripped them open too.

Jinga held out the torn bags of skin to Gaggau. 'Study them well, hunter,' she snarled. 'They are as empty as the tracks you seek to follow – as empty as the answer Manu brings you back.'

She allowed Gaggau to look at them for a moment.

He had just time to see that there was nothing in either the hare's stomach or its womb. Then Jinga hurled the entrails in his face. She turned and left the cavern.

Gaggau squatted in the dusk, blood trickling down his cheeks.

31

Gaggau opened his eyes.

He glanced instinctively at the cave's entrance to check the position of the stars. It was very early. The moon had gone, but the sky was still almost black. Behind the arch of rock, Gaggau could just make out the constellation he knew from its twisted shape as the writhen juniper with the bright beacon owl-star above. Dawn was approaching, but the sky wouldn't start to lighten until the owl-star vanished.

Gaggau turned his head back.

Tana was asleep beside him on the great heap of dried skins. He could hear the steady pulse of her breathing and smell the night scent of her skin. Gaggau sensed the stirrings of desire. He ran his hand down Tana's body, feeling the soft swell of her breast, the supple flatness of her stomach, the dampness as he explored the space between her legs.

He withdrew his hand and licked his fingers. The taste was sweet and salty. He waited, hoping desperately that the smell and taste would transfer the urgency in his mind to his body. It did not happen. Below his waist, below the thick grey pelt and the bulging belly, he remained as limp as a spent caddis fly floating on one of the mountain streams.

Angry and frustrated, Gaggau rolled away, lowered his feet to the ground and heaved himself upright. As he stood, one of the thorn clips Tana had put into the wound on his leg burst from the skin. He felt the blood well out, and winced. Snorting furiously to bury the pain, he limped into the darkness.

Outside, he'd expected to be alone. To his surprise he saw a silhouette squatting on the earth by the cave's entrance. He sniffed and recognized the smell. It came from Soru, the youngest of the ranging's hunters.

'What are you doing here?' Gaggau demanded. 'I said we would leave in the time between the owl-star's falling and the sun's rising.' The hairs on his pelt bristled and rose.

The ranging's young males only came to the main caverns in search of a chance to mount the females who sheltered there. The females, from Gaggau's old and barren mate Jinga to the young Tana, belonged to Gaggau or to the mates they'd been given. Any unmated male who tried to mount them challenged not only Gaggau's property – they threatened his very life.

Soru placed his hands flat on the ground in a gesture of submission. 'I came only to be here when you rose,' he said. 'I wanted to learn as you read the wind.'

Gaggau approached the young yeti and sniffed him warily. If Soru was chasing one of the females, the scent of seed would be on him. There was nothing. Gaggau grunted. Soru was impetuous and inexperienced, but he was keen. One day he would make a good hunter – if there was any prey left for the holding to hunt.

Gaggau lowered himself on to a rock. 'Do not come here again before the time,' he said. 'Today you may stay.'

Soru raised his hands and squatted on his haunches. 'And you will tell me?' he asked eagerly.

'When I am ready,' Gaggau answered.

He rolled back his head, closed his eyes and inhaled the night air so deeply that his already massive chest seemed to expand to twice its size. Then slowly he let the air out, and concentrated.

Burra, his mother, had taught him.

Although all the ranging's females learnt the rudiments of hunting from childhood, they rarely became skilled hunters. There was no need. In normal times, times of plenty, the males could kill enough prey to feed everyone. Nothing about Burra was normal – neither her childhood, nor her personality, nor the time she lived in.

Gaggau's grandfather never seeded a son. Burra was his only child. He brought her up like a male, teaching her obsessively as if to compensate for her gender. Burra was a superb pupil. Intelligent and fearless, she was a better hunter than her father even before she reached puberty. For fifteen years afterwards she refused to mate. Instead she hunted with the patriarch, first as a companion and later, as he aged, as the ranging's leader.

When he died, Burra finally chose a mate – Gaggau's father. Burra took his seed. When her belly swelled with Gaggau, she dismissed him. Much later, far beyond the normal limit of child-bearing, she briefly took another mate and to the astonishment of the ranging her belly filled again. She gave birth to Manu, then rid herself of Manu's sire as swiftly as she had done with Gaggau's.

Gaggau barely knew his father. He was just one of the ranging's hunters who would stand, in a dawn like this, waiting to hear what Burra had read in the wind. The air Gaggau blew out from his lungs was laden with information. As the air passed through his nose, the sensitive hairs inside his nostrils picked up the messages it carried, decoded them and relayed them to his brain.

The coming dawn was cold. Until daybreak, frost would harden on the hill flanks. The morning that followed would be unusually warm – the wind building from the west already carried traces of damp. Before the sun came up there might be rain showers. Afterwards the day would be hot and still.

The night's frost had penned the mountain prey creatures within the rocky sanctuaries they had chosen before darkness fell. There was no reason for them to venture out, for there was nothing for them to eat. The daylight, the early rain and the warmth would change that. The buds on the trees and undergrowth would swell and open, the grass shoots on the high pastures would thrust upwards. The animals would spread out to feed.

Gaggau closed his eyes again. Imprinted on his mind was a three-dimensional map of the hunting grounds. He unrolled it behind his shuttered eyelids. Sector by sector, feature by feature, colour by changing colour, he ran it through his brain. He saw the gullies and ravines, the tree copses and the slopes of scree, the streams and the snowfields. He overlaid the map with the wind, rain and sun. Then he tried to plot the movement of the animals according to the conditions that would change hour by hour over the hunting day.

In the past Gaggau would have had a starting point. He would have known where the animals were. The mass of their bodies as they herded together would have given off a smell as clear and distinctive to his mind's retina as shadow or sunlight. The animals no longer herded together – there were not enough of them. They existed now only as individuals or, at best, in groups of two or three. Their bodies didn't generate enough scent spores for the smell to reach him. Gaggau had to guess not just where the pattern of the day would lead the prey, but where they were in the first place – or even if they were there at all.

Squatting at his feet, Soru cleared his throat. 'Where do we hunt, Gaggau?' he asked.

Gaggau had fallen into a trance, trying to scan the secret spaces of the hidden hill flanks. He blinked at the sound of Soru's voice, turned and shook his head angrily. The anger passed. Soru was young, Gaggau remembered, and anxious to learn. He should teach the young male just as Burra had taught him.

'The wind brings nothing,' Gaggau said. 'There are perhaps one or two musk deer does with kids climbing from the lower valleys. Also maybe some muntjacs. They follow the grasses as the snow line retreats. We will cast first towards the peaks for the musk deer. If we do not find them, we will head down for the muntjac –'

As Soru listened intently, Gaggau explained his reading of the night, the wind and the temperature, and his forecast for the day's hunting.

He was still talking when Raku appeared, followed a few moments later by Penga. The two joined Soru and squatted down at the patriarch's feet. Gaggau repeated his forecast for the benefit of the new arrivals, then heaved himself off the rock and stood up.

'Raku will lead,' he said. 'Penga travels to the sun-side, Soru to the side of the stars –'

Gaggau was leaning on his knobbled staff of juniper wood. He rocked back and balanced himself on his good foot, raised the staff in the air and shook it.

'Today we kill.'

He tucked the staff back under his armpit. Dragging his club-foot behind him, he limped away.

Gaggau was wrong about the musk deer. He was wrong about the muntjac too.

Neither of the deer were there. The gullies and corries, the winding, rope-like coils of the woodland, the little plateaux, were barren. The high shelves of grass were thick with sweet, succulent plants. Flowers bloomed. The Himalayan primrose, glowing a fragile lemon-rose amidst the snow, was everywhere. All that was missing were the animals.

They had always been there. Now they had gone.

Gaggau wiped the sweat from his face. It was mid-morning, and he and the hunters had been out for seven hours. They had roamed backwards and forwards, systematically sweeping the grounds. In the past, under Gaggau's direction, they would have killed within an hour of leaving the caves. Not today. Today, as so often since the spring began, they were empty-handed.

Gaggau glanced down. The three young hunters were squatting in a ring at his feet. Their faces were expressionless but he knew what was going through their minds.

Hunger. Hunger was more deadly than anything. Only hunger could destroy the ranging. Without food they could neither breed nor hold their territory on the crests. Now the gnawing ache in their bellies had risen to torment their minds. Gaggau the great hunter had not led them to prey. He said the prey was not there, but perhaps the fault was his. Gaggau was old and lame – perhaps he had lost his old skills.

Perhaps it was time for someone else to lead the ranging.

That, Gaggau knew, along with the pangs of hunger, was what filled their thoughts. He looked at them with contempt. They were children. They knew nothing. Under the leadership of any one of them, the ranging would be doomed before the year's snows came. Anger welled in him. He narrowed his eyes and raised his club to punish them for their arrogance and stupidity – to knock them off their haunches and bruise their backs.

Gaggau stopped. Suddenly a memory of his mother, Burra, came back to him. He was very young and it had been another time of famine. Not as bad as this one, but bitter and threatening all the same. Then, too, the ranging had hunted for days without success. At the darkest moment, when they hadn't eaten for days, Burra took Gaggau aside.

'Do not be frightened,' she said. 'The ranging will live through these days. There are places where a few prey can always be found. The animals go there to feed. The places are small and secret. We will hunt them if necessary, but the hunger is not yet great enough. The places must be kept secret and saved for the worst. You should know where they are. The worst will not come now, but it may come in your time.'

Burra told him where the secret places were. Next day she led the hunters to a kill. Slowly that year the game returned and the famine ended. Burra was right. She never had to use the secret places.

It was so long ago that Gaggau had forgotten their existence until now. It had needed the arrival of the worst – and the hunger was beyond anything in the ranging's history – to bring them back to him. As Gaggau remembered, his tiredness slipped away and a surge of triumph flooded through him. Burra had never been wrong. If she said the secret places always held prey, they would hold prey now. Only he, Gaggau, knew where they were.

He pushed himself away from the rock. 'I said we would kill today,' he bellowed. 'The day is not over. We will kill!'

Moving faster than he had for weeks, he limped away up the ravine. Startled by the confidence in the old patriarch's voice, the three yeti leapt up and followed him.

Burra had made Gaggau memorize the positions of seven hidden sites where the animals fed, all of them on the remote edges of the ranging's hunting grounds. The one he headed for was the furthest of all from the caves, but the closest to where the day's fruitless search had led them. It was still a long distance away.

Gaggau headed on unerringly. The ache in his club-foot no longer troubled him, and the pain of the wound from yesterday's hunt was forgotten.

Almost sixty full seasons had passed since Burra described the place he was searching for. Gaggau had never once been there, but it made no difference. Burra had told him the sun's angle above it at different times of the day. The changing star-set at night, the rise and ebb of the snow's thickness in winter and the upland grass in summer. The sinuous folds of the ravines and corries, the drift of the winds and the flight patterns of the birds they carried.

Gaggau had stored the information in the locked caverns at the back of his mind. His frustration and anger had broken the locks, and the long-buried knowledge had spilt out into the light. With Burra to guide him, he could have found the place in winter or summer at any hour of the day or night.

Gaggau came upon it soon after darkness fell.

He knew they were close. Every instinct, every one of the instructions he'd been following, told him so.

Raku, the eldest of the three hunters, confirmed it. 'There is a deer beyond the ridge,' he whispered.

Gaggau paused. His sense of smell was fading with the years. The younger hunters had much keener noses – it was the only concession he made to them. Gaggau sniffed the air. Faintly he picked up a trace of the musky smell of a muntjac buck. Raku was right – the buck was feeding close to them.

They had reached Burra's secret place.

Gaggau didn't need any more help. He knew what Raku didn't – the nature of the site where the buck was grazing. It lay beyond and below them on the far side of the ridge, a small grassy bowl with hill flanks on three sides, and mountain streams flowing down through steeply rising corridors of trees. The fourth side, the side where the buck had climbed up from beneath, was open. Burra had told him that and she'd also told him how the bowl should be hunted.

Gaggau turned and whispered his instructions to the three hunters, then watched them vanish into the darkness. He waited until he knew they were positioned where he wanted before edging silently up to the top of the ridge and looking down.

The buck was feeding at the centre of the bowl beneath him. Gaggau inhaled, rasping his breath out in the muntjac's hoarse bark of alarm. As the sound echoed across the grassy floor, the deer whirled round, lifted its head and for an instant stood quivering. Then it plunged downwards.

The animal had three possible escape routes. The one it chose was guarded by Soru. As the buck raced towards him, Soru rose from the ground and clubbed it across the muzzle. The force of the blow made the buck's forelegs buckle. As it stumbled and dropped to its knees, Raku and Pemba appeared from either side, threw themselves across the deer's back and brought it to the ground. Raku's bone killing knife flashed twice in the moonlight across the deer's throat. A moment later the animal was dead.

Gaggau saw the deer crumple into stillness, and laughed – a deep rumbling laugh of contentment. The sort of laugh he hadn't given since the snows lifted that season, perhaps not for many seasons before. The hunters had killed, and this time not a goat but a deer. They were far from the caves but when they carried the meat back the holding would eat, even the hollow in his own belly would be filled.

For the moment the famine was over – and he, Gaggau, had ended it.

Gaggau stood up. Dragging his foot behind him, he limped down towards the other three who were already starting to butcher the carcass. He had covered half the distance when he stopped abruptly. There was a strange flickering glow behind the rocky shelf on the far side of the clearing. Occupied with the deer the other three hadn't seen it. Gaggau tensed. He narrowed his eyes and peered forward.

The yellow light came closer. The night wind had been blowing from behind his back. Suddenly it changed direction and swirled round. It brought with it the fearsome, sickening stench of what Gaggau knew as the dark storm's child – fire. An instant later a line of figures appeared on top of the rocks, silhouetted against the sky. The figures were forked and upright like the people. They were running, and in their hands were blazing branches.

Gaggau blinked at the flames' brilliance. Fierce blind anger swept his body. Launching himself into a hobbling run, he hurled himself down the slope.

He knew who the figures were. They were not the people, nor were they shumbi – if they had been, Gaggau would have scented them long ago in spite of the wind-set. They could only be the oduna and they were out to rob him of his prey.

As he reached the floor of the clearing, Gaggau slipped on a clump of dew-laden grass. He fell back, skidded on, and tumbled over twice before he could get to his feet again. Stiff and aching, he scrambled up. The three young hunters had become aware of the oduna only seconds before. Terrified by the burning brands, they had abandoned the deer and were racing away. Gaggau roared at them to stop.

The oduna were shouting and howling now and the hunters, either too frightened or unable to hear him in the uproar, ignored Gaggau and ran on. Raging, Gaggau threw himself forward again. He reached the carcass at the same instant as the three leading oduna and confronted them over the deer's half-dismembered body. Gaggau gave a long challenging growl and tried to meet the oduna's eyes. He failed. They held the fiery branches in front of them, and their eyes were hidden by the glare of the flames.

Gaggau stretched out his arm and gripped one of the deer's haunches. Still howling, the nearest oduna hurled his brand at the holding's patriarch. The branch struck Gaggau in the stomach. The flame set fire to the front of his pelt and flared up his body. He felt an agonizing pain and smelt the stench again, stronger and harsher now. Keeping hold of the haunch, he roared defiantly again.

More brands rained down on him. Tormented and maddened, he let ago of the haunch and picked up one of the brands, intending to hurl it back. But he had grasped it by its burning end. As he raised it above his head, he felt the worst pain he had ever known. His hands blistered and sizzled, and his head swam dizzily.

Gaggau tried to toss the branch away but it seemed to cling to him. Frenziedly he shook it. Eventually it dropped to the ground, taking strips of his skin and flesh with it. Gaggau turned. Stumbling and swaying from side to side, he hobbled away, and reeled up to the top of the ridge. Cowering in the grass Raku, Penga and Soru were waiting for him in the darkness.

Gaggau dropped to his knees. He could smell blood, his own blood, and the terrible cloying smell of the oduna's firebrands as the sparks continued to sear his flesh.

'Carry me to the ranging,' Gaggau muttered.

He slipped unconscious on to the grass.

32

Manu glanced down at the child. 'The crests are far,' he said. 'Do you wish to ride on my shoulders?'

They had crossed the river from the island at the start of their journey to the ranging. During the swim Iona had been forced to cling to Manu's neck. When they reached the far bank the yeti had put her down so that he could shake himself dry. Now he was standing gazing down at her.

'No,' Iona snapped. 'I'll walk.'

She stared up at him bitterly. All the island yeti had betrayed her, but because she'd instinctively come to trust him more than any of them, even more than the blind Kekua or Churinga, Manu's betrayal was the worst of all. His eyes no longer seemed bright and golden, they had become clouded and devious. His strength that had once been her shield and safety was oppressive and threatening. His strong, open features looked cunning and dangerous.

Babilla growled and Iona's glance slid towards the leopard. Babilla was growling only in irritation at the spray from the water that was cascading round her, but to Iona the animal appeared to be siding with her master. For the first time since she'd realized that the great rose-patterned cat was no different from Misty, Iona hated the leopard.

Manu frowned and lifted one of his huge arms, arms that to Iona still looked like great tree branches covered in mahogany-coloured hair. For a long time he rubbed his hand thoughtfully against the side of his head in silence. Then he spoke.

'It is not of my choosing that you go to the crests,' he said. 'I do not belong on the island any more than you do. But I am still of the people and Tonemetapu is wise and I must do as he says. Also, the crests are where I was born. They are my home. I would like to take you there with me, not because Tonemetapu instructs me, but because it is my desire.'

Manu stopped.

Iona stared at him again. It was the longest speech the yeti had made to her. His face was grave and his features were set in a look of earnestness, of hope, almost of pleading. For an instant Iona closed her eyes. She was still a prisoner and everything in her still fought against being sent to the unknown clan in the mountains, but Manu hadn't betrayed her. He was simply obeying Tonemetapu's orders. More important, far more important, Manu wanted to show her his home. He could only want to do that because she was his friend.

Iona opened her eyes again and a radiant smile flooded her face. 'You may carry me,' she said.

Manu smiled back. As the yeti swung her up on to his shoulders again, there was a splash behind them. Manu and Iona turned their heads together. Wengen had plunged into the river and was swimming over in their wake. He climbed out and shook himself, but he didn't approach them. His face expressionless, Wengen stood apart.

'Wengen travels the same path,' Manu said quietly. 'Yet he will travel behind us and alone. Yerto has ordered it shall be so –'

Manu turned. 'Come!' he said.

With Babilla leading, they set off.

Manu and the leopard smelt it at the same instant.

Manu stopped in mid-stride and flared his nostrils. Beside him Babilla pricked her ears, growled and flattened herself on the ground. Behind them Iona came to a halt and glanced round, puzzled. Then she wearily rubbed her legs.

It was just after dark on the second evening after they'd left the island. On his own Manu would have made the journey to the crests without a break. With Iona he had to travel more slowly. They paused often during the daylight hours and rested for most of the night. In spite of that Iona was exhausted.

The first day, when they'd crossed the great bowl of the plain, hadn't been too difficult. The trouble started that morning when they began to climb. Beneath the tree canopy the snow lay thick and the dusky air was bitterly cold. On the open hill flanks the sun blazed down and sweat poured off her. For hour after hour she struggled upwards, alternating between the icy chill of the forest and the searing heat of the rocky slopes.

Again and again Iona would haul herself on to the top of some ridge that seemed to be brushing the foot of the sky itself, only to find the wall of a valley falling almost vertically on the other side. Beyond would be another, higher ridge. The only way to reach it was to descend into the valley and painfully climb up again.

With each ridge they climbed, the air grew thinner and harsher. Iona started to cough. She had blisters on her feet and her muscles throbbed. From time to time, giddy and bleeding, she asked Manu to carry her. Each time after fifteen minutes she begged him to put her down. It was bad enough making her own way, but however carefully the yeti climbed it was even worse being jolted and bruised on his shoulders.

Wengen was somewhere behind. As Manu had promised her, the big island yeti never drew near to them, not even when they stopped at night. He walked, fed and rested alone half a mile to their rear. Yet Iona was constantly aware of his shadowing presence. The realization made her uneasy and whenever a gap opened up between her and Manu, she would hurry to catch up, however tired she was.

Now, her chest heaving, Iona clutched the lightning-blasted trunk of a rhododendron for support. She peered ahead. 'What is it?' she asked.

Manu glanced round. 'Can you not smell it?'

Iona sniffed the air and shook her head. She could smell nothing except the metallic scent of the evening's frost and the now familiar smells of the undergrowth – the resin from the crushed mastic, the pollen from the primroses, the dusty odour of the oxidized red earth.

Manu strode back to her. He broke off one of the blackened branches from the tree beside Iona. He gnawed at the outer covering of charred bark, raised the branch to his face, and winced. Then he held it under the child's nose.

'It is that,' Manu said.

Iona sniffed again. She could just detect the acrid scent of the long-dead fire which had ignited when the lightning struck.

She lifted her head and scanned the night wind with her nostrils as the yeti had done. The smell on the breeze was very faint, so faint she had to close her eyes and concentrate with every fibre before she was sure she had picked it up. She sucked in the mountain air, and slowly she became certain.

To Manu it was pungent and repulsive. To Iona it was no more than a few scent spores which registered at the extreme ranges of her senses. The spores signalled fire.

'It's only a –'

Iona stopped. She'd been about to say it was only a fire, but she'd forgotten the yeti word for fire. Frowning, she thought for a moment. Then it came back to her.

'It is the dark storm's child,' Iona said, 'but it is old and dead.'

Manu shook his head. 'We are close to the ranging. This comes from within their hunting grounds not far from where they have their shelters. It is alive and dangerous –' He paused. For the first time since Iona had known him, Manu looked tense and worried.

'When the storm drops it from the clouds and it breathes, it can eat everything,' Manu went on. 'Today there have been no storms.'

Bewildered, he winnowed the air again. The stench he caught from the wind made him recoil, and he rinsed his mouth with his tongue and spat. Babilla was equally distressed. Manu stooped and stroked the leopard's neck. 'We must change our course,' he said. 'We must move away from it.'

'No!'

As she snapped out her reply, Iona felt a sudden surge of confidence. It was the first and only time she had defied any of the yeti. This was something she knew about and they did not.

Manu stared at her. 'We cannot go on. We will walk straight into it.'

'You say it eats everything,' Iona answered. 'If it's not stopped, won't it eat the trees and bushes of the ranging's hunting grounds?'

Manu nodded.

'Then we must stop it.'

'You don't understand what this is,' Manu replied, his face grim. 'This is stronger than anyone. It will eat until it is fed. Only then will it go away. No one can stop it.'

'I can stop it,' Iona said firmly. 'All shumbis know this creature. We call it "fire" and we know how to drive it away. Take me to where it is feeding.'

Manu was silent.

For a long time he gazed down at her. Iona gazed steadfastly back. She had no idea what was going through the yeti's mind. She didn't know how far away or how big the fire was, let alone whether she would be able to put it out. She didn't know what it would mean if she succeeded. Nor did it matter to her that she was challenging Manu, the one yeti above all whom she trusted.

All Iona knew was that for once the advantage had passed to her. The yeti, she had learnt, were terrified of fire. She was not.

Eventually, reluctantly and unhappily, Manu nodded. He had no idea whether even a shumbi could control the creature, but he had seen the devastation it had caused before. The season was high summer. The upland trees and bushes of the ranging's hunting grounds were drying out – they were already vulnerable. If the creature from the skies was allowed to feed unchecked, the last of the animals would vanish. There would be nothing left for them to feed on, and Gaggau would have an irresistible case for sharing the valley with the holding.

Manu turned. With Babilla loping fretfully beside him and Iona following, he set off again.

Too tired to wonder where they were heading, Iona trudged upwards through the darkness. With every step the scent of smoke grew stronger. Sometimes, when they dipped into a gully, she lost it for a few minutes. Then they climbed out and the smell returned, acrid and unmistakable now on the night wind. Finally Iona saw the two silhouettes, Manu and the leopard, come to a stop above her. She scrambled up and stood beside them.

They'd reached the rim of a grassy plateau. Before them the ground stretched out under the cold silver glow of the rising moon. On all three sides ahead, thickly wooded ravines ran down from the mountains. Each of the ravines was a watercourse. Iona could hear the rustle of the falling streams, and see the occasional shimmer of spray as the wind plucked at the foam on the torrents of snow-melt.

She narrowed her eyes. As she stared intently ahead, the words of Duncan, her uncle's old stalker at Killiemurchan, came back to her.

'Don't look for the beasts, lassie,' he'd said when he'd taken her up into the hills above her uncle's estate. 'Look for where the beasts want to be. They're just like us. Food and drink is what they're after. Look for pasture and a wee burn or two, and ye'll find them.'

Iona and Duncan were searching for the red deer of the Scottish Highlands. Duncan had guided her to a place just like this. A couple of highland streams, a swathe of grass in the moorland, and the sheltering hills all round. The deer were there, just as Duncan promised.

The Himalayan deer and the other mountain animals should have been here too. They were not. The plateau was deserted and the reason was obvious – at the centre of the little plain was a spreading circle of fire.

Iona ran forward. Behind her Babilla snarled in fear and Manu hung back beside the leopard. Iona reached the edge of the fire. Orange and scarlet flames were licking across the ground. The night's dew had crystallized into fans of glittering frost which had slowed the flames' advance, but the fire was gnawing at the icy whiteness and devouring the grasses beneath. As Iona watched, the blaze rolled remorselessly on.

If the fire reached the ravines, the drying undergrowth beneath the trees would carry it all over the mountains.

'Here!' Iona shouted.

Manu hesitated, then he ran forward to join her. He stood blinking as the reflected glow flickered over his face. Babilla had followed him. The leopard patrolled the ground in restless circles, growling in fear whenever a column of sparks erupted upwards.

'We can stop the creature with water and our feet,' Iona said. 'I'll use my feet. Fill your gathering bag from the stream and come back!'

Manu unslung the bag from his shoulder. Unlike the birds'-nest containers used by the holding, Manu carried a large bag made out of the dried stomach of a deer. As Iona started to stamp on the ring of burning grass, he raced over to the nearest stream.

'What do I do?' he asked when he returned with the bag bulging with water.

'Pour it over the creature wherever it's feeding,' Iona instructed.

Manu looked at her anxiously. 'Will that not anger it?' he asked.

Iona opened her mouth to try to explain, then stopped. 'Give me the bag,' she said.

She took the bag from him. For an instant her knees buckled under its weight, then she straightened herself, tilted it over her arm and began splashing the grass from its mouth.

'Look,' she said. 'The water is killing it.'

Manu stared down at the ground where the flames were sizzling and dying. He furrowed his face, trying to take it in, and shook his head in bewilderment. Then he seized the bag and began to copy Iona.

Iona had no idea how long it took them – an hour perhaps, maybe more. If Manu had been a man rather than a yeti it would have taken twice as long. As it was, his strength and speed enabled him to run tirelessly and swiftly backwards and forwards from the stream. He filled the bag, emptied it over the flames and raced back to fill it again.

The two of them worked their way round the blaze. Iona trampled and stamped, while Manu drenched the ground with water. Eventually they came back to where they had started. A few plumes of smoke were still lifting into the night and the occasional spark flashed away on the wind, but the fire was out.

Iona glanced at the yeti. His face and most of his body were coated with flakes of soot. She touched her own face, and looked at her fingers. They were black too. Iona brushed her hands on her jacket and grinned.

'I told you,' she said. 'It's not easy and it's dirty, but the creature can be stopped.'

Manu looked round the plateau. His eyes scanned the corridors of woodland that led up to the snow line. Manu was a hunter. He knew the animals the woodland harboured, and what would have happened if the trees had been destroyed.

He looked back at her gratefully. 'The trees are saved. I will remember how it was done. In cloud-time I will tell of it –'

Manu broke off and his head jerked round.

With the fire extinguished, Babilla had plucked up enough courage to cross the smoking grass into the centre of the plateau where the blaze had begun. Now the leopard was tugging at something and growling hungrily. Manu ran over. He bent over Babilla and plucked what looked in the moonlight like a bone from the ground beside the leopard.

Manu inspected the bone and tossed it away. He began to cast left and right, tracing wider and wider circles round the feeding leopard. From time to time he stooped and knelt to sniff the earth. Once he licked his finger, drew it across the ground and tasted the soil that clung to his skin. Then he set off again, restlessly prowling from side to side.

'What is it?'

Iona came up to him. Manu, squatting on his haunches, was studying a patch of soil between the clumps of burnt grass.

'There was a killing here,' he said. 'The ranging hunted and found prey. Gaggau himself led them. Raku was with him. Young Penga, too, and also Soru.. Look, these are their tracks –'

Manu pointed. Iona looked down. She could see nothing except a few ridges and furrows in the earth.

'They killed and then they were challenged,' Manu went on. 'There are other tracks. They were not made by hunters of the ranging.'

'Then who made them?'

'The oduna.'

Iona frowned. 'Who are the oduna?'

Manu told her.

As he finished Iona was still frowning. She didn't really understand what he'd said. All she'd gathered was that there was a third group of yeti, of the 'people' as Manu called them, whom no one had mentioned before. They belonged neither to the holding or the ranging. Instead they seemed to be outcasts from both.

'That is not all,' Manu added. 'There has been fighting. Look!'

He gestured at the ground. Dark patches stained the earth and crusted the grass stems. Iona had no need to ask what caused them. It was blood.

'The blood scent is Gaggau's,' Manu said. 'The oduna called down the storm's child to help them drive him off his prey. Gaggau was wounded and the hunters carried him away. The oduna do not know about water and the trampling of feet. The storm's child has taken for itself much of the deer Gaggau killed. All the signs are here.' His hand flickered over the burnt grass in the moonlight.

Iona saw the charred logs of a fire and the blackened bones of an animal that had been roasted on it. Manu had interpreted what had happened according to his own knowledge and experience. Iona did the same.

There had been no summoning of lightning from the sky. The oduna had used fire, she guessed, to frighten Gaggau and the ranging's hunters from the deer they'd killed. The fire alone hadn't been enough. The oduna had had to fight the mountain yeti too. But the flaming branches they'd hurled at the hunters had turned the battle in their favour.

Gaggau had been wounded, and the hunters had carried him away. Afterwards the oduna had piled the branches together, and roasted the animal over the flames. That was why the smell of cooked meat still hung trapped in the icy air above the little plateau. It was not the dark storm's child which had eaten the deer.

It was either the oduna, or someone who had taught the outcasts about fire.

'We must get to the ranging,' Manu said urgently.

33

'Stay here,' Manu said quietly.

Iona stopped.

For the last half-hour they had been climbing up a tiny winding path that clung to the mountain flanks above a gorge. The gorge was so deep that the roar of the river below sounded as faint as the humming of distant bees. Once or twice Iona peered down. Far beneath in the darkness she could see occasional flashes of white foam that glittered as remotely as the stars overhead.

Iona felt dizzy. It was as if she were balanced on a tightrope suspended midway between the sky and the earth. She licked her lips and swallowed. Pressing her shoulder against the rock face and concentrating on the flicking tip of Babilla's tail, she forced herself to walk on.

Now they had come out on to a broad open ledge. The gorge and the river were still on one side, but much further away now. On the other side the mountain sloped up to the crests. For a moment Iona couldn't see more because Manu was standing in front of her. Then, as he strode away, the view before her opened out.

Set into the mountain flank where it reared up from the ledge were a number of jagged spaces of blackness. Iona peered at them. They were the mouths of caves. Outside the cave mouths, the ground was littered with boulders. One of the boulders seemed to move, then another, then a third. She narrowed her eyes, stared forward again, and tensed.

They weren't boulders – they were yeti. Iona realized there were twenty or thirty of them. She had reached the ranging. The caves must be their shelters. Manu told her that Wengen had overtaken them for the first time after they had put out the fire on the little plateau. He had gone on ahead to warn the ranging of her arrival, and everyone had come out to inspect her, just as they had in the valley below – but that had been in daylight.

Frightening enough by day, in the darkness it was worse. The moon was high and full, but the mountain flank was in shadow and all Iona could make out were dim, occasionally moving silhouettes. She had questioned Manu about the ranging during the journey, but she'd learnt little.

'They are also the people,' he said. 'They are like the holding, except they hunt and eat meat.'

To Iona hunting and meat-eating conjured up images of blood. Manu himself came originally from the holding. She had seen him hunt and eat meat, but Manu had become familiar over her weeks on the island. In the darkness the shapes of the new yeti in front of her were as strange and menacing as Manu's had once been.

Iona waited. The wind on the ledge was icy. Her breath came out in plumes of steam and her legs throbbed with tiredness. Minutes passed, her teeth started to chatter and she shivered uncontrollably.

'Gaggau wishes to see you.'

Manu had returned. He beckoned and she followed him forward.

While Iona waited the moon had climbed higher. Now its light shone down over the ledge. In the cold metallic glow she saw the members of the ranging watching her. She glanced at them warily. They were the same height as the yeti of the holding, but leaner and more muscular. They had Manu's dark pelt and his gleaming yellow eyes. Otherwise, at first glance the two clans seemed identical.

Yet there was a striking difference. Iona stared at them and realized that the contrast lay in their faces. The faces of the valley yeti were plump and confident, those of the ranging gaunt and harrowed. The young of the holding had been stilled into silence when Iona appeared from the river on Manu's shoulders. Here they mewed and sobbed in spite of everything their parents did to quiet them. Iona thought their distress must be due to fear of her, a shumbi. Quickly she realized it wasn't. The children here were hungry, as was everyone else. That explained their sunken features and staring eyes. The ranging was starving.

'I have brought her to you,' Manu said.

Iona's head jerked round. Watching the yeti, she hadn't noticed where Manu was leading her. Now she saw that they were standing at the entrance to one of the caves. Manu stepped inside.

'So this is the shumbi.'

The voice came from somewhere close to the cave's mouth.

Iona gazed into the darkness. For several moments she could see nothing. Then the moon rolled further up the sky. As the angle of its light changed, it began to illuminate the cavern. The glow crept across the sandy floor and up on to a bench of rock piled with animal skins. Lying on top of the skins was an old male yeti.

It could only be Gaggau. The moonlight spread over him, and Iona saw the ranging's leader.

He was old, as old as his fellow patriarch, Yerto, in the valley below. His fur was speckled with grey. In places – on his chest, at his groin, along the inside of his thighs – it was almost white. But in the few places where his pelt showed through, the base colour was in sharp contrast to Yerto's.

Yerto's fur was silky and had the valley's colouring, the pale translucent colour of ripening wheat. Gaggau's pelt was coarser and darker, darker even than Manu's. The hairs were oaken-brown and had the deep gnarled texture of the bark on the great trees that lined the drive at Mainwarden. They stood out from his hide, bristling defiantly and aggressively under the whiteness that cloaked them like snow.

Iona sometimes thought of the stiff-boned Yerto as a knotted log washed up by the river on to the island's shore and bleached dry and silvery by the sun. Gaggau gave the same impression of weathered age. He might have been a twin piece of flotsam though the mountain years had ground him harder and sharper. He wasn't a log, he was a misshapen stone, grey-white like Yerto but coloured by the driving snows of the crests, not the softer flow of the river's water.

Gaggau inspected her for a long time in silence. Behind him Iona could see the glow of two other pairs of eyes also watching her intently. The other yeti were too deep in the shadows for her to see whether they were male or female.

'So this is the shumbi,' Gaggau rasped eventually to Manu. 'Tell her I am wounded.'

'The shumbi is named Iona,' Manu answered. 'She has learnt the language of the people. She hears what you say.'

Gaggau glanced at Iona. 'The oduna made the creature from the skies attack me. What can you do to heal me?' he demanded.

Gaggau held out his hands. They were swollen and blackened, and blood was oozing from his palms. The oduna must have pelted him with blazing branches. Ignorant of fire, Gaggau had obviously seized one of the branches and tried to throw it back. In half a dozen other places the fur on his body was charred, and the skin was raw beneath.

Iona looked up. Gaggau's face was sunken and contorted with pain. She racked her brains. Even if she'd known how to treat burns, she had no medicines with her. The yeti was in agony, but there was nothing she could do.

Iona shook her head helplessly. 'I can't heal you,' she said.

'It is not so!' Gaggau roared. 'I have spoken to Wengen. He knows from Tonemetapu that you can do anything. You must heal me! Without my hands I cannot hunt. You are hiding your powers to keep them for the holding!'

In fury Gaggau struggled to lift himself off the great pile of skins. As he threw himself forward the skin ruptured beneath the burns, and runnels of bright blood flowed down his pelt. He howled and fell back.

Iona stood frozen in fear.

The two yetis whose eyes Iona had seen watching her ran forward. They were both female, one young, the other old and wrinkled. They swung Gaggau's legs back on to the skins. Gaggau moaned and snarled. As the young one tried to comfort him, the older yeti swung round towards Iona.

'I am Jinga, mate of Gaggau, so listen well!' Her voice was hoarse and her eyes gleamed venomously in her haggard face. 'Gaggau must hunt so we may eat. He needs his hands. Give them back to him, little shumbi. If you do not, we must eat what we can find.'

Jinga's eyes ranged up and down Iona's body.

Iona stared back at her. For an instant panic paralysed the child. She had thought the yeti of the valley were monsters. In comparison with the ranging, they were not. These were the true monsters, the creatures that had prowled her dreams. They were hungry, ready to kill and eat her as she had always known they would.

Iona fought the panic back. Deep inside her she knew she had to live, and living meant conquering the terrible malevolence of this creature in front of her. Living meant healing Gaggau. It meant giving him back his hands, allowing him to hunt, allowing the ranging to eat. Desperately Iona thought again.

Once when she was very small Mr Simpson had given her a potato to bake in an autumn bonfire of leaves at Mainwarden. When

Iona smelt the potato's warm smoky scent, she tried to hook it out from the fire with a twig. In her eagerness she fell forward into the embers and scorched her arm. It was only a small burn, but she screamed in pain. Mr Simpson picked her up in his arms and ran with her to his cottage.

His wife took one look at the hot red patch on Iona's skin and reached for the butter dish.

'It's the air that hurts,' Mrs Simpson said, spreading butter over the wound. 'Keep the air out and the germs can't get in either. Seal a burn like you're potting shrimps, that's what I always say. It'll mend soon enough underneath.'

Mrs Simpson was right. The pain vanished. Three days later the burn mark had vanished too.

Butter. That was all Iona could think of. She glanced frantically round. It was pointless. The yeti didn't use butter – they wouldn't know what it was, let alone how it was made. At least Iona knew that – old Angus had taught her in the dairy at her uncle's house in Scotland. To make butter one needed milk. The yeti didn't even have that.

She turned back. Gaggau and the old female yeti, Jinga, were gazing at her, the one in anguish, the other with hooded, greedy eyes. Panic surged up in Iona again, and she almost choked. She forced the terror down. Milk. She had to have milk. Suddenly it came to her.

It was early summer, and the yeti females had given birth to their young. Iona had seen them in the holding and again outside the caves. In the valley the mother's breasts had been large and full. Here on the crests they were much smaller, but they still held milk. Wherever it came from, milk had to be the same. It could still yield butter.

Iona drew in her breath, and explained what she wanted.

Jinga stared at her disbelievingly. 'You will take the food of the young, when there is no food for anyone?' she shouted. 'It is as I thought. You have not come to heal Gaggau. You have come to destroy us all!'

Gaggau had fallen back on the pile of skins, and Jinga was squatting at his feet. She leaped up to throw herself at the child. The rage and bitterness she exuded were as strong as the buffeting gusts of the night wind that intermittently whipped through the cave.

White-faced, Iona recoiled. Her back bumped against the rocky wall and she stopped. It flashed across her mind that there was nothing more she could do or say. She had tried and failed. Now, confronted with this demon, she was helpless. She closed her eyes and waited for Jinga's attack.

'Listen to the shumbi, Jinga. Tonemetapu says she comes from the stars. Do as she says. For Gaggau it is the only hope.'

The voice was Manu's.

Iona opened her eyes. She had forgotten about Manu. The yeti had stepped forward and was standing between her and Jinga. Beside him, crouched on the floor of the cave, was Babilla. The leopard's eyes were fixed on Jinga and it was growling warningly.

Jinga's gaze moved across the three of them, Manu, the leopard, and Iona in the shadows behind. She rinsed her tongue round her mouth and spat furiously at the ground.

'Let the shumbi do what she can,' Jinga said. 'She has the night for her affairs. When daylight comes we must hunt. To hunt, the ranging must first eat. I know what shall feed it.'

She stormed out of the cave.

As she went, Iona saw Manu lift his hand and beckon towards Gaggau's couch where the young female yeti squatted. She rose and came forward slowly and Iona saw that her pelt had the pale colouring of the holding. The yeti reached out and shyly gave Iona the holding's greeting, stroking the child's nose and then her face.

'She is named Tana,' Manu said. 'She will do what you ask of her. Tell her what you want.'

Iona looked at Tana. The young yeti's face was open and candid, her eyes level and calm. Framed in its fair soft fur, Tana's face reminded Iona of home – not her own home, but the place she'd come to think of as home. The holding.

Iona smiled. 'I want milk from the suckling females,' she said. 'Tell them it is to save Gaggau.' She explained again. When she finished, Tana nodded.

'They will understand,' Tana said. 'You will have what you ask for.'

Iona bumped the container rhythmically up and down on her hip.

The container was a tube of bark from a lightning-felled tree. One end was stoppered with chipped wooden laths, bonded to the bark with resin and mastic. The ranging used it to catch the blood when they cut the throat of a slaughtered prey animal. There had never been any need to stopper the other end because the blood was drunk within hours of the animal's death, so Iona had improvised a lid by tearing a length of material from her jacket, and binding it round the top.

She had no idea if it would work. She had no real idea what she was doing at all. She could only cling desperately to what she remembered old Angus telling her. He used to take her into the dairy at Killiemurchan when Morag, the dairymaid, was making cheese. Morag used a heavy churn on an iron tripod which she swung over and over with a wooden handle, but Angus had shown Iona how it was done in the old days when he was a child.

Now Iona was copying what she'd seen Angus do then, praying that it would work for her as it had for him.

She stopped and lifted the container to her ear. Across the small cave close to Gaggau's, Manu and Tana squatted on their haunches watching her intently. Iona shook the bark tube and listened. The milk inside was no longer slopping backwards and forwards like water. It was rolling more slowly. It was curdling.

Briefly Iona closed her eyes in relief. She set to work again.

It was almost dawn when she finished. She removed the lid and poured the last of the whey on to the ground. Then she dipped her finger into what was left, and cautiously raised her finger to her mouth. The flavour was unlike anything she had ever tasted. It was warm and honey-sweet with a strange wild scent of the upland herbs. It was also unmistakably butter.

Iona got to her feet. She stumbled from weariness and almost dropped the container. Then she recovered her balance and rubbed her face.

'It is done,' she said to Manu. 'Let us go to Gaggau.'

Manu led the way outside.

It was icily cold on the mountain shelf. Hoar frost covered the rocks and the sand beneath their feet was frozen. The yeti of the ranging were still there. Looking blearily at them, Iona realized that they must have been there all night. She saw the nursing females who had given Tana their milk, their eyes dull and hungry and heavy with anxiety. At their breasts the new-born young were mewling.

She tried to smile encouragingly. It was impossible – she was too tired and still too frightened. She felt her lips part in a glazed and meaningless grin. Then she stepped into Gaggau's cave behind Manu and Tana.

Gaggau was lying on his heap of skins, either asleep or unconscious. Sweat was running down his body in spite of the cold and he twitched convulsively. There was no sign of Jinga, but Iona thought she caught the gleam of eyes in the darkness at the back of the cave.

Tana went forward and squatted beside the old yeti. She picked up one of his swollen hands and examined it carefully, sniffing at the cracked and bleeding skin. Then she glanced back imploringly at Iona, her eyes filled with tears.

'If you can do anything, you must do it now,' she said. 'Maybe Gaggau will survive. His hands will not, and without them he cannot hunt. He is nothing.'

Iona knelt beside her. She gestured and Tana held out Gaggau's hands. Iona coated them with the butter from the bark container. She did the same with the burn marks on Gaggau's body, anointing them one by one as Tana – with Manu's help – turned the patriarch from side to side.

When all the wounds had been smeared with the thick oily paste, Iona put her hands on the ground and pushed herself upright. As Manu and Tana stood beside her, Iona gazed down at the old yeti. Whether the treatment would work, she had no idea. But she had done her best. It was what Mrs Simpson would have done, and to Iona Mrs Simpson was infallible.

Iona turned and headed for the cave's entrance. The sun was rising and although the dawn wind was still cold it smelt fresh and sweet. She drew the air deep into her lungs. It carried the scent of blossom from late-flowering mountain trees, and there were birds singing everywhere.

She took another step forward, dropped to her knees, toppled over, and slept.

34

Iona opened her eyes and blinked.

The darkness was so intense that for a moment she could see nothing. She turned her head and a patch of the night sky came into view. The sky was framed by a black arch of rock. She frowned and realized she was inside one of the ranging's caves. Beneath her was something soft. Iona explored it with her fingers.

She was lying on a deep, comfortable pile of animal skins. Someone must have carried her there, and draped some of the skins over her as she slept. The air in the cave was bitterly cold, but she lay surrounded by a cocoon of warmth. Reluctant to move, she stared at the blackness of the cave's roof.

'You are awake?'

The voice was Tana's. Glancing to her left Iona saw the young yeti standing close to her silhouetted against the stars.

'Yes.'

'I have brought you something to eat.' Tana held something out towards her.

Iona sat up. She hadn't been aware of it before, but now she realized that she was ravenously hungry. She fumbled for Tana's hand in the darkness, took what the yeti was holding, raised it to her mouth and bit into it.

As far as she could tell it was a piece of dried meat. It smelt like venison, and tasted strong and salty. Iona didn't care what it was. Her stomach was churning, her body was calling out for food, and she chewed at it greedily.

'In the valley you will have eaten much better, but this is all we have,' Tana said apologetically. 'It's what is left of last winter's stores. Some remained when the snows lifted. Otherwise there would be nothing.'

Iona finished the meat. She was still hungry and she longed to ask for more, but it was impossible. When she thought of the sunken faces of the yeti she'd seen on her arrival, she knew she'd been lucky Tana had given her anything. She glanced at the cave mouth again. To her surprise the sky outside seemed a little paler. It wasn't night-time, as she'd assumed when she woke, but the start of dawn. She'd slept for nearly twenty-four hours.

Iona's head swung back towards Tana. 'How is Gaggau?' she asked.

'Like you he has slept,' Tana answered. 'He too has just woken, and he is better. I stayed with him after you covered his wounds with the curd you made, then he sent me away and called for Manu. That is why I am here. Often, when Jinga allows it, I sleep by his side but this is my cave. This is the shelter I was given when I came from the holding.'

The early morning light was growing stronger every moment. In its still chill and silvery glow, Iona propped herself up on her elbow and looked at Tana more closely. The yeti was squatting on her haunches beside the pile of skins. Tana was slim and graceful. In human terms, Iona thought, she would be considered beautiful. She had long supple limbs, broad hips, firm breasts, and wide candid eyes set in a fine-boned face.

Iona thought of the valley where Tana came from. Compared with the crests it was warm and lush and hospitable.

'Don't you want to go back to the island?' she asked.

'Yes, of course I do. Sometimes it is all I think about.'

'Then why don't you go? You're grown up now. The ranging can't keep you. If they want another child, they can ask the holding for one.'

'Gaggau will not let me go. He wants to mate with me. He tries but he cannot rouse himself to place his seed. He will not accept that. He will go on and on trying until he dies. His pride will not let him stop.'

Tana's face was stricken.

Iona stared at her, appalled. She knew little about mating except what Dougal had taught her when he put the rams, the 'tups' he called them, to the ewes in her uncle's flock. That and the whispered information that had been furtively exchanged in the corridors of her school. Dougal's tups, mounting the ewes and leaving a scarlet smear on the backs of the sheep to show they had seeded them, made much more sense to Iona than what she'd heard in the corridors.

'What about Manu?' she demanded. 'Doesn't he want to return to the ranging?'

Tana nodded. 'He will not speak of it. But, yes, I am sure he does.'

'Then if you both agree, who can stop you?'

'Jinga,' Tana said bleakly. 'Jinga is Gaggau's mate. She is barren. That is why she has to allow Gaggau to lie with me. But she knows his seed will never root. She wishes me away, but she does not want Manu back. She has her own ideas for the ranging.'

'What ideas?'

Tana shook her head. 'I do not know. All I know is that Jinga thinks and plans. When she is ready she strikes like the snakes of summer as they take the birds from the trees.'

The cold crept up on Iona. She shivered, pulled the hides up to her chin and wriggled down beneath them.

In a way, she thought, both Tana and Manu were hostages. The holding and the ranging had exchanged the one for the other as children as the clans had apparently always done. The old seer, Tonemetapu, said it was for peace and to strengthen the bonds between them.

Iona could understand that. She understood now why Manu hunted with the leopard, and why he had offered her meat from his prey. It came naturally from his background. What puzzled her was why the two of them, Tana and Manu, had become trapped in the wrong places. They were both adults, they both wanted to return to their own homes, yet they were prevented. There had to be another, stronger reason than Gaggau's wish to sire a child and the fearsome Jinga's determination to keep Manu away from his birthplace.

Iona asked the female yeti. Tana thought for a long while before replying.

'Often I have wondered myself,' she said. 'Now I think perhaps I know. Here in the ranging Gaggau says the prey have vanished from the crests this season alone. It is not so. The animals have been retreating almost from the time I came here. I have a gatherer's eyes, and I have seen the loss each season in what the hunters bring back. Gaggau deceives himself in saying it is new, so does everyone, even in the holding below –'

Tana paused and frowned. Her clear, vivid eyes were also, Iona realized, intelligent and thoughtful.

'The world of the crests is changing for ever,' Tana went on. 'So, maybe, is the world of the valley. Manu and I belong to the time before the changes began, the changes no one will accept. If they let us go, if other children take our place, both the clans will have to acknowledge what is happening, for nothing can be the same again. No one wishes to do that. That is why they cling to us.'

As she struggled to take in what the slender female yeti had said, Iona's mind went to Manu. Iona had been right. Both Tana and Manu were in a sense prisoners – but it was Manu the child cared about.

'You said that Manu is with Gaggau?' she asked.

'Yes,' Tana answered. 'Manu has been waiting until Gaggau woke. Now he speaks with Gaggau alone – alone, that is, apart from Jinga. Sleep again while you can, for I think soon she will come for you.'

Manu squatted on the ground close to Gaggau's great couch. Jinga was somewhere in the darkness at the back of the cave. Manu could smell her and occasionally hear a rustle as she moved.

'I come to speak to Gaggau,' Manu said, addressing himself to the blackness beyond. 'I bring word from the holding. I speak for Yerto.'

'I stay by Gaggau's side to hear the word,' Jinga replied.

Her voice rasped with anger and challenge. Manu paused. He wished with all his heart she wasn't there. From his earliest childhood, even before he was sent to the ranging, Manu had felt her malevolence towards him.

At first it had baffled him, but slowly he began to understand the reason for it. Jinga bitterly resented her barrenness. She had grown no male to lead the ranging when Gaggau's powers failed. She blamed Gaggau for that. By some twist in her mind she also blamed Manu – and blamed him much more fiercely. She hated the fact that Manu and Gaggau were half-brothers, although in age an entire generation separated them. She hated Manu for being the natural heir to the leadership. Above all, Manu had come to realize with a shock, Jinga simply hated.

Her hatred didn't need a reason. It was a dark, destructive force which permeated her life and being. She might have chosen any target for it – Manu was the most obvious and provocative. He distrusted her deeply, yet it was something more profound than distrust that made him wish her away from the cave.

What Jinga was doing was against all custom. Manu had brought a message from the holding to the ranging, from one patriarch to the other, a message of such grave importance that Manu doubted there was any precedent for it. It concerned the very survival of both the clans. Messages between the clan leaders, even over much lesser matters, were always exchanged through their trusted couriers in private.

Later, after considering and reflecting, either patriarch might consult the whole clan. If he had a wise and experienced mate, as Yerto did in Ryena, he would certainly consult her. But the passing of the messages took place alone between the males. Jinga had no right to be in the cave. Her presence there violated all the traditions of the past.

There was nothing Manu could do about it. If Jinga had decided to stay, she would stay. Her malevolence was reinforced by her immense strength and determination. Not even Gaggau, brave old hunter that he was, would dare order her out. Manu looked at the patriarch.

Gaggau was lying back on his couch, his hands resting palms upwards on the hides. His skin was still blackened, but the blood had stopped flowing and the swelling seemed to be reduced. He was breathing more easily too, and there was less sweat trickling down his face.

'How do you feel?' Manu asked.

Gaggau grunted. 'The creature sank its teeth deep. Now perhaps its jaws are loosening.'

'That was the shumbi's doing,' Manu said.

'The shumbi? What shumbi? What has a shumbi to do with this – ?' Gaggau propped himself up on his elbow. He stared vacantly at Manu.

Gaggau's mind, Manu realized, was lost and empty. The attack by the oduna and the pain afterwards had sliced through his memory like the cut of a sharpened bone. A moment later, to Manu's surprise, Gaggau's face cleared, and he frowned.

'The shumbi,' he said. 'You brought her to me. She is small and dark and lacks fur. She sees clearly. She has eyes as green as the young reeds by the streams of snow-melt. Her eyes are steady like a hawk's and she knows the tongue of the people. Yes, I remember now. She prepared something. She spread it on where the creature gnawed at me –'

Gaggau glanced at his hands. 'Now the wounds are better.'

Manu nodded and breathed in deeply. This was the moment he had dreaded even more than when he had taken Gaggau's demand down to the valley. He had to say it. He had to get it over with. He had to do it knowing that Jinga was listening.

'The holding sent you the shumbi,' Manu said. 'They cannot allow the ranging to share the gathering of the valley. There is not enough to feed both the clans. But they wish well to the ranging, they wish to do all they can to support it through the famine. The shumbi was given to them by the snows and the river. They pass her on to you. She is the most valuable gift they can make. Thus says Yerto. Thus says Tonemetapu.'

He had spilled the words out in a flood. When he stopped, he felt as weak and drained as if he had raced all the way up to the crests to deliver the message. Now he waited.

He had expected an outburst of anger from Gaggau. There was none. The old silverback lay gazing at the cave's roof. Too tired or too confused by the pain of his wounds, he didn't seem to have taken in what Manu had said. Manu also expected an outburst from Jinga – it came with a vengeance. Jinga erupted from the blackness, ran forward and confronted him with a wild, snarling fury.

'So Yerto says we cannot share the valley?' she screamed. 'What of the bonds? Where does he think we shall eat? You have seen the females and the young. They are the same as the hunters. The animals have gone and they are all starving. How shall they feed?'

Manu scrambled to his feet. He was taller, much taller, than Jinga. Confronted with her implacable fury he felt like a child. He shook his head. There was no answer he could give her.

'Listen to me, both of you –'

It was Gaggau. Manu and Jinga turned to look at him.

'Quarrels will do nothing,' Gaggau said. 'The ranging must eat. That is all that matters. The holding have sent me the shumbi. How do you call her?'

'She is named Iona,' Kanu said.

'Iona.' Gaggau's voice stumbled awkwardly round the word. 'Very well. The shumbi Iona has healed my hands. Maybe she can find the prey that we cannot. Take her with you, Manu, and hunt.'

Gaggau paused.

'Your mind is lost!' Jinga shouted. 'The child cannot find prey. There is no prey left to find.'

'The shumbi has seven sunrises,' Gaggau said. 'I have spoken. Hunt, Manu, hunt!'

As the old patriarch dropped back on the hides, Manu glanced at his mate. The expression on the old yeti's face was dark and violent. Manu recoiled. Then he turned and walked out.

He headed for the cave to which he had carried Iona. He had no more faith than Jinga did – and that alone united them – that he, Iona and the hunters would find prey, but Gaggau had spoken.

He, Manu, and the shumbi would hunt together.

'The men are ready,' Jinga said. 'They are waiting for you.'

Iona blinked in the darkness of the cave and sat up. She could just make out the contours of Jinga's face. The old yeti's features were set in an expression that was both anxious and hostile.

Jinga was fearful of her, Iona could see that. There were pinpoints of apprehension in her eyes and puckers of worry at the corners of her mouth. She was also savagely angry. The tendons of her neck throbbed and the vein pulses flickered at her temples. Iona had no idea why. She only knew that for the first time since she had entered the valley, she had found an enemy.

'The men wish to hunt,' Jinga went on. 'Lead them to a prey.'

Iona went outside. In the beginnings of the thin morning light she could just discern the silhouette of Gaggau. The clan's patriarch was standing awkwardly, supporting himself by a branch tucked under his shoulder. Tana knelt on the ground beside him, massaging the old male's deformed foot.

Behind Gaggau were gathered the ranging's hunters. There were at least a dozen of them, all armed with hardwood clubs with a hollow notch at their bulbous ends. Into the notches had been set a piece of granite roughly chipped in the form of an axe-blade. The granite blades were bound to the shafts over and over again with dry willow fibres.

Round each of the hunters' waists was a leather loop. Some of the loops contained as many as six or eight lengths of leather, making them look like thick belts of coiled rope. The younger yeti had nothing hanging from their belts. Suspended from those of the older ones were throwing spears. Identical in shape and construction to the clubs everyone carried, the spears were much lighter and the granite blades much sharper.

'So,' Gaggau irritably pushed Tana aside and limped forward on his crutch, 'where do we range today?'

Iona stood very still.

The entire ranging was assembled behind the old yeti in the gathering dawn, not merely the hunters, but the females and the children too. It was like the evening of her arrival, but with a vast difference. Then they had assembled to inspect her as an extraordinary curiosity, an alien, a creature which had dropped from the skies into their lives.

Now they wanted something from her. She was a shumbi. She was the first to enter the valley in the memory of any of the yeti. She was a portent, a talisman, a token from the stars. She had brought, so it was said, gifts to the valley-dwellers. She had saved one of their children, and they had decided she must be shared with the crests. It was only right and proper. The ancient agreements of the cloud-time meant that they could not keep her for their own.

The holding had sent her up to the crests, with Manu as her guide and companion. That was right and proper too, for Manu belonged to the crests. Now the shumbi, the stars' gift, had to show what she could do for the mountain-dwellers.

Iona closed her eyes and trembled. She could do nothing.

35

'But what do I do?' Iona's voice was plaintive, almost despairing.

'I will be with you,' Manu answered. 'Babilla will be there too. If there is prey on the crests, between us we will find it.'

He looked at her reassuringly. Iona shivered.

Beyond the cave's mouth the sky was still dim with the last of the night. It would be an hour or more yet before the morning sun lifted over the crests. Iona clapped her arms against her chest for warmth. Her stomach felt even colder than the bitter dawn air of the ridge.

'Manu hunts with you –'

It was Gaggau's voice. Iona stared at the ranging's patriarch.

The old yeti had thrown aside the prop of his branch and dropped to the earth. Tana was crouched beside him, massaging his deformed foot again. Behind him Iona could see Jinga. The old female's eyes were penetrating and hostile.

'Go with Manu,' Gaggau went on. 'Find him prey, lead him to it. He will kill and we will eat.'

Gaggau heaved himself up and waved his hand dismissively. As he turned away Iona saw his cheeks. Their hollowness owed as much to hunger as to age.

Babilla growled. The leopard was crouched at Manu's feet. He stooped, stroked her and whispered something. Babilla's ears pricked and her tail snaked backwards and forwards. She stiffened, and for an instant stood quivering. Then she uncoiled her muscles and bounded away.

Manu's eyes followed her until the sinuous flowing shape of the animal had disappeared. Then he turned to Iona. 'The leopard leads,' he said. 'Let us hunt.'

As he beckoned to the gathered hunters, Iona reached out and took his huge splayed hand, just as once in a world so far away now it seemed to belong to dreams she'd taken Duncan's hand when they'd headed up towards the high tops, or Mr Simpson's when they'd set off into Mainwarden's woods.

Manu glanced down at her and smiled. Iona squeezed his fingers gratefully as they moved away in Babilla's tracks. She had never needed Manu's comforting presence more, but even as she felt the warmth of the thick fur on his skin she was filled with foreboding. She remembered Tana describing how the animals had been disappearing for seasons now. Instinctively, after a bare forty-eight hours of knowing her, Iona liked and trusted the young female yeti with her graceful body and her calm clear eyes. She believed what Tana had said. The rest of the yeti thought Iona was a witch, a magician, a sorcerer – perhaps even Tana thought so too.

Iona was none of those. If the animals had really left the crests, nothing would be able to conjure them back, least of all Iona herself.

They hunted for seven days.

The first morning it was almost daylight when they set off. After that they left in the darkness well before dawn. By the time they returned it was always dark again. They ranged in great sweeps along the ridges and into the upland valleys through every point of the compass. Iona didn't know the mountain landscape, but she could always tell where they were, or where they were going, by the position of the sun. The direction of their journeys changed every day.

Those days were the most exhausting Iona had ever spent – far worse than her climb up to the crests. Whenever they ascended the almost vertical wall of a gully, Manu offered to carry her. Previously she might have refused, now she accepted gratefully. She no longer minded the painful jolting and bumping as Manu heaved his way up. Anything was better than the dizzying strain on her legs.

The tiredness was the smallest part of her ordeal. Day after day her body ached, her lungs heaved and struggled for air, her eyes blurred and watered. She could have dealt with these physical demands. What she found intolerable was the burden, the pressure, that had been placed on her.

She was there as a totem, a talisman. Because she was a shumbi, she was possessed of magic. She was there to halt the yeti's hunger, to find game and fill their bellies.

There was no game.

Carrying Iona with them, Manu and the hunters scoured the crests. They criss-crossed the ravines and woodlands. They searched the high saddles, and the lonely hidden pastures by the watercourses. They ventured into territory the ranging had never hunted before. They cast Babilla in front of them and watched to see whether the leopard could scent what they did not.

Babilla sniffed the air. She drew it in through her nostrils, examined the messages it was carrying, and discarded them. There was nothing to engage her hunting instincts. Puzzled and uncertain, she turned and loped back to Manu. She lay beside him, panting. Manu reached down and scratched her head. The leopard's ribs were as hollow and sunken as any of the hunters'.

The days weren't entirely barren. Twice Babilla put up a wild boar sow with a litter of young. The first time the sow escaped, although the leopard killed four of the litter. On the second occasion the hunters managed to trap another sow in a gully, and they killed nine animals including the mother. Most days one of the hunters – it was almost always Manu – felled a bird or a monkey with his throwing club.

Every prey, however small, was carefully divided. The first part was given to the leopard. It was vital that Babilla kept up her strength since, apart from Iona, she was their best hope of finding game. The next share went to the hunters themselves. It was almost as important that they fed as the leopard did, for if they lost their strength the whole ranging would fail. Then if any food remained, it was carried back to the caves.

It wasn't enough, it was nothing like enough. What they killed wasn't even adequate to feed themselves, let alone the old, the females and the young of the ranging for whom they were hunting. It was exactly the same on the seventh day as on the first. They returned empty-handed.

The time Gaggau had given them had elapsed. The shumbi's spells were powerless. The crests held no animals and the ranging were left hungry.

That last evening they came in slowly as the dusk gathered. Propped on his club, Gaggau waited outside the cave mouth watching for them.

Raku, leading the final sweep through the forest line, was the first to appear. The summer grass was rising thick and green and sweet in the glades between the trees. It was there, earlier in the week, that the leopard Babilla had flushed the two sets of boar. At the week's end, with the meadow cover higher and more succulent still, there should have been not only boar but wild goats, muntjac, musk deer, perhaps even bear and their cubs.

There was nothing.

The hunters had trawled the woodland behind Raku and crossed it in silence. Silence from them and silence from the glades. At the end, standing on a mound beyond where the trees fell away, Raku looked back at them and spread his empty hands wide. Manu nodded grimly. He raised his arm and pointed in the direction of the caves.

The grounds were empty and the hunt was over.

Raku vanished. He was tired and his belly ached with hunger. He set off for the caves to call in his day's share of the cloud-time stores – it would be meagre enough but it was better than the emptiness that was shrinking him now. Behind him Penga and Soru followed. They had each led one of the wings of the sweep, and they had seen Manu's command. They too were famished.

The other younger hunters, the apprentices of the ranging, trudged wearily after them. Manu turned and scanned the trees for Iona. He had been carrying her, but he had put her down for the final drive. He saw her now. She was kneeling by a thicket of rhododendron with her arm over Babilla's neck, stroking the leopard's head. Manu called to her and Iona came over to join him, Babilla padding behind.

'Nothing?' she asked.

His face sombre, Manu shook his head. 'We go back to the caves.'

'What will happen tomorrow?'

'That is for Gaggau to decide. He may tell us to try again. Perhaps he could even lead the ranging to a new territory.'

'He would take them away from the caves?'

Iona was startled. Somehow she'd sensed the ranging had inhabited the caves for ever. She couldn't conceive of them living anywhere else.

'It has happened twice in long-ago seasons,' Manu said. 'We talk of it in cloud-time. When the game returned then, the ranging came back to the caves. Now it will be more difficult –'

He lifted his head and scanned the horizon. Iona followed his gaze.

The distant peaks glittered white in the setting sun. Between where they stood and the distant snows, the evening mist was already filling the ravines. It swallowed up the woodland and the mountain flanks and the soaring twisting ridges, until only the crests were left above the grey obscuring haze.

'New grounds will be hard to find,' Manu finished.

'But there is the valley?'

Manu nodded grimly. He didn't speak.

Iona looked at him. She knew Manu was torn between his allegiance to the ranging, his birthplace, and to the holding, where he'd grown up. Whatever happened in the dispute between the two clans, one of them would suffer. Manu would suffer anyway. He was suffering now.

'I have failed you, Manu,' Iona said miserably. 'I could not find game.'

'You have failed no one,' Manu said. 'I trust Babilla to find the animals when I cannot. Even you and Babilla could not find them. If a shumbi and a leopard together cannot find prey, the reason is clear. The prey has gone. It is no fault of yours –'

Manu glanced down at her. At that moment Babilla raised her head and licked Iona's fingers. Unthinkingly, frowning in concentration, Iona rubbed the leopard's cheek. Babilla's eyes narrowed contentedly.

Manu laughed. He stretched out his hand and touched Iona's hair. 'Look,' he said. 'Babilla is as hungry as anyone, but she doesn't blame you. She trusts you. Babilla trusts few and frightens many. In both the holding and the ranging, most will not come near her.'

'Then they're stupid,' Iona answered. 'Babilla's just a cat. I've got a cat at Mainwarden, at home. She's only got one eye and she's called Misty –' She stopped. For an instant her eyes blurred with tears.

Mainwarden and everything it stood for – from her mother to Misty, from Mr Simpson to the summer smell of the strawberries in the walled garden, but above all for its safety – had never left her for an instant since she was swept down into the valley. Mainwarden haunted her dreams. It hovered beyond the trees in all her waking hours beneath the Himalayan sunlight. Until now it had seemed lost and remote, the centre of a world she had known in another life.

Not any longer. Touching the leopard's cheek, saying Misty's name, suddenly brought it back to Iona with a physical shock. Mainwarden was very close. It was with her now. The shelters on the island and the caves on the crests were the rooms of Mainwarden. The leopard was Misty. The monsters which had prowled into Iona's nightmares along Mainwarden's corridors were all round her in the valley and here on the crests.

Manu was one of them. Manu who a moment ago had laughed and ruffled her hair. The blind and gentle Kekua was another. So were the placid Churinga and the doe-eyed Tana. Iona shook her head and blinked away her tears. Everything had changed. Everything that once was clear and simple had become confused.

'Why has it happened, Manu?' she demanded. 'Why have the animals gone?'

'I do not know,' Manu replied. 'No one knows. But for myself I believe it may be because of what is also spoken of in cloud-time. Many, many seasons ago there was a time when prey thronged the grounds as never before. There was food for everyone. The ranging grew in numbers. The more the ranging grew the more mouths there were to feed. The hunters were out every day. Eventually the animals could not support the killings made among them. The prey dwindled and retreated. As they did, so the size of the ranging fell because of starvation. At the end the ranging was smaller than when it started.'

'But the ranging is already small,' Iona objected. 'And still there are no animals.'

'It is not the ranging who are killing now,' Manu said. 'The killing is happening outside the grounds, although it moves always closer. It is being done by the oduna and maybe others. Whoever it is, the result is the same. The animals are vanishing.' He was silent.

They had reached the top of the last ridge before the caves. Below them the ground sloped down to the mountain shelf that housed the ranging. The rest of the hunting party had returned. They were gathered in the last of the sunlight in a circle round the unmistakable figure of Gaggau, his pelt gleaming white and his body tilted awkwardly over the branch he was using to support himself.

As they watched, Gaggau turned and shouted something towards the entrance to his cave. Jinga appeared. She seemed to be speaking to the patriarch, although she was too far away for either Manu or

Iona to hear her voice. As she finished, Gaggau stiffened. He stood for a moment, frozen, then he caught up his crutch and hurled it at the female yeti. Jinga vanished back into the cave.

As Gaggau let go of the branch a great roar echoed up the mountain flank. Iona tensed. It was a sound unlike anything she'd ever heard, full of mingled fury and anguish. At her side Manu tensed too and Babilla pricked her ears and growled.

'Quick!' Manu said urgently. 'We must go back. Something has happened – something very bad.'

He bounded away down the slope, the leopard racing ahead of him. Leaping from rock to rock, Iona hurried after them.

36

Wengen appeared on the path that led up to the caves.

It was two days earlier, the morning of the sixth day of the hunt. As usual the hunters had left before dawn and wouldn't be back before dusk. Hidden by the shadow inside the cave mouth, Jinga watched Wengen intently.

The big yeti from the valley came closer, walking with the slow, ambling stride of the holding. As he passed the cave mouth she backed deeper into the darkness. He disappeared from her sight and Jinga came forward again. She peered cautiously out into the spreading sunlight.

Wengen was climbing up above the caves. Jinga, who had been watching him ever since his arrival, knew exactly where he was going. For some reason Wengen liked to place himself on a vantage point. He'd chosen a spur above the caves, where he could survey the activities of the ranging without anyone being aware of his presence. Jinga also knew what he would be doing now.

Wengen would be feeding. Saliva dribbled from Jinga's mouth at the thought.

Wengen was a gatherer. He took his carefully apportioned share of the ranging's cloud-time stores – the swiftly dwindling stock of last season's wind-dried meat on which they'd all been forced to depend – but he gathered too. Jinga didn't know what he gathered. Gathering was a skill she'd never learned. It belonged to the valley. Whatever Wengen gathered, it was enough to keep him sleek and healthy – much healthier than any of the ranging yeti.

Wengen never shared what he found on the ledges of the crests. He kept it for himself. Apart from Jinga, the yeti were too preoccupied with their hunger to wonder what he was doing as he set out day after day, let alone why he remained so full-bellied. But Jinga knew. She knew that for Wengen not to share his cropping was a violation of the bonds. Jinga didn't resent it, though her own stomach was aching to be filled.

Wengen was cunning. He could feed himself even in a time of famine. She respected him for that, more than if he'd parcelled out his gatherings with the ranging's infants. Unlike Gaggau, Wengen was a survivor.

Gaggau.

Jinga glanced round at her mate with contempt. The old patriarch was asleep. The shumbi had dressed his wounds three times since she'd first made the strange yellow paste from the females' milk. The wounds seemed to be healing now. At least the shumbi had done that. It was all she had done – and it was unimportant. With his club-foot and the whitening burden of the seasons, Gaggau would never hunt effectively again whether he were healed or not.

What the shumbi hadn't been able to do was find prey for the ranging. The hunters had gone out on six mornings now. Each night they'd returned almost empty-handed. Even the vaunted Manu had been unable to kill. Jinga knew why. What was left of the prey had migrated to the valley. If the ranging hunted there, they could kill and eat as they'd done in the past.

All that stopped them was the stubbornness of the holding's patriarch, Yerto. His stubbornness – and his deceit. He'd sent them the shumbi as a gift from the stars, so he claimed, to be shared. Yerto was lying. The shumbi wasn't a gift. She was a half-drowned rat who'd been washed into the valley from the distant mountains.

The shumbi had certain skills, that was all. What the ranging needed was not a shumbi child's skills, but prey. The child had shown she was incapable of giving them that.

Jinga looked at Gaggau again. Now he was snoring. She sneered derisively, then paused and thought for a moment. Absently, she picked up a twig from the cave floor. The twig's bark had been worn away and the wood beneath was shiny with grease. Jinga frowned. Then she recognized it.

It was the twig Gaggau used to draw his elaborate maps in the sand showing where the hunters were to go, and how they should follow their quarry. The maps were a fantasy. There was nowhere for them to go, no quarry left to follow. Jinga snapped the twig between her fingers and tossed it away. Suddenly, her mind made up, she rose to her feet. Without another glance at Gaggau, she walked out of the cave.

*

'You have fed?' Jinga asked. She was squatting opposite Wengen on the spur above the caves.

'The ranging feeds me,' Wengen replied. 'I feed well.'

When Jinga appeared Wengen had risen and greeted her with the nose-scratching gesture of the holding. The old female had returned the greeting. Now they faced each other on their haunches.

'You do not feed well here,' Jinga said bluntly. 'You feed on the leavings of our cloud-time stores. So do we all. The leavings will not last much longer. You have the knowledge of the valley. You can gather.'

Wengen gave her a slow sly smile. 'I do not wish to be a burden on the ranging, so I gather what I can.'

Scattered round his feet were the husks of nuts and the skins of berries. Jinga looked down at the litter and up at Wengen's face again. 'The winter fat cloaks you deep and well.'

Wengen lifted his shoulders and glanced away. He said nothing.

It was true. Unlike the emaciated bodies of the ranging yeti, Wengen was well fleshed and his pelt gleamed. Again Jinga felt no envy, only admiration and respect.

'For the sixth day Manu hunts with the shumbi,' Jinga went on. 'Apart from "insects", they have not killed yet. They have brought us back nothing. They will not kill today.'

Wengen gave another silent heave of his shoulders.

'The reason is simple,' Jinga continued insistently. 'The animals are not here. They are in the valley. That is where our clan should be hunting. We should be sharing the valley with the holding. Yerto forbids it.'

'So I have heard.' Wengen spoke at last. 'My father does not consult me. He shares his counsels with one of your people, with Manu. I am only here as companion to Manu and the shumbi.'

'Gaggau is old, your father is old,' Jinga said. 'Both of them are old and foolish and full of pride. Between them they will destroy us all. They must be stopped before they do so.'

'How are they to be stopped?' Wengen asked. He still managed to appear only mildly interested.

Jinga knew it was nothing more than a façade. Wengen was Yerto's eldest son. He was deeply and passionately involved in what was taking place, but his position as Yerto's heir to the leadership of the holding was being eroded daily by Manu. His status in the hierarchy of the clan, his entire life and future, depended on the outcome of the dispute between the two patriarchs.

'Your father does not trust you,' Jinga said brutally. 'He trusts only Manu. Yerto has disowned you. If he has his way, Manu will lead the holding and you will be nothing. Here on the crests, Gaggau has no one to follow him. He holds blindly to Tana because he still believes he can seed her. He will believe it until he is carried out to the birds.'

'Even if this is true,' Wengen said, 'what can I do?'

He no longer feigned lack of interest. His face was alert and flushed with anger and Jinga knew she had touched him on the rawest parts of his being.

'Take Tana away from here,' the old female said softly. 'Take her back to the valley. It is where she comes from, where she belongs. On the way, cover her and seed her –' She paused and licked her lips.

'The seed spills out of you, Wengen. I sense it, I can almost feel it,' Jinga hissed. 'Would that such seed had been poured into me, but the old one is barren. Fill Tana with your seed instead, and present her to Yerto, swelling. He has no choice but to accept that. On the crests you will have broken Gaggau's dream of the girl, and she will be lost to him. The old cripple, too, will accept that. All he can do then is call Manu back from the island. With Manu gone, the holding is yours.'

Wengen gazed out into the gathering dusk.

Apart from sexual arousal he rarely felt excitement, least of all in matters needing thought. Wengen was shrewd but cautious. His mind worked slowly and methodically. He sifted carefully through a problem until he found the answer, then he acted on it. Now for once he felt excitement, instant exhilarating excitement, pour over him.

From the moment he'd seen Jinga, Wengen sensed the haggard old female was an ally. He didn't know why. Maybe it was her eyes – pitiless and unforgiving, they were like his own. Perhaps it was the set of her mouth – greedy and tight with suppressed anger, that was his, too. Or was it just something she exuded – a hardness, an implacable determination, a ruthless desire to succeed and conquer?

Whatever it was, it had found echoes deep inside Wengen. Now he understood why. Jinga was filled with hatred. So was he. They both hated the same things – Gaggau, Yerto, Manu, the shumbi, the whole elaborate network of deceits that bound the ranging and the holding together. The difference was that the old female could define them and make them plain. More important, she had an answer to them. Jinga knew how to deal with the hatreds.

'I cannot take Tana,' Wengen said slowly. 'She would not come. If I tried to carry her away by force, she would alert the ranging. They would seize her and bring her back.'

'Not if I am with you,' Jinga answered. 'Tana will come with me.'

'With you?' Wengen stared at her. 'You will come too?'

'As far as I am needed, yes,' Jinga nodded. 'When you are beyond the caves, when you have seeded her, I will return. After that you have nothing to fear.'

'When is this to be done?'

'Tomorrow,' Jinga said. 'It is the last day Gaggau has given the shumbi to find prey. All the hunters will be out with Manu and the child. After they leave in the morning Gaggau sleeps again. Listen –'

Wengen leant forward and listened.

'Tana!' Jinga called softly to the young yeti.

Tana turned from where she stood by Gaggau's couch. It was not yet dawn but the hunting party had long since left. The old patriarch had watched them stride away, the little shumbi walking ahead, before returning to his cave. He had fallen asleep again, and Tana was covering him with hides to protect him from the cold until the sun rose.

Jinga stood at the cave mouth, beckoning. For an instant Tana stared at her, puzzled. Her relationship with Jinga was marked on the old female's side by anger, hostility and abuse. It had always been so, but for once Jinga looked almost kindly. Tana arranged the last hide and walked warily over to join her.

Jinga took her arm and led her away from the cave until their voices couldn't waken Gaggau.

'He is better?' Jinga asked.

Tana nodded. Iona had twice more made the paste from the females' breast milk and anointed Gaggau with it. The paste was working slowly, perhaps because of Gaggau's age, but each day Tana could see the wounds healing.

'That is good,' Jinga said. 'But he needs more than the shumbi's skills. Gaggau needs food.'

That was true for the entire ranging of course, Tana thought. But Jinga was right – Gaggau, old and wounded, had even more urgent need of food than the others. He was eating a fraction of what he normally ate at that time of year. Until there was enough to feed him properly, Gaggau would never recover.

'Maybe the hunters will kill today,' Tana suggested.

'They will not kill,' Jinga said crisply. 'Not even a shumbi can find game when the game has gone –'

She paused. 'There is another way to feed Gaggau and make him well.'

Tana glanced at her, startled. 'Another way?'

Jinga nodded her head on her thin neck. 'Wengen came with you from the valley. He is a skilled gatherer. Even here on the crests he has been gathering. Have you not seen his condition, the way his pelt gleams? Have you not wondered why? Did you think he survives on his share of the cloud-time stores?'

Tana frowned. She hadn't thought about it until then, but it was true. When Wengen arrived just ahead of Manu and the shumbi, his plumpness contrasted starkly with the hollow ribs and sunken faces of the ranging. Now the ranging yeti were even more emaciated, while Wengen remained as sleek and well fleshed as when he had first appeared.

'Wengen has found places to harvest,' Jinga continued insistently. 'He has offered to share his harvesting so we may feed Gaggau. There is not enough for everyone, so you and I must gather with Wengen alone. No one else must know. But Gaggau is the son of the great hunter, Burra. If we return him to health, he will find game even where the shumbi cannot. Then all the ranging will eat.'

Tana hesitated. She understood clearly what Jinga had said – and she knew it was wrong. It was wrong of Wengen to have gathered for himself alone without sharing with the ranging. It violated the bonds. But Wengen at least came from the valley. He was a stranger to the crests, and his membership of the other clan gave him some excuse for his behaviour.

There was no such excuse for Jinga and herself. Jinga came from the ranging. Tana herself, even if she was born in the valley, had grown up on the crests. She belonged to the ranging as much as to the holding. If either she or the old female yeti found a source of food, they were bound to share it – with the ranging's skeletal hunters, its dull-eyed mothers, and their feverish, swollen-bellied children.

'I must think,' Tana said desperately.

'You have no time to think,' Jinga answered brutally. 'Wengen has made his offer. He wishes to save Gaggau and the holding. He is waiting now to show us the hidden harvest and how we may crop it. I know where he will meet us. Do you come with me or not?'

Tana closed her eyes.

For most of her life Gaggau had been a father to her – the father she'd lost when she left the valley. He had to be fed. If he wasn't, he would never hunt again. He wouldn't even survive the coming cloud-time. She was doing wrong, a far graver wrong than Wengen, but she had no choice.

Miserably Tana nodded.

'Then come with me.'

Jinga caught her arm again. Tana tried to turn back towards the cave, but Jinga tugged her away. 'You need nothing from there,' she said abruptly. 'We go now.'

She drew Tana along the shelf and down one of the paths that led to the ravines below.

Wengen waited for them in a clearing not far from the caves.

It was still dark and he was standing beneath a tree. He remained deep in the shadow until they were only a few paces from him, then he stepped out into the open. Tana halted in mid-stride. The dawn wind was blowing from the crests behind her and she hadn't scented his presence. She peered at him uncertainly.

Although he came from the valley, Tana had no memory of Wengen. He must have been a presence in the holding during her early childhood, but when he arrived at the caves it was as if she was seeing him for the first time. He was tall and heavily built with a smooth strong body overlaid by thick layers of fat. Supple and confident, with a glowing pale-haired pelt, by the standards of the valley yeti he was a perfect example of their best young males.

For some indefinable reason Tana didn't trust him. There was something sly and arrogant, even menacing, about Wengen. His pale eyes were close-set and sleepy. The morning hunting conferences were vitally important to the ranging. Wengen listened to them with a casual, almost contemptuous indifference. When the hunters set out he departed on what Tana knew now were his own gathering expeditions – selfish expeditions that the bonds forbade.

Tana swallowed. She was about to do exactly what in her mind she had been accusing him of, even if in her case it was on behalf of Gaggau. Trying to shake off her anxiety, she hesitated.

Wengen came forward. He looked at Jinga and nodded. The old female had been holding Tana by one arm ever since they left the caves. Now Wengen took her other arm. Between them they began to hurry Tana further down through the darkness.

They moved so quickly, Wengen on one side and Jinga on the other, that Tana barely knew what was happening. So far, she had felt only guilt and apprehension. Guilt at the secrecy about the harvest they'd come to collect, and apprehension about Wengen. Now, stumbling on the path in the gathering dawn light, she sensed she was being swept up in something more furtive and dangerous. Frantically Tana tried to calm herself.

Jinga was Gaggau's senior mate. Wengen was a member of the holding like she was – he was even the patriarch's son. If the two of them were guiding her down from the caves, how could it be wrong? But if it wasn't wrong, why had they, one from the crests and the other from the valley, joined forces in the night? Why did their hands grip her so tightly that her arms felt bruised and aching?

Bewildered and frightened, Tana ran on between them. Twice, when they paused to check their direction against the star pattern and the thin scent drift, she tried to question them. Each time Jinga harshly cut her off.

'Am I not Gaggau's mate?' she demanded. 'Is not Wengen from the holding? Are we not going to gather to save the old hunter?'

Distraught, Tana nodded.

'Then you are safe,' Jinga went on. 'Trust us. We are doing what is right.'

The three of them plunged on again. Tana knew only that they were heading down towards the valley.

As dawn came they stopped. 'Rest here,' Jinga instructed Tana. The old yeti moved away.

Tana sank to her haunches. The ranging's females didn't accompany the hunters, and she was unused to the pace she'd been forced to keep up over the past hour. She leant back wearily against a rock, feeling increasingly confused and frightened. Jinga had said they were going out to gather for Gaggau. They hadn't gathered. Instead Wengen and the old female had dragged her between them away from the ranging almost as if she had been a prisoner.

Tana glanced over at where the two were standing together, speaking to each other in whispers. She fought down her tiredness and unease, and gathered her courage. She would challenge them. She would demand to know what they were doing. If they were going to gather for Gaggau in an effort to help the patriarch recover, then they should start immediately. If they weren't, she was going to return to the caves.

Tana began to get to her feet. As she moved, the other two swung round. From the ferocity of their expressions, Tana thought in bewilderment, she might almost have been a prey animal trying to escape. Wengen strode quickly towards her. With her eyes fixed on Wengen's face, Tana didn't see where Jinga went although she sensed the old female had scurried behind her.

As she looked at Wengen, Tana's stomach went cold and she felt the hairs rise and prickle on her neck. Wengen's eyes were narrowed, and his features were set in cold, brutal triumph.

'The time has come for you to be taken back to the holding, Tana.' Wengen's voice was gloating. 'It is also time for you to be seeded. It is for me to do both.'

Wengen was fondling his groin. Appalled, Tana glanced down. She saw him swell and harden until what seemed like a thick branch was spearing out between his thighs. Her head lifted again dizzily.

It had all been a lie. There was never any intention to gather for Gaggau. Only a plan made by the two of them to trick her away from the caves, so that Wengen could mount her and carry her back seeded to the holding. It was worse than a lie, worse even than the deceit of gathering for the patriarch without sharing with the others.

Tana could only be returned to the island or given for seeding by the clans' two old leaders. What Jinga and Wengen were doing was the worst violation of the bonds Tana had ever known. She opened her mouth to scream. At the same instant she started to whirl round to run for the safety of the crests.

Tana was right – Jinga had slipped behind her. As Tana screamed but before she could move, Jinga's hands seized her elbows. The female was old but she was still strong. She used her strength swiftly and viciously, kicking Tana in the knee and then hurling her sideways as Tana's legs buckled with pain.

Tana fell to the ground. She lay on her back half stunned. Before she could move, Wengen was on top of her. She tried to fight him off but he was too heavy and powerful. She slipped back, her legs parted, and felt the big yeti force his way into her. He entered her and pumped savagely up and down, gripping her throat with his hands until Tana began to lose consciousness.

She choked. The raw hurt between her legs, the suffocating weight, Wengen's short greedy grunts echoing in her ears, the pressure of his hands, all of them were unbearable. Her last memory before she lost consciousness was Jinga's excited voice screaming as she urged Wengen on.

Tana had no idea how long it was before she opened her eyes again. She felt a different pain this time, a pain like a club rhythmically battering her head. Her eyelids fluttered and opened. She was still lying on her back. Blood and saliva were trickling down her chin. There was a shadow above her, Wengen's shadow. Jinga had vanished but the big island yeti was kneeling at her side and slapping her face.

'Get up!' Tana heard him shout violently. 'We go to the holding. I am taking you as my gift to my father, Yerto. The old one has always wanted a male child seeded by me. Perhaps this time his wish is granted.'

Wengen's pale eyes blinked and he laughed. He pulled Tana to her feet and set off. Tana wept. Helplessly she trudged downwards behind him.

37

'No! No! No!'

Manu and Iona had heard Gaggau's shouts from the ridge above. They were still ringing out when the two of them reached the caves, terrible incoherent bellows of fury and despair. The other yeti of the ranging had backed away from him. They were squatting in a circle in front of the caves, watching Gaggau in terror and awe as he raged backwards and forwards in frenzy between them.

Manu looked at him. Then he glanced swiftly back at Iona. 'Wait here!' he said. 'Gaggau is dangerous. Do not go near him. Guard her!'

His eyes engaged the leopard's. His hand was outspread and pointing at Iona. Babilla snarled and lowered herself on to her belly with her head resting on Iona's feet. The warning growls lifting from the leopard vibrated through the child's body.

Motionless, Iona waited.

Manu strode behind the circle of the transfixed yeti and entered Gaggau's cave. He did not have to call for the old female. Jinga had seen him coming, and was waiting for him.

'It was not me,' she said. 'I had nothing to do with it.'

Her eyes were fierce and her voice was defiantly aggressive, but there was almost a whine in it too. Manu knew at once that whatever she said, Jinga would be lying.

'What has happened?' he asked.

'Wengen has taken Tana back to the holding,' she answered. 'He has seeded her and he will present her to Yerto seeded. That is all.'

Manu looked at her in disbelief.

Tana had been given in guardianship to the ranging, just as he'd been given to the holding. Only the two patriarchs could sanction the return of either of them, and their decision depended on the assent of a full council of the clans and an agreement to a new exchange of children between the island and the crests. It had never been otherwise from the time the first Burra, the great hunter from whom Manu's mother took her name, led the ranging up from the valley.

'Who decided this?' Manu asked quietly.

'Hunger,' Jinga answered. 'The hunger that we have. The hunger that you in the valley do not know. You are living, but we die. Wengen knows it. You do not. You were born here but you do not belong here –!' The old female's voice rose to a scream. 'You do not belong anywhere among the people, Manu!'

Jinga broke off. Manu was silent.

After his many seasons' absence from the crests, Manu knew he was considered almost a stranger among the caves. Jinga was a true member of the clan. She was much older than Manu and she was mate to the patriarch, his brother Gaggau. She was feared by the ranging, but she was also respected for her cunning and hardness. Everything about Jinga, not least at that moment her violence, should have made Manu fear and respect her too.

It did not.

In the hunting vocabulary of the ranging there was a word, 'ka-kanawai'. The hunters used it to describe a plan or a device for luring and trapping prey in places where the animals would not normally go. Manu had explained it to Iona while they'd been quartering the mountain flanks, and she had quickly grasped its meaning. To her it stood for a trap, a decoy, a stratagem. Above all, it stood for deceit.

Jinga was using ka-kanawai. She and Wengen had planned something together – Manu didn't know why or what its final purpose was. Across his mind flashed the possibility that perhaps even Wengen didn't fully understand. But Jinga had devised a plot whose end would be deadly, and the realization removed any fear of the old female that Manu might have had.

He stared at Jinga for a moment longer. Then, without speaking, he turned and walked out of the cave.

The entrance to the shelter in the mountain flank was low and as Manu emerged he had to duck his head beneath the natural lintel of the rock. He stood up on the starlit surface of the shelf and glanced round. The energy that had fuelled Gaggau's rage and grief was spent. The patriarch was slumped against a boulder with his club-foot propped out in front of him.

The torment that had goaded him into madness had stretched and broken open some of the unhealed wounds on his legs. The thorn clips had parted and runnels of blood flowed down his skin. The blood congealed quickly in the cold of the approaching night, but when the sun rose after dawn it would begin to run again.

Manu went over to him. Gaggau's eyes were open but his head was lowered on his chest and he was muttering vacantly to himself.

'The night's cold is coming fast, Gaggau,' Manu said quietly. 'Here you will be chilled. You must go to the cave.'

He tried to lift the old yeti, but Gaggau's huge inert weight was more than he could manage to raise without wrenching him awkwardly. Manu turned and snapped at the nearest two young hunters. 'Help me!'

The glazed expressions vanished from their faces. They leapt to their feet and ran over.

'No!'

Suddenly, inexplicably, the torpor left Gaggau. He pushed Manu aside and heaved himself to his feet on his own. Balancing himself on his one good leg, he blinked and stared round the shelf, his gaze taking in the circle of the yeti and Manu standing at his shoulder.

'There is no prey,' he said. His voice was dull and slurred, but life was coming back into his eyes.

'None that we can find,' Manu agreed.

'Wengen has taken Tana,' Gaggau went on. 'He has mounted her. Your hunting and my sleep allowed him to do it. Do you know that?'

Manu said nothing.

'It is true.' Every moment Gaggau's eyes grew clearer and his voice sharper. 'But Wengen does not act alone. Yerto is behind him. Yerto is behind everything. He wants to keep us from the valley. He sent us the shumbi pretending she would show us animals. She cannot. Now he takes the best of his young females back. He knows I have no child and he denies me the last chance to seed one. He is doing all he can to weaken the ranging.'

Gaggau broke off.

Manu waited. Everything Gaggau had said was wrong. It wasn't Yerto who'd sent Iona to the crests, but the old seer, Tonemetapu. Yerto hadn't ordered Tana back to the valley. That was something, Manu was certain, Jinga and Wengen had agreed between them. He didn't know why, he only knew that the old female was devious and dangerous.

Manu looked at Gaggau. There was no point in telling him the truth. The patriarch was alert again, but the strangeness still lay on his face. He had made up his mind, and nothing was going to change it.

'What will you do now?' Manu asked.

'We will go down to the valley,' Gaggau answered. 'Yerto has tried to stop us, but he has not succeeded. Now he must accept the bonds. We cannot feed here, so we must share with the ranging. You will go first with the shumbi and tell him we are coming –'

Gaggau stopped again. He glanced round as if he were searching for something, then saw what he was looking for. It was his hunting club, the club Manu had seen him hurl in frenzy at Jinga. It was lying outside the cave mouth.

Gaggau lurched away from Manu to pick it up. He took one step and almost toppled to the ground. Manu reached out and gripped him before he fell. Gaggau twisted his head round and shouted at Raku.

'Bring it to me!'

Raku ran forward. He gave Gaggau the club and returned to the circle of the squatting yeti. Gaggau supported himself on the club and pushed Manu away.

'I am Gaggau, so listen well!' he shouted. 'You have hunted and you have not found. The shumbi has hunted and she has not found. The prey has left us. The prey favours the valley –'

Gaggau began to tap the head of the club rhythmically on the ground. 'So we will go to the valley. We will hunt and find and kill. In the valley we will eat! In the valley we will eat!'

To the drumming of the club, Gaggau chanted the phrase again and again. The yeti began to call it out too. Their feet picked up the club's rhythm and they began to stamp. Rocking from side to side they rose. The circle closed in on Gaggau, retreated, then surrounded him again.

The sound of the shouts and the drumming feet increased. It echoed off the mountain wall, and spilled away like tumbling water into the ravine below. The noise sucked the rest of the ranging – the old, the females and the children – from their caves. They gathered behind the hunters and added their voices until the chant was deafening.

'In the valley we will eat! In the valley we will eat!'

In the darkness behind the tramping, eddying circle, Iona stood very still, her hand still resting on Babilla's neck. Beneath her fingers the leopard's hairs rose and bristled.

38

'I am sorry, sir, it is the dispute with India –'

The trim young Nepali woman smiled brightly and apologetically at Robert Cabot from behind the area of the reception desk which enclosed the hotel switchboard.

'All our international calls must be routed through there. Since the border troubles there are often delays. Please be patient and I will try again. As soon as there is a connection, I will tell you.'

Cabot swore under his breath. He started to glower at the young woman, but she was too pretty to be angry with and he knew it wasn't her fault.

'I'll be in the bar,' he said. 'Page me there. Whatever happens, keep trying because I'm going to stay there until you get through, even if it takes the whole goddamn day.'

'Yes, sir.'

Walking away across the lobby Cabot heard her dialling again. He went into the hotel bar, slumped down in a chair by the window and called for a whisky. He was tired and when the drink came he sipped it gratefully. As the alcohol seeped into him and began to take the edge off his fatigue, he swung round and gazed out over Kathmandu.

Cabot had returned there less than two hours ago. He wasn't sure how long it was since he'd been in the city last. Three weeks? Four? Or even a lifetime? He didn't know and although at that moment a lifetime felt most likely, it was probably only a month. If it was, it had certainly been the worst month of his life. Without Roshan he would never have survived it, not without losing his sanity.

Although Cabot had travelled with the Sherpa for years, it was only over the past few weeks that he'd really come to know the man. Ever since Iona's disappearance Roshan had advised him, guided him, counselled him, and above all restrained him – restrained him first when in a frenzy of worry and impatience Cabot had been about to attack the demented scarlet-eyed Welshman, and then again and again as the days and then the weeks passed.

'I have friends,' Hughes had said with his maniacal laugh. He wouldn't explain any further. Soon afterwards he left the ridge, promising to return in forty-eight hours.

After Hughes disappeared, Roshan checked Cabot for the second time. Cabot believed the Welshman – the evidence of the prints in the snow was impossible not to believe – but he didn't trust him. He wanted Hughes followed and Cabot couldn't do it himself. He was too lame and in any event he didn't know the mountains, but Roshan and the other Sherpas were well capable of tracking the man wherever he went.

Roshan shook his head. 'No, sir,' the Sherpa said. 'If the yeti have Miss Iona, they will know we are coming long before we are close to them. They will take her away. We will not find her.'

'For Christ's sake, Roshan, if they know we're coming, they'll know he's coming too.'

'He says he has friends, sir. Maybe they protect him.'

'Friends? Who the hell are these friends?'

Roshan rubbed his chin. 'I think this man knows more than he tells us. Not about Miss Iona, but about the yeti. I think maybe he has a way of coming close to them that we do not –'

The Sherpa paused and shrugged. 'I think we must trust him, sir.'

Hughes didn't return after the promised forty-eight hours. Cabot allowed another day to go by and then at Roshan's urging yet another. When there was still no sign of the Welshman as dusk fell on the fourth day, Cabot's patience snapped.

'Roshan!' Cabot called out and waited impatiently for the Sherpa to come to him.

By then nearly a week had passed since the storm and the appalling realization that the child had vanished. The mood in the camp was dark and sombre, almost one of mourning. The porters and the other Sherpas no longer talked and laughed by the fire at night, they sat hunched over the flames in silence. Sharma, Roshan's wife, who unlike her husband spoke no English, occasionally came across to Cabot and touched his shoulder in silent sympathy. Her beaming smile had gone, and her plump face was harrowed with grief.

In Cabot himself the torment had become almost unendurable. He blamed himself for not insisting the child slept in his own tent – although he knew that Iona was an energetic and capable child on the verge of womanhood and the blame was entirely irrational. At times, even more irrationally, he blamed himself for bringing her to the Himalayas at all. He thought of her mother, his niece Dorelia, and he was haunted with guilt. The prospect of trying to tell Dorelia what had happened to her daughter while she was in his care chilled him far more than the icy temperatures of the mountain nights.

Above all, deep inside himself, Cabot felt an aching sense of loss. He had never married, he had no children, the self-contained little girl with her fearless green eyes and her direct enquiring mind was his only stake in the future. No one else had that relationship with the child, yet somehow he had let her slip not just through his own hands but, if Hughes were right, into the grasp of creatures from pre-history.

'Yes, sir?'

Roshan had come up to him and was squatting down by the fire in the darkness.

'We've waited long enough, far too long,' Cabot said. 'That man, the Welshman, he's mad. Christ knows what he was doing, but he's not coming back. I should never have figured he would. At first light tomorrow you're going to send your best runner back to Kathmandu. I'm going to call in all the helicopters they've got, the military, everything. We're going to search this place like it's never been searched. I should have done it right at the start. If the kid's alive we're going to find her –'

Cabot paused and a shudder ran over his body. 'If she's not, we'll still find her.'

'No, sir.'

Roshan's voice was quiet and emphatic. Cabot gazed at him in astonishment. Roshan had never questioned, let alone challenged, one of his orders before. In the firelight the Sherpa's face was grave but intractable.

'The nights freeze, sir, and Miss Iona has no food,' Roshan said. 'Alone, a child could not survive this long in the mountains. By now she would be dead and the vultures would have come for her –'

He paused. 'There have been no vultures.'

It took Cabot several moments to realize what Roshan meant. Then it began to dawn on him.

'Are you telling me you've been watching for vultures and you haven't seen any?'

Roshan nodded. 'We have all been watching, sir. From here we can see everywhere, and we have looked at the sky from morning to night. There are many vultures on the crests but this season there are few animals, fewer than I have ever known, and the birds are hungry and thin. If any creature had died, even a mountain hare, the vultures would have risen and flocked. They have not –'

He looked steadily at Cabot. 'Miss Iona is alive, sir. I think the man with the red eyes is right. She has been taken by the yeti, and they are giving her food. I think he will return here for he has no reason not to. I do not know whether the man can bring her back, but if you bring in soldiers and helicopters, then I know we will lose her.'

Cabot looked back at the Sherpa. He wasn't sure whether to shed tears in relief or at his own blind stupidity. Vultures. To a country people, a people of the mountains, the flight pattern of the wheeling scavenger birds conveyed better information than a thousand helicopters could ever bring back. A vulture's sight was so acute it could register from the clouds the carcass of a mouse ten thousand feet below it. If Iona had died within miles of the ridge the sky would have been dark with flapping silhouettes.

Cabot closed his eyes and shook his head. To Roshan it was so obvious he hadn't even mentioned it. If the Sherpa was right about that, the rest of what he'd said would prove correct too.

'We'll wait, Roshan,' Cabot said huskily.

Roshan had restrained him for the third time. Geraint Hughes was back next morning.

Cabot was woken by Roshan with the news. He didn't stop to dress. He simply pulled on his woollen dressing gown, hurried out of the tent and limped over to the fire in the icy dawn air.

The Welshman was squatting on a log, cradling a cup of coffee in his hands. He cast his bloodshot eyes over Cabot. Before Cabot could speak, he let out a peal of wild laughter that echoed through the trees.

'Questions you want to ask me, sir, is it? Well, here are your answers. Yes, the yeti, the people as they call themselves, are down below us in the valley. Yes, I am sure they have the young lady and this one thinks as I do –'

He stabbed out a finger towards Roshan. 'We have been talking about vultures, bach, vultures. I watch for them, too – we both know the ways of the mountains. Your granddaughter isn't carrion for the birds, sir, not yet, at any rate.'

The strange high-pitched laughter rang out again. Roshan nodded and smiled uneasily at Cabot. Cabot clenched his jaw. The fact that Iona wasn't his granddaughter was unimportant. All he wanted was to know she was still alive, and to find out how he could get her back.

'How do you know the yeti are in the valley, Mr Hughes?' he asked quietly.

'Because they killed one of my friends, didn't they? They killed him, but we ate him. And the next time my friends almost killed one of them.'

The laughter grew stranger and wilder every moment. This time Hughes hugged his ribs and shook with delight until he almost toppled off the log.

Cabot thought of Iona and dread flooded over him. He felt his temper beginning to slip away, but his eyes caught Roshan's and under the Sherpa's steady gaze he controlled himself.

'I want the child back,' he said between his teeth. 'How are you going to do that?'

'Time, Mr Cabot, time, you must give me time –'

Hughes stopped laughing. The red tide ebbed from his eyes, and briefly his sing-song voice was clear and rational. His arm reached out and gestured over the valley.

'They have her somewhere down there, sir,' he said. 'They will not harm her, no, bach, they will not touch a hair of her head. They will think she brings them luck and call her a shumbi –'

Cabot glanced sharply at Roshan, raising his eyebrows and silently asking him to translate the word. The Sherpa gave a small shrug of his shoulders. He had no more idea what it meant than the American did.

'The animals they feed on have gone, sir. The ridges and crests are deserted. I have seen it for myself. Ask your sirdar and he will tell you the same –'

Hughes's head jerked round and he spoke in Gurkhali to Roshan. Roshan grunted in agreement.

'The yeti will believe the child can bring them back,' the Welshman went on. 'She cannot. Soon, before the snows come, they will be forced to leave the valley to hunt. Maybe all of them, maybe a few, maybe just one. But when they come, whether it is one or many, my friends will know and take me to meet them. I will give them food and obtain the child in return. That is how it will be.'

He stopped, and in the silence that followed Cabot glanced at Roshan again. The Sherpa was frowning. Cabot sensed he was torn between believing the Welshman and doubting him. Cabot felt the same.

The game animals, the animals the yeti were supposed to prey on, the musk deer, the wild boar, the muntjac, the bear and mountain goat, were certainly far fewer than he had known in the thirty years of his Himalayan expeditions – in fact they had virtually disappeared from the high ridges. Their scarcity could only be explained by the felling of the forest, and the devastation of the mountain landscape as the remorseless pressure of human occupation edged up towards the Tibetan plateau.

On the other hand the yeti, if they existed – as Cabot was now certain they must – wouldn't depend on hunting alone. They would be gatherers too. They were among the ancestors of man and all man's ancestors had combined the two activities. The yeti would be no exception. The absence of prey wouldn't drive them out of the valley, they would feed off the harvest from the bushes, trees and grasses. It would take something else, a meteor or a portent, to dislodge them from their feeding grounds.

Cabot looked up and his gaze met Hughes's. As he stared at him, Cabot saw blood begin to fill the Welshman's eyes again.

'Dhu, dhu, dhu!' Hughes cried. 'You do not trust me, is it? You are wrong. Give me time, sir, give me time. With the help of my friends, the child will come back to you. Well, she will return if the creatures have not eaten her first!'

Another crazed burst of laughter lifted into the morning sky. He spoke again in Gurkhali to Roshan. A moment later, without further explanation, he was gone. Cabot heaved himself upright and opened his mouth to shout after him, but Roshan caught his arm.

'It is all right, sir,' the Sherpa said. 'He has told me where he goes and what we should do.'

Cabot sat down again and listened.

'There is a village on the far side of the valley,' Roshan went on. 'It is many miles from here, and many miles beyond the valley itself. I have never been there, but I know of it. It is the last place people live before the upland plains of Tibet that lie beyond the mountains. I told the man that in three weeks the helicopter comes to take us back to Kathmandu –'

Cabot's head jerked up. He had almost forgotten about the date he had arranged for the helicopter to collect them.

'If the man has news between now and then,' Roshan continued, 'he will come back here to the ridge. When the helicopter comes, we will break camp and discharge the porters. The helicopter will take us to the village. Afterwards the man will make contact with us there. It is high summer now but soon, for it always comes soon in the mountains, there is winter. The village is a better place for him to find us as the snows approach.'

'Us?' Cabot glanced at him, puzzled. 'What do you mean, Roshan? You've done your job and I'm grateful, most of all for keeping me sane. But you've other treks ahead and you'll get paid off with the porters like before.'

Roshan looked at the ground, frowning. Slowly he raised his head and gave Cabot a slow, reflective smile. His features showed the strain of the past week, but his expression was resolute and inflexible.

'I am a Sherpa from Everest, sir,' he said. 'We do not leave anyone lost in the mountains, yet I do not stay for that. Miss Iona belongs to you and it is still not because of that. It is because she is rare, more rare than any of the flowers you search for. I stay until the child is found.'

In the hotel bar in Kathmandu, Cabot called for another whisky.

He seldom drank and never before at this hour of the morning, but today he needed the whisky almost like a drug. As he waited for the barman to return, he swung round and peered at the reception desk which he could just see beyond the arch that separated the lobby from the bar. His eyes caught the telephonist's. Smiling and shaking her head apologetically, the young woman mimed that she was still trying to place his call.

Cabot grunted in frustration. The whisky came, he picked up the glass and heaved himself stiffly round to look out over the hotel garden again.

The three weeks had passed, and Hughes hadn't returned to the ridge. The helicopter arrived, the camp was struck, the porters and the other Sherpas were paid off and lifted out in relays. Cabot had stayed with Roshan until the end, hoping against hope that even as the two of them waited on the silent and forlorn space of ground where the tents had been pitched for the helicopter's final flight out, Hughes might still turn up.

Long after the machine lifted into the air Cabot's face was pressed to the scarred glass, scanning the earth below. As the ridges and hill flanks fell away there was no sign of any life beneath, let alone of the crabbed figure of the Welshman. Cabot slumped back in his seat as the helicopter swung south and flew on. It put down briefly to deposit Roshan in the lonely mountain village on the far side of the great misty bowl of the secretive valley. Then it returned to Kathmandu with Cabot still aboard.

Cabot always had liked the ramshackle little capital with its jerry-built architecture, its open drains, its cosmopolitan inhabitants and its bustling, vividly scented markets. But now the first time he found the town irrelevant and oppressive. He didn't want to be in Kathmandu – he wanted to be with Roshan in the remote village in the crests.

The helicopter was waiting at the airport to take him there, but before he could leave he had to speak to Dorelia.

'Sir, sir, we have a connection!'

The young woman had come out from behind the desk and was hurrying towards him, waving her arms excitedly. Cabot drained the glass and levered himself to his feet. Limping, he set off towards the desk.

How, he wondered grimly as he made his way awkwardly between the chairs, did he tell Dorelia that her daughter had fallen into the hands of what, in spite of his observations to Iona, could only be called monsters?

39

'For Christ's sake, Charles, what the hell is this? Are you playing some game with me or what?'

Dorelia Howard's eyes blazed with mingled anger and bewilderment. She stared at her lawyer for a moment, then swung round towards the window.

Lefanu watched her as she walked away.

She was wearing a tailored skirt and jacket in heavy black shantung silk. He had begged her to dress conservatively for the hearing, and the suit was her concession. Being Dorelia she had also put on a white blouse with a plunging neckline, her cabuchon emerald earrings and heavy gold bracelets on both her wrists. Her breasts lifted beneath the clinging sheen of the whiteness, and the green and the gold flashed round her like a halo.

Dorelia looked exactly what she was – magnificent and provocative. She did not look like a responsible and careworn mother battling for custody of her child. Inwardly Lefanu sighed.

'No, Dorelia, I'm not playing any sort of game with you,' he said. 'They've made an approach and we should consider it very carefully. Your brother-in-law's death has changed things somewhat. Bluntly, it's strengthened your husband's hand.'

'We happen to be dealing with my daughter, not with that bastard's dead brother,' Dorelia said icily over her shoulder. 'I never liked Harry. He was arrogant, he drank, he was probably gay, he and Michael were unhealthily close –'

She glanced back. 'What the hell has Harry's death got to do with Iona?'

'Possibly quite a lot, Dorelia. It may have opened a window –' Lefanu stopped. As he polished his glasses, he assembled his thoughts.

A month had passed since the start of the custody hearing. Dorelia's appearance in the witness box had been an unmitigated disaster. She had undermined her case with almost everything she said.

After the court rose that first day with Dorelia still being questioned by her husband's counsel, Lefanu had spent the evening trying to devise a reason for requesting an adjournment when the court sat again the following morning.

He failed to come up with anything. In the event it hadn't mattered. Within fifteen minutes of the court reconvening and as Lefanu was grimly waiting for the process of Dorelia's destruction to start again, the judge was taken ill and the court rose. By late afternoon it became clear that although the illness wasn't serious, it would be a month before the hearing could resume under his direction.

Using every skill he had acquired over the years, Lefanu managed to persuade the opposing side to wait for the judge's recovery rather than have the case started again before someone else. Now the month was up, the judge had recovered, and within half an hour, according to Lefanu's watch, the court would be ready to sit again.

All was exactly as it had been four weeks earlier apart from two totally unexpected developments – the death that week of Michael Howard's elder brother, and the approach from Michael's solicitors which had only reached Lefanu the evening before. Lefanu tried to contact Dorelia at home as soon as he read the proposal. Predictably, as he learnt from Cummer the butler, she was out. She was still out when he telephoned for the last time at midnight. Lefanu smiled wryly and went to bed.

Only now, just before the court sat and as they waited in the conference room was Lefanu able to put it to her.

'With your brother-in-law's death, Michael inherits the family estates in Scotland,' Lefanu said. 'Michael of course already owns Mainwarden. According to his solicitors he does not envisage marrying again after the two of you are divorced. Be that as it may, it is irrelevant to their proposal.'

'And just what is this proposal?' Dorelia demanded.

'Michael Howard intends making over both Mainwarden and the Scottish estates to Iona irrevocably. He will live in Scotland, you will naturally live wherever you want, and Iona in the interim will have Mainwarden –'

Lefanu paused. 'The condition is agreement to joint custody of Iona.'

'Joint custody – ?' Dorelia looked at him as if he were mad. Very slowly she walked back to the table.

'I may live in a sick world where a mother has to fight to get custody of her own daughter, but I'm not sick myself,' she said. 'You think Michael can make a deal by promising Iona those two dumps? They're not worth a pitcher of warm spit! If Iona wants them when she grows up, then I'll buy them for her. But I'll tell you this for free –'

Dorelia bent and stared down at the old solicitor, her eyes dilated and her cheeks white with anger.

'I'm not sharing Iona with that creature. I'm paying you to see the child stays with me. If you're suggesting I accept joint custody, I don't even need to think about it. All I need to think about is where I find another lawyer!'

As she finished Dorelia's voice rose until she was almost shouting.

Lefanu looked back at her. 'Iona,' he said quietly.

'What do you mean, Iona? Who the hell do you think I've been talking about?'

'About yourself, Dorelia, not your daughter –'

Lefanu pushed back his chair and got to his feet. Now from his much greater height he was gazing down at her. He knew what he had to do, but before he committed himself he would make one final attempt to get her to change her mind.

'Listen carefully,' he said. 'To the judge your husband's proposal will make a great deal of sense. What you call "dumps", he will see as a major inheritance of land and ultimately responsibility. Joint custody will allow Iona to visit her other inheritance and grow into understanding it. Meanwhile Mainwarden, which goes to the child immediately, will in effect be common ground –'

Lefanu's voice hardened. 'I said at the start that although it would be difficult, I thought we might just win outright. After the use the other side made of your friendship with Mr Ryan, I began to feel we might have to settle for a joint order. This news has changed it again. If you refuse, your husband will argue it demonstrates a total lack of reasonableness on your part and an equally complete lack of interest in Iona's future. I think he will apply for sole custody. He might get it.'

He broke off. Dorelia looked at him with loathing. Her face was set inflexibly and her breathing had quickened.

'I am not going to let that creep get away with it. You're obviously too goddamn weak to stand up to him, or maybe the bastard paid you off. It doesn't matter. What I'm going to do –'

Lefanu raised his hand and stopped her before she could go on.

Anger, Lefanu discovered long ago, was something clients could afford, not their lawyers. For the first time in his career, Lefanu felt angry. Dorelia was wild, imperious, an uncontrollable force of nature. Her features, though contorted with rage and frustration, were still more beautiful than any he had ever seen. He loved her but there was someone, he realized, he loved even more – the child he had never really known but who in his mind had always been his. Mirrored in Dorelia's extraordinary eyes he saw the slender elfin child that she and her husband were mindlessly bent on breaking on the anvil of their mutual hatred.

It wasn't Mainwarden or the land in Scotland that mattered, although Iona would get both. What the child needed was time, safety, and a measure of peace between her warring parents. Lefanu couldn't guarantee the peace but, when the dust settled, the proposal from the other side offered a chance to all three of them of finding it. The chance was fragile but it was the best they had – the best, above all, Iona had.

He had to give it to her. It meant Dorelia was no longer his client. The child was.

'If you were going to say you're dismissing me, Dorelia, you can save yourself the trouble,' he said quietly. 'I'm resigning as your legal adviser here and now. The hearing begins in approximately twenty minutes. You will, I fear, go into court unrepresented, but I wish you well.'

'Jesus Christ, you're as big a shit as he is – !'

The words erupted from Dorelia as a scream of abuse. Lefanu had expected it and he ignored it, just as he'd ignored her previous insults.

'Get the hell out of here!'

He turned and walked towards the door.

His hand had already begun to turn the heavy brass handle when he heard a sound behind him. Lefanu paused and listened. It was the sound of weeping. He waited with his back to the room. The weeping went on for several minutes, then it died away. After a short silence he heard Dorelia's voice. The fury and bitterness had vanished. Instead as she spoke she sounded like a plaintive wounded child.

'Charles,' she sobbed. 'Please come back.'

*

Out of the corner of her eye Dorelia noticed someone slip in at the back of the court. It was Lefanu's clerk. He bowed to the judge and hurried forward to Lefanu's side. Dorelia watched him incuriously.

It was half an hour later, and the judge had only just taken his seat. Lefanu had told her the process would be swift and undemanding – with the custody issue settled by consent, the court would be anxious to get on with the endless other cases waiting to be dealt with. As Dorelia had been in the witness box when the hearing adjourned, she had to be there when the court reconvened. Within minutes and without needing to answer any more questions, she would be dismissed.

There were still details to be agreed, Lefanu said, but he would work those out with Michael Howard's lawyers. To all intents and purposes the matter had ended, and so had the marriage.

'You blackmailed me, didn't you, Charles?' Dorelia had said earlier through her tears after Lefanu turned from the door and came back to the table.

'Lawyers don't resort to blackmail,' he answered. 'Sometimes they employ a little gentle persuasion.'

'Why?'

'In this instance because I love your daughter and, in my judgement, the settlement is in her best interests. I believe she needs both her parents. I'm glad the whole distressing business is over, I'm glad Iona's missed it, I'm glad she knew nothing about the rupture between you and your husband. If I remember rightly she returns this week from Nepal –' Lefanu smiled. 'Most of all I'm glad she's safe in Mr Cabot's hands.'

They had gone into court then. As she sat down in the witness box, Dorelia still felt a tremor of resentment. She had set her mind on outright victory, and she'd been frustrated. On the other hand, as Lefanu had pointed out, in every practical respect she'd won. Iona would live with her during termtime, which occupied two thirds of the year. Dorelia might have to accompany the child in the holidays to dowdy, gloomy old Mainwarden, and she might lose her occasionally to Michael, but Iona was growing up fast. As soon as she was eighteen the child would be able to take her own decisions, and Dorelia hadn't the slightest doubt about where and with whom she would choose to live then.

As Dorelia watched, the clerk whispered in Lefanu's ear. She saw the white-haired solicitor stiffen. He leant forward and tapped her counsel on the shoulder. A moment later Dorelia's barrister stood up.

'My lord, something has just been communicated to me which materially affects this hearing. I would respectfully request a brief adjournment so that your lordship, my learned friend and myself can consider it in your chambers.'

Dorelia barely took in what happened next.

The judge nodded. The court rose. The two leading counsel with their juniors following them swept out in the judge's wake, and a hum of puzzled conversation filled the air. Then Dorelia became aware that Lefanu was standing by the witness box.

'Come with me, Dorelia,' he said.

He took her by the arm and led her quickly out of the courtroom. Outside they were joined by his clerk. The corridor was thronged with the reporters who had covered the hearing from its start. Ignoring their questions, Lefanu shouldered his way through and turned into the conference room they had left only minutes, it seemed, before. Lefanu slammed the door behind them, leaving the clerk outside to guard it.

Dorelia looked at him, bewildered. 'What is this?' she said. 'What's happened?'

'Sit down.' Lefanu pointed at a chair.

His voice was uncharacteristically harsh and his face sombre. Somehow, Dorelia sensed, his attitude had nothing to do with the quarrel between them earlier. It was a cover for something else – something that had frightened Lefanu.

'Please tell me,' she asked imploringly.

'It's about Iona,' he answered. 'Your uncle, Robert Cabot, called my office from Kathmandu thirty minutes ago. He tried to reach you at the Boltons, but was told you were in court. He spoke to my clerk instead –'

Lefanu leant forward and took Dorelia's hand. 'Dorelia, you're going to have to be very strong. Iona's disappeared. She was camping with your uncle and their porters on a ridge in the Himalayas. Four weeks ago there was a violent snowstorm during the night. When everyone got up next morning, Iona's tent was empty. She'd vanished.'

Dorelia looked at him disbelievingly. 'I don't understand.' Her face was blank. 'Robert loved Iona. He'd never let anything happen to her –'

She broke off. Suddenly her voice rose and she began to scream. 'People don't just disappear, for Christ's sake! She must be somewhere! Where the hell is my daughter?'

'Dorelia!'

Lefanu was still holding her hand. He clenched his fingers until his nails were almost cutting through her skin. Dorelia winced in agony but Lefanu's grip was unyielding, and the pain brought tears to her eyes. It also snapped through her hysteria.

She calmed herself and tried to think. There was something puzzling, something wrong, and she suddenly realized what it was.

'Why has it taken four weeks for Robert to tell me?'

Lefanu swallowed. He seemed confused, almost tongue-tied.

'Two days after Iona vanished, an old man came to Mr Cabot's camp,' he replied. 'The man's a European who's lived in the Himalayas for forty years. He says Iona has been abducted. He claims to have seen her tracks in the snow before the storm obliterated them. He also saw other tracks – the tracks of the people who took her away.'

'Who took her away?' Dorelia stopped. She shook her head in confusion.

'The man says Iona's been abducted by the yeti.'

'The yeti?' The word meant nothing to Dorelia. 'Who are they?'

'They're sometimes popularly known as the abominable snowmen.'

'Abominable snowmen – ?' Dorelia stared at Lefanu. She didn't know whether to weep or laugh or scream again. It was madness, utter madness.

She'd vaguely heard of the abominable snowmen. They were a myth, a fantasy, creatures of dreams and nightmares like mermaids or fire-breathing dragons. The idea that Iona, her often wayward and troublesome but always four-square, flesh-and-blood human daughter, could have been seized by monsters – Dorelia could think of no other word to describe them – was unbelievable. Lefanu might just as well have told her that Iona had been taken by fairies. Hysterically Dorelia started to smile, a terrible glazed and frozen smile. The smile vanished on her lips.

'Abominable snowmen don't exist,' she whispered. 'Tell me that, Charles. Tell me my daughter hasn't been captured by monsters. Please, Charles.'

Lefanu swallowed again. He kept hold of Dorelia's hand. Now he was doing it as much for himself as for her. Lefanu was lost, out of his depth in a world beyond his knowledge or comprehension.

'Dorelia, I can only tell you what I've been told.' He felt the inadequacy of the words even as he struggled to answer her. 'Your uncle is extremely sensible and highly experienced. If he accepts this man's story, however bizarre it seems, for the moment we must do the same. With the man's help Mr Cabot has been searching for Iona. They will go on doing so for however long it takes, and I have to warn you it may be some time. All that matters is that Iona is apparently still alive.'

'Alive? In the hands of monsters?' Dorelia shouted at him. 'How can a child deal with monsters? If they haven't killed her already, they'll frighten her to death.'

She stopped. Suddenly she broke down. She tore her hand away from Lefanu's and flung herself forward over the table, sobbing uncontrollably.

40

'Why did you do it?'

Ryena's voice echoed round the shelter as she looked down at Wengen.

Her son was squatting on the floor in front of her. The big yeti gazed back, his eyes hooded and expressionless. 'Was it not time, Mother?' he asked quietly.

The stare he gave her was direct and fearsome. For an instant Ryena glanced away, trying to shut out the terrible blank intensity of Wengen's gaze. Children grew up, they came to maturity, they mated, built their own shelters and moved away, but she knew no child should ever look at a parent as Wengen looked at her. The old female shook her head.

It was mid-morning. Almost the entire holding had left before dawn to gather in the distant pastures to the west of the island. Despite his lameness, Yerto had gone with them. Increasingly worried about the ranging's threats to come down into the valley, Yerto had taken to going out with the gatherers. He had become obsessively determined to ensure that the holding's cloud-time stores were larger than they had ever been, in case they had to be shared with the clan from the crests.

Ryena was one of the few yeti left on the island. The wind was blowing strongly towards the mountains and Wengen had been only an hour's travel away when she first caught the scent of his approach. Ryena had sniffed the air and frowned. There was another yeti with him. Its scent was vaguely familiar to her, but for several moments Ryena couldn't identify it.

Then she remembered – it belonged to Tana. Ryena had last seen Tana when she left the island as a child many seasons ago. No wonder Ryena hadn't recognized her smell. By now Tana must have come to breeding age, and as an adult her scent pattern would have changed almost beyond recognition. Almost – but not quite. There was enough left in the drifting spores to bring back the laughing crawling infant who had been carried away to the mountains.

Briefly Ryena smiled. Then the smile faded and she frowned. Tana was the holding's gift to the crests, just as Manu had been the ranging's to the valley. Tana should not have been returning without Yerto's knowledge – and Yerto knew nothing about it. Her face creased with anxiety, Ryena left the shelter and ran down to the river. The opposing wind was stronger than she'd realized, and Wengen and Tana were much closer than she'd thought. The two were already in sight. As she stopped, they pushed their way through the reeds on the far side and paused on the bank.

Ryena stared at them, appalled.

It had been seasons since she'd seen Tana, but Ryena recognized her instantly. The young yeti had matured into a supple and well-framed breeding female. Everything about her from the sheen on her pelt to the strong flat cage of her pelvis sang out that she was ready to be seeded. Everything – except the bitter bruised look in her eyes and the crusts of dry blood on the inside of her thighs.

Tana had been mounted. She had been mounted, Ryena knew, by Wengen and against the female's will.

Shocked and sickened, Ryena gazed at the pair. Then Wengen plunged into the river and swam across, pulling Tana behind him. They climbed out and shook themselves dry. Tana looked at Ryena – a look filled with guilt, confusion and pain. Without giving the old yeti a chance to speak, she ran away up the bank. Ryena's head turned to follow her.

It must have been twenty full seasons since Tana had seen the island, but she seemed to know unerringly where she wanted to go. Pushing the reeds aside, she headed upwards. On the top of the bank she hesitated, a hesitation that lasted barely a moment before she launched herself forward again and threw herself into one of the shelters. The shelter was Kekua's. Twenty seasons after Tana had last seen the blind yeti, she'd unerringly chosen Kekua's sleeping-place as sanctuary.

Ryena looked back at Wengen. 'Tell me what has happened,' she said. Trembling she walked up to her own shelter with Wengen beside her. He told her what had happened, while Ryena listened with growing fear and disbelief. Now she forced herself to confront him again.

Ryena had never understood her son. From the moment she dropped him, something had set Wengen apart. Even as an infant the other young of the holding had been wary of him. He grew up with them, he played with them, he was taught the same skills. He was Yerto's son and he should have been their leader.

It had never happened. Wengen remained in the background, a cautious prowling figure first in their games and later in the gatherings. When the other young yeti were let loose on the valley, Wengen always stayed behind. The others ranged free, while Wengen wandered behind them. It wasn't as if he lacked strength – he was taller and stronger than any of them. It was something else, something dark and strange.

Sometimes, in those early seasons of his life, Ryena wondered in terror if she hadn't given birth to the most fearsome creature of all – a neuter. She hadn't. His seeding of Churinga proved that. Wengen should never have mounted Churinga after his father had given her to Manu, but in her relief at discovering he carried seed, Ryena had managed to overlook how it had taken place. Such violations by young males had happened before when the grass rose, they would happen again.

This was different. This was more than a violation – it was a defiance of the bonds. It suddenly occurred to Ryena that she had reared something much worse than a neuter, something that was ominous and unfathomable.

'Yerto must be told,' she said. 'Yerto will decide.'

Out of habit she rested her hand on Wengen's shoulder as she'd done ever since he was an infant. Now her fingertips seemed to grow cold as she touched his pelt.

'Yerto will know everything,' Wengen answered. 'He will know about this and more. The old one has much to learn. He will learn it all from me.'

There was a chilling certainty in his voice. He glanced up at his mother, his gaze brutal and complacent. Ryena removed her hand from his shoulder. She no longer wanted to be near him.

Ryena shuddered and walked away.

Yerto stared across the earth.

The holding's patriarch was propped up on one elbow on his bed of dried ferns and grasses. Wengen squatted opposite him under the bow-branch of the entrance. Outside it was dusk. Inside it was almost dark. All Yerto could see of his son was Wengen's silhouette and the occasional gleam of his eyes when the evening wind plucked a gap in the plaited reeds of the roof and the early starlight filtered through.

Yerto had returned from the gathering with the others as the light faded. He swam across the river, shook away the water and limped up to his shelter. Ryena was waiting for him. As soon as he saw her Yerto knew something had happened. For a while Ryena refused to speak of it. She made him shuffle up and down until his pelt was dry, then she led him inside and helped him on to his couch. Only then did she tell him.

Afterwards, as Wengen waited in his favourite place in the thick grass on the spine of earth above the holding's shelters, Ryena called to her son and he scrambled down.

Yerto looked at him as he came into the shelter. 'It is impossible,' he roared. 'It is –'

He broke off, reaching out as if he could seize words from the air to replace those that refused to come to his mouth. There were none. The air was empty.

The old yeti fell back and rolled on to his side. Stiffly he drew his knees up to his chest until he was lying in a foetal position. It took only an instant for his mind to tell him that he was abdicating. That was impossible. No leader of the holding ever abdicated – that would mean the holding's destruction.

Leadership, succession, continuity, they all had to be ensured. The holding's health depended on them, the stored knowledge had to be passed on, it was Yerto's task to do so. And the logical, the proper vehicle through which it should be done was squatting close to him. Wengen.

As his knees protested with pain, Yerto hauled himself upright again. It was even darker now and he could barely make out Wengen's shape. As he searched for his son's outline, Yerto's mind was a dizzying whirlpool of confusion, like one of the river's foaming and spinning eddies when the spring snow-melt was in full spate.

The river resolved the turbulence of its whirlpools. In all the great duration of the holding, Yerto knew that none of its leaders had ever been confronted with a question as dark and deep as this. As the patriarch he would have to find an answer. Like the river he would have to resolve it.

'Why?' Yerto's roar had sunk to a whisper.

'The time had come,' Wengen answered. 'It is past time that a new child be exchanged. Tana is grown. She has been ready for seeding for two seasons now. Gaggau tries to mount her, but his vigour is gone. He denies it, but his mind has gone with his seed. He is spent. Tana has been left barren on the crests as another belly to be fed –'

Wengen paused. 'I saved her,' he finished.

'You saved her?' Yerto looked at him disbelievingly. 'With whose word to speak for you did you save her?'

'I needed no word,' Wengen answered. 'There is hunger on the crests. Hunger has no words. The ranging cannot feed themselves. I have lifted the burden of a mouth from them, and brought back a breeding female to the island –'

Wengen stopped again. 'Did you not always want a male child of my seed – a child from your own seed? Tana is made to swell with a male infant.' His eyes were narrow and accusing.

Yerto swung his head away. The patriarch felt weak and old, confused and tormented almost to the point of madness. Much of what his son had said was true. Yerto wanted Wengen to seed a child, he wanted it desperately. It was true too that Tana must have grown to maturity. Yerto remembered her vividly as a bold, well-made child. As an adult she would now be in her prime as a breeding female.

Tana should have returned to the island. She should have been replaced in the ranging by another child. Only Gaggau's stubbornness, the vanity of a foolish and wilful old male who had never seeded his own child, had kept her in the crests. Yerto tolerated that because he wished to keep Manu. If Tana had returned, Manu would have had to go back to the mountains – and Manu was more valuable to the holding than any female.

Now Manu would have to leave. As the realization came to Yerto, the weakness and the confusion left him. Tana's abduction wasn't something that had happened by accident, after some sudden hardening in Wengen's groin. It had been planned. Planned not by Wengen alone – Wengen was cunning but not clever enough for that – but by Wengen and someone else. Someone determined to damage the holding at its heart.

'Who told you to bring Tana back?' Yerto demanded.

'No one,' Wengen replied. 'I did what was right both for the ranging and for the island. I did what I thought you would want me to do.'

He looked up at Yerto. For a moment his face was defiant, then his eyes slid evasively away.

Yerto didn't need to ask more. He knew his son. He knew what the sideways movement of his eyes meant. Wengen was lying. He hadn't acted alone. He had been encouraged, guided and helped, and Yerto knew who was responsible. Not Gaggau. Gaggau was old and vain and crazed by his desire to seed, but he still held to the bonds.

However hungry the ranging, however much he wished to eject himself in Tana and seed a child for himself, Gaggau would hold to the old ways for as long as he lived. His mate, Jinga, would not. Only Jinga could have been the force behind this – Yerto could see it clearly. Jinga wanted the ranging to invade and hunt the valley. Tana's seizure from the caves would goad Gaggau into leading the mountain clan down to the island. At the same time it would prise Manu away from the holding.

Afterwards the embittered old female would be able to do whatever she wanted. Yerto had no idea what she had planned, but he knew there would be nothing to stop her.

Suddenly Yerto laughed.

Wengen glanced up in surprise. The patriarch seldom laughed, but strength and energy had somehow come back to him. His laugh was as chill and deep-throated as the last of the winter snows when they broke and swept down in avalanche from the mountains.

'You think I do not understand,' Yerto said. 'You are wrong. I know Jinga and I understand it all. You mounted Tana because Jinga led you to her, but I tell you this, Wengen – if you have seeded her, it will gain you nothing. Tana is mine to give, not Jinga's. Even if Tana swells, the child will not be yours. The child will belong to whoever I give Tana to. Not by Jinga's choice, but *mine* – !'

Along with strength and energy, anger had returned to Yerto. He heaved himself off his bed and began to roar again. 'I give her now! I give her to Manu!'

As Yerto's bellowing voice echoed round the shelter, Wengen narrowed his eyes so tightly they might almost have been closed. They gave nothing away – he could have been asleep on his feet. Yet he studied the patriarch with a steady, unblinking gaze.

Jinga was cruel, malicious and vengeful. That suited Wengen. What Jinga had taught him, what he'd done to Tana as a result of her urging, had opened a lost and hidden part of his mind. Jinga had the clear-sightedness to bring out into the open all the desires and ambitions Wengen knew lay inside him, but which he'd never been able to define or express.

All his life he'd held back. He'd held back as a child, distancing himself from the other yeti young. He'd held back in his youth, and he'd held back as an adult. No longer. Jinga had unlocked his mind. Through her guile she had made him see what had been pent up in him for so long, like the river's flow blocked and deadened by the winter's ice.

The ice had melted. The river flowed through him. Its waters carried a surge of confidence and power he had never known before.

Yerto was old and spent, just like his fellow patriarch, Gaggau, on the crests. The two greybacks were dying. A new time was coming. Wengen had thrust himself into Tana and discharged his seed, and however much Yerto shouted and blustered, Tana was his. Soon the holding would be his too.

All that stood between him and the holding's leadership was Manu, but Manu was doomed. He was a stranger on the island. Manu had tried to seduce the holding's young males with his hunting skills, but now that Wengen had brought Tana back to the valley Manu's time was past. He had no choice but to leave and return to the crests. There he could talk to his brother Gaggau – so far apart were the two in age it always astonished Wengen to remember they had Burra as a mother in common. It didn't matter what their relationship was, nor what they decided. From now on they would have to treat with Wengen about the vanishing prey on the crests.

Yerto's roars faded into rumbles and then into silence. The patriarch began to cough, a painful wheezing sound, bred of the old yeti's age and the river's damp, which echoed hoarsely round the shelter.

Wengen looked at his father with contempt. 'I have mounted Tana,' he said. 'My seed is lodged in her belly. If Manu wishes to take her, then he will have to fight me.'

Without giving either the patriarch or his mother, Ryena, the chance to speak, Wengen left the shelter.

Yerto struggled to take in what Wengen had said. As he did, his face became rigid with shock. At his side Ryena closed her eyes in anguish. All the bonds were inviolable but apart from killing another member of the people, two were more sacred than any of the rest – that the clan's leader should never be challenged, and that its members should not fight with each other.

Wengen had announced he was going to defy them both.

41

'Let me carry you again,' Manu said.

Iona had sunk down on a rock. She sat with her elbows propped on her knees, and her head buried wearily in her hands.

'No,' she replied.

'For a short distance,' Manu pleaded. 'Just to the end of this gully. Afterwards the ground levels. It will be easier then, and you can walk again on your own.'

'No!' Iona repeated defiantly. 'I don't want to be bumped around by you and I don't want to walk anywhere. I just want to rest.'

Her voice had a fierce stubborn edge of anger. Manu gave up. He squatted on the ground and waited.

Iona glanced at him through her fingers. The expression on his face was resigned. A few weeks ago Iona wouldn't have dared defy him. She had been terrified of all the yeti – they were the monsters of her nightmares made real, even more frightening than the creatures of darkness which prowled round her bed. Those other creatures no longer came to her when she slept. There was no room for them when real monsters surrounded her all day and lay beside her at night.

Now most of her fear had gone. Some of the yeti still frightened her, as Gaggau had when she first saw him, wild-eyed and angry and bleeding. The ferocity of Gaggau's appearance and behaviour, and the way she had suddenly come on him in the cave like a great angry beast from the beginnings of time, had made her mouth dry and her stomach cold. She was still wary of the mountain patriarch – his snorts and bellows recalled the fire-breathing dragon of fable – but she'd started to attribute his threatening behaviour to pain and to his anxiety about the vanished animals.

Jinga and Wengen were different. Watching Iona through hard cold eyes, the old mountain female and the big male yeti from the valley troubled and unnerved her. The other yeti were huge and strange, yet each of them had emerged as a different and recognizable individual – the blind Kekua, the gentle, plump, slow-witted Churinga, Tana with her grace and her clear level eyes whose colour, like all the island yeti, mingled the cold grey of the frost-strewn boulders with the magical blue of the dawn sunlight. Above all the strong and skilful Manu, who smiled so often and sometimes even seemed to tease her as Iona noticed the parent yeti did with their young.

Jinga and Wengen remained animals. Jinga had the gaze of a reptile, Wengen the silent brooding strength and the ferocity of a rabid wolf. She distrusted both of them with a fear that sometimes made her physically weak.

At last Iona had discovered that she had a certain power over the yeti, the dangerous and threatening, the friendly and trustful.

The realization came to her slowly. She was a shumbi, the first who had ever been washed up by the river. At the start she thought it was only because she was strange and alien. Then as her terror faded, she saw the yeti looked at her not just with spellbound curiosity but with awe and fear. Even Tonemetapu's voice was hushed and careful when he spoke to her.

Iona was an intelligent, resilient child, with a child's swift, acute perceptions. It dawned on her that she wasn't just a prisoner of the yeti – she was a gift to them, a portent sent down from the stars. She had magic which could change the lives of the holding and the ranging – and she had been sent to them at a time of crisis for both the clans.

Iona didn't know what the crisis was, nor, she sensed, did the yeti. The disappearance of the prey from the crests and the troubles between the clans were part of it, but only its visible, its most obvious manifestation. Behind that was something much darker and more troubling. Even in the brightest summer sun, its presence hovered over the valley like shadows cast by the wings of circling vultures.

A rough damp tongue rasped across Iona's wrist.

Iona blinked. The leopard had crawled up beside her and was licking her hands. Iona scratched the animal's chin. Babilla was hungry – she wouldn't eat until they got back to the island, when Manu would feed her from the cache of wind-dried meat he kept for her. Babilla was asking Iona to go on.

Iona stood up. Eagerly Manu got to his feet too. 'Are you ready to go on?' he asked.

Iona nodded. 'You may carry me, too.'

Manu swung her up on to his shoulders. Iona settled her legs round his broad, powerful neck. A head of them was another of the steep jolting corridors of rock and shale that formed part of the track between the valley and the crests. Iona gripped Manu's head.

'Step carefully,' she said, 'or I will make you put me down, and we will have to halt again.'

'I will tread slowly,' Manu answered.

Moving with caution he started to descend the gully. With a growl of approval, Babilla set off behind them. Rocking gently on Manu's back, Iona smiled.

Although it had taken the child a long time to realize it, she wasn't entirely helpless in the yeti's hands. She was the shumbi washed down from the snows, the herald of something unknown, the bearer of magic. The magic didn't always work – she had saved Churinga's baby, but she'd failed to find prey on the crests – yet whether it worked or not she was still a talisman, she had power.

Iona didn't yet know how to use it, but in the turmoil darkening the yeti's world she sensed the time was close when she would discover.

They made the journey back to the island in good time. As they reached the river at dusk, Manu paused on the bank and frowned. Their approach would have been scented long ago, and most of the holding should have been waiting on the far bank to greet them. There was no one. The sloping shelf of earth was empty, and silence hung over the reeds beyond.

Iona had been walking for the past few hours. Manu swung her up on to his shoulders again. His face troubled, he waded into the river and swam across, Babilla paddling steadily behind them.

On the other shore Manu set Iona down. Together they walked up to the circle of shelters and Iona looked round in surprise. Normally the open space of ground in front of the yeti's dwellings would have been filled with sound and movement – with children playing and squabbling, and the adults talking. Now the holding seemed to be deserted and the silence was oppressive and disturbing.

A tremor of fear ran over her. Worried, she glanced at Manu but before she could speak he said abruptly, 'Stay here.'

He gave the guard command to Babilla and the leopard bounded forward, crouched by Iona's side and lowered its head over her feet. Iona heard the familiar warning growls lift from the animal's throat. Manu strode across the beaten earth and entered Yerto's shelter.

Iona heard voices. They were too quiet for her to make out what they were saying, but there were echoes of bewilderment and anger in the sounds that rolled across the ground. Tense and frightened, Iona waited.

'There was no one on the shore,' Manu said. 'There is no one on the common ground. Why?' He spoke softly.

Yerto gazed at him through the shadowy twilight inside the shelter. The patriarch was lying on his bed of dry reeds, Ryena squatting at his side holding his hand. Both their faces were harrowed with anxiety. Manu glanced from one to the other. Yerto, he knew, was old and grey and failing. With a shock he realized the same was true of Ryena.

Manu had thought the old female was somehow invulnerable to age. From the moment he'd first seen her, Ryena had been warm and strong and glossy-pelted. He'd been a child then. Over the seasons that followed, Ryena had become the mother he'd never had. As he grew up she was the one unchanging element in his life. Manu believed she would never change.

Now he saw that her features were haggard, her pelt almost as grey as Yerto's, her body shrunken and wasted. The change, he knew, must have taken place over a long period of time, but seeing her always as he'd seen her first, Manu hadn't noticed it. Yet there was something else, something that had nothing to do with Manu's blindness to what was happening to the old female as the seasons passed.

Ryena had been wounded to the heart. The wound had aged her far more than the passage of the snows. It was recent and raw, and it bled still.

Manu's eyes switched between the two of them. 'What has happened?' His voice was still quiet but his tone was urgent.

'Wengen has returned,' Yerto answered. 'He has brought Tana with him. He says he has seeded her.'

Manu nodded gravely. 'I learned so on the crests.'

'Wengen has violated the bonds. Even Gaggau did not know what Wengen planned. Gaggau is lame and foolish, and the ranging is hungry. The emptiness in Gaggau's belly has risen to his head –'

Yerto raised himself on his elbow. 'Gaggau dreams. In his dreams he will bring the ranging down to the valley. So Wengen tells me. Is it true?'

Manu nodded again. 'I was sent back with the shumbi to tell you the ranging follows us.' He paused. 'But they do not come to share the gathering. Gaggau comes to hunt.'

Manu heard the sharp intake of Ryena's breath.

Until that instant the old female hadn't believed the ranging would come down from the crests. The club-footed Gaggau's pleas and demands, she thought, were empty bluster. At the very worst the ranging would come to the valley only to gather. She'd been wrong. For the ranging to hunt the gathering grounds was worse than the worst. It would lead to the death of the valley.

The old female squatted motionless in the darkness.

'If Gaggau comes, he and I will talk together,' Yerto said vaguely.

The patriarch plucked at the reeds beneath him. He hadn't taken in the implications of what Manu had just said. Yerto's mind was fixed on something else, something that for the moment was even more important to him – something that obsessed him.

'Tana comes from here,' Yerto went on. 'In seizing and seeding her Wengen has not only broken the bonds. He has defied me, his father –'

Yerto's voice began to rise in fury. 'He shall not do it. Tana is not his to take. She is mine to give now, just as she was as a child when I gave her to the crests!' he shouted. 'I have told him this. I have told him he shall not have her. I have told him I am giving her to you.'

Manu's head jerked up in astonishment.

It was Yerto's right to give Tana as a mate to whoever he chose. Old Gaggau had the same power over the young breeding females of the clan on the crests. But Tana came from the holding, and he, Manu, from the ranging. As far as Manu knew, no patriarch of either clan had ever given one of his own as a mate to a member of the other.

'How did Wengen answer?' Manu asked, bewildered.

Yerto didn't reply. The patriarch's anger and the gathering torment of the events since the shumbi's arrival seemed to have drained him of energy. He fell back on his bed of reeds and stared at the shelter's roof, mumbling to himself as he traced the passage of the stars in the cracks overhead. It was left to Ryena to answer.

The old female pushed herself off the ground. She limped forward to Manu, her limbs creaking and her muscles aching and protesting as the evening's chill enveloped them.

'Wengen denies his father,' she said. 'Because he is our son and both he and Tana are from the holding, Wengen says he has the right to take her. If you dispute it, Wengen says he will fight you for her.'

Manu was silent. He had passed beyond amazement. Once, climbing to the crests many seasons ago he had lost his footing on a winter rock face. For what seemed an eternity he plunged downwards, slithering and tumbling as ice sprayed up around him. Eventually he slammed into a boulder and the world dissolved in darkness. A long time later he recovered consciousness. As he tried to stand, his knees buckled weakly, he felt cold and sick and dazed, and he vomited helplessly on to the snow.

Manu felt the same numbing chill and confusion now.

The yeti did not fight each other, neither within the clans nor between the clans. Fighting was destructive and unnecessary. It was a violation of both the clans' worlds, using up energy needed for the gathering in the valley and the hunting on the crests. It achieved nothing except waste. It was an obscenity to be avoided at almost any cost.

Sometimes it was unavoidable. On those rare occasions the cause was always either territory or mating. Dazed and grieving, Manu knew one of those occasions had arisen now.

He looked at Ryena with a last desperate appeal. 'Is there no other way to stop this?'

Ryena gazed back at him. As Manu had seen, she was old and frail and haggard. He had asked her about her first and only son. Implicitly he had asked her to condemn Wengen, to halt him on the savage and destructive course on which he had embarked.

Ryena shook her head. 'If Wengen is not halted, the holding will die. You must go out and fight him as he demands. You must defeat him.'

Her voice was implacable. Manu looked at her for a moment longer. Then he lowered his head and nodded.

'When dawn comes I will fight him,' he said.

Manu called first from the thick grass just beyond the invisible circle that ringed the holding and its shelters.

'It is I, Manu!' he shouted. 'Manu, Manu, Manu!'

The sound cut through the morning air like the scream of an eagle defending its nest.

Manu expelled his breath and shivered. The grass lapping round his waist felt as cold as the river's waters in the snow-melt. Blood was pounding in his head and there was an empty sickness in his stomach. Everything inside him urged him to turn from the island and head for the crests – to run from the valley and climb back into the silence and loneliness of the mountains. He had been born there, he belonged to the ranging, he would be safe there.

Clenching his jaw, Manu fought the impulse down. He was no part of the holding, but he had been caught up in its life. Now he could not escape from it. He waited.

He did not have to wait long. Almost before the echoes of his fierce, high-pitched call had faded across the valley, the members of the holding had started to tumble out of their shelters. Everyone appeared, males, females and the young. Even old Yerto came stumbling out into the daylight. He stood like the others, peering at the long grass from which Manu's call had come.

Only one of the yeti didn't emerge, but remained stubbornly inside his shelter. Manu knew he was there from the scent spores that drifted up to him from the flattened earth floor. He would have known anyway from instinct and the fear that had made Manu himself want to run – not fear for his own life, but rather terror of the consequences for everyone of a battle, whatever its outcome.

Manu had been sent from the mountains to the valley as a child to be a token of peace, a constant reminder of the sanctity of the bonds. Now he was about to fight the son of the island yeti's patriarch. Devastated, he forced himself to shout again.

'Manu, Manu, Manu!'

The call swirled across the holding. It rippled through the grass and was hurled back by the trees. It struck the eddying pools of the river and was thrown up to the sky. There was no response from the one place at which Manu had directed it – the dark and silent shelter at the holding's northern tip.

Manu made a final attempt. He came down from the grass and walked slowly round the clearing. As he passed, glowering, snarling, baring his teeth and heaving his shoulders in the ritual gestures of aggression, the members of the holding shrank back, pulling their children behind them. Even old Yerto retreated.

He was Manu, the yeti from the crests. He was dark-furred with golden eyes, and the snow-pelted leopard padded in his shadow. He was lean and strong, and until now he was kind. He patiently built shelters, he taught the young males to find small game on the plains, he laughed and played with the children. He found the little shumbi by the river, brought her back to the island and took her to the mountains.

Suddenly he had changed. He was no longer the Manu the holding had known. He was a hunter and he was hunting the island for a quarry, Wengen, whom all the holding disliked and distrusted, even hated, yet who was one of their own too. Breathless the island yeti waited.

Iona waited too.

The evening before, the evening of their return from the crests, Manu's face had been both tormented and resolute when he emerged from Yerto's shelter. Refusing to answer Iona's questions, he released Babilla from her guard over the child, told Iona curtly to find Kekua, then strode away. His shadow seemed to stretch out forlornly and alone under the rising moon before it vanished beneath the trees.

Although taut with anxiety – the disturbing voices from the patriarch's shelter still echoed through her mind – Iona was exhausted. She had fallen asleep immediately. Kekua must have come while she slept, because the blind yeti was there when Iona woke in the sharp darkness that came just before dawn. Kekua was sitting up staring with her sightless eyes at the arc of fading stars beyond the bow-shape of the shelter's entrance.

'Wengen has declared he will fight with Manu for Tana,' Kekua said, anticipating as so often Iona's question. 'You may hear much, but close your eyes, your ears and your nostrils to it all. Stay here in the shelter and be safe. This is a matter for the people, not for a shumbi.'

Kekua's voice was dull and flat with a sadness Iona had never known in her. Propped half upright on her hands, the blind yeti advanced to the shelter's entrance and squatted down beneath the the roof support, blotting out from Iona's sight what lay beyond. Over her shoulders Iona could see the early sunlight begin to fill the clearing.

Iona crouched on the mat of ferns and grasses that formed her bed. Mist from the river had seeped into the shelter as it did every morning before the sun rose. Swirling round her and half hiding Kekua, the grey haze turned into coils of fear. Mesmerized, Iona gazed at the silhouette of the blind female. For the first time since she came to the valley she felt terrified not for herself but for one of the yeti, for Manu.

Frozen and dry-eyed Iona waited and listened.

Outside on the circle of earth between the shelters Manu ignored all the watchers of the holding. He completed three circuits, calling his name all the while. At the end of the third circuit he paused. Close to him he could hear the whimpers of a frightened infant. From somewhere far off came the caws of crows above carrion. He could smell ripening summer fruit, the fragrance of grass and the thin metallic scent of fish feeding off the river's surface.

The sounds and smells billowed over him, warm and close and comforting. Manu absorbed them and was flooded with anger. As the rage pulsed through him, he did something he had never done before except as a gesture of respect to Yerto. He bunched his hands into fists and dropped forwards, so that he was supported on all fours.

Manu ran forward, then stopped and reared up. Scything out with one arm, he swept the bow-shaped support of the shelter away. The plaited grass roof fell in and a cloud of dust lifted over the earth. Wengen crawled out of the wreckage and rose to his feet. There was no fear on his face. His expression was sly and confident.

'So,' he said. 'You come from the crests and you destroy my shelter. Why?'

'I come for Tana,' Manu answered.

'Tana is of the holding,' Wengen replied. 'You are of the ranging. You have no claim on Tana. If you wish a mate, go back to the caves and ask your brother Gaggau to give you one from among your own. Tana is mine.'

'Tana has been given to me by Yerto,' Manu said quietly. 'Yerto has the right to give the holding's females to whom he chooses.'

'Yerto is old,' Wengen said with contempt. 'He no longer knows what he does. Even if he did, Tana is not his to give. She has grown to seeding time among the crests far beyond the holding's grounds. I needed no one's permission to take her from there except perhaps Gaggau's. Gaggau is even older and weaker than Yerto. He will be glad to have one less mouth to feed.'

'Did Tana share the wanting with you?'

Manu's voice was still quiet, but he gazed at Wengen with a ferocity that made the other yeti's eyes slide away.

'Wanting?' Wengen laughed. 'What is wanting when a male knows the time has come to mount? A female accepts the seed that is placed inside her. That is all –'

For an instant he had been unnerved. He recovered his confidence and looked at Manu again, his voice hardening as he went on.

'You have been here too long, Manu,' he said. 'Tana is mine, not yours. She has returned to the island. The exchange that was made between the two of you is ended. You have no reason to stay now. Go back to the caves where you belong. Your time with the holding is finished.'

Manu stared back at him. His anger had surged and fallen like the press of the river's water. Now it rose again as the waters did when flash-floods poured down from the crests and boiled over the river's banks.

Everything Wengen had said was untrue. Yerto and Gaggau were old, but they were still the clans' patriarchs. Wengen had no right to take Tana as a mate without their agreement and unless the two clans agreed, and another child was sent from the island in her place. And he had no right to mount Tana without her consent.

The patriarchs chose the first mate. Almost invariably the female accepted the breeding partner selected for her, but she was given the chance to refuse him. Mismatched pairings produced flawed children, and the female alone was said to know whether the chosen seed was right for her or not.

Tana had never had that choice. She had been seized, abducted and brutally mounted like a muntjac doe in the autumn rut.

Manu had never seriously considered Tana before in any way, let alone as a mate. She had simply been a shy and friendly presence in Jinga's shadow whenever he visited Gaggau in the caves. Now she stepped out of the shadow and stood vividly at the centre of his mind. He saw her slender, almost childlike body, her light smiling eyes, her slow graceful walk that contrasted so strongly with the awkward muscular movements of the ranging, her capable hands as she tended Gaggau and the gentleness with which she had treated the old yeti's wounds.

Manu saw her as if for the first time.

He saw her and she called silently to something long hidden deep inside him – hidden by his years as hostage to the holding, just as Tana had been hostage to the ranging. Hidden by the years when he'd learnt ineptly to gather while all the while he had been longing to hunt. Hidden as Yerto came to depend on him, and Manu increasingly found himself treated not as the gift of the crests to the island, but as Yerto's natural son.

He wasn't Yerto's son. Yerto's son was standing in front of him. Yerto's son had broken the bonds, humiliated his father, violated Tana, and scornfully instructed him, Manu, to return to the crests.

Like the river's floods, Manu's rage swirled over the banks of his control.

'Until Yerto tells me to leave the island, I stay where my shelter is made,' Manu said, his voice no more than a whisper but a whisper charged with menace. 'I hold to the bonds. I take Tana because she has been given to me, and I believe the wanting between us is shared. Your shelter I have destroyed. Build another where you will, but let it not be here. If you cut even one more reed on the island, it will be the last you cut anywhere.'

Something flared at the back of Wengen's eyes. Without warning he sprang at Manu's neck. From all round the clearing a low dismayed murmur rose into the morning air. A moment later the two yeti were locked together, and tumbling over and over across the earth.

On the rare occasions when the yeti fought, the battle was more of a ritual contest than a true fight. If fighting itself was bad and wasteful of energy, inflicting damage was worse. A wound threatened the sufferer's ability to hunt or gather. Instead, after much roaring and bluster, heaving and buffeting, the stronger emerged as the winner and the loser retired unhurt. Manu had never fought before, but he knew this battle was different.

Wengen fought in silence with a concentrated, implacable fury. Wengen wanted to do more than wound – Wengen was out to kill.

Manu realized this when he felt Wengen's hands round his throat. Like all the holding yeti, Wengen was heavier than his counterparts from the crests. He managed to turn Manu on to his back and straddle himself across Manu's chest. Wengen's thumbs gouged deep into Manu's windpipe until he was barely able to breathe. He felt himself becoming limp. Dizzily he thought Wengen, too, would know he was weakening, and release the pressure.

Wengen did know it. His narrow eyes blazed again, saliva trickled from his mouth and he bore down even harder.

On the point of losing consciousness, Manu knew he was about to die. He tried to draw his knees up to his stomach, but his legs felt as if vast mountain boulders had been piled across them. Straining and heaving he somehow cast the boulders off. He arched his back and kicked out. One of his knees caught Wengen in the groin. Wengen grunted in pain and his hold on Manu's neck relaxed.

Manu knew it was his last chance. One of his hands was free, and he struck at Wengen's nose. Wengen blinked in pain and his eyes watered. Manu twisted sideways with the speed and desperation of a trapped otter. He kicked again, broke away from Wengen, squirmed across the ground and climbed to his feet.

Manu swayed and stumbled. His head throbbed and his heart was pumping wildly. Frantically he sucked in air. He was young and strong and fit, he knew he only needed moments to recover and he had won himself those precious moments. When Wengen came at him again, Manu was ready. He was more than ready – he had learnt his lesson.

At close quarters on the ground Wengen, the heavier yeti, was stronger. In the open the advantage lay with Manu. He was faster and more agile, and he had the stamina of the mountain hunters. As Wengen plunged forward like a charging bear, Manu swayed and stepped aside. He braced his arm and struck at Wengen's face. His forearm caught Wengen across the cheek, jolting his head back. Wengen staggered, and rocked on his heels. Then he snarled and went for Manu again.

An instant before, Manu had been in front of him. He was no longer there. Moving on the balls of his feet like the shadow of a wind-tossed leaf, he had slipped away. He turned and swung round behind Wengen, then hit him again, hammering his arm into Wengen's back beneath his rib cage. This time Wengen snorted in pain and his legs buckled. He recovered and hurled himself at Manu once more.

Wengen reeled to a halt. Where Manu had been standing, there was nothing but the morning air. As Wengen gazed in murderous confusion across the clearing, another chopping blow from behind pitched him forward. He staggered and dropped to his knees, his eyes no longer blurred, but streaming with tears.

He shook his head, then opened his mouth and roared, a roar not of challenge or aggression, but of pain and self-pity. He felt tormented and humiliated.

Above him Manu raised his foot. One small kick to Wengen's spine, Manu knew, and he would pitch the other yeti forward on to his face in total abject defeat. Across his mind flashed everything Wengen had done. His muscles contracted, he aimed his foot at Wengen's back – then suddenly he stopped.

Manu didn't give himself time to think. He swung away and, his chest still heaving, walked over to Yerto. He went down on his arms and greeted the patriarch with the holding's nose-scratching gesture.

'I declare the wanting,' Manu said. 'I ask for Tana.'

Yerto's face was bleak. He glanced at his son Wengen, still crouching in the swirling dust at the clearing's centre where the fight had taken place. Then Yerto looked back at Manu, and his gaze softened.

'Tana has already been given to you,' the patriarch said. 'All that was needed was the wanting. Now she is yours without condition. Go and breed well.'

Manu backed away. Suddenly he felt very tired. All he wanted to do was sleep. When he woke he would cleanse himself in the river, and life would start again.

He stood up. Stumbling slightly he headed for his shelter. Just before he stooped to step inside, something pricked his nostrils. He straightened up and sniffed the air. A trail of scent was drifting towards him from the direction of the crests. The other yeti in the clearing had caught it too, and were standing with their nostrils flared. Manu inhaled again. The source of the scent spores was still far off, but now he recognized it.

It came from the ranging. The mountain yeti had left the caves and were on their way down to the valley.

Kekua had also picked up the scent. She climbed to her feet, walked away from the shelter and turned to face the mountains. For the first time since the fight started Iona could see the clearing. The blind yeti had told her to stop her ears, but it was impossible. Iona had heard the scuffle of battling limbs, the furious grunts, the sound of blows and the gasps of pain.

She had tried to identify where each one came from. Whenever she thought Manu was hurt, she trembled. Now she crawled forward and peered out. The first thing she saw was Wengen. The big powerful yeti was squatting on his haunches at the clearing's centre with blood trickling down his face. There was an air of defeat about his bowed shoulders and lowered head, but his hooded eyes were still dark with venom.

Iona's gaze moved away. She wasn't interested in the hateful Wengen. All she minded about was Manu. She searched for the lean dark-pelted yeti, and found him at the entrance to his shelter. He was standing gazing towards the north, scanning the air from the mountains. His chest was heaving with effort, and there was blood on his face too, but he was upright and he was safe. It was all that mattered.

Tears filled Iona's eyes and flowed down her cheeks.

42

The yeti of the ranging came within sight of the island as the sun rose over the crests behind the trail that had taken them down from the mountains.

Two groups of the younger hunters came first. Waiting for their arrival on the bank with the holding, Iona recognized Raku at the head of one group, and Soru leading the other. The hunters threaded their way through the bushes and stopped on the edge of the river. Then Gaggau came into sight. He hobbled forward awkwardly, supporting himself on a branch and lurching from side to side as he dragged his club-foot behind him. After the mountain patriarch came the dark scuttling silhouette of Jinga, and following her the old, the females and the young of the clan.

Gaggau came to a halt on the bank midway between the two groups of hunters, and looked across the water. Tired by the waiting, Yerto had dropped forward to support his upper body on his bunched hands. When he saw Gaggau, he heaved himself upright and gazed back over the river. Minutes passed while the two patriarchs studied each other. The eyes of both were hazed with age, but their stare was level and unblinking.

Suddenly, without exchanging a call or even a gesture, both of them turned. Gaggau limped away into the bushes, Yerto climbed stiffly back towards the shelters. A moment later the two clans followed them, the holding streaming upwards after Yerto and the yeti of the ranging vanishing in Gaggau's wake.

Iona blinked and glanced round. She was alone on the bank. She shook her head, bewildered.

The meeting between the clans was unprecedented. They came together in cloud-time although Iona still had no idea what cloud-time meant, except that it belonged to the snows, to the icy, wintry space between the seasons. But never before, as both Manu and the blind Kekua had told her, had they faced each other in summer. To all the yeti it was an encounter almost as extraordinary as Iona's own appearance, the arrival of a shumbi washed down from the heights.

The encounter had taken place, the clans had looked at each other, and without exchanging a word they had silently retreated. Now all round Iona there was nothing except the rippling flow of the river and the rustle of the summer grasses.

Iona turned and ran after the others. She caught up with Kekua at the back of the procession.

'What's happening?' she asked. 'Why did no one speak?'

'Yerto and Gaggau will speak later,' Kekua answered. 'This morning the ranging showed themselves to us. We saw their number, what condition they were in, how many old and young were with them. They saw the same of us. Now Gaggau and Yerto will consider.'

'What are the ranging doing now?'

'They are making their own shelters for their stay in the valley.'

'When they speak, will Gaggau come here or will Yerto go to him?'

Kekua shook her head. 'Neither. They will meet at a place that Tonemetapu has chosen. It is over there.'

Iona looked in the direction of Kekua's outstretched hand. She was pointing at a clump of trees half a mile from the river on the far side of the island from where the ranging had stopped.

'All the valley belongs to us,' Kekua went on, 'except the space of ground beneath the trees. That belongs to no one. We may pass through the trees, we may listen to them, but we may not gather there. It has always been so. On the crests, too, there is a place of trees where the ranging may not hunt. That also has always been kept apart.'

Iona frowned. It was almost as if Kekua were describing a church. The only churches Iona knew were built of stone. At her father's insistence she'd gone to morning service every Sunday for as long as she could remember, either in London or at Mainwarden. The churches in both places were grey, cold and smelt of damp – even in summer her breath seemed to mist in front of her face as she sang the hymns.

The trees Kekua had pointed at were glowing green-gold in the morning sun, and throbbing with life and sound. As warmth rose from the earth their branches stirred and seemed to dance. Birds darted in and out of the canopy of leaves, their songs drifting across the plain to the island. If the trees were the yeti's equivalent of a church, they made a much more attractive one than any Iona had seen.

She glanced back at the blind female. 'When will they meet?' she asked.

Churinga was walking on the other side of Kekua with her infant, little Tumba, held to her breast.

'Tell me, tell me, tell me!' Churinga said. 'You learn to talk, you go to the crests, you come back, and still you are the same, little shumbi!' She laughed.

'Be patient, Iona,' Kekua said. 'Because the valley's grounds and the river are ours, and the ranging must use them both to come to the trees, it is for Yerto to decide. When he has decided, Gaggau will know. You will know too because you also will be there.'

Her face flushed, Iona walked on.

Yerto's choice for the time of the meeting between the two clans was the late afternoon.

The holding's patriarch advanced slowly towards the clump of trees, his eyes narrowed against the waning light and his hips creaking painfully. He longed to drop forward, to remove the aching weight of his upper body and prop himself on his bunched hands. He could do that on the island when only the holding were there to watch. Not now. Gaggau was waiting for him and Gaggau would know that for Yerto to use his hands was a sign of age and weakness. Gaggau, or more probably his mate, Jinga, would exploit it ruthlessly.

Yerto kept to his feet. Manu was at his side. Shaking off his supporting arm, Yerto stepped into the trees' shadow.

To get there Yerto had crossed the river on its deeper, swifter-flowing western side for the first time that season. Until he entered the water and began to swim, he hadn't realized how much he had stiffened, how fast his strength was fading. Only last season he had been able to surge through the foam-flecked current as swiftly as any of the holding's young males. Sometimes for the sheer exhilarating pleasure of it, Yerto made the crossing a race. He gathered the young males together on the bank beside him and launched them all into the water together.

Yerto always won the race. However hard the stream was running, he was always first to the bank on the far side. No longer. Once or twice today his head had sunk beneath the surface, plucked down by the river's remorseless pull. Only the watchful Manu at his side had saved him. Manu gripped him, lifted him and carried him forward. Choking and gasping, Yerto waded into the shallows. He collapsed in the reeds and lay there for a long while. Finally he heaved himself on to his feet.

With Manu at his side he had set off again, knowing that from this point he must not stumble. Gaggau was waiting for him.

On Tonemetapu's instructions, Manu had visited the copse during the morning. In the last snows several of the older trees had fallen, and three of them lay across each other in a rough triangle. Manu had cleared the undergrowth that had sprung up between them, leaving an open space of earth framed by the trunks. He'd glanced round and nodded, satisfied. The old patriarchs could use the natural wooden benches to support themselves.

Gaggau was already resting on one of them when Yerto and Manu appeared. His mate, Jinga, was there too, sitting further back in the shadows. The two of them had crossed the river earlier in the shallows upstream from the island. Gaggau, although he wouldn't acknowledge it, had also needed help in the water. Raku and Soru had been with him to provide it, but they had been left outside the trees to wait. The two mountain yeti looked expressionlessly across the little clearing as the party from the island appeared.

Yerto and Manu led, with Ryena behind them. Slowly but steadily, the old female had swum the river on her own, without help. After Ryena strode Wengen. Neither of his parents had acknowledged Wengen's presence when he joined the party on the island bank, yet each – with silent anger in Yerto's case, sorrowfully in Ryena's – accepted his right to be there.

The conference between the leaders of the two clans was historic, and its outcome for both incalculable. Whatever Wengen had done, he remained Yerto's son. There was no turning him away. Like Manu – in the absence of a son to Gaggau, Manu was heir to his half-brother – Wengen could claim an inalienable right to attend the meeting of the holding and the ranging.

Iona came last.

Whenever she'd crossed the river before, Manu had carried her on his shoulders. This time, as they came down to the bank, Manu's eyes had switched uncertainly backwards and forwards between her and the old limping patriarch. He hesitated, then he made up his mind. He called to the leopard, gave Babilla a curt instruction, and waded into the water beside Yerto.

Babilla looked up at Iona. The leopard gave a rumbling growl, caught the sleeve of the child's jacket between her teeth and tugged her towards the river. Iona followed the animal. They entered the water and Iona began to swim. A moment later the swirl of the current caught her and tore her sleeve from Babilla's jaws.

As she felt herself being swept away, Iona reached out and clutched the leopard's neck, sinking her fingers into Babilla's fur. Breathless and coughing she wrapped herself against the leopard's body, clinging desperately to the animal's ribs. Spume from the river's surface, steel and silver and a foaming coppery-white, clouded her face and blinded her eyes.

Babilla seemed oblivious to Iona's panic. Sinuous and powerful, she forced her way through the river's downward press, and pulled the child ashore. On the far bank the leopard shook herself dry, then turned her head and inspected Iona for a moment through her opaque and watchful eyes. If she had been given a task to perform, Babilla decided she had completed it. She bounded off behind Manu.

Iona followed her. By the time she reached the trees, the two parties had met and greeted each other. She saw Yerto propped against a trunk on one side and Gaggau on another. Dimly in the shadows she could make out their mates and Wengen behind the two great silverbacks. Iona's eyes caught Manu's. As the mountain yeti silently indicated she should wait and llsten, the child dropped to her knees, Babilla crouching beside her.

Gaggau was speaking.

'We asked soon after the season's start to share in the gathering,' he said. 'We knew then the prey had gone from the crests. You denied us. You said there was not enough in the valley for us both. We continued to hunt, but again we found nothing. We asked you once more, and you denied us again. Instead you sent us the shumbi –'

Gaggau broke off and looked at Iona. The face of the mountain patriarch was gaunt. He examined the child with angry puzzled eyes, and Iona shivered. She reached out and stroked the leopard's neck for comfort almost as if it had been Misty's. Babilla bristled and rubbed her cheek against Iona's leg.

'She was given to you by the river,' Gaggau went on. 'You said you would share her with us, and she would find prey. Again we hunted. With the shumbi to lead us we crossed the grounds from end to end. There is not a feeding place we have not searched and watched and searched again. There is nothing. The prey has vanished from the crests. Not even the shumbi can trace its spoor.'

Old Yerto grunted. So far there was nothing he could question. All Gaggau had said was true.

'Now I have brought the ranging down to the valley,' Gaggau finished. 'We have no choice. On the crests we starve, and every day the hunters lose strength. The little they find is not enough to sustain them alone, yet they must share it with all the ranging. Soon the old and the young will die. Our breeding females will follow them to death. Perhaps one or two of the hunters will survive on the birds and monkeys they fell. What use is that if there are no females for them to seed? The ranging is at an end –' Gaggau shifted painfully on the trunk.

Iona watched him intently. His wounds from the firebrands were still not fully healed, and the long trek down from the crests had bruised and wearied his deformed leg. The years were closing in on him, she knew, and for a moment as the shadows played across his features his massive head looked almost skull-like.

Finally he found a more comfortable position. The breeze swung the shadows away and his face became recognizable again, the hair on it white as if touched by hoar frost. He gazed at Yerto once more, and this time there was anguish in his eyes.

'Even if no seed links us, Yerto, we are brothers, you and I,' he said. 'The bonds join us. You cannot let the ranging die. You say the valley's gathering will not feed us both. Very well. The animals have gone from the crests, but they are still here in your gathering grounds. Let my hunters follow them. If we take from you, we will share with your people. I ask only that we may hunt.'

Gaggau stopped. Yerto stared back at him.

Iona's glance switched between the two patriarchs. The anguish and confusion that strained Yerto's face was as great as that on Gaggau's. Yerto opened his mouth to speak, but no words came. He turned and looked imploringly at his mate, Ryena.

Ryena stood up slowly. She was stiff and old, almost as old, Iona guessed, as Yerto. But unlike Yerto, Ryena handled the burdens of age with grace and confidence. There were none of Yerto's awkward angry movements as he tried in frustration to make his body do what it was no longer capable of. Ryena lowered herself to the ground from the treetrunk that had been supporting her. She steadied and composed herself carefully, then equally carefully she began to speak.

'We grieve for you and the ranging, Gaggau,' she said. 'We know your prey has gone. We know you starve and must be fed. The bonds say we must share the valley with you, and we accept that. But for you to hunt here is no answer. If you take the valley's animals, you will take the valley's life. I am Ryena, mate of Yerto, so listen well –'

The old female swept out her arm, indicating the grounds beyond the trees. 'Here the birds and animals harvest beside us. They eat and take seed from the bushes and meadows. They expel the seed and the seed flowers. They crop the young trees and the trees stay small, so the grasses flourish beneath them. These grounds belong to the creatures as much as they do to us. If you hunt them, the grounds will die. Then there will be nothing left for either the ranging or the holding.'

Ryena paused. 'We have gathered stores for cloud-time,' she went on. 'When cloud-time comes, share those stores with us. Before the snows, harvest what is left in the valley at our side. We will divide equally grain by grain, fruit by fruit, berry by berry. All I say is: leave to the valley what you call prey. I am Yerto's mate. I have bred. Listen to me well!'

Ryena thought for a moment, her face wrinkled in concentration. Then, without another word, she stepped back. She sat down in the shadows as slowly and gracefully as she had stood up.

'The ranging hears the words of Yerto's mate –'

The voice was Gaggau's. He paused. To Iona the pause seemed endless. Then Gaggau continued, and his words were edged with hardness again.

'We have listened but we have no choice. We cannot gather as the holding does, we have neither the skills nor the time to learn them. We hunger. We must hunt the valley or die. The bonds say we cannot be denied.'

He stared at Yerto. The two grey-backed patriarchs faced each other, immobile and silent.

Iona waited, her arm resting loosely across the soft hair of Babilla's shoulders. After a time a wagtail flicked its tail in a patch of sun-speckled grass beneath the trees. Babilla's ears twitched. A day-hunting owl brushed through the leafy canopy. The sun moved slowly across a full quarter of its day's arc, and still the clans' leaders had not moved.

Again it was Ryena who finally broke the silence.

'What says Tonemetapu?'

At the question Babilla stiffened. Iona could feel the leopard's hackles rise and the muscles bunching along its spine. The great cat's dark ear-tufts were alert and angled forward. Iona followed the direction of its gaze.

In the deep tree-shadows at the end of the clearing was what Iona had taken for a small mossy boulder. She narrowed her eyes. It wasn't a boulder. The grey lichen-patterned shape resolved itself into the silhouette of a squatting yeti. The silhouette belonged to the old seer, Tonemetapu.

Iona tensed in surprise. She had thought Tonemetapu was so much part of the writhen juniper at the island's head, of the trunk and roots and saplings which formed the little arch of darkness where he sat, that he was bonded to the tree like the moss which clung to his body. He was not. The island yeti must have picked him up, swum with him across the river and carried him to the copse.

A lizard darted across the dust at his feet. Tonemetapu waited while the reptile hunted and seized a fly. The lizard swallowed its prey, its tongue flickered round its mouth, then it scuttled away. Afterwards Tonemetapu spoke.

'There is death in the gathering,' the old seer said. 'The holding and the ranging come to this place of peace with blood-rage upon one of them. I cannot speak, nor will there be resolution between the clans until the blood-rage is cast out –' He paused and raised his withered arm. 'I see the death-anger pounding there!'

A horrified murmur ran round the circle of the yeti. Iona's eyes widened in fear and a low growl came from Babilla. Tonemetapu was pointing at Wengen.

Yerto rose slowly to his feet, and stared down at his son. Under the patriarch's dark implacable gaze, Wengen started to back away.

'Is this so?' Yerto demanded.

Wengen said nothing. As Yerto's eyes continued to burn into his face, he slid further and further back. Wengen looked to Iona like a huge brown snake mottled grey by the tree-shadows trying to hide itself.

'I ask you!' Yerto shouted. 'Is it so?'

Still the terrified Wengen remained silent.

Yerto thought for a moment. Death-anger among the yeti emerged only in fighting. It almost always vanished when the fight ended. If it didn't, if the blood-rage remained afterwards, then so did the presence of death in the clan. Wengen had fought only once – he had fought Manu.

Yerto looked at Manu. 'Was the death-anger on Wengen when you fought?' he asked.

Manu stood up. He looked steadily back at the patriarch. The memory of Wengen's hands tightening round his neck had not left him – it would not leave him until he died.

'It was on him,' Manu answered bleakly.

Briefly Yerto closed his eyes. His face was contorted with horror and grief, and for a moment he swayed. Iona watched him, mesmerized. Then Yerto recovered and turned back towards Wengen.

'In spite of all you did, you were still my son,' Yerto said huskily. 'I thought the blood-rage had passed when the fight ended. I did not know the rage had led to the death-anger, and it is on you still. You are my son no longer. You no longer belong to the holding, nor to the people. Providing you keep yourself apart, you may stay until the sun lifts in the sky tomorrow. Then you do not exist. By the time the light enters the valley you wlll be gone –'

The patriarch seemed to choke. He recovered himself again and his voice rose to a hoarse, chilling shout.

'I send you to the oduna, Wengen! Go now and for ever!'

Yerto collapsed on to the trunk. As his head dropped to his chest, another ripple of shock and dismay ran over the clearing. The sentence of exile had been pronounced. To the yeti, exile was death just as surely as the death-anger itself.

An instant later the heads of all the yeti swung towards Wengen. Iona's head jerked round too. Wengen had wriggled away until twenty paces separated him from the others. There was a rustle and he stood up. As his pale eyes flickered round the gathering, he looked at once terrified and vengeful.

He opened his mouth to speak. A look of pleading crossed his features, but no words came out. He hesitated, a spasm shook his body, and he stumbled. Trembling, he turned and walked away. The walk became a trot and then a run. A moment later the yeti plunged into the bushes and vanished.

Iona listened.

Echoing through the clearing were the fading beats of his footsteps, but the child could hear another sound too. It was a strange threatening noise, like the rising hum of a swarm of wasps disturbed at their nest and gathering to attack an intruder with their poisonous bites. For an instant Iona couldn's place it. Puzzled, she glanced back and scanned the trees. Then she realized where the sound came from – Jinga.

The old female was rocking backwards and forwards on her haunches, muttering to herself. Her arms were clasped round her knees and her eyes were closed, but her wrinkled face was convulsed with anger and pent-up violence. Iona had never seen any creature so consumed with rage and hatred. Shivering, the child tore her glance away and looked back to the clearing's centre.

'It is done –'

The voice breaking the silence was Tonemetapu's. The old seer's words drew everyone's attention.

'The presence of death among the people has been removed,' Tonemetapu said. 'It is time to resolve the quarrel between the ranging and the holding. I have heard what both the clans have to say. Before I can decide what shall be done, I must consult the star without a name –'

Tonemetapu raised his face towards the tree canopy through which wavering shafts of sunlight were lancing down from the morning sky. He seemed to study the sky for a moment. Then his head dropped and his glance swung between Yerto and Gaggau.

'Withdraw your people from the trees, both of you. Leave me here alone. When evening comes and the star appears, send Kekua to me. Kekua is without sight. She is also wise. The star will speak to me, and Kekua will bring you its true answer.'

The grass rustled as the yeti stood up. With Babilla at her side, Iona followed them out on to the plain. Together they settled down to wait.

*

'I lay it here,' Kekua said.

She knelt and put the bird's nest on the ground. She had lined the hollow of down feathers at its centre with fresh leaves. Inside she had placed a handful of late summer berries and nut kernels from the day's gathering. It was only a tiny handful, a young child's portion, but it would be more than enough for Tonemetapu.

Kekua remained on her knees. Dusk was close and the space beneath the tree was already in deep shadow. She searched the evening air, reading off the messages it gave to her through the patterns and pulses it left on her skin and in her nostrils. Mist was beginning to rise from the river. A late-hunting falcon had dipped down to perch on the upper branches. Night-flowering orchids were opening on the far bank, and their scent was rich and dizzy in her nose.

Kekua shook her head. She could sense or scent them all. She could even detect the faintly beating wings of a swallow-tailed butterfly that had alighted on a branch high above her head. What she couldn't pick up was the presence of Tonemetapu. She frowned, concentrated and tried again, swinging her head and her sightless eyes from side to side.

Then Tonemetapu spoke. 'You come for my answer,' he said.

His voice was very close. As Kekua's mind measured the distance between the sound and her ears, she knew he was less than an outspread arm's length from her. The butterfly overhead was five times as far away. She had heard the butterfly, but not Tonemetapu. Pressed against the trunk, the old seer was as silent as the tree itself.

'Yerto has sent me,' Kekua replied. 'But I come for Gaggau too. I come for all the people.'

There was a rustle. Tonemetapu was pulling the nest towards him. He examined its contents. As he sifted through the berries and nuts, Kekua's nostrils picked up the distinct smells of each. He began to chew on something, and Kekua wrinkled her face. He was eating a plump sweet cranberry. She knew exactly where she had found the fruit, she even remembered the spiny twig from which she had plucked it.

'What should my answer be?' Tonemetapu asked.

Kekua frowned. It was the last question she had expected the old yeti to put to her. She was only a messenger. The decision must be Tonemetapu's alone.

'I do not know,' she replied uncertainly. 'It is not for me to say.'

'My sight is almost gone, Kekua,' Tonemetapu said. 'As blindness comes on me, I learn to see with my mind. You are wholly without sight and you always have been. You have had long seasons with your full blindness, and you have learnt to see further than me. That is why I asked that you should come here – ' He paused. 'I ask again. What should my answer be?'

Kekua was silent in thought. She could feel the radiation of warmth from Tonemetapu's body. It was almost imperceptible, less tangible than that of the butterfly that was still perched on the branch overhead, but now that Kekua had picked it up, she knew where to direct her words.

'The ranging starve,' she said. 'They wish to hunt the valley. Because of the bonds they cannot be denied, but a season might come when the harvest fails round the island. Then the holding would need to gather the crests, and the ranging would have to agree. It is the same for both the clans. And yet –'

Kekua stopped. She felt the weight of something troubled and confused lying deep inside her.

'Continue,' Tonemetapu prompted her softly.

'Since Manu came to strength, the young males of the holding have watched him,' Kekua went on. 'He hunts and they learn from him. Sometimes they hunt too. At night they talk and laugh and tell stories about how they chased and trapped the animals they found. Yerto is too old to halt them. The others on the island are content. A sambur buck gives the same as a week's combing of the grounds. The children are learning too –' Kekua hesitated again.

'Manu is strong and brave and intelligent. All he has done for the island is good, and Yerto trusts him. That is why Manu has been kept here long after the time for him to go back to the crests. Although he does not know it, Manu is changing the holding. He is just one. If the ranging hunt the valley too, the change will be greater, far greater. All the holding's males will take to hunting. So will the children. The gathering skills will be lost. Then the holding will be lost.'

Kekua broke off. She gazed at Tonemetapu through her sightless eyes. The old yeti looked back at her.

'I have heard Yerto's mate, Ryena, I have heard you,' he said. 'You are both wise. Ryena because she knows what will happen to the valley, you because you know what will happen to the people. And yet the bonds must be kept, the ranging must be fed. Look upwards, Kekua –'

Kekua heard the faint rustle of bones creaking in his neck as Tonemetapu raised his head. She followed his glance towards the tree canopy and the night sky beyond.

Kekua could see nothing, but her skin registered every shifting window in the leaves above, every drift of air, every shadow cast by the hunting owls. She also registered the movements of the stars beyond. The constellations were wheeling up from behind the crests and printing the dark canopy of the air with brilliance. The pulse of one star was stronger and more vivid with the radiance of the Himalayan night than she had ever felt on her skin before. She almost recoiled at the brightness it flashed through her pores and into her mind.

'The light comes from the star without a name,' Tonemetapu said. 'It has spoken in agreement with you and Ryena. It shines so brightly because the snows are close. Only one turning of the moon separates us from cloud-time. Until then, the star says, the ranging may hunt. They may share with the holding, and the two clans may harvest the valley side by side together. But when cloud-time comes the sharing must stop –'

Tonemetapu's head dropped. Kekua's eyes lowered with his as she sensed the change in the angle of his face.

'In cloud-time the people must find a new way of living together, of sharing the harvest of the crests and the plains. They have one last moon to prepare themselves for their choice. Go and tell that to Yerto and Gaggau and all the people. Tell them to listen well for I, Tonemetapu, have spoken through the star without a name –'

The old seer's voice grew faint with tiredness. It sounded like the fragile murmur of the reeds on the river's bank when the last light winds of autumn rustled them before the winter storms set in.

'Tell them,' Tonemetapu finished, and though Kekua's hearing was acute she had to lean forward to catch his words, 'the little shumbi is their peril and their salvation. They must make peace with her, or she with them. Whichever way it falls, the choice will be hers.'

Tonemetapu fell silent.

Kekua stood up. The patriarchs of the two clans were waiting anxiously and expectantly in the darkness beyond the ring of the trees. Threading her way between the trunks by touch and the play of the starlight on her skin, Kekua set off to find them.

She had much to tell them. But the essence of Tonemetapu's message was clear – they had one turning of the moon to share the valley and prepare for cloud-time, and the little shumbi, the half-drowned creature washed up on the river's bank, was the key to the people's survival.

43

Squatting on her haunches Jinga waited.

In spite of the intense darkness under the trees, the old female could see clearly. Like Manu she had the golden night-hunting eyes of all the ranging. Unlike the island yeti, whose sight by day was as sharp as the falcons and eagles which hunted the valley in the light but whose vision dulled as evening came, Jinga's pupils were backed by the reflecting discs of the mountain owls.

The discs gathered in every tiny pulse of luminescence from the night, even the faintest rays from the most distant stars. The light they absorbed defined images, and the images were transmitted to Jinga's brain. The old female registered them as trees, flowers, birds, insects and animals. She saw the landscape in the thin fitful glow of the sickle moon as clearly and vividly as the holding's gatherers did under the sun.

She scanned the valley now. The trees surrounded her. The island was immediately ahead, its shores washed by the twin arms of the river. She could hear the monotonous roar of the water as it cascaded over the headland rocks, divided into two streams, and surged together again as it eddied away. Beyond the pulsing river lay the plain. Most of the valley was hidden from her by the ridge at the island's centre, but in the far distance the mountains sheered up into the night sky. Laced with fields of snow and ice, the crests glittered in the starlight.

Somewhere – and it was too far for even Jinga's eyes to pick out – the black mouths of the caves opened on to the ledge above the ravine. She thought of the deep beds of warm hides inside them, of the winter stores, the wind-dried meat that used to be piled from the ground until the stacks reached the rocky roof, and she ran her tongue round her lips.

The caves were her home, but the stores were no longer there. The ranging's larders were empty. The food that should have filled them was called the cloud-time stores, although it wasn't eaten then.

The yeti required nothing in cloud-time, because the cold of the snows fed them. The stores were needed after cloud-time ended, when the melt began and before the crests came back to life, and the harvest and the prey animals returned. It was then that the ranging – and the holding too – were at their most vulnerable. The yeti's bodies were at their weakest, and there was nothing to hunt or to gather. Without the hidden caches of the year before, the hoarded meat and the painstakingly accumulated stocks of nuts, berries and grain, they would die.

Jinga clamped her arms to her chest. Although the night air in the valley was nothing like as cold as on the crests, the year was passing and each day the temperature fell. Jinga's pelt walled out the cold. It was the hunger ahead that seemed to chill her blood. This season there would be no caches, there was nothing to hide. She gazed into the darkness again.

'I have come,' Wengen said. He walked into the triangle of cleared earth where the clans had met that afternoon.

Jinga dropped to the ground. Unlike the valley yeti she didn't depend on smell. If she had, she would have scented his approach several minutes before. As it was, a casual scan of the darkness allowed her to pick him out as the big, powerfully muscled yeti came forward through the trees.

'Sit,' Jinga said.

Wengen lowered himself on to the fallen trunk where his father had sat earlier. Jinga examined him. Wengen's pelt glistened with beads of water from the river, and she knew he must have come straight from the island to the trees.

'You have until daylight,' Jinga said. 'What happens then?'

For a moment Wengen didn't answer.

Yerto had declared him an outlaw. To be exiled from the holding was an event so rare that none of the yeti on the island knew the fate of the outlaw.

'I will cross the valley,' Wengen replied eventually. 'I will climb to the crests. Then I will turn and follow the rising sun.'

Jinga snorted contemptuously. 'You think you will find food on the crests or in the sun's path?'

'I will search.'

Wengen shrugged his shoulders wearily. All the tremulous defiance he had shown Yerto had vanished. He looked shrunken and dazed. Only now, hours after Yerto's pronouncement, had the full impact of the patriarch's edict begun to strike him.

He was an outcast. He had nowhere to go except into a landscape without food.

'You will search!' Jinga grunted in scorn again. 'You will find nothing, just as we have found nothing. You will starve like us, Wengen. Unless –'

She came close to him and paused. Wengen could just make out her shape in the darkness. Jinga was heaving her arms angrily like an ancient flapping crow.

'Unless you can find people who will feed you.'

'Who will share their food with me?' he asked.

'The oduna,' Jinga snapped.

'The oduna?' Wengen looked at her appalled.

To be declared an outlaw, as Yerto had declared him, was almost inconceivable. But it had happened, and somehow Wengen would have to deal with it. If he was to survive he would have to forage, gather and hunt on his own. He would have to live without the support of the clan, scouring the ridges and the valleys that were supposed to lie beyond the great valley where the island lay.

The world of the oduna was different. Lost and alien and fugitive, they lived at the edges of the yeti's imagining. They belonged to the darkness beyond the darkness, beyond even the reach of the stars. To be cast among them was to be cast into a world of nightmare.

Wengen shuddered.

Jinga turned from him and scuttled across the clearing like a tree-crab, scratching her face.

'Gaggau was wounded on his last hunt before the little shumbi came,' she said. 'You saw his marks. The oduna made them. They threw spears at his body. The spears were lit with the dark storm's child. The oduna cannot call down the creature – only the shumbi can do that.'

Wengen frowned.

Jinga sneered at his stupidity. 'They have been taught by a shumbi, Wengen,' she said slowly. 'There must be a shumbi with them. He leads the oduna, he has taught them how to hunt for him.'

Wengen thought about what the old female had said, and realized she was right. The oduna, however horrifying, were only exiled members of the people. They didn't know how to call down and use the dark storm's child any more than the ranging or the holding did, but they had held it in their hands when they challenged Gaggau. They had used it to drive the hunters off the prey, and seize the animal for themselves. The oduna couldn't have done that on their own.

They could only have been led by a shumbi.

Wengen's face grew perplexed again. Even if Jinga was right, he couldn't see what difference a shumbi's presence among the oduna on the remote crests made to him. He started to say so, but Jinga cut him off.

'The ranging say the river gave our shumbi to the valley. The river washed her down from the crests, and Manu found her. But the shumbi is young, a child. How did the river find her?' Jinga asked.

Wengen didn't know.

'Do not our children, from the island and the crests, sometimes fall into the running water? Are they not swept away? Do not we search for them, all of us, until we find them? Do we not go on searching however long it takes?'

Wengen nodded. The children of both the clans were not only vital to the future – they *were* the future. Whenever a young child fell into one of the turbulent streams and rivers that threaded the valley and the crests, every activity was abandoned until it was found. Rescuing the child took precedence over everything. It was even more important than hunting or gathering. Lost children were beyond any price paid in the effort, energy, and danger needed to return them to their clans. Without their young neither the ranging nor the holding would continue to exist.

'It is true,' Wengen said.

'Then is it not true of the shumbi, too?' Jinga demanded.

Wengen was silent. The old female's mind was running on much faster than his.

'The child fell into the waters. That is why the river brought her to the valley – it could not have been otherwise. Can you not see, Wengen? Have you not looked at her shape and her legs and how on her breast she is starting to swell? Soon she will start to bleed –'

Jinga's voice was harsh with exasperation. 'The shumbi is like us. She is a child lost to the river. The adult shumbi will be searching for her as we would search. To them she is as valuable as a child of the people is to us.'

Wengen closed his eyes. He felt dizzy.

The old female was brutal and malevolent – Wengen knew that. He had shared in that brutality and malevolence when he had seized and raped Tana. He'd thought it would benefit him, but he'd been wrong. It had led only to his fight with Manu and his exile from the holding.

The fault was Jinga's. He should disown her, never listen to her again. He should walk away from her for ever, just as in a few hours when daylight came he would have to walk away from the holding. Except, he thought bitterly, she had left him with nowhere to go.

Wengen swung round. He set off towards the rim of the trees, took three strides and stopped. He hesitated and turned back. 'What are you saying?' he asked.

It wasn't only desperation that halted him. It was the echo of Jinga's last words. He didn't know what she meant, but with nothing else to hold on to, Wengen clung to the resonance of her voice as it faded among the branches overhead.

Jinga inspected him in the darkness. With her night-seeing eyes she could see him far more clearly than Wengen could see her. Wengen thought the darkness hid him. To Jinga he was as vivid as if he stood before her in the full light of day. His face was drawn, his pelt prickled with fear, his posture was stiff and awkward.

Jinga opened her mouth and let out a deep-throated cackle, a cackle of scorn, of humiliation. She intended it to be so.

'Here –' She patted the trunk where she was squatting. As if he were in a trance Wengen came over and heaved himself up on to a branch facing her.

'Go to the crests,' Jinga said. 'Look for the oduna's tracks. Follow them. When you find the oduna, you will find food. You will also find the shumbi who leads them. Tell him you know where the little shumbi is.'

'But how can I speak with him?'

Jinga spat scornfully at the earth. 'If he taught the oduna to use the dark storm's child, he must know our speech –' She paused, then went on. With every instruction her voice grew more insistent and compelling.

'Say you will take him to the little shumbi. Say that in return he must do what you want. He must help you.'

'Help me with what?'

'Help you become leader of both the holding *and* the ranging,' Jinga said. 'There is no space for two clans any longer. There is not enough food anywhere. From now on the ranging must hunt the valley as well as the crests. When the two clans feed together, the ranging will be stronger. It must be so. The hunters are always stronger than the gatherers. Look at what happened today. Yerto agreed we could hunt the valley. He said it was because of the bonds, but he lied. He agreed because he could not refuse us. We are stronger than you, Wengen.'

Wengen stared at her, hypnotized. 'How will the shumbi make me leader?' he asked.

'For giving him back the little shumbi, he must kill Gaggau, Yerto, Ryena and Manu for you. With the dark storm's child it will be easy for him. He will throw it at them and they will die. And when they are gone, who is left to lead the clans? No one but you –'

Jinga's voice dropped to a whisper. 'You have nothing, Wengen,' she hissed. 'You are an outcast. At best you will become one of the nameless oduna. At worst you will starve to feed only the vultures. But if you do what I say, you will return to lead both the clans. You will have Tana. You will have whatever you want.'

Wengen's eyes jerked away. He couldn't look at the old female any longer. Terror filled him, terror of the darkness and what was happening to him, terror above all of Jinga.

Wengen had thought nothing could be worse than the sentence of exile Yerto had pronounced on him. This was worse, much worse. He knew that he had violated many of the laws by which the clans lived. He had defied Yerto and Ryena. He had raped Tana. He had challenged Manu to combat. When they fought, Wengen had tried to kill Manu.

Yet what Jinga proposed was a graver violation than any of these – Jinga denied all the bonds. She had told him to ally himself not only with the outcast oduna, but with a shumbi – a creature that throughout the yeti's existence, as the clans were reminded again and again in cloud-time, they were bidden to avoid at whatever cost.

And Jinga had instructed him to kill. Not with his own hands, but using the shumbi as his weapon. Yerto, Gaggau, Ryena, Manu, the identity of the victims was irrelevant – the deaths, the killings, were what mattered. The bonds tolerated much: theft of food or roofing reeds, mounting another's mate, keeping secret a prime gathering ground, all could be explained and forgiven.

Not killing. Killing was inexcusable. Like a child lost to the waters, killing was the clans' destruction. That was the reason for his exile.

Wengen glanced back at the old female. She perched on the branch, huddling her knees in her arms. With her dark pelt and her glittering eyes she looked more than ever like a crow.

She spoke before Wengen could. 'So you will go?' she said. 'You will go to the crests, find the oduna, and the shumbi with them? And then you will do as I say? You will become leader of the clans?'

Jinga's voice rose in excitement, the excitement of lust, and suddenly it infected Wengen, pouring over him in waves of desire.

All his fear and hesitation vanished. In his mind he saw the two old greybacks lying dead with Ryena and Manu beside them, and he exulted. He saw Tana, Churinga and the young females of both the clans, and he felt himself harden. He saw the huge territory of the two clans with their combined grounds reaching from the snows to the island, he saw the hunters and the gatherers setting out, and he saw himself at the centre of it all, directing, ordering, praising and, above all, punishing.

He remembered the humiliations and frustrations of the past, and he no longer resented them – he treasured them. Every one would be slowly and brutally avenged. Jinga had been right. She had entered his life late but alone among all the influences on him she had consistently seen and spoken the truth to the deepest parts of his being. Now she was giving him triumph.

Jinga didn't need to wait for Wengen's answer. She saw his pale eyes flash with eagerness, she saw the long firm swelling at his groin, and she gave a husky cackle of laughter.

'Go now! When you return, come back to me as leader!'

Wengen swung himself off the branch and strode away through the darkness beneath the trees. As he reached the border of the plain he stared round, orientating himself by the stars. The southern crests stretched in a crescent ahead and to his left. Somewhere up there he would find the oduna and the shumbi who had taught them about the dark storm's child.

Tall and purposeful and murderous, Wengen headed on, the long-drawn-out peals of Jinga's laughter echoing behind him.

44

'What have you done with her, Robert? Where the hell is she?' Dorelia's voice erupted in a scream that echoed round the room.

Cabot rubbed his chin. Dorelia had flown through the night and taken the morning flight to Kathmandu. From the pallor of her cheeks and the dark rings beneath her eyes, she had barely slept during the long eighteen-hour journey.

Before replying Cabot turned and limped across the room.

The elegant porcelain plaque on the door outside announced it was the salon of the Maharajah Suite. Left to himself Cabot would have been much happier with his usual quarters in the smaller, quieter hotel close to the market, where he and the child had stayed. Dorelia always demanded the best which for her meant the most expensive. As soon as she'd told Cabot she was flying out, he had booked the suite and moved into the hotel himself to be close to her.

It was less than an hour since he had met her at the airport. Dorelia had been accompanied by what Cabot assumed was her new partner, a paunchy rumpled man who'd been introduced as Sean Ryan. Ryan, Dorelia told him, was a writer. Even as they shook hands Cabot knew that he was going to dislike the man. He had a growling aggressive voice, the stench of alcohol came off his skin like a spray, he chain-smoked and he swore constantly. Knowing Dorelia, Cabot reflected, it was almost inevitable that once she'd rejected the cold and bloodless Michael Howard, she'd turn to his opposite, a foul-mouthed, beer-swilling figure like Ryan.

The three of them spoke little on the journey from the airport into Kathmandu, and as soon as they reached the hotel Ryan headed for the bar. Now Cabot and Dorelia were alone.

'Iona's in the valley I told you about when I called, Dorelia,' Cabot answered. 'It's a huge space of land that lies below the ridge where we made our camp. Where exactly in the valley she is, I don't know. But we'll find out and we'll get the kid back.'

'And she was taken there by these –' Dorelia hesitated, searching for a word she could understand and accept. She couldn't find it so she fell back on the one she'd been trying to shut out of her mind. 'These monsters!'

'Except in people's imaginations, or more likely in their nightmares, monsters don't exist, my dear.' Cabot spoke as quietly and reassuringly as he could. 'In the real world there are only animals like ourselves. Iona seems to have been taken by a group of animals we call the yeti. There's no reason to think they won't be feeding and caring for her as one of their own.'

'The yeti?' Dorelia stared at him. 'I got Sean to ask about the yeti in London. Sean's worked for newspapers, he's got sources everywhere. He's spoken to scientists, to the Natural History Museum, to everyone. He says no one believes the creatures exist.'

'I wasn't sure myself, Dorelia, until I saw the prints in the snow. Then even I was convinced.'

'And you still let her go? You let her wander out into the night with these appalling animals all round her?'

'No, Dorelia, it didn't happen like that –' Cabot paused.

He could have guessed Dorelia would try to make him shoulder the maximum amount of blame for Iona's disappearance. In fact, although in her selfishness Dorelia was blind to it, there was no need. Cabot had tormented himself with guilt ever since that appalling morning after the storm. He knew his feelings were irrational and misconceived but the haunting sense of responsibility, the suspicion that if somehow he had acted differently the child wouldn't have been lost, never left him for an instant.

He realized now that Dorelia felt guilty too. She blamed herself for suggesting that Iona went with him, and her accusations were an attempt to transfer her own guilt onto him. Instead of anger, Cabot looked at her haggard face and felt only pity. With all Dorelia's faults, in her own way she loved her daughter. The story she'd been asked to accept might well have unhinged a far more stable and generous mother than Dorelia would ever be.

Cabot came back to where she was standing. He took her hand and told her again about the night of the storm. When he finished Dorelia wept. She clung to him sobbing for a while, then she stepped back and wiped her eyes.

'Why did she do it, Robert?' Dorelia asked in a hurt, bewildered voice. 'Iona and I don't always get along, Christ, what mother and daughter do? But I know the child. She's sensible, down-to-earth, careful.'

Cabot managed a wry smile. 'I'm glad we're talking about the same child, Dorelia, because that's exactly how I'd describe her, and those qualities are going to be her greatest strengths wherever she is now.'

'Then why the hell did she get dressed and go out into the night in the middle of a storm?'

It was the question that had baffled Cabot ever since he'd searched Iona's tent and found her clothes, her boots and her survival belt missing. He'd spent nights lying awake trying to find an answer. Finally one possibility had occurred to him, a possibility so strange and contradictory in terms of all he knew about the child that his immediate reaction was to dismiss it. Only when he was left with nothing else did he reconsider it.

He'd assumed the child had dressed because she was going somewhere. He'd thought she must have had a goal, a plan, a private expedition she was set on completing whatever the weather, but perhaps he was wrong. Perhaps she was *escaping* from somewhere. The only place she could have been escaping from was the tent, and the only motive that could have driven her out from the tent's safety into the blizzard was fear.

It was just possible, thought Cabot, that his goddaughter, the competent, level-headed child he'd believed was fearless, had chosen the storm in preference to the tent through sheer terror. But not of the yeti – Hughes had emphatically demonstrated that the creature hadn't been closer to the camp than where its prints crossed Iona's. Roshan agreed. The yeti, the Sherpa said, never approached a human dwelling. That meant that the terror must have been inside Iona herself, something she had brought with her to Nepal.

Cabot looked at his niece. He was about to tell Dorelia his theory, but stopped himself. Dorelia was under enough pressure already without facing the possibility that the child she'd sent with him to the mountains was so weighed down with fear before she left London that she'd walked out into the dark fury of a Himalayan storm to escape it.

Instead Cabot said simply, 'I don't know, Dorelia. When she's back with us, we'll find out. Let's leave it until then.'

Dorelia looked at him, distraught. 'She will come back, won't she, Robert?' she asked despairingly.

'Sure as hell she'll come back,' Cabot replied with a confidence he didn't remotely feel. 'Hughes isn't exactly the guy you'd choose to run the Federal Reserve Bank, but he knows the mountains, he knows these animals, he'll find her. I figured that out and Roshan agrees – and if Roshan thinks so, you can put your money on the table that the Welshman will bring her home.'

'But when, Robert, when?' Dorelia's imploring voice began to crack.

'Roshan's waiting in a village called Nanga Purna. It's a little hamlet high up in the mountains not too far from the valley to the south. Roshan's got other Sherpas with him. As soon as he gets any news from Hughes, he'll send a runner back here. Nepal's a vertical country, but it's also a tiny one. We'll know within a couple of days when the child's been located.'

'And then?'

'We'll go out there and wait for Hughes to bring her in. Meanwhile, you'll just have to bite on the bullet and be patient.'

Dorelia closed her eyes and shivered. 'Without Charles I don't know how I'd have survived this.'

Cabot frowned. 'I thought it was Mr Ryan. Who's Charles?'

'My attorney, Charles Lefanu,' she answered. 'Sean loves Iona too and she loves him, she told me so, but it's been Charles who's really kept me going over this. Of course he's known Iona much longer than Sean. It was Charles who got the hearing adjourned again so I could fly out here. I guess they all love her, even that bastard Michael, but maybe Charles most of all.'

Cabot was silent. He took off his glasses, polished them and put them back on his nose. There were many things he might have said, but it wasn't the moment to say any of them. He managed to give his niece another quizzical smile.

'I'm delighted, my dear,' he said, 'that Iona has so many close and loving admirers. With any luck this old stranger in her life who clearly isn't part of the magic circle may be able to reunite her with them.'

Dorelia didn't seem to hear him. Her cheeks had sagged and her eyes had filmed with tears again.

'For Christ's sake, where is she, Robert? What is she doing – tell me!'

45

Iona opened her eyes and lay blinking on her bed of grass and reeds.

Something had woken her. Inside the shelter the darkness was as deep as it always became as soon as the sun set behind the bowl of the mountains and the last of the light faded from the evening sky. Iona listened. The usual noises of the night had vanished – the shrill double whistles of the little pearl-spotted owls as they hunted for insects above the island, the whisper of the flying squirrels' wing membranes as they floated through the trees, the squeak of bats and the occasional distant cough of a deer.

Now Iona became aware of a new sound. It filled every corner of the shelter as if the wings of a thousand moths were beating against the roof. She frowned – it could only be rain. Sometimes at Mainwarden she had hidden in the haystack at the end of the cattle barn. When rain fell on the packed dry grass it made exactly the same noise as it was doing now on the shelter.

Wide-awake now, Iona raised herself on her elbow.

It was the first rain that had fallen on the valley since her arrival. Rain in the Himalayas, she knew from Kekua, was one of the signals that the summer was ending and the season was moving quickly towards winter. After a while the drumming died away, and the clouds overhead parted. Through the bow-shaped hoop at the entrance, Iona glimpsed the moon.

On the night Kekua came back with Tonemetapu's decision, the moon had been new, a slim silver sickle above the trees where the clans had met. Now it was half full. The old seer had given the clans a month to share the valley's harvest and prepare for cloud-time. Only two weeks remained. Iona thought back to the meeting and the days that followed.

The morning after the clans met, Iona went down to the river bank at dawn with Kekua and Churinga for the daily conference of the gatherers before they set off into the valley's grounds. They waited for Yerto. The patriarch appeared, not as before from the direction of the clearing but swimming across the river from the far side with Manu at his shoulder.

Yerto clambered ponderously out of the water. Once his foot slipped in the mud and Manu had to grip his elbow to prevent him from falling. Stiffly Yerto shook himself dry. The burden of exiling his son Wengen still lay heavily on him. The old yeti's face was gaunt and harrowed and his eyes were dull. Several times when he spoke he stumbled over his words.

'I come from meeting Gaggau and his hunters,' he said. 'We have discussed how the valley shall be shared between the holding and the ranging, so that neither interferes with the other. Gaggau and I are agreed. The grounds will be divided. Each day the two clans will use different pastures. One will hunt, the other will gather. The next day they will change. So it will continue –' Yerto's head dropped wearily on his chest. He gestured at Manu and added, 'Manu will speak for me where the holding starts today.'

Yerto set off up the bank. He took a few steps and stumbled, half sinking to his knees. Manu ran to his aid but the patriarch's mate, Ryena, was there first. She helped Yerto back to his feet and walked beside him, almost as stooped as he was, up to the clearing.

Manu returned to the water's edge and addressed the gatherers, giving them their instructions for the day. Then he plunged back into the water with the leopard behind him. The ranging had come down to the valley, and Manu was going to hunt with his own people.

Through the frame of the shelter's entrance Iona looked at the circle of the clearing lit by the light of the half-moon.

When she came to the island the space between the shelters had been grassy and sweet-smelling. Now the grass and the scents had gone. In the urgency to gather in the cloud-time stores, the earth had been trodden flat and bare by the constant passage of the holding's feet.

Day after day the ranging hunted and the holding gathered. For the first week all the efforts of Gaggau's hunters were devoted to acquiring enough prey to fill the clan's bellies and repair the damage done by the hunger on the crests. Everyone, from the hunters themselves to the old and the children, needed protein. Once they were fed, once their strength had begun to build back, the ranging turned its energies to the demands of cloud-time.

Cloud-time. The phrase had come up again and again. Iona had asked Kekua, Churinga, Manu, all of the yeti she had come to know and trust, what cloud-time meant. She still didn't know.

'It is where we go when the snows come,' Kekua said. 'It is for the people to be together and dream. You will learn, little shumbi, when the time comes.'

Churinga had said the same, so had Manu. Puzzled and dissatisfied, Iona knew there was no point in pressing them further. Whatever cloud-time was, it was something they couldn't explain.

What Iona did learn was that the stores weren't for cloud-time itself. They were needed for the weeks that followed, when the snows were melting but the new season's growth hadn't yet started. Without anything to eat then, the yeti would have starved. In a way, Iona thought, the stores were like the caches of nuts the squirrels at Mainwarden gathered against the winter.

Each evening as she returned at dusk with the gatherers, Iona would see the hunters coming back too. Much of their prey were the birds Uncle Robert had taught her to recognize. Their thonged carrying belts bulged with emerald-winged flycatchers, scarlet minivets, blue-feathered magpies and jays, larks and warblers and even the occasional kingfisher. On good days they killed animals – musk deer, a sambur buck, hill foxes and jackals, serow antelope, sloth bears, and once a black bear with her cubs.

Yerto no longer left the island but old Ryena continued to come out with the gatherers. She would look anxiously at the dead birds and animals as the ranging passed.

'She and her young should be filling themselves with the valley's fruit.' Ryena pointed at the carcasses of the bear and her cubs slung on poles the hunters were carrying on their shoulders. 'That is why they come here. As they forage, they leave the seeds in their droppings. The seeds are spread and next season they grow so we may crop them –'

Ryena's face clouded and she shook her head. 'It will not be so in the season that comes. The ranging must eat, they must prepare for cloud-time, but there will be little fruit to harvest in the valley when the sun returns.'

Sorrowfully she walked on.

In the shelter Iona glanced up. The moonlight had vanished from the clearing and the drumming on the roof had started again. The rain had returned. Iona lay back and tried to sleep, but her mind was restless and Ryena's words kept echoing through her mind. The child sat up and gazed into the watery darkness once more. Beside her Kekua slept untroubled.

Iona wasn't sure why, but she knew instinctively that Ryena was right. The ranging were recovering from the season's disastrous famine. They would have to share the gatherers' stores when cloud-time ended, but both the clans had enough to last them through the coming winter until the sun came back. Next year it would be different.

The valley was being plundered. If the animals returned to the crests and the ranging were able to hunt their grounds again, the land would recover. If the animals didn't return and the ranging were forced to go on sharing the valley, the valley was doomed. It didn't have the resources to support both the clans. In one of Uncle Robert's favourite phrases the valley would 'degrade and die'. If that happened, the yeti would die with it.

Iona reached for Bear. Hugging the ragged little animal to her for comfort, she stared at the falling rain and shivered.

It wasn't just the possibility of the valley and the yeti dying that haunted Iona. It was what Kekua had said when she walked out of the trees with Tonemetapu's decision. She'd given the old seer's message to the patriarchs, their mates and the yeti who accompanied them. Then she'd turned towards where Iona was crouching in the darkness with her arm resting on Babilla's neck.

Kekua picked out the child unerringly. She gazed at her with her sightless eyes and spoke as if she could see her. 'Tonemetapu also says the shumbi will be either the people's peril or their salvation. That is for her to decide.'

Iona knew she couldn't harm the clans. She was a child in a world she still barely understood, floating among the yeti like a reed bobbing on the tumbling river. She had thought that learning their language would give her a pathway to escape. She was wrong. Speaking the tongue of the people had only anchored her more firmly in their lives.

Briefly she'd thought she had power over them because, washed down from the crests and the stars, she was magical. But she had no magic to offer the gatherers – in the feeding grounds she was clumsy and inept. She had no more magic on the crests – the prey animals remained stubbornly absent however far she travelled with the hunters. She could not even use fire.

Twice Iona had tried to strike her matches and twice she had drawn back. Fire in the valley would be deadly. It would be the end of everything. She couldn't impose herself on the yeti, and she couldn't help them. She could do nothing at all. And still Tonemetapu insisted she could be their salvation.

Troubled, bewildered, and guilty for reasons she couldn't fathom, Iona lay down. Clutching Bear in her arms she slept.

When Iona woke again the rain had stopped.

She crawled to the shelter's entrance and sniffed the morning air. Her nostrils filled with the rich loamy scent of warm wet earth. The valley floor was hazed with a soft white mist, and the yeti, stretching themselves in the dawn light, seemed to be floating in clouds. She glanced round the clearing.

Manu was just emerging from his shelter. He stood up, spread out his arms and yawned. His dark pelt had the sheen of silk, and as he shook the sleep from his eyes his face was frank and bold and eager. Three months ago Manu was an unknown monster who had invaded the living world from the darkness of Iona's nightmares. Now he was familiar and, as the muscles rippled under his hide and he balanced himself lightly on his feet, he was almost beautiful.

Iona plucked her gaze away from him.

She climbed the ridge and pushed her way down through the undergrowth to the river. The grass seemed to have grown an inch in the night. The willow bushes and clumps of maidenhair that lined the path were hung with spiders' webs, glistening with droplets of dew like the pearled tiaras on the heads of the women in the old family portraits at Mainwarden. In spite of the gathering radiance of the morning, the air was sharp and chill.

Iona shivered. Kekua had said the rain heralded winter, and Iona could feel snow in the bright air.

She stopped on the river bank. Beyond the inlet where she washed every morning was a deep pool in which Iona had occasionally glimpsed a mahseer, the slender, speckled, trout-like fish which the holding yeti sometimes speared with their pointed gathering sticks. Today after the night's rain the pool had become a well of dark indigo water whose depths were thronged with mahseer. There must have been hundreds of them, perhaps even a thousand.

Iona waded out to the pool's edge. She plunged her arms into the water, and felt the lithe silvery bodies brushing against her skin. She tried to catch some of them, but the fish slipped through her hands. Frustrated, she went back to the shore and stood for a moment thinking.

The fish were not only beautiful. To the yeti they were a prized source of food – and Iona had begun to think like the yeti. Several hundred mahseer, wind-dried like the meat of the prey animals, would be a valuable addition to the cloud-time stores. To catch the fish before they dispersed would need a net – spearing was much too slow for a concentration as big as this one.

Even better, it occurred to Iona, would be to build a pen like the ones in the fish farms that lined the West Highland lochs near her Uncle Harry's house in Scotland. The fish in this shoal were small. If they were penned for a while they would almost double in weight – Iona knew that because Uncle Harry had taken her to one of the fish farms, and explained how it worked.

It was too late to pen the mahseer this season. The best that could be done was to catch as many as possible, and Kekua would know how to make a net, Iona was sure of that. But next year a pen could be made and that would change everything. The yeti wouldn't have to rely on the occasional catch from their gathering sticks. The fish would fatten on their own, and the yeti could haul them from the water whenever they were needed.

Iona headed back for the clearing to look for Kekua.

Afterwards she could never be sure whether she got the idea from the shoal of mahseer or from what happened later the same day. It wasn't important. What took place that day was to change the lives of the yeti for ever. Even as it started, Iona knew that she was the cause of it.

On her return from the river Iona found Kekua. The blind yeti knew exactly what was needed to harvest the fish, a basket-like container woven from willow saplings. She, Iona and Churinga fished the pool for an hour before the mahseer vanished. The fish were gutted, split, skewered on sticks and left to dry on the ridge. Then the three of them set off to join the day's gathering party.

That evening, as they headed back for the island, their path crossed with the returning hunters close to the ranging's camp.

Manu was at their head. The hunters had had a barren day until half an hour earlier when they'd put up a wild boar sow with the year's half-grown litter. Normally the hunters killed and butchered a prey animal where they found it. Occasionally, if the hunt ended close to the caves or, as now, to their camp in the valley, and if the animal could be captured alive, they took it back and slaughtered it there so that the other yeti of the ranging could drink its blood.

Manu glanced up at the gathering party. He saw Iona and beckoned. 'Come!' he shouted. 'Share the blood with us!'

The gatherers led by Ryena changed direction and followed Manu to the ranging's camp.

When they arrived, two of the hunters, Raku and Penga, had the sow pinned down on the ground by her ears and Soru was gripping the animal's haunches. Each of the other hunters held one of the screaming struggling piglets, and Manu stood close to them with a stone-bladed killing club in his hands. A couple of the ranging's females came forward with clay-stoppered lengths of hollow branches in their hands to catch the blood.

Raku and Penga wrenched the sow's head round so that the animal's neck was exposed, and Manu raised the club above his head.

'No!' Iona shouted.

The heads of all the yeti swung towards her. Manu hesitated. He lowered the club and stared at her, astonished. Iona walked forward.

Dusk was settling down over the valley and the stars were already beginning to appear. The air was chill and owls were calling. Kekua, Churinga and the other gatherers watched her, as tense and bewildered as the yeti of the ranging.

'Put away your club, Manu,' Iona said. 'Take the thongs from your hunting belt, bind them together and make a leash. Put the leash round the sow's leg and tether her to a tree. Let her range and feed where she can roam. The litter will not escape. They will stay with her. When they are fat, you can kill them, but keep the sow because the boar who seeded her will find her and she will have another litter. Then you can do the same again –'

Iona paused and gulped for air. She felt breathless and she was trembling.

Whether it was the fish that morning or the wild boar and its litter now, she had no idea. One or the other had triggered something inside her, an instinct she knew was right. There was an answer to the valley's problems, to the demands placed on it by the presence there of the ranging as well as the holding. It was an answer so simple, so obvious, so deeply embedded in all her life and past that Iona couldn't believe it hadn't occurred to her before.

Used carefully, the valley's resources were enough to feed both the clans. What they needed was the knowledge of how to husband them. Iona had only a fraction of that knowledge, absorbed unthinkingly throughout her childhood. Uncle Harry explaining about the farmed salmon, Tom discussing the cattle and sheep at Mainwarden, old Silas gauging the year's hay through his shrewd narrowed eyes, Mr Simpson examining the vegetables in the walled garden and gruffly pronouncing on their condition.

What they had passed on to Iona was enough to provide what Tonemetapu had asked of her – the people's salvation.

'It is a new way,' Iona finished. 'Whatever happens next season, whether the prey animals return or not, it will let the ranging and the holding share the valley so neither is hungry. In the world of the shumbi it is called farming.'

Manu was silent. For a long while he stared at the child. Iona gazed back at him.

For the first time, she was looking at one of the yeti not just on equal terms but from a position of strength that owed nothing to her being a shumbi, to possessing what they believed was magic. She had something the yeti hadn't. It wasn't anything concrete, like the matches. It was something in her mind. She might lose the matches, but she could never lose what she knew and they did not.

She *did* have power over them. And because power was magic and the two were inseparable, she did after all have magic too.

Manu turned to Raku and Penga. 'Do as the shumbi says. Make a leash with your thongs and tether the animal to a tree. And you –' He glanced at the hunters holding the piglets. 'Put the sow's young down. Let them feed from her belly. Tomorrow you, Soru, stay here and guard her. When the sow has cropped, take the leash to another tree –'

Manu looked back at Iona. 'We will do as you say. The hunters will follow a new spoor.'

The new ways were to apply to the gatherers, too.

Next morning after the holding had crossed the river, but before they entered the grounds that Yerto had allotted them for the day, Iona went up to Ryena.

'I wish to speak with you before we gather,' Iona said.

Ryena stared at her. The old female's head was bowed and her eyes were sunken and weary. Finally she nodded and the two of them walked away from the other yeti.

Iona had slept little during the night. For hour after hour she had tossed restlessly in the darkness of the shelter, her mind in tumult.

She still couldn't understand why the answer to the ranging's deprivations hadn't come to her earlier. Now she had found it, the possibilities were almost endless. The hunters already used the natural funnels and gullies of the crests to trap prey. It was only a step from there to fencing the gullies, to building stockades and penning the animals so that they could breed in captivity.

But tethering and penning didn't solve the hardships of the holdings' gatherers, who relied on harvesting the wild. The fruiting trees and bushes, the tubers, berries, nuts and seeds, and the plants that bore them, couldn't be penned and tethered. They were scattered across the grounds at random, depending for their survival on the vagaries of the sun and rain and wind, and the birds and animals that also cropped the valley.

Or so Iona thought. Towards dawn she realized her mistake. The solution that came to her was even more dizzyingly obvious than the penning of the animals.

If the animals could be farmed, the valley's pastures could be sown.

'You spoke of the bear,' Iona said to Ryena. 'You said how it ate the fruit and expelled the seeds and kernels as it returned to the crests, and that when the season turned again you harvested what had grown from its scatterings. Is that not so?'

Ryena nodded.

'Then why do we not do as the bear? We have no need to eat and expel the seeds. We have only to gather them when they are ripe and place them in the earth. We can sow them wherever we want – close to the island so they are at hand to crop. We can do what the bear does, but we can do it better.'

Ryena made no reply. The old female rubbed her face. She examined the gathering pouch of a weaver's nest in her hand, then looked back at the river and up at the crests. She gazed at the other members of the holding, waiting fifty paces away from them. Then she turned to face Iona again.

Iona held her breath. She knew what was going through Ryena's head. It had been hard enough to persuade Manu, but Manu was younger, his mind was more open and flexible, Iona knew him much better and she knew that he trusted her. Ryena was old. She was being asked to change the habits and convictions not only of a lifetime but of all the long generations of the yeti who had gone before her.

Ryena gathered from the earth so that she and her people could eat. Iona was asking the old female to gather – and then put back into the ground what she'd so painstakingly taken from it. Watching the yeti's trenched and perplexed face, Iona thought that perhaps the gap between the two of them was so vast it was unbridgeable. A chasm separated them that neither could cross.

Then Ryena raised her head and smiled. 'We will gather today as before,' she said. 'Half will go to the cloud-time stores, the other half will be given back to the earth, and placed as you direct.'

Ryena reached out and scratched Iona's nose. Iona lifted her hand to return the greeting – then stopped. Instead she threw her arms round the old female and hugged Ryena to her.

'How do you know when cloud-time has arrived?' Iona demanded.

The gathering party had returned early from the grounds, and she was standing with Kekua before the shelter in the evening light.

The month Tonemetapu had given the clans was almost over. Each day the two groups had combed the valley with increasing urgency. Normally by then the holding's work would be done. The cloud-time stores would be gathered in, and the yeti would be enjoying the last days of sun before the winter set in. This season was different. The hunters had barely had enough time to build up their stores of body fat against the snows, let alone to prepare for the barren period when the winter ended. The island yeti had to provide not only for themselves but for their companions from the crests.

Every day the air was colder. Twice over the past week Iona had woken at dawn to find the clearing white with ground frost, and once the morning wind had brought a flurry of sleet.

Kekua didn't answer Iona for a moment. The blind yeti stood with her head tilted towards the sky and the intent frowning expression on her face that Iona knew meant her senses were alert to something.

'Look!' Kekua pointed suddenly. 'Up there in the trees among the branches.'

Iona glanced up. She caught a flash of brightness and saw it was a butterfly. Its wings were a deep golden-yellow dappled at the edges with splashes of jade green. Whenever she had watched the valley's butterflies before, they had always flown swiftly, swooping and fluttering like quick jewelled sparks over the grass or among the leaves. This one was beating slowly and languorously overhead as if it were half-asleep.

'Have you found it?' Kekua asked.

'Yes,' Iona replied, marvelling once again at Kekua's ability to read the world of the valley as easily as if she could see.

'The yellow butterflies tell us of cloud-time,' Kekua said. 'They share it with us. They know when the time has come and they fly to the place where we and they can dream. They tell us too when cloud-time is over. It is the brushing of their wings that wakes the people after the melt begins. That butterfly is early, but it is on its way, it is already dreaming. When more follow behind, then it is time for us to go.'

Iona followed the butterfly's flight as it disappeared towards the setting sun. She shivered. It wasn't only the evening chill that made her tremble, although tonight was the coldest evening on the island yet. She'd remembered something her Uncle Robert had told her once. Some butterflies, he said, could survive the bitterest winters by becoming part of the winter themselves. Perhaps the yeti could do the same.

All Iona knew was that cloud-time was close – and she was neither a butterfly nor a yeti.

46

Geraint Hughes stopped and stood motionless.

The creature was about two hundred yards away and higher up the slope he was climbing. It stood in the open in a clearing between the trees, making no attempt to hide.

The leading oduna behind Hughes had spotted the animal too and gave an uncertain hiss of alarm. One by one the other oduna, following in a line, also saw it, and the single hiss became a chorus of anxiety. Hughes glanced over his shoulder and cursed them furiously into silence. Then he looked ahead again. Although he had never seen one before, Hughes knew instantly that the creature was a yeti.

The yeti still hadn't moved. It was staring down at him intently. Hughes waited for one minute, then two, then ten. He wasn't conscious of registering the yeti's appearance – he was only aware of its still, calm presence above him. Finally he realized that his first instinctive reaction – which he hadn't even admitted to himself – was right.

Hughes hadn't found the yeti – it had found him. It wasn't going to run – it was waiting for him.

Hughes shrugged off his pack and dropped it on the ground. Behind him the oduna had sunk to their haunches and started to whisper among themselves. He swung towards them again. 'Stay here,' he said. 'Be very quiet. Do not move a step further. If anyone does, then it will be this.'

Hughes tapped the sheath where he kept his ivory-handled folding razor. Its blade administered the most fearsome and dreaded punishment he dealt out – the severing of an ankle tendon. He had only used it twice in forty years. Now he was prepared to use it on every one of them.

The oduna remembered the two of their tribe who had limped ever since, dragging useless legs behind them. As they shrank back, Hughes turned and began to climb the slope. The yeti was still immobile in the clearing between the trees.

As Hughes trudged up through the snow he began to take in its appearance, which was strangely close to the image he'd created long ago and carried in his mind ever since. It was very tall, well over six and a half foot, Hughes guessed. It had broad bowed shoulders, long arms and a thick pelt of fur. Its forehead protruded above its eyes and its lower jaw stuck out in a great lantern-like sweep.

To some extent, it resembled the pictures in Hughes's childhood schoolbooks of Neanderthal man, the fleshed-out forms of the early human skeletons found in the Neander valley. Yet even a hundred yards away, he could see that his image didn't match the reality. The artists' drawings suggested a coarse-haired lumbering creature, heavy-jointed, slow-witted and primitive.

The yeti was nothing like that.

For a start the creature's pelt wasn't coarse and rough. It was fine, almost silky, and its colour wasn't the dark bear-brown Hughes had imagined. It was a pale wheaten ochre, reminding him of the high valley meadows at the end of the Himalayan summer. Then, although the yeti hadn't stirred, Hughes sensed that in spite of its size its movements would be swift and graceful. Finally there were the animal's eyes.

The yeti stared at him steadily and fearlessly as Hughes approached. Its light slate-grey pupils were thoughtful and intelligent, almost cunning, their gaze so penetrating that Hughes felt a momentary shiver of uncertainty. The eyes seemed not merely to stare at him, but straight through him to the oduna huddled whispering behind.

Compared with them, the yeti might have come from a different race.

Hughes stopped five yards away. The oduna always made a gesture of submission at the appearance of a human, squatting, lowering their heads and waiting until they were told to stand. The yeti made no such gesture. It continued to examine Hughes for a moment, then it walked forward, stretched out its arm and scratched the side of Hughes's nose.

He stiffened as the creature towered above him, and the hair prickled on the back of his neck. He swallowed his fear. There was nothing threatening in what the yeti had done, but Hughes knew it meant something – something he had to respond to. His mind raced. If the scratching was a greeting, he would have to return it.

He lifted his arm and warily scratched the yeti's nose. It gave a small grunt, the first sound the creature had made. As far as Hughes could tell it was a grunt of approval, and he breathed out silently in relief. The yeti stepped back.

'I am Wengen, so listen well,' the yeti said. 'I have come from the valley to find you. This is the cause –'

The yeti spoke in the tongue of the oduna, the system of communication Hughes had worked out and taught himself years before when he first came upon the creatures. The language depended not only on words, but on sounds and intonations and gestures. Many of those employed by the yeti were unknown to Hughes. The oduna's version of the language was crude and simple. The yeti's was more subtle and complicated.

From time to time Hughes lost what the yeti was saying to him. Then he would hear a familiar phrase or sound – a fluting whistle or a soft bark like the warning call of a deer to her kid – and he would pick up the central thread of the story again. Motionless, he listened.

As far as the Welshman could make out, there were two tribes of yeti. Wengen came from the tribe which inhabited the great misty bowl of the valley that Hughes had looked down on from the ridge. On the crests above lived another group. The mountain yeti depended on hunting animals for food, and that season the animals had deserted the crests and come down to the valley to hunt. Bitter disputes had broken out between the two groups.

'Basha' was the word Wengen used. The oduna used the same word to explain their own plight as outcasts. Misfortune, disaster, or occasionally at its worst, evil, was how Hughes translated it to himself. Whatever it was, basha had been visited on Wengen with a vengeance. For some reason the yeti had been caught up in one of the worst of the conflicts. He was blamed for the trouble, and exiled by the tribal leaders.

That was why he came to be standing in front of Hughes, or rather that was the background to his appearance. The real reason he was there, the reason he had tracked the oduna and found Hughes, was different. As Hughes heard the yeti state it, the hairs on the Welshman's neck rose and prickled again.

'Before all of what I have told you,' Wengen said, 'something happened to the valley. The river brought us a shumbi –' Wengen hesitated as if Hughes, although a shumbi himself, might not know what the word meant. 'You know what that is?'

'Yes –'

It could only be what the oduna termed a 'shambay', their word for a human. The oduna used it to refer to him.

Hughes pointed at his chest. 'It is one like I am.'

Wengen nodded. 'This shumbi was a child, a female child near to breeding age but not yet with blood on her legs when the moon changes,' Wengen went on. 'Manu found her on the river's bank and carried her back to the holding. The people of the holding say she was given by the snows. Even Tonemetapu says that. I say she tumbled into the waters and was washed down to us –'

Wengen's voice was suddenly defiant. Hughes was silent, waiting for the yeti to go on. Eventually he did.

'I say she was lost to the river by her own people. I say I know where she can be found. I am Wengen, so listen well!' The yeti's voice rose and hardened as he finished. Then he was silent.

Hughes stared at the creature. He felt blood starting to cloud his eyes, and he massaged them furiously with his fingertips.

He was no longer afraid of Wengen. He was afraid of himself. His eyes misted with the opaque redness only when the madness began to invade him. Normally Hughes accepted its arrival with delight. He revelled in the hot, turbulent tide that surged across his body. He laughed and shouted and struck out wildly at the oduna. The more they cowered and whimpered, the more furiously he beat them. He bellowed at the moon. He cursed the stars. He spat on the snow. He howled at the trees, silencing the owls' song. When the demons had danced him into a frenzy, he collapsed exhausted on the ground. Then the oduna wrapped him in skins and placed him before the fire he had shown them how to make. Afterwards, retreating and squatting on their haunches, they waited for daylight and his awakening.

Now Hughes shuddered. Madness was part of him, was at the core of him, but today he must neither tolerate nor acknowledge it. He forced it down, packing it deep inside himself, slamming shut the heavy lid of his mind and throwing home the bolts. Madness belonged to tomorrow. Today he had heard the story he had waited all his life to hear. Today he had to remain sane.

'Why did you search me out?' Hughes demanded.

'Jinga told me to do so.'

'Jinga?' Hughes frowned. The word seemed to be a name, but it wasn't one the yeti had mentioned before. 'Who is Jinga?'

'Jinga is mate to Gaggau who leads the ranging, the people of the crests,' Wengen answered. 'All are against me except Jinga. She said that if I found you and offered to show you where you could find the shumbi child, you would help me return to the valley.'

Hughes was silent.

The yeti was far more intelligent than he had believed possible, more intelligent than even the complexity of his speech suggested. Hughes was being offered a bargain that was almost human in the thinking behind it.

'How can I help you return?'

'You have the power to call down the dark storm's child,' Wengen said. 'Come with me to the valley. I will show you the shumbi's shelter. Call down the wounding brightness on Gaggau, Yerto, Manu, and the others I shall signal out for you. Then I shall have the two clans, and you may take the child.'

'What do you mean by the dark storm's child?' It was another phrase unknown to Hughes.

Wengen looked at him, puzzled. Silently he raised his arm and pointed. Hughes glanced over his shoulder. The yeti was pointing at the fire that still smouldered on the slope beneath them, and the Welshman understood.

Hughes remembered the two mysterious night-time clashes his oduna had had since they came to the ridges. In the first, one of the oduna had been killed. In the second, the outcasts, wielding fire-brands, had driven some hunters from the body of a recently killed prey animal. The pack claimed that on both occasions they had been confronted by yeti, but Hughes hadn't believed them. He guessed their enemies had been nomadic mountain tribesmen who he knew from the oduna's stories had killed many of them in the past.

He realized now that he'd been wrong. The oduna had indeed been attacked twice by the yeti. The second time the oduna had driven them off with the fire he'd taught a few of them to use. Wen-gen knew about fire – the dark storm's child, as he called it – but he evidently didn't know how much more lethal a rifle could be.

'These people you speak of,' Hughes said, 'you wish me to kill them?'

Wengen nodded. 'Their time is at an end.'

'And in return you will give me the shumbi?'

It had already been said, but it was so important that Hughes wanted it repeated and confirmed.

Wengen nodded again. 'We have no use for her. She can neither find game on the crests, nor gather on the plains. The child is yours.'

Hughes said nothing for a long time. He closed his eyes and breathed in deeply.

He was right. The first set of tracks belonged to a human child, the child who had disappeared from the American's camp. Hughes knew Cabot would give anything to have her returned to him. He would pay, by Hughes's standards he would pay hugely. That was important because for the first time in his forty years in the Himalayas Hughes had a purpose for money.

Money would buy him permits, porters, equipment, everything he needed. What it couldn't buy him was the second set of tracks, the tracks of the yeti. Nothing could have bought him those. He had come across them through fortune, fate, the spirit of the mountains – Hughes didn't know. All he knew was that after forty years he had found not only the tracks, but the creatures who made them.

He had found the key to Everest.

Hughes opened his eyes. He felt dizzy and he knew the madness was close to him once more. He caged it behind the bars of his mind and looked at Wengen again.

'I will call down the dark storm's child,' he said, 'I will kill those you signal to me. I want the shumbi, but I want more.'

'What do you ask for?'

The yeti's eyes narrowed. They gazed at Hughes with a cold suspicious glare. At each exchange between them, Geraint understood increasingly how much he had underestimated the intelligence of the creatures from the heights.

'After we have finished, after I have the child and the people you signal are killed, I go to the crests,' Geraint answered. 'Not your crests here, but the high distant crests to the north. I go to the highest crest of all.'

Wengen wrinkled his face, puzzled. 'The highest crests are far above the tree line. There is no food there, only snow and ice.'

'Nonetheless, that is where I go. I take my own food with me. I need your people as guides, to show me the way and tell me how I may climb there. Can they do that?'

Wengen inspected the shumbi as if he were mad. From somewhere deep down in the yeti's stomach a sound rumbled up that might have been a laugh.

'Our people came from the stars,' he said. 'The first to seed us was the star without a name. We can climb back to where he was born in dreams, in cloud-time, whenever we wish. We can climb anywhere –' Wengen paused. 'How is it named, this crest you wish to climb?'

'The shumbi name it Everest,' Geraint answered.

'Kill for me, give me the clans, and I will take you there.'

47

'Tell him nothing has changed,' Hughes said to Roshan. 'She is there, she is alive.'

Roshan had dark penetrating eyes. There was a fearsome intensity in them as he stared back at the Welshman and Hughes was glad he was telling the Sherpa the truth – or at least what he had to believe was true. For some reason the child seemed to evoke an allegiance that was almost chilling in its strength in everyone involved with her. Hughes had sensed it in the tall white-haired American, in the Sherpas who'd waited with Roshan in the village – now he felt it in the sirdar.

'Bring Miss Iona back,' Roshan said. He paused. 'I will be waiting for her and for you.' He looked at the Welshman again, then he turned and walked away down the slope to the clearing where the helicopters had landed.

The helicopters had arrived barely thirty minutes before, although it was forty-eight hours since Hughes had come down to the village, spoken to the Sherpa and watched Roshan's runner set out for Kathmandu. Hughes had never liked villages and Nanga Purna was no exception. He hated the cloying smell of animal fat as it burnt on the cooking fires, the raucous cries of children, the clamour and press of the adults, the bellowing of the water buffalo and the grunting of the hogs.

As soon as the runner left, Hughes had retired to the shelf of rock and wiry mountain grass, frosted and sprinkled now with the first scattering of the winter's snows, high above the village where he had made his camp. The oduna were sleeping further away and higher still – nothing would have persuaded them to approach the settlement apart from hunger and a desire to seed. Hughes had fed them and with the onset of winter the impulse to breed had died.

Where the yeti, Wengen, was, Hughes didn't know. He was probably waiting even higher on the crests. Hughes wasn't concerned about the tall, powerful creature. He had seen the anger, the cunning, the vengeful bitterness in those pale translucent eyes. When he called for the yeti, Wengen would come to him. Wengen had terrible scores to settle in the valley – he would wait for ever to bring them to account.

Hughes glanced down and examined the throng of people which had gathered below him. There must have been almost thirty of them. Perhaps eight were Europeans. Apart from Roshan he could identify only one – the American, Robert Cabot. At Cabot's side was a woman in her early thirties. She was dressed in an expensive quilted skisuit, and her face was drawn and anxious. She could only be the girl's mother.

Standing close to her and holding the woman's hand was a short burly man with a heavy paunch, prematurely greying hair and shrewd hooded eyes. Hughes had no idea who he was. From his protective attitude towards the girl's mother, he should have been the child's father, but somehow Hughes sensed he wasn't. The girl's father, Hughes guessed, was the much taller man at the back whose angular face was almost as harrowed as the woman's.

Between the tall man and the couple in front were the other Europeans. Apart from the helicopter pilot, unmistakable in his leather jacket, the rest must be diplomats from Kathmandu – half of them from the American embassy and the remainder British. Everyone else was Nepalese. A dozen of the Nepalese were in military uniform. Two of them carried on their jacket lapels the red insignia of senior officers and one had the gold crowns of a general.

The oldest of the American diplomats murmured something to Cabot, then the two of them turned and spoke to the Nepalese general, who waved his arms and raised his voice. Hughes couldn't understand what he was saying but he sensed an argument was taking place. Cabot ended the dispute quickly and emphatically.

'No,' he snapped, his voice echoing up to Hughes. 'All that matters is that we get the child back. If that means doing what I say, then for Christ's sake everyone's going to do what I say.'

The general shrugged his shoulders sullenly. Cabot turned and strode towards Hughes. The American diplomat tried to follow him, but Cabot abruptly waved him away. He walked past the Welshman and headed on, beckoning Hughes to follow him. A hundred yards up the slope and well out of hearing of the others, Cabot stopped.

'What happened?' Hughes demanded. 'Trouble, is it?'

'Of course there's trouble.' Cabot was snapping at the Welshman now. 'You say you've found the child and she's in the hands of the yeti. If she is and we get her back, everyone wants to be part of it – not to mention being the first to see the yeti. What the hell did you expect?'

'I tell you this, bach, the only chance of bringing that child home is if I go after her alone.' Hughes's voice was angry and suspicious. 'Alone apart from my companions, that is. If anyone else tries to follow me, she's lost for ever. The yeti will run with her. She'll never be found.'

'I accept that.'

'Then why did you bring this whole bloody crew with you?'

Cabot looked down at the little Welshman, trying to control his own impatience and anxiety. 'You asked for money,' he replied. 'The only way to get it quickly to you here was by helicopter, and the only helicopters in Nepal belong to the government. Then there's Iona's parents, particularly her mother. She's almost been destroyed by worry. Finally there's Iona herself. It's over three months since she disappeared. Even if she is still alive, she's probably sick or wounded. She may have to be airlifted straight to Kathmandu –' Cabot paused.

'Jesus, Hughes!' he burst out violently. 'I want that child back. If I have to bring in an army to get her, then that's what I'll do.'

Hughes stared back at him silently.

The child had vanished from Cabot's camp. The limping white-haired American, Hughes realized, felt deeply guilty about her disappearance, blaming himself for what had happened during the storm. Hughes wanted only the money – there was no need for a helicopter. Cabot had brought in the Nepalese government and the embassies too, and Iona's parents, to prove to everyone – and above all to himself – that he would do anything to get her back.

Hughes gave a short harsh laugh. He might be mad, but he wasn't the only one. The guilt Cabot felt had made the American crazy too. They were equal now, united in their different worlds of madness only by the girl.

The laughter faded from Hughes's face. 'Whether or not you bring an army,' he said, 'I still go alone. Otherwise I do not go at all.'

Cabot nodded. 'I have told them all that. Even the general has agreed.'

'You have the money?'

Cabot was wearing one of his favourite garments, a thigh-length linen bush jacket long since grown worn and shabby with years of use. He felt for the inside breast pocket and pulled out a bundle of dollar bills. 'You asked for twenty-five thousand dollars,' he said.

Hughes nodded. It was what he'd demanded as they stood on the ridge above the uncovered tracks in the snow. In terms of Cabot's own wealth the sum was so small that the American hadn't thought to ask what it was needed for. As the price for Iona's return it lacked any meaning at all.

To Hughes it was a fortune.

During the forty years of his wanderings, Hughes had largely lost touch with the value of money. When he wanted something, he bartered or traded for it. In the subsistence economy of the Nepalese uplands, a European with a rifle was a rich man. Hughes had a rifle. He also had a natural authority which he wielded over the mountain tribes. And he retained the shrewdness of a boy who had grown up in the Welsh valleys as the depression of the thirties bit deep into the heart of the principality.

Twenty-five thousand dollars was a figure he plucked from the air. He wasn't sure exactly how much it would buy. He would only find out by descending into the markets of Kathmandu, but that wasn't necessary. All he needed were porters, food and equipment. From his knowledge of the high villages and their markets, Hughes knew he could buy all he wanted for a fraction of the sum.

Twenty-five thousand dollars was a magical guess, a plunge into the darkness of the American's wallet. He looked at the bundle of bills in Cabot's hands and he laughed. Magic was what he had been given.

The American began to count from the roll.

'I will give you five thousand now as a token of good faith,' Cabot said. 'You will have the rest of course as soon as you bring the child back.'

Hughes stared at the money Cabot had counted out. He waved his hand dismissively. Blood had started to film his eyes and he was still laughing.

'I trust you, bach,' he said. 'Hold it all in your safe-keeping. Where I go, I have no need for it. Keep it for me until I return with the child. Give it to me when she is back in your hands.'

48

Iona saw Kekua coming down the path that slanted over the ridge towards the head of the island.

The blind yeti moved with her usual sure-footed grace, but there was an urgency in her walk that Iona hadn't seen before. It was late afternoon. The sun had already dipped behind the crests, and the sky was darkening. She watched Kekua cross the clearing and approach the shelter.

Iona sat cross-legged on the ground outside. Churinga squatted beside her, holding her child against her breast. It was the last day of the month Tonemetapu had given the two clans to share the valley, and for the fifth day in succession the wind was blowing from the north. The air felt raw and chill, but insulated by their pelts, Churinga and the infant yeti seemed impervious to the sudden drop in temperature. Iona had been shivering since the wind rose at dawn.

She had got up with the gatherers, but for the first time since the ranging came to the valley she hadn't gone out into the grounds. She'd returned to the shelter and pulled bundles of dry reeds over herself, but she couldn't ward off the cold. If Kekua had been there, Iona would have huddled against her, but the blind yeti had disappeared on her own at the same time as the gathering party crossed the river.

The only time Iona crawled out of the shelter during the day was to go down to the river to wait for their return. Chilled and miserable she wanted the presence and comfort of someone she knew and trusted. With Kekua away and Churinga busy with the infant Tumba, it left only Manu. He was the last to wade out of the water with Babilla behind him. As always the leopard shook herself, showering Iona with icy water from her rose-patterned hide.

Manu began to laugh as the child backed away, but when he noticed the paleness of her face and the grey pimples of cold on her skin the laughter stopped and he stared at her with concern. He stepped forward and touched her nose and cheeks with his fingertips. Feeling the chill lying on them, Manu caught her up in his arms and ran with her towards the clearing.

Iona lay huddled against his chest. For the first time since the north wind began to blow, she felt warm and comfortable. Part of that warmth and comfort came from Manu's own body heat, but the rest, the greater part, came from the simple fact that he was carrying her. She felt safe in his hold. There were strange and complicated feelings stirring inside her, feelings she had never known before and didn't understand. She knew only that she was where she wanted to be.

Manu carried her first to his own shelter. He laid her on the ground and disappeared inside. A moment later he reappeared carrying a bundle of skins. Some were small and light, the pelts of muntjac deer and mountain foxes. One was much larger, the skin of a black bear. Manu wrapped the smaller skins round her in layers, then enveloped Iona in the bearskin, carried her across the clearing to the shelter she shared with Kekua and placed her on the earth outside the entrance to catch the last of the sun.

The yeti looked at her anxiously and touched her face again. The colour was already seeping back into the child's cheeks and her skin had lost its chill.

'Now you will be well again,' he said.

He waited for a moment as she huddled down into the cocoon of warmth, then he smiled and walked away. Peering over the rim of the furs that encircled her, Iona watched him go. Inside herself, she felt an ache that was quite distinct from the cold.

She longed for Manu to stay. She hadn't needed to tell him she was cold when she greeted him on the bank – he had realized it as soon as he saw her. He had simply picked her up and run with her to the shelters. The skins, she knew, had been cleaned and dried by Manu himself. He was a hunter and alone in the holding he had the skills to cure them. They were his gift to her.

The pelts warmed her, but Iona wanted more than the warmth. She wanted the strength and safety of Manu's massive shoulders, the stir and prickle of his chest hairs against her body, the questing stare of his eyes as he scanned the landscape, and the flare of his nostrils as he read its scent messages. She wanted Babilla padding beside them, growling with pleasure as the yeti scratched the leopard's throat.

Most of all she wanted Manu's arms round her again, but there was no chance of that until she went out with the clans again. Manu had gone for the night, and he had other concerns on his mind. He had gone to join Tana, Iona thought bitterly, in the shelter he had built for his new mate.

It was then that Kekua appeared. When she stopped in front of Iona, she was panting slightly and Iona could see a pulse beating on the side of her neck.

'I have been listening to the butterflies all day,' Kekua said. 'Again and again I followed them from one side of the island to the other. For a long time I was not sure. Then as the sun began to set, they flew to the west and I knew. I went to Tonemetapu and he had seen them fly too –'

Kekua paused. 'The year is ended. We go to cloud-time.'

At Iona's side Churinga drew in her breath sharply, and clutched the tiny Tumba to her breast.

What happened next was so swift and certain, Iona had difficulty in taking it in.

The yeti simply left the island.

There were no final preparations, no collecting of supplies for the journey in front of them, no dismantling of the shelters that had been their home all summer. Within minutes of Kekua's message reaching the clearing, the entire clan had assembled on the bank with old limping Yerto at their head. They plunged into the water and swam across. Then, like migrating swallows answering some irresistible call, they were gone. One instant they were there, the next they had departed.

Iona, bewildered, was swept up and travelled with them.

They walked all that night. Within the first hour they came across the clan of the ranging who must also have abandoned their camp at the same moment, and set out in the same direction. From then on the two clans walked together. Towards dawn they reached the base of the mountains that encircled the valley and for a while they climbed through the foothills. Just as the sun was rising they entered a narrow gully. Halfway along its steep walls was the deeply shadowed entrance of what appeared to be a cave.

Kekua took Iona's hand as one by one the yeti began to lower their heads and file inside. 'This is the place of cloud-time,' she said.

Drawing Iona after her, Kekua stepped into the cave. As Iona followed she felt something patter across her back and took a last quick glance behind her. The dawn sky had darkened with cloud, blotting out the sun, and snow was falling. It was, she knew, the first snow of the coming winter. She shook the flakes from her shoulders and headed on.

Iona lost all sense of time. The cold and darkness of the tunnel were so intense they swallowed up her senses. She could see nothing, hear nothing, smell nothing. Her mouth was so numb she could barely feel her tongue against her lips. She was aware only of the occasional pressure of Kekua's hand on her own, and once or twice when she stumbled a giddy realization that she was still moving.

Finally she bumped into Kekua and realized the yeti had stopped. A moment later Kekua drew her on again, this time more slowly. The impenetrable blackness was gradually fading and giving way to a misty greyness. Iona blinked. As her eyes became used to the growing twilight, she saw that they had entered an immense cavern. Its roof was hidden in the dusk, but from somewhere far above her enough light was filtering down to illuminate her surroundings. Her gaze ranged round the vast cave. Its sandy floor shone with hoar frost and its walls were lined with columns of twisted and fluted rock. The spaces between the columns were filled with ice and at random intervals flares of gold and bronze and green sparkled out of the ice, as if jewels had been buried deep in the glittering whiteness. Iona peered at them, but the light was too dim to see the source of the dancing shimmers of brilliance.

She glanced down. During the journey Tonemetapu had been carried on a litter of branches by four of the young male yeti. They had taken him to the end of the cavern and carefully placed the old seer on a shelf of stone set deep in the wall. The rest of the yeti, the members of both the island and the mountain clans with all their young, had gathered in a semi-circle round him. They squatted on their haunches, the two patriarchs and their mates at the front, and the others ranged behind in order of age.

Iona, her hand still in Kekua's, was immediately behind Yerto. At her other side was Manu. As Iona knelt, Tonemetapu began to speak.

'The snows have come, so listen well!' Tonemetapu said. 'The stores are gathered. They are in place for when the season turns again. Then the star without a name will call the clouds to send down rain. The rains will come, and all will be well for the people.'

'All will be well,' the yeti replied softly.

To Iona the murmured response sounded like an incantation, a reply that might have been given by a congregation in church.

'The holding and the ranging are met, and we go now together to cloud-time,' Tonemetapu went on. 'This season there is more than ever that we must dream. The prey that has been lost to the crests. The hunger of the ranging, and the hunting of the valley. Above all, the new ways that the little shumbi has brought to the valley. All this we must dream.'

'All this we must dream,' the yeti repeated.

Tonemetapu paused and Iona whispered to Kekua, 'What does he mean?'

Kekua wrinkled her face as she tried to explain.

'When the deep cold comes and cloud-time is on us,' Kekua said, 'we can talk to each other without speaking. Tonemetapu starts by telling us the past of the people from the beginning with the star without a name, all through the many seasons since then until the one that has just ended. Do you not see warmth in the ice?'

Kekua raised her hand. By warmth Iona knew she meant light – to the blind yeti they were the same.

Kekua was pointing at the strange shimmers in the cavern's walls. Looking more carefully at the columns of ice, Iona could see now that they were embedded with objects. Some of the objects, those the light was reflected from, were metal. Iona stared again. She could make out a richly engraved sword, a winged helmet of bronze, a jewelled belt and a silver drinking mug. There were many others, some as simple as a crude iron sickle, and they were all immensely old.

'What are they?' Iona asked.

'Across the long-ago seasons, other shumbi have passed by the valley,' Kekua replied. 'Those are what they left behind. The people collected them and gave them as cloud-time gifts to the star without a name, so that he would send the rains again. Each marks a season in our past that Tonemetapu will tell again for us –'

Kekua lowered her hand. 'When Tonemetapu has finished, we dream to each other through him. If there are quarrels, they are explored and healed. If there are problems, they are considered. If there are new ways and new plans for the season that comes, they are agreed. We hunt and range apart, but in cloud-time we are one people. Cloud-time makes the bonds between us.'

Iona struggled to understand Kekua's words, but the air in the cavern seemed to be getting colder every moment. In spite of the skins wrapped round her, she was trembling and she could feel her mind numbing. Then she saw the holding's patriarch, old Yerto, rise to his feet in front of her, his grey-haired back shining like frosted iron in the dusk. He turned and gazed down at Iona. She stared back at him, bewildered.

'He asks for a gift for the star without a name,' Kekua said softly. 'The leaders of both the clans must offer him something. Because you were found by the holding, he looks to you.'

'But what can I give him?' Iona asked frantically.

'Only you can decide how much you value the star,' Kekua answered.

As the great bulk of Yerto towered silently and lopsidedly above her, Iona tried to think.

Manu had rescued her from the river. If he and the leopard hadn't come across her, she would have died. Afterwards the holding had looked after her, had given her warmth and shelter and food. She had gone to the crests and Tana had taken care of her. She owed the yeti her life. The people belonged to the star without a name, but she owed the star even more – she owed him the most precious thing she possessed.

Iona tugged her belt round and unzipped the pouch. She pulled out the battered and almost hairless Bear and held him for the last time. Then she offered him up to Yerto. The patriarch took the tiny furry animal and examined it for a moment. Apparently satisfied, he limped over to one of the ice columns.

Using his gathering mattock, Yerto chipped out a small shelf in the ice. He placed the bear on top of the shelf and limped back to his place. Iona could see a slow trickle of almost freezing water running down the column. Within days the bear would be encased in ice like the other objects in the cavern.

'The holding has given,' Tonemetapu said from his bench. 'Now it is for the ranging.'

Tonemetapu looked down at Gaggau. The moss on the seer's skeletal body glowed green and luminescent in the twilight, giving the impression that he was cloaked in fireflies.

Gaggau tried to stand but failed. Age, his club-foot, the wounds from the oduna's attack, but above all the constantly thickening cold, kept him squatting stiffly and painfully on the ground. As Iona watched he tried to pass his gift to his mate, Jinga, for her to offer in his place. Iona couldn't see what the gift was. She saw only Jinga's hot fierce eyes, and the contemptuous gesture with which the old female brushed the offering aside.

Then Jinga was on her feet. A frenzy of rage and bitterness carried her forward as she ran towards Tonemetapu. She crouched in front of the seer and shook something in his face.

'I bring my own gift for the star!' she cried. 'I will place it in the ice so the people will know that now and for ever everything has changed. The little shumbi has brought nothing except ruin –'

Jinga thrust out her hand at Iona. 'The animals went from the crests when she came here. She will bring the same hunger to the valley. What she teaches about herding prey and putting fruit in the ground are tricks. Next season there will be nothing for any of the people to eat. Only Wengen can save us –'

Jinga coughed and spat on the cavern's floor. 'There is a shumbi who walks with the oduna,' she continued. 'Wengen has gone to find him. He will bring that shumbi back so that this one may be taken away. When the child has left, Wengen will lead the clans. The ranging will hunt where they choose, and the holding will gather where they can –' Jinga paused and drew in her breath. When she went on her voice rose to a vengeful shout.

'The people are Wengen's now! I taught him that it should be so. He returns to the valley as I speak. He will be here before the snows have closed the passes. Wengen comes back not only with the shumbi and the oduna – he returns with the dark storm's child!'

Jinga lifted what she was holding. It was a fragment of charred wood that must have stuck to Gaggau's pelt when the oduna rained down their fire on him. The old female gazed in savage triumph over the throng of the yeti. She scurried across to the pillar of ice and placed the wood alongside Iona's bear then she returned and squatted down beside Gaggau. The fierce glare faded from her eyes and her pupils seemed to cloud over.

Iona gazed at Jinga, appalled, before swinging round to Kekua. The blind yeti's head had slumped down on her chest.

'Didn't you hear what she said?' Iona cried. 'Wengen is on his way back. He brings the shumbi and fire with him. He'll destroy everything!'

Kekua appeared to take no notice of her. Iona was still holding the yeti's hand, and she tugged at it furiously. Kekua didn't respond and her palm felt strangely cold, almost as if all the blood had drained from it. In a frenzy Iona turned to the other side.

'Manu!' she screamed.

Manu's head had dropped on to his chest too. Like Kekua he ignored her. Iona slapped his face. There was no reaction, and Iona could feel that his skin was icy beneath her fingers. She glanced round at the rest of the yeti. They were all motionless, their heads sunk and the breath barely stirring their bodies.

Suddenly Iona realized that the air had grown still colder. It was so cold that even her trembling had stopped. She was suspended in a chrysalis of ice that was winding round her body. The chill had already taken all the feeling from her feet and legs. Now it was starting to climb over her stomach.

Desperately she shook her head, trying to clear the numbness that seeped across her brain. She gazed at the yeti again – and she understood.

They had drifted into hibernation. She remembered what Uncle Robert had once told her. Hibernation was a state that over millions of years certain animals had learnt to adopt to defend themselves against the winter cold and the starvation it brought. Their body temperature plunged, their systems slowed until they were torpid, to all intents and purposes they entered a sleeping coma, midway between life and death, where they had no need of food. When the seasons turned and warmth came back to the earth, they came to life again.

The yeti hibernated. They called it cloud-time, and they used the silent communication they could direct to each other through the icy torpor to hold themselves together as a people. They had assumed – Kekua, Manu, Yerto, all of them – it was a world that Iona, bundled in hides to compensate for her lack of a pelt, could enter and share with them.

They were wrong. Iona could not.

Her body was different from theirs. Initially she could withstand the cold of the cavern for longer than the yeti. That was why she was still conscious, while they had slipped into their winter sleep.

But when her own system had exhausted the reserves it was pumping up to fuel the functioning of her heart and lungs, it was left with nothing. The yeti could hibernate, she could only die.

Instinctively Iona knew it. To stay alive she had first to keep her blood circulating, and then to escape from the cavern. She forced herself to stand. Rocking on her feet, she shook her arms and beat her hands together. The action rattled something in her pocket.

Dimly she realized it was the box of matches. She paused. With every moment that passed her mind was working increasingly slowly, but she knew the sound was important. She pulled out the box, examined it carefully, then glanced round. Manu was still squatting hunched at her side. There was some connection between the yeti and the box. She searched her mind and remembered what it was.

Manu had given her meat and she had tried to cook it. Cooking required a fire and fire was painful – it had almost destroyed Gaggau. As if in a dream she fumbled the box open, struck one of the matches, lifted Manu's arm and held the flame to the soft pink skin of his armpit.

The stench of burning flesh lifted into the icy air. Manu stirred. He flinched and moaned. Then, swatting at himself as if attempting to beat off an irritating mosquito, he staggered to his feet. Mumbling and blinking, he reeled as if he were drunk.

Iona caught his hand and pulled him behind her across the cavern floor.

49

Iona never knew how she found her way back to the cavern's entrance.

The tunnel was pitch-dark, darker even than the blackness at the end of her bed where the monsters had once prowled to haunt her nightmares. She groped her way along the walls, guiding herself round the twists and bends in the rock with her hands. Occasionally she came across gaps where smaller satellite tunnels ran off to the sides.

Twice Iona mistook them for the main tunnel and blundered on until she found her way blocked by an unyielding wall of stone. Then she had to retrace her steps to the main tunnel, where the only way of checking her direction was to light one of her swiftly dwindling store of matches and search for the faint print of her boots in the sandy floor.

All the while she had to keep tugging Manu onwards as he reeled and stumbled behind her. Several times when she was lost, Iona slapped and shook him. Once in a rage of frustration she screamed and kicked him as hard as she could. The toe of her boot bounced back off the massive muscles of his leg but there was no reaction from the yeti. The cold and the thin icy air of the cavern had chilled him into a coma.

Iona swore. She used all the words her mother had told her she mustn't use – the forbidden words she'd learnt from overhearing Mr Simpson when the rabbits burrowed into the walled garden at Mainwarden, the strange and violent Gaelic ones that Angus spat out when the red deer came down in autumn to raid her uncle's in-bye fields of wheat. She cursed the yeti with them. Then she dragged Manu on.

Finally the tunnel ended and they came out into the open. Iona's knees buckled. She managed to stiffen them and hold herself upright. She closed her eyes, and stood under the sky gulping in great lungfuls of air.

She had known they were close to the entrance – with every step forward the mixture of oxygen in the air had grown stronger. Now it invaded her, flooding her blood, surging through her body and washing the torpor away like a cascade of champagne. Iona swayed giddily, then regained her balance and glanced back at Manu.

Manu had toppled forward as they came out of the tunnel and now lay face-down in the snow. As Iona watched, he lifted his head and blinked. His mouth opened and he drew in great mouthfuls of the outside air as she had done. He pushed himself off the ground and staggered to his feet, staring round him in a daze. Then he saw Iona, and frowned uncertainly as if he were seeing her for the first time.

Suddenly Manu recognized the child and the frown became a smile. He tossed his head, shaking off the last effects of the cavern's air, and stepped forward. Iona didn't wait for him to reach her. She threw herself at the yeti, caught him round the waist and buried her face in the warm dark hair at his stomach. Iona wept.

She didn't know how long she cried for. Eventually she felt Manu's hands cradling her face and pushing it away from his body. Iona brushed away her tears. She stared up at him – and suddenly, terrifyingly, everything came back.

'Manu!' she said. 'Wengen is coming!'

Manu peered down at her. 'Wengen?' he echoed.

'Don't you remember what Jinga said?' Iona cried. 'That Wengen has gone to the crests beyond the grounds? That he is going to find the oduna and the shumbi that leads them, and bring them into the valley?'

Manu shook his head. 'Gaggau has sent Wengen away,' he answered. 'That is all I remember.'

'Wengen is on his way here!'

Manu looked bewildered.

Iona clenched her hands. In a frenzy she hammered them against Manu's ribs. The blows had as little effect as those she'd rained on him in the blackness of the tunnel. At least he'd been in a torpor then. Now he was awake and alert, but the effect was the same – Manu continued to look at her, bemused. Despairingly Iona turned away.

What had happened in cloud-time had congealed in ice and sunk to the bottom of his mind. The yeti had no memory of it. From the moment the clans entered the tunnel everything had been frozen and lost in the mists of the cavern. Iona gazed out over the mountains.

She hadn't noticed it until then, but snow was falling. Moment by moment the flakes dropped thicker and faster and even as she looked the trees and ridges began to vanish under a swirling grey-white mantle. Within minutes the entire landscape had disappeared. All that remained was a soft rustling twilight, the colour of the wings of wintering geese and as razor-edged with cold as the frost that glittered on the river's dry reed beds.

A storm was gathering.

As Iona gazed ahead, a sound caught her ears. For an instant she thought it was part of the storm. She listened and the sound came again. It didn't belong to the storm, although it had the deep rumbling intensity of the wind that was sweeping the snow forward. She glanced at Manu. The yeti was leaning forward listening intently too.

Suddenly Manu opened his mouth. 'Babilla!' he called.

A moment later the leopard appeared. Babilla had been left outside by Manu when they entered the cavern. Now the leopard came bounding forward through the falling snow. She brushed against Iona in greeting, then she stopped in front of Manu. The rumbling in Babilla's throat softened to small growls of pleasure, she half closed her eyes and pressed her head against Manu's thigh.

Manu laughed and bent down to ruffle the leopard's neck. As his hand touched Babilla's fur, something extraordinary happened. A charge seemed to pass from the leopard to the yeti – and Manu remembered. He stiffened and his head jerked up.

'Wengen is coming,' he whispered. 'He brings the oduna and the shumbi who leads them to the valley. Jinga told us.'

Iona gazed at him through the tumbling snowflakes, and a wave of relief surged over her. Babilla had succeeded where she had failed. Somehow the leopard's appearance and the feel of her pelt beneath Manu's fingers had unshackled the events imprisoned in cloud-time and now they were rising to the surface of Manu's mind like corks released from the depths of the sea.

'The valley cannot feed them,' he said. 'They must be told to turn back –' His face was taut and anxious, and his eyes quartered the darkening snow-strewn air.

'We should go now to meet them,' he went on. 'I will speak to

Wengen and the oduna. You must talk to the shumbi. Between us we will explain there is not enough food here. We must hurry!'

Impulsively Manu stepped forward. Iona caught his arm. Digging her feet deep into the snow that was already beginning to build round her ankles, she managed to pull him round to face her.

'It will not be like that, Manu,' she said. 'The shumbi has no need of the valley to eat. He wants something else. Jinga says it is me. I think it is more than that. Wengen wants something too. He wants the leadership of both the clans –'

Iona paused. 'Don't you remember what else Jinga said? They do not come to share. They come to kill.'

As Manu looked at the child in horror, the last of the forgotten fragments of cloud-time came back to him and he remembered everything. Iona was right. Wengen was returning to claim both the holding and the ranging. He could only do that by killing the patriarchs and anyone else who opposed him. With the help of the shumbi and the oduna he might succeed.

'How do we stop them?' Manu asked grimly.

Iona's mind raced. Only force would halt Wengen and the others from reaching the valley. Manu couldn't stop them on his own, he would need other yeti to help him. Even then they would be faced with the shumbi, the man. He would certainly be armed, and if he used his gun it wouldn't matter how many yeti faced him. They would be doomed.

The only chance was to ambush and rout them before the man could fire.

'You're a hunter, Manu,' Iona said. 'Think like a hunter. Think of the shumbi as a prey animal. The shumbi cannot climb like the yeti, so Wengen will have to lead him into the valley by a track he can travel. Where would that be?'

Manu was silent, his face was furrowed in concentration. Then he nodded almost to himself.

'Both times when the ranging encountered the oduna on the crests,' he said, 'the oduna were advancing from where the sun sets. That is where they will come from again. On that side there is only one path leading down to the valley. Many animals use it to reach the pastures below. That is the path they will use to bring the shumbi in.'

'And if the shumbi was an animal, where would you hunt him?'

Manu thought again. 'Close to the valley's floor the path is steep,' he answered. 'Any creature who uses it must travel slowly. I would wait for him there.'

'Can you find the path?'

Manu nodded. Then he glanced at Iona and frowned.

'To hunt just one animal needs more than a single hunter. Wengen, the shumbi and the oduna are many. They are more than I and Babilla can stop, even if we take them by surprise on the path.'

'There will be others of your people with you,' Iona said. 'We will go back now and get them from the cavern.'

Manu looked bewildered. 'The people are asleep in cloud-time. Nothing can waken them until the season turns again.'

'I woke you. I can wake them.'

She caught Manu's hand and pulled him towards the entrance to the tunnel. As they reached it, Manu stopped and peered back through the snow that was still falling in canopies of silent murmuring whiteness.

'What is it?' Iona asked impatiently. Manu was scanning the air through his flared nostrils as she'd seen him do so many times before.

'The pass where they will come,' he said. 'In summer I could find it from anywhere in the valley, even in my sleep. I had forgotten the snow. The smells have vanished and the air is dead. I cannot be sure where it is.' His voice was raw with anguish.

'You must be able to find it!' Iona shouted at him.

Mutely and miserably Manu shook his head.

Iona peered at him through the tumbling flakes. The torment in his words was etched on his face. Manu was a creature of sunlight and scents – summer was his compass. The winter cold took the compass from him, and when the snows fell he slept with the other yeti in cloud-time until the ice melted from the mountains. In winter, Manu was lost.

'Isn't there one of the yeti who can find it, even in the snow?' Iona asked imploringly.

Manu started to shake his head again. Then he stopped, his eyes widened and he swung towards Iona. 'Kekua,' he said. 'She can find it.'

'Kekua?' Iona was bemused. 'Kekua's blind. She uses sounds as well as scents to find her way. There are no sounds when the snow's falling. In the snow she's worse off than you are.'

'Kekua has the knowledge of the valley inside her,' Manu insisted. 'It is held in her mind. She needs nothing, neither scent nor sound, wind or sun. She will take us to the pass.'

The snow was clouding Iona's eyes. She had no idea whether Manu was right, but she knew they couldn't hesitate any longer.

'Then Kekua is the first we must wake,' Iona said. 'Breathe, and breathe deeply!'

They both filled their lungs with air, and ducked beneath the deeply shadowed arch of rock. In Iona's pocket the remaining matches rattled in their box.

Manu led the way unhesitatingly to the cavern.

By the time they reached it Iona's eyes had started to adjust to the blackness. She glanced round. The cavern was filled with the same grey twilight as before, but the air seemed to be colder and duskier now. The yeti were still squatting motionless, but a dank mist had seeped out of the stone and spread over the floor to the height of their shoulders so that their heads appeared to float in an icy rippling sea.

Iona shivered. She searched for Kekua. The mist was rising every moment, and in the twilight all the yeti's faces looked alike. 'Where is Kekua?' she asked Manu.

Manu raised his arm and pointed, and Iona saw that he was trembling. She knew she had little time – if the torpor of cloud-time invaded Manu again, everything was lost.

She pushed her way between the silent yeti, sending waves of mist coiling in front of her, until she found Kekua. The blind female was squatting hunched like the others, her eyes closed and her head sunk on her chest. Iona pulled out the box of matches and struck one. As the match head flared she gripped Kekua's elbow, lifted her arm and held the flame to the tender hairless skin of her armpit.

The smell of scorched flesh lifted into the air again. Kekua stirred and moaned and tried to jerk away from the pain, almost pulling Iona over. The child clung to her elbow and kept the flame against Kekua's skin until the yeti's eyes flickered and opened. Suddenly she heaved herself to her feet and stood swaying and swatting at her armpit as if an insect was biting her.

'Come over here and hold her!' Iona shouted at Manu.

Kekua was in the same state as he'd been, upright but comatose. Manu lurched over and took her hand.

'Who else?' Iona demanded.

One by one Manu pointed them out. He chose the strongest of the young males, half of them from the ranging and half from the holding. Iona ran between them striking matches, goading them out of their hibernation sleep and leading them over to him.

She stopped. She was panting and in spite of the cold she could feel trickles of sweat on her body. She counted the yeti she'd woken. Including Kekua there were fifteen of them. Iona glanced down at the matchbox. There were only two matches left. She would have to keep one in case they needed to make fire.

It meant she could rouse only one more yeti.

'I've got one match left!' she called to Manu. 'Who shall it be?'

Manu didn't answer. As Iona stared at him she saw him stagger and his mouth begin to sag. She knew she had only moments left – she would have to make the choice herself.

Her eyes swept the cavern, searching desperately for a last suitable candidate. Her gaze travelled on, stopped, and swung back. It came to rest not on a male, but on Tana. For an instant Iona studied the young female, then she ran over to her. A few moments later she was at Manu's side, pushing Tana in front of her.

'Out!' Iona cried frantically. 'Out!'

Led by Manu the column shuffled away into the blackness of the tunnel.

'Can you find it?'

'Little shumbi, you have known me since the last of the snow-melt. In all that time have you ever seen me lost?' Kekua smiled. 'Yes, I can take you there.'

Iona threw her arms round the blind yeti's waist and buried her face in the soft hair at Kekua's stomach.

It was an hour later. All the male yeti Iona had roused were clustered round Manu in the swirling snow outside the tunnel's entrance. The two females, Kekua and Tana with Iona between them, stood in another group to one side.

The second journey through the tunnel had been even harder than the one Iona had made alone with Manu. Twenty yards from where the last of the winding passages came out into the open, the cloud-time cold had felled Manu again. His breathing became shallow, he stumbled and reeled, then he collapsed. As if the cold were contagious, the other male yeti behind him began to topple too. Within minutes all fifteen of them were lying inert.

Iona was at Manu's shoulder when he sank to the ground. She peered down at him. Every second he lay there his body heat was being sucked away into the earth, making it increasingly difficult to revive him. Iona's head jerked up. At the end of the tunnel she could see a tiny window of grey light. She caught Manu's arms and frenziedly tried to drag him towards it.

Without Kekua and Tana, she would have failed. The limp weight of Manu's body was too heavy for her, and tears of despair filled her eyes. Then, as she was about to give up, the two females appeared beside her. For some reason their threshold of tolerance to the cold was higher than the males. Clumsy and vacant-eyed, moving stiffly like huge wooden puppets, they gripped Manu and helped her to pull him out into the air.

The three of them went back and dragged out the next yeti. But by the time he was in the open Manu had recovered. He took over, and soon all the yeti had been pulled out of the tunnel. Gradually, as they breathed in the fresh, oxygen-laden air, they too regained consciousness.

Now their eyes were alert and their faces anxious but resolute. Wengen was returning with the oduna and a shumbi to invade the valley. If he succeeded, the clans would die. Wengen had to be stopped.

'Are you ready?'

The question came from Manu. He left the young male yeti and strode across the space that separated them from the females. Iona thought he was speaking to her – he wasn't. He was looking at Kekua, who nodded.

'Then we go.' Manu reached out and touched her lightly on the nose in the holding's greeting. 'Take us there safely, Kekua.'

Sightlessly Kekua stared back at him, and her arm reached out. As Iona watched, Kekua fumbled for Tana, found her hand and held it tightly. 'I will take you there safely so you may return safely, Manu,' she replied quietly.

Her blind white eyes were the colour of the falling snowflakes. In the winter storm, Iona knew, she was their only compass and guide. Kekua knew it too, but her gesture had said more than that – Kekua was giving Tana to Manu.

'We leave now!' Manu shouted abruptly.

As the yeti hurried forward, he turned back to Iona. 'The way is hard,' he said. 'It is better if you travel on my shoulders.'

Iona shook her head. 'I will walk beside Kekua.'

She took the blind yeti's other hand and they set off into the snow.

50

'There!' Wengen stretched out his arm and pointed.

Geraint Hughes looked down.

Often when the blood flooded the broken veins in his eyes, Hughes could barely see further than a few dozen yards in front of him. It happened whenever he descended from the crests to the mountain flanks below and his madness was always worse then too. Neither his brain nor his eyes could tolerate the thickened air pressure of the lowlands.

Today he was standing on a ridge at 16,000 feet. The tormenting red mist that blurred his sight and savaged his mind was no more than a memory. Hughes felt calm and alert, and his eyes were clear. The problem was that beneath the yeti's hand there was nothing to see. Where they were standing on the ridge the sun shone coldly from a winter sky, as pale and luminous as a pool in one of the rivers that threaded down from the mountains. Below them the landscape was cloaked in eddying clouds of snow. A storm had swept down from the crests. It had left the peaks and ridges clear, but it was raging over the ravines and across the upland plains. Beneath the storm the ground was invisible.

Hughes swore, and glanced furiously at Wengen. He felt the familiar tide of rage begin to rise in him, and drove it down. The storm was no fault of the yeti's. For the first time in forty years, Hughes was involved in something far too important to be put at risk by anger.

'The valley is beneath the clouds?' Hughes asked.

Wengen nodded. 'It is there.'

Hughes's eyes ranged round the circle of crests that stood out above the coiling grey mist. He recognized every one. Over the years he had climbed the network of animal tracks that linked them all like an immense and intricate spider's web. In the furthest distance he could even see the hog-backed ridge where the American had camped, and where he had found the tracks of the yeti and the child. What he couldn't see was the valley below – the valley, hidden now by the storm, into which he'd never descended.

The valley where the yeti were keeping the child.

'How do we get down?' Hughes demanded.

Wengen raised his hand to his face. He rubbed his nostrils, trying to draw a message from the wind blowing across them, but the wind gave nothing back. Winter had come, and the air was barren.

Wengen frowned. As a member of the holding yeti, he depended on sight and above all smell to orientate himself and navigate his way across the valley. From the start of spring to the end of summer he could have crossed the holding's grounds with his eyes closed. Now every scent had been burnt out by the cold, and the valley was lost under the snowstorm.

There was another difficulty. On his own Wengen would have searched for one of the precipitous tracks trodden out by the musk deer to find his way down from the crests. Once he reached the valley's floor, he would have trusted himself somehow to find his way back to the island. He wasn't on his own – he had the shumbi to lead, and the shumbi was old. In Wengen's eyes, he was also half crippled. The shumbi would never negotiate the musk deer's tracks.

It was imperative that the shumbi not only got down to the valley, but arrived there unharmed. The shumbi had within him the secret of the dark storm's child, and he also carried his smoking branch – Wengen had learnt about that from the oduna. He had nothing but contempt for the outcasts. Unrecognizable to Wengen as yeti, they were small, timorous, dirty, and barely capable of speech. They could no more hunt or gather in the sense Wengen understood except with the fumbling clumsiness of one of the holding's infants. Whenever possible Wengen stayed apart from them, but occasionally he had forced himself to speak with them. He wanted to learn about the shumbi. The oduna were in awe of the big pale-pelted yeti, and they answered his questions eagerly, breaking off to chatter among themselves in a mongrel tongue Wengen couldn't understand.

Wengen had found out about the smoking branch the first time he talked to them. Yes, the shumbi could call down the dark storm's child, the oduna told him. He could make it do whatever he wanted, but the branch was even more powerful. The shumbi could gaze out at a prey animal, hold up the branch, and when he told the branch to roar, the animal would fall.

What was important, the oduna added, was that the shumbi was calm and quiet when he spoke to the branch. Often a redness filled his eyes, a redness the colour of the falling river willow leaves at the summer's end. When the redness was in him his hand shook and he screamed and the smoking branch roared not at the prey, but uselessly to the sky. Then the shumbi abused them violently too.

Wengen nodded. He understood what they were saying. He understood, Wengen thought, as they did not, what caused the shumbi's anger. The shumbi desired the moon. That was why he had made the condition that the people should guide him to the peak he named Everest in the shumbi's language. On Everest, the shumbi believed, he could reach up and catch the moon and hold her in his arms.

Walking away from the oduna, Wengen smiled to himself. Between dreaming of the sun and the clouds, the star without a name had yearned for the moon. The star had never found her, nor would the shumbi – the moon was beyond reach, however high he climbed. The shumbi would find that out for himself. It did not matter. What mattered was that the shumbi entered the valley with his knowledge and his smoking branch, and without the redness in his eyes.

The only way for him to do that was through the pass.

'There is a cleft close to where we stand,' Wengen said. 'Once, I think, a river ran down it. Now the river has gone. Deer use the cleft to enter the valley to feed. The way down is not easy, but it is better than the other paths from the crests.'

'Then for Christ's sake, let's take it!' Hughes snapped.

Cautiously, with Wengen leading the way and the oduna following, they headed downwards.

51

'Here!' Kekua called. She pointed upwards.

Stumbling through the snow behind her, Iona didn't realize for a moment that the blind yeti had spoken. Manu caught Iona's arm and pulled her to a halt. As she stopped, Kekua's cry filtered into her consciousness. Wearily the child lifted her head.

She didn't know how long they'd been climbing. In the unending snow and darkness it seemed like days. In spite of her earlier determination to walk, for much of the time Manu had carried her. Bumping on his shoulders with the snow blinding her eyes, Iona had no idea where they were going. Nor did Manu or the other yeti trailing in a line behind them. The bitter cold had robbed the air of smell, the storm had blotted out the landscape, the journey was unfamiliar to all of them.

Without Kekua they would have been helplessly lost within the first hour, but the blind yeti never hesitated. Deprived of sight from birth, she had made the island into her compass. She used it to recall and locate every scrap of information about the landscape which had come to her through her nose, her ears or her skin, and which since childhood she had stored in her memory.

Light reflected from a distant mountain flank would reach her face as a tiny pulse of warmth. From long experience she had learnt to calculate exactly the height of the light's source and its distance from the island. She did the same with wind currents, rainfall, birdcalls, the barking of deer, the scent of Himalayan primroses, with a myriad other reference points that changed season by season, and often hour by hour.

Kekua did it instinctively, without conscious thought. Daily she added to the vast body of information she held within her. Over the years it had built up into an immense three-dimensional map of the valley and the surrounding ranges, so detailed and complete that it showed not only the shape and contour of every crest, ravine and peak, but the position of individual rocks and trees.

The map was invulnerable to storm or snow, to the loss of scent or sound. It lay across Kekua's brain, functioning independently of everything except the blind yeti's existence. Kekua had navigated by it ever since they left the cavern. She led them up tortuous gullies, over long moraines, across streams starting to freeze with the onset of winter, down boulder-strewn clefts, and then up again through dense thickets of pine and rhododendron.

Kekua set an unrelenting pace. She knew where they were heading and she knew how to lead them there. Now they had arrived.

Manu let go of Iona's hand and walked forward to Kekua's shoulder.

'The musk deer come this way,' Kekua said. 'Maybe there are grass plains below on the other side of the crests where they feed in summer – I do not know. What I do know is that as summer ends they climb towards the crests and follow the hill slopes. Here they turn down towards the valley –'

She turned her head and stretched out her arm in the direction from which they'd come. 'From here there are many paths downwards. We have climbed one, but there are many more. For anyone who seeks the valley, this is the pass they must cross first to find them.'

'Wengen will come this way?' Manu asked.

Kekua nodded. 'With the shumbi he has no other choice.'

Manu gazed up.

Briefly the storm had lulled. The snowflakes were still falling, but there were breaks in the dense clouds as the wind-rush parted them and from time to time a brilliant crescent moon shone down from the night sky. In the shafts of moonlight Manu saw a gorge rising above him. From where he stood it looked almost vertical. Once it must have been a watershed, carrying the melting snow from the crests down into the valley every spring. Then the press of water from above had changed its course and now, when the snows poured down, they spilt elsewhere. The change had left the gorge rearing up above Manu like a gaunt abandoned staircase, its steps formed by huge boulders.

Manu's eyes ranged left and right. On either side for as far as he could see there were sheer cliffs, notched at their tops with V-shaped indentations. Across the centuries other streams of snow-melt had carved a way through the rocky battlements to spend themselves on the plain below. Those cliffs were impassable to any creature. Kekua was right – only the lost dead gorge above him gave access to the valley.

Manu examined it again. This time he looked at it with a hunter's eye, tracing the path the musk deer took. They had avoided the obvious stepping-stones of the boulders, because here on the shadowed northern side of the valley the boulders would have been slippery with dew, even in high summer. Now, at the start of winter, they were coated with frost and more treacherous still. Instead the deer had trodden out a track on the earth between the rocks. It zigzagged as it dropped, spearing first one way and then another, apparently at random but always continuing its winding descent. Finally it led to the area of open ground where Manu was standing. From there, as Kekua said, a dozen or more tracks led further downwards to the valley.

Manu frowned, trying to assemble his thoughts. Taut and uncertain he sifted through them, searching for a pattern – a hunter's pattern – that would tell him what to do.

Wengen, the oduna and the shumbi – they were the factors he had to deal with. Manu knew little about the oduna, nothing about the shumbi. Like ghosts they haunted the darkest, most remote limits of his imagination. Manu excised them from his mind. Wengen, on the other hand, he did know.

Wengen was a gatherer. He was strong and cunning, but he wouldn't know cloud-time had arrived. Only the movement of the butterflies could have told him that. Far back behind the crests which was where, Manu guessed, he must have been searching for the shumbi, Wengen wouldn't have seen the sleepy flight of the bright sun-winged insects.

Wengen had left the island when both the holding and the ranging were still in their different camps. He would surely not realize that they'd moved. He didn't even have to worry about the shumbi's smell – the storm would have blotted that out just as it had all the other scents of the valley. There was no reason for him to be cautious. Wengen would bring the shumbi straight down the staircase of the cleft, certain that they had hours to travel before they came close to the yeti.

Manu got no further in his reasoning. Behind him he heard Kekua's voice.

'They are coming,' Kekua said quietly. 'They have entered the pass and are climbing down.'

The hairs on Kekua's body, as sensitive as the antennae of a moth, had picked up the vibrations from their approach long before Manu had even begun to listen for them.

Manu swung round. There was no time to plan, no time even to think. He could only whisper instructions to the yeti as he'd done so often in the past when he was leading a hunting party on the crests and he'd suddenly spotted an approaching prey animal.

The yeti backed away and lowered themselves into the snow. Furiously Manu waved Iona and Kekua back too and snarled a soft command at Babilla. The leopard padded over to the child and settled down beside her. Manu looked for Tana, but she had disappeared.

Manu cast a final glance up into the swirling white funnel of the gorge. Then he, too, crouched in the snow and waited.

52

Wengen paused at the top of the gorge.

Flurries of snow were still falling but the storm had started to move away from the crests and travel northwards towards Tibet. Between the flurries there were longer and longer intervals when it was possible to see the landscape in the moonlight.

The wind was blowing from behind him, carrying the storm before it. Wengen scanned the air with his nose, searching for any smells that might have been thrown back by the gusts swirling up from the ravines, but it was too cold. Every trace of scent had been scoured away by the frost. Instead, in frustration, he had to depend on his eyes.

He gazed down over the valley. For some indefinable reason he was wary.

He could see neither the river nor the island. They were too far away, and even in full daylight it would have been difficult to pick them out amid the valley's plains. Nor could he see the caves of the ranging which were almost as distant and in any event hidden by the curve of the mountains. He looked up towards the gorge he'd climbed on his journey out of the valley, then down to the little snow-covered plateau at its foot and the ravine beyond that dropped to the plain – all were silent and deserted.

Wengen was still alert and cautious. There were no tracks in the snow below him, but he sensed a presence there. He studied the snow minutely but if anything had trodden the plateau the drifting flakes had buried its spoor, and only the reflected moonlight shone back at him.

Uncertainly, Wengen lifted his head and glanced back.

The Snowman, as the oduna called the shumbi, had been following him. The oduna, moving in a pack, were further back still. The Snowman had trouble with his eyes. He walked stiffly, sometimes losing his balance and plunging into the drifts along the path Wengen had chosen. The oduna had no such problem, but for them Wengen had nothing but contempt.

Watching them over the three days since they'd left the shumbi's camp, Wengen found it difficult to believe they had ever belonged to the people. Physically they were strong. Under the Snowman's direction they had felled trees and made bridges across the rivers they had had to cross. Inside themselves the oduna were timid and clamorous. They chattered monotonously with each other, they clung together, they looked up fearfully whenever Wengen or the Snowman approached them.

Wengen looked at their shadows advancing on him under the moonlight. He rinsed out his mouth and spat on the ground. He despised them.

The Snowman reached him first.

'This is the pass down to the valley?' Geraint Hughes asked.

Wengen nodded.

'Where is the little shumbi?'

Wengen pointed. Hughes peered in the direction of the yeti's outstretched arm. He could see nothing but a vast bowl of blackness hazed with the occasional scatter of tumbling snow.

'The river and the island are below us at the plain's centre,' Wengen said. 'They are too distant to be seen, but they are there. That is where the shumbi will be.'

Hughes gazed out again. He could still see nothing. The moonlight glittering off the nearby banks of snow stung his eyes. He lowered his head and rubbed his face, then he glanced at the yeti.

'You are certain?'

Wengen paused for an instant before replying. 'Yes,' he said.

Hughes caught the brief hesitation. 'What's the matter?' he demanded fiercely. 'Is the child there, or is she not? Tell me, for Christ's sake!'

He caught the yeti by the chest, his fingers clawing into Wengen's hide, tightening until the yeti's fur stood out between his bunched knuckles. Wengen towered over him by more than twelve inches and the yeti's body weight was almost twice his own, yet Hughes shook him as if Wengen was no more than a rat clenched in the jaws of one of the valley terriers of the Welshman's childhood.

Wengen managed to tear himself away. He stared down at Hughes, panting. Finally understanding the oduna's terror of their leader. The shumbi's eyes were flooded scarlet with rage, and foam slid down from the corners of his mouth. The Snowman was more dangerous than any peril in the valley or the mountains. The Snowman came out of the dreams, the bad dreams that occasionally haunted the sleep of Wengen as they did all the yeti. In his brutal fury the shumbi, the Snowman, was a monster.

'She will be there,' Wengen said. 'It is only that when the snow comes to the valley, the people retire to the cavern for cloud-time.'

'Cloud-time?' Hughes shouted. 'What's that? And where the hell is the cavern?'

Wengen's glance swung back over the valley. The river and the island were still far beyond the reach of his gaze, but the snow was thinning every moment, the storm rapidly drifting away.

The yeti turned to Hughes again. From speaking to the oduna, Wengen knew that cloud-time had been lost to them in the distant past when their ancestors were exiled from the valley. Now they barely knew what it was. Wengen tried to explain it to the shumbi.

'Cloud-time is when the people gather together for the winter,' he said. 'The cavern is where they meet. For a moment I thought they might already have assembled there, but I was wrong, the snow confused me. This is only the first storm of the winter. The people wait for the snow before they move from the island. It is only when the animals retreat, the butterflies leave the trees and the last of the plants die, that they move –'

Wengen paused. 'The little shumbi will be where I told you, but we should hurry to find her.'

Hughes stared at the yeti through narrow suspicious eyes. Looped round a leather thong on his shoulder was what the oduna called the 'branch that smoked'. The Snowman had used it several times on their journey to the pass, each time levelling it against a mountain deer or boar. He had squeezed the curved twig at the branch's base – Wengen had seen the Snowman's knuckle whiten with the pressure. A chilling roar, a spurt of flame, and the animal had fallen.

The oduna had warned Wengen about the branch but the first time he heard the roar he'd thrown himself to the ground. Lifting his head he'd seen the oduna running forward to cluster round the corpse of a deer. A moment later Wengen stood up and joined them. Shouldering the oduna aside, he'd stared down at the animal disbelievingly. The animal had been dead when it fell – the oduna were butchering its carcass.

Although the roar still sent ripples of fear through his stomach,

Wengen no longer hurled himself down when he heard it. He had no idea what the branch was, or how the Snowman guided the force inside it. He knew only that the force was deadly. It allowed them all to eat without either hunting or gathering. It also gave the Snowman, the branch's master, a terrifying power.

As Wengen watched, the Snowman lifted the branch and shrugged off the thong. Leaning forward aggressively, he tossed the branch up and down in his hands. 'Touch it!' he said.

He thrust out the branch towards Wengen. His eyes held by the Snowman's ferocious glare, Wengen cautiously placed his hand on the frost-furred blue-black stick set into the branch's wooden base.

Wengen winced. The stick was the coldest object he had ever touched. Far colder than ice, it seemed to cling to and try to eat through his skin. He sprang back and sucked his fingers.

The Snowman chuckled. 'It bites you, doesn't it? It kills people just as easily as animals.' He slung the branch back over his shoulder. 'We'll go down. Remember, I'll be behind you every step.'

Wengen removed his fingers from his mouth. His skin was still burning, and he looked back at the Snowman, shaking his hand in pain.

'The rocks are too dangerous,' he said. 'We will take the path the deer use where it runs between the rocks. I will go first to kick away the snow. Once we reach the plateau below, we can walk safely, but until we get there it will not be easy. Two of the oduna should be with you for support.'

Hughes stared down into the gorge and nodded. He turned and slapped his hand against the roaring branch's base. Half a dozen oduna ran forward. Hughes picked out two of them and waved the others back. He spoke curtly to the two he'd chosen, and they positioned themselves on either side of him.

'I am ready,' Hughes said.

The yeti took a final glance at the Snowman. 'Give me time to clear the path,' Wengen said. 'When you can see the way clear, follow me.'

Wengen set off down the gorge's precipitous winding corridor, kicking and shovelling away the snow with his feet as he went. He was fifty feet below the ledge before he heard the Snowman set off in his wake. Wengen raised his head and listened.

He could hear the Snowman's angry mutters and the soft, almost silent press of the oduna's feet as they guided him down. Wengen paused. Inexplicably he was still uneasy. He scanned the air with his nostrils once more, but the air gave him back nothing. He probed the ground below with his eyes. Apart from the fresh-fallen snow mantle, there was nothing there either.

A stone, dislodged by the foot of the Snowman or one of the oduna, skittered past him. It bounced off the frozen surface of the drift at his side and plunged silently downwards. The tread of the three came closer, and Wengen headed on down.

He saw Manu when he was only a few steps above the plateau.

Squatting in the shadow of a boulder at the gorge's foot, Manu had watched Wengen's descent.

He had listened to the exchange between Wengen and the shumbi at the head of the gorge, every word funnelled down to him through the night air as clearly as if they had been speaking at his side. Wengen's voice was immediately recognizable. The shumbi's voice was alien and unfamiliar.

Manu had listened carefully. The shumbi spoke the language of the people, but coarsely and roughly. When he menaced Wengen, Manu felt the threat vibrating through the sounds he made, although for a time Manu lost the meaning of the words. As Wengen replied, Manu picked up the sense again.

They were coming down through the gorge. Wengen would lead, the shumbi would follow with two of the oduna to help him.

Manu waited behind the boulder. The storm had almost passed, and the moon was high above the crests. Its bleak and icy light glittered off the wind-driven snow banks that had silted up around the rocks. Each time Wengen kicked the snow away from the deer's path, the angle and pattern of the luminescence changed.

Wengen came nearer. As the gorge funnelled out on to the plateau his shadow appeared on the ground, closely followed by those of the other three, the shumbi and the two oduna. The four shadows danced across the snow, mingling, separating and coming together again. With every moment they grew sharper and closer. Manu drew in his breath. Overlying the shadows now were other flickering patterns cast by the rest of the oduna as they climbed down behind their leader. Manu concentrated on the dark black shapes cast by

Wengen and the shumbi.

When Wengen rounded the last of the boulders above the plateau, Manu stood up.

Wengen saw him instantly. So did the shumbi and the oduna, and the flickering shadows froze. Manu walked forward until he was standing directly in front of them at the gorge's foot.

'Go back, Wengen!' Manu said. 'There is no place for you among the people, nor is there food in the valley for those with you.'

He spoke quietly but in the stillness his words echoed up the gorge as if he had shouted. Wengen stared down at him, as always his face expressionless and his eyes opaque. After a moment he lifted his head and searched the plateau, then his gaze returned to Manu.

'Who is with you?' Wengen demanded.

The only tracks in the snow were Manu's. Wengen didn't know how or why the mountain yeti had come to be waiting for them at the foot of the gorge, but he was sure he wouldn't have come alone.

'The young of both the clans are with me,' Manu answered. 'We are many. We are here to deny you the valley and the crests.'

Wengen nodded. Manu was a hunter of course. He was accustomed to setting ambushes for animals. Whoever was with him would be hidden among the rocks and trees scattered across the plateau. That was why Wengen could see no trace of them.

'Where is the little shumbi?' Wengen asked.

'She is safe.'

'Fetch the shumbi,' Wengen said. 'Give her to us. If you do, we will depart and leave you the valley. If not, we will come down and take her.'

Manu gazed up at him. Wengen was lying, Manu knew that. The exiled yeti hadn't returned only for Iona. He had come back to take both the valley and the crests. Even if he had been speaking the truth, it would have made no difference. Iona was neither Manu's to give nor Wengen's to take. Iona belonged to the snows which had sent her to the valley.

'I am Manu, so listen well – !' Anger began to fill Manu, fuelled not only by Wengen's lies, but by his arrogance. His voice rose.

'The little shumbi has a name. She is called Iona, and she has become a member of the people. She has chosen to stay with the clans. You try to take her at your peril. Go back!'

A smile crept over Wengen's face, and Manu's pelt prickled with distrust.

Now Wengen's face was flushed with greed. His mouth was twisted down at the corners with tight narrow lines of cruelty. His pale eyes were no longer shuttered and opaque – they were bright with hatred and what appeared to be triumph.

Wengen raised his arm. For an instant he held it above his head – then he swept it down. Behind him there was a flash, a puff of smoke, and the loudest, most terrifying sound Manu had ever heard. Dimly he realized it came from where the shumbi was standing. Trapped inside the gorge the noise echoed off the rocky walls like the roar of an avalanche. At the same moment something invisible moaned past Manu's head with the speed and venom of a striking snake.

Every instinct in Manu's body screamed for him to run and hide with the other yeti behind the boulders. Somehow he stood his ground. A shock wave of air buffeted his face, and Wengen leapt down on him.

Disorientated by the noise, Manu had no time to dodge. He could only raise his hands in front of his chest before Wengen landed on him. The valley yeti was heavier than Manu and he had dropped from six feet above Manu's head. Manu's knees buckled under the impact. Staggering backwards he twisted and fell. As snow buried his face, Manu felt Wengen's fingers claw at his throat.

When they'd fought before over the seeding of Tana, it had been in the open on dry firm ground. Manu was faster and more agile than Wengen, but even then it had been a desperate struggle before he'd won. This battle was entirely different.

The initiative lay with Wengen. He was heavier and stronger than Manu, and they were fighting in snow where there was no purchase for Manu's feet. Behind Wengen stood the shumbi with his smoke and flame and the devastating roar of the branch in his hands. Above all, it wasn't a battle about the seeding of a female, vicious and deadly though that contest had been. They were fighting for the valley. They were fighting for their own lives, and the lives of all the yeti.

As he struggled to lever Wengen off him, Manu knew it was a battle which would end only with the death of one of them.

Twenty yards away, in her chosen hiding place, Iona watched with an appalled and helpless fascination.

When they reached the plateau Manu had found a haven for her in a cluster of rocks a hundred paces back from the gorge's foot. He told her carefully what he thought would happen. Wengen, the shumbi and the oduna would appear at the top of the gorge. Because Wengen knew the valley and its approaches, he would come down first, leading the others behind him.

Manu would be waiting at the base of the gorge. He would tell Wengen to retreat. If the encounter happened as Manu hoped and believed, Wengen would turn back. If it didn't and Manu had to call on the other yeti to repulse him, Manu wanted the child as far away as possible.

Iona shook her head stubbornly.

She was the prize, the reason Wengen was returning to the valley with the shumbi. When Manu rose to challenge them, Iona was determined to be as near to him as possible. She didn't know why – it was a determination born of instinct. She chose her own position, a rock only yards away from the hiding-place Manu had picked for himself. Unable to move her, Manu had been forced to agree, and Iona scooped away the snow and settled down to wait.

The snow continued to fall. It obliterated the tracks of everyone – Manu crouching in front of her, Kekua huddling behind another rock to Iona's right, the rest of the yeti scattered across the plateau in the shadows of trees and boulders. When Wengen appeared high on the lip of the gorge above them, Iona saw everything.

She saw Wengen speak to the shumbi, watched them climb down together, guided by two of the oduna with the rest of the creatures scrambling behind. She saw Manu rise and confront Wengen, heard the deafening roar as the shumbi fired his rifle, and saw Wengen plunge down on top of Manu.

Iona's breath caught in her throat, almost suffocating her. Wide-eyed with terror she watched the two yeti grappling frantically on the ground. As they fought, snow lifted and blew away like spume above their heaving bodies. Twice Manu managed to throw Wengen off him, but each time, as he struggled to rise, his feet slipped, he sank to his knees and Wengen leapt on him again. Using his greater weight and driven by a ferocity Iona had never witnessed in any animal before, Wengen bore down on Manu.

Spitting and snarling, his teeth sought Manu's neck and his fingers gouged at Manu's eyes. Lashing out with his legs, Manu managed to heave him off, and for the third time tried to stand. The snow around them was compacting into ice now in the bitter air and once again his feet slid from under him. He tumbled and fell limply on to his side.

Wengen balanced above him, the hands that had raked across Manu's face wet with blood. He brushed his fingers dry against his pelt and laughed.

'I have come to take the valley!' he shouted. 'Now it is mine!'

As Wengen hurled himself forward, Manu searched for the ground with his foot, found the earth beneath the snow and drove his heel against it. The heel buckled weakly and an agonizing pain ran up his leg. As he'd twisted away from Wengen's last attack, he must have broken his tendon. He lay half crippled and helpless in the scuffed and trampled whiteness.

Straddled across Manu's back Wengen bore down, searching again with his mouth bared for the mountain yeti's neck. His teeth found the soft skin at Manu's throat, his jaws clamped together and blood began to spurt up over his face.

Iona screamed, pushed herself up from the hollow where she'd been lying, and hurled herself forward. Her legs were stiff with cold and she moved with the terrible slowness of someone running in a nightmare. She drove herself on, scattering great sprays of snow in front of her stumbling feet like a boat wearily butting into the waves of a storm. Then she became aware that someone was running at her side.

Iona turned her head. It was the blind yeti, Kekua. As Iona saw her, the child lost her footing and fell. She struggled to her knees, spat the snow from her mouth and stared.

Kekua wasn't so much running as floating over the drifts with the speed and grace of a wind-driven leaf. Her eyes unseeing, Kekua overtook the child. She reached the two struggling yeti, and launched herself at Wengen. Unerringly her arms folded round his lowered head as his teeth tore across Manu's throat.

Wengen hadn't heard Kekua's approach. He grunted in surprise and let go of Manu's neck. He tried to look up, but his head was pinioned between Kekua's arms. Half turning, he glimpsed Kekua's face. He could hear the heaving of her chest, he felt the warmth of her breath on his pelt, he saw her eyes, milky-white and as chill and pitiless as the snow. Most vividly of all he saw the ice-hard set of her features and the implacable line of her mouth.

Terrified, Wengen knew she was going to kill him.

He made a last frantic effort to escape. He kicked and heaved and struggled, but Kekua was above him and her strength seemed limitless. She held him down, her gaze directed not at Wengen but into the sky above the pass. She seemed to be watching the stars as Wengen squirmed and wriggled beneath her. Suddenly she cut Wengen's struggles short.

'It is over,' she said.

She hauled up Wengen's head, twisted it quickly to one side, and snapped his neck. As Wengen fell limply into the snow, Kekua struggled to her feet and stood above him.

Iona had plunged to a halt in a deep drift of snow a few yards away. Panting, she stared at Kekua. Numb and shocked and bewildered, Iona could barely take in what had happened. Her face sorrowful but strangely exultant, the blind yeti seemed to be gazing back at the child, then she turned from Iona and looked down at Manu.

For an instant the milky opaqueness that clouded her eyes dissolved, and it was as if she had been given the power of sight. She reached down and felt for the wounds in Manu's throat. Iona could see her touching the torn flesh tenderly, trying to staunch the flow from the lacerations of Wengen's teeth. Blood flowered on her hand before it congealed and darkened in the night air. As Kekua stood there, stooped over Manu, there was another deafening explosion on the slope above her. Kekua spun round as if she'd been kicked in the spine. Her legs splayed out and she reeled from side to side. Shuddering and coughing, she reached for the air, clutching at the ladders of the falling snowflakes as if they could hold her upright.

The snow vanished between her clawing fingers, and Kekua toppled and fell across Manu's body.

A scream rose in Iona's throat. Before it could burst out, there was a metallic click higher up the slope and the urgent, compelling shout of a human voice.

'Don't move, child, or you'll be shot too! Stay where you are! I'm coming down for you! I'm seeing you safe, cariad, I'm taking you home!'

The shumbi, the man, came lurching headlong down the twisting path between the boulders.

Iona stared up at him in frozen horror. Even in the moonlight she could see his eyes were scarlet and swept with madness. Behind him, following him, came a pack of sinewy scampering shapes. She could see their eyes glowing too, not golden like Manu's or the clear translucent grey of the island yeti, but with a dull, hungry gleam.

The child stood there, rooted and helpless. The man was like a crazed pied piper with a horde of huge greedy rats scrambling in an irresistible tide in his wake. He was worse than any of the monsters from her nightmares, and she knew he wanted her more than anything in the world. The man came closer. His feet struck a rock, and Iona saw a spark flare beneath his cleated boots and the starlight flash off the barrel of his rifle.

She closed her eyes. Suddenly something cannoned against her ribs and hurled her aside so that she pitched forward face down in the snow. Choking and sobbing, she struggled back to her feet, brushed the snow from her eyes again and peered up.

It was Babilla.

The leopard had been crouching at her side. When the shot that killed Kekua echoed over the pass, the animal must have waited an instant. Then it had sprung forward, knocking her down as it leapt. As Iona watched she saw Babilla racing upwards, covering the ground in great soaring bounds towards the point where a small puff of smoke was still slowly drifting away in the almost motionless air of the bank thirty feet above.

Iona heard the metallic click of a bolt being pumped again. Before the man could squeeze the trigger, Babilla was on him. Iona saw the leopard leap in a great arc from the snowdrift below. She saw the moonlight flash on Babilla's teeth as the creature opened its mouth and snarled. She saw the surging flow of its rose-printed pelt and the spread of its outstretched claws.

Iona knelt and hid her face in her hands.

Later, she didn't know how much later, she felt something butting at her thighs. She opened her eyes. It was Babilla. The leopard was lying beside her with its head on its paws, nudging her gently. There was blood on Babilla's face, and the animal was giving little satisfied growls.

Iona stood up, trembling. She gazed round the clearing and up the pass. When she had last looked up, the cleft had been filled with the flickering shadows of the oduna. Now it was empty. The oduna must have fled when Babilla killed the man with the rifle – she could see his body spread-eagled like a dead and dried starfish on the scuffed whiteness of the snow.

The yeti had risen from their hiding places and seemed to be everywhere. One of them was directing the others. Iona peered forward and saw it was the graceful young female, Tana. As Iona watched, one group of young males picked up Manu on Tana's instructions, and began to carry him down towards the valley. Another group lifted the body of Kekua and followed the first. Wengen and the shumbi were left lying where they had died in the snow.

The two groups tramped past Iona, Tana walking behind them. Iona tried to see Manu's face. His eyes were closed and his pelt glistened with blood, and Iona burst into tears. As she stood shivering and sobbing in the darkness, she felt an arm round her shoulder.

'Do not cry, little shumbi. Manu is badly hurt, but I will tend him and he will recover.'

The voice was Tana's. Iona wiped the tears from her eyes and looked up at the young female.

In less than an hour Tana had changed. The shyness and uncertainty had vanished from her face. She looked calm and strong and confident. The scars of her brutal violation by Wengen seemed to have been wiped away by his death. She had a mate of her own wanting now, a wounded mate she would have to look after. Tana exulted in her task.

'You must rest, Iona,' Tana went on. 'I will carry you.'

She reached down and swung Iona up. Iona tried to protest, but she was limp with tiredness and drained of everything except the desire to sleep. Cradled in the yeti's arms, she huddled against Tana's breast, and wept again.

53

Iona screamed in her sleep.

The sound of her voice woke her. She jerked upright and peered round her in terror. The last time she'd been woken by one of her own screams – apart from the night of the snowstorm – the sound had rung through the nursery floor of the house in the Boltons. Iona had wondered fearfully if it had been heard by her mother's sharp-eyed, sharp-tongued maid, Hartley.

The terror began to ebb away. This time there was no Hartley watching television on the floor below, no draughty corridors leading off the landing outside Iona's bedroom door, no darkness beyond her bed where the monsters had prowled. Instead Iona found she was lying wrapped in a bearskin cloak on a bed of moss beneath the stars.

As she blinked and tried to work out how she came to be there, Iona heard a voice saying, 'What is it?'

It was Tana.

Everything came back to the child then. She wrapped the heavy bearskin round her and scrambled to her feet. It was still night, but dawn was close, and in the glow of the approaching sunrise off the snow, Iona saw she was in a glade in the forest. Tana must have carried her down there from the pass, gathered the moss for her bed and folded the hide round her against the cold. Judging by the waning stars Iona must have slept for six hours.

'How is Manu?' Iona asked anxiously.

'I have bound his wounds with mud and leaves. He is tired and weak, but better. In a moment you may speak to him –'

Tana paused and glanced curiously at the child. 'You called out in fear,' she said. 'Why?'

Iona looked up at her.

It had been a nightmare. Like the nightmares of the past it had retreated to the furthest, almost forgotten recesses of her mind within seconds of waking. It would return when she slept again, nightmares always did. But this one had been different from her previous dreams. These had been peopled by the monsters – this one by the man with the rifle.

In her sleep Iona had seen him lift the gun and fire the shot which killed Kekua. She saw Kekua stagger and fall, but the nightmare hadn't ended there. The man had reloaded and pointed the gun at Manu. Inexplicably there was no Babilla to save the yeti, the leopard had vanished and the man was aiming again. Iona couldn't make out his face but she could see his finger tightening on the trigger.

It was then that she screamed, a scream of warning to tell Manu to escape and hide.

Iona closed her eyes. Everything had changed, everything had been turned upside down. In the nightmares in London the threat had come from the monsters. Inside herself, alone in bed in the darkness at night, Iona had clung to people to protect her from them – to old Mr Simpson, to pudding-faced Kate, to anyone who was safe. Now it was the yeti who were threatened, and it was people who were attacking them.

People like the man with the gun would go on attacking them for as long as Iona remained in the valley.

'Take me to Manu,' she said suddenly.

Tana led her through the trees to where Manu lay on a bed of moss like the one Tana had gathered for Iona. Round his neck was a great collar of summer-dried but still supple orchid leaves held together with clips of thorn. Beneath the leaves the mud Tana had applied to his throat was seeping over his chest and shoulders, and down across the other wounds left on his body by Wengen's teeth.

Manu must have lost a large amount of blood. His cheeks were sunken and his breathing shallow, but his eyes were open and he recognized Iona immediately. He tried to lift his hand to give her the nose greeting, but his arm refused to move. He wrinkled his face irritably, and Iona smiled. She leant down and gently gave him the greeting herself, then she stood up and turned to Tana. 'I wish to speak to Manu alone,' the child said.

Tana stared at her for a moment before swinging round. Several of the other young male yeti had gathered by Manu's bed at the shumbi's approach. Tana waved them back and walked away with them.

'Tana says you will heal,' Iona said.

'I am healing now. I will hunt again.' Manu's voice was hoarse and frail.

'Wengen is dead, the shumbi is dead, the oduna have gone,' Iona said. She tried to smile. 'You have guarded and kept the valley –' Iona paused, and looked down into Manu's eyes. She drew in her breath, and held it in her lungs until she felt dizzy. Then she breathed out slowly.

'I am going from the valley, Manu,' she said.

For a moment Manu didn't understand what she meant. He looked at her, puzzled, then, as he finally took in her words, he tried to heave himself upright.

'You cannot leave us!' The croak that came out of his mouth was the closest he could manage to a shout. 'You are part of the valley now. You saved Churinga's child. You helped make peace between the clans. You are teaching us how to hunt and gather in ways we knew not before. You belong here, Iona!'

The effort was too much for him. He coughed, spitting out blood, and fell back on the bed of moss onto his side.

Iona said nothing, and the silence went on. His chest heaving, Manu studied the child's face. There were tears in Iona's eyes and her expression was anguished. It was also resolute. He knew she had made up her mind and nothing would change it.

'Why?' he asked eventually.

'While I stay here, there will be no safety for the people,' Iona replied. 'The shumbi who came for me is dead, but other shumbi will follow him looking for me too. They may not come with killing branches as he did, but they will come and find the valley and there will be nothing left for the people. The only way to stop them is for me to go.'

It was Manu's turn to be silent. What the child had said filtered slowly through his mind. Iona had seen clearly and spoken the truth, Manu realized. If either of the clans lost a child, the people would abandon everything and search until it was found however long that took and whether the child was alive or dead. The shumbi were the same with their own young – except that where they searched, death and destruction followed.

Manu rolled over on his back and gazed up at the stars. The sky had cleared but he sensed that more snow-clouds were moving down from the mountains.

'If you go, you must go swiftly,' he said. 'The shumbi must have come from one of your people's shelters. His tracks, and the tracks of Wengen and the oduna, will surely lead back there. Two of the young males will take you to the top of the pass. Afterwards travel alone. Follow the tracks before the snow comes again, and you will be safe.'

In his voice there was resignation and an immense sadness.

Briefly Iona felt only gratitude. Manu hadn't questioned her, he hadn't argued or tried to stop her. Weak and in pain he had considered her decision calmly and thoughtfully, and accepted it without comment. He was concerned only with the practicalities of the journey that lay in front of her.

The gratitude faded, and the tears in Iona's eyes welled up and flooded down her cheeks. Dropping to her knees by his side, she broke down and sobbed. 'I don't want to go, Manu.' Her words were choked and husky. 'I want to stay with you.'

'The people grieve when one in the clans goes to the stars,' Manu said. 'The grief passes quickly. It is like the harvested fruit which grows again. With the climbing to the stars, it is the same. We know the one who has gone grows there, and we will come together again –'

Manu raised himself on his elbow. 'You do not go to the stars, little shumbi. You go to your people, to your own shelter. But you have another home now, here in the valley. This is where you can always return.'

He dropped back on the bed of moss again. His eyelids fluttered, and he looked pale and exhausted. Iona knew the effort of speaking to her had drained almost all his strength. The longer she stayed there, the wearier he would become.

She reached out and scratched his nose for the last time, then she stood up and turned away. As she moved Iona heard his voice again.

'You had one firestick left to use in the cavern,' Manu whispered. 'You asked me whom you should wake. I was cold and could not answer you. You chose Tana. Why?'

Iona glanced back at him.

Beneath the collar that enclosed his wounds, Manu's pelt lay thick and glossy over his hard-muscled body. She thought of him hunting, with Babilla bounding ahead. She thought of his bold bright eyes quartering the grounds, and his quick incisive movements when

Babilla scented prey. She thought of his laughter, and the care he had taken of her from the moment he had picked her up on the bank.

She remembered him swimming the river so many times with her arms clasped round his neck, how he had stood between her and Jinga when the old female had been about to leap for her throat. She remembered the days they had fruitlessly hunted the crests, and his constant good humour in spite of her failure.

Iona wept again. 'I wanted to look after you,' she said. 'I just knew Tana could do it better.' She was sobbing and her voice was barely audible.

Manu reached down towards his thonged hunting belt. He pulled something out and held it up to her. 'Take this from me,' he said. 'It was given me by my mother Burra from the ice of cloud-time. She said it came from the first animal hunted by the star without a name. She said whoever had it would always hunt with success and safety.'

Her eyes blurred, Iona took the object from Manu's hand. She tucked it into her pouch. Then she turned and ran from the clearing.

54

Iona saw them long before they spotted her.

She didn't know how long she'd been walking since she left Manu. Two of the young male yeti had helped her up the almost perpendicular stairway of the gorge. At the top, on Manu's instructions, they had left her and returned to the valley. Since then she must have travelled for thirty-six hours, perhaps more.

At the start as she climbed away from the valley the going had been very hard. Although she was fit and strong after the months she'd spent there, it was the most difficult journey she had ever made. Several times, at the foot of a sheer icefall or wading through waist-deep snow along an exposed ridge, she'd almost despaired, but always, even at the worst moments, Iona had been driven on by Manu's directions.

'Wengen led the shumbi and the oduna to the pass,' he'd said. 'You can take the same way out. Their tracks will guide you. But whatever happens, you must keep moving. If snow falls again before you find your people, you will be lost. As a shumbi in the mountains, nothing can save you then.'

The prints of Wengen, the shumbi and the oduna had stretched out mile after winding, precipitous mile before her. Iona followed them, struggling upwards through the snow. Finally she came to the crest of the highest ridge she had scaled. Dizzy and breathless, she rested for a few minutes in the lee of an ice-sheeted boulder. As she huddled there a torpid chill began to seep over her bones and muscles.

Iona shook her head. She heaved herself to her feet and forced herself to set off again.

Afterwards it was easier. The icefalls and rocky couloirs were as steep as before, but she was travelling downwards now. Twice she lost her footing and gashed her skin as she slid. The cuts ached painfully as the blood coagulated in the chill air, but she struggled on. Later the fall of the landscape flattened out and she could move faster. Tana had given her a pouch filled with dried cloud-time stores which the yeti had brought with her to the pass from a cache close to the cavern. Every few hours Iona paused and ate hungrily. Then she stumbled on.

As she travelled Iona glanced constantly at the sky. At dawn it had been clear but by mid-morning clouds had started to gather. Now, in what she guessed was the early afternoon, the clouds were massing on every side, thick, grey and menacing, and pregnant with snow. Within minutes of the snow falling the tracks would vanish.

Iona hurried on again. The snow held off, the night passed, and day came again with watery sunlight and a bite in the air that seemed even fiercer and more bitter than during the hours of darkness. Finally, just as the light was starting to fade for the second time, Iona found what she was searching for.

Something glittered ahead of her. It was too distant and too far below for her to make out what it was, but the sparkle was dark and metallic against the whiteness of the ice and snow – it came from something man-made. Iona quickened her step. A few moments later she stopped and peered down. She could see everything clearly now.

Half a mile beneath her was a small open bowl in the mountains. At the centre of the bowl and straggling away up the slope beyond were wooden houses, with little columns of smoke rising from their roofs. It was a Nepalese village. Three helicopters were parked in an open area – the flare of light had come from their canopies – and a group of people were standing in front of what looked like an inn.

Iona was still too high to see who they were, but several of them wore European clothes. Then one of them walked forward. The figure was smaller than the others and its silhouette seemed to be a woman's. A thin shaft of light broke through the clouds and swept across the clearing, briefly touching the woman's head.

The woman's hair was a deep gold.

Iona's heart surged up in her chest until she felt she was choking, and tears blurred her eyes. In front of her everything vanished and she swayed and almost fell. She caught hold of a pine sapling, and stood there sobbing. She had no idea how long she wept for, but eventually she pushed herself away from the tree, and walked on.

'Iona!'

Her mother saw her first. Dorelia Howard shouted and started to run. Behind her there were other shouts and other people running, and then Iona was overwhelmed. She felt her mother's arms envelop her and her mother's tears wet on her cheek. She heard her father's voice mingled with other voices, some of them speaking in English, some in Gurkhali.

'Darling, are you all right? Let me look at you –'

In the confusion and uproar, Iona was aware of her mother pushing her away and staring at her.

'Oh my God, you're so brown and thin! What did they do to you. Did they – ?' Her mother broke off, her face suddenly taut with dread.

'I'm all right, Mum,' Iona said. 'No one did anything to me. I'm fine.'

'Oh, my God!' Weeping, Dorelia clutched her again. Iona started to cry too, and they stood together clinging to each other.

The next hour was a blur. Iona remembered going inside the inn. Vaguely she remembered too being examined by an American doctor in an upstairs room. She heard him tell her mother what Dorelia already knew, that she was thin but apparently in good health. Then Iona was taken downstairs again.

Everyone had streamed into the inn behind her, and the big low-raftered room was crowded and noisy with excited talk. The air outside was darkening, and candles and a fire had been lit. Iona was sat down at a table and a large bowl of food was placed in front of her. She had long since finished the contents of the pouch Tana had given her and she hadn't eaten for more than twelve hours, but she was too tired and dizzy to be hungry. She took a few mouthfuls and pushed the bowl away. Instead she sipped at a mug of hot smoky tea.

'Darling.' It was her mother's voice again. 'You remember Sean, don't you – ?'

Iona glanced round. She saw her mother with the heavy-shouldered figure of Sean Ryan at her side.

'Sean's a writer, as you know, darling,' her mother went on. 'He wants to talk to you. He wants to hear all about this extraordinary story of you and these creatures while it's still fresh and immediate in your mind. Tell him about the yeti.'

Iona looked at Sean – and froze. A chill of fear ran through her as she stared at him. Shrewd and pale and calculating, his eyes reminded her of Wengen's. Like Wengen, too, his presence was somehow violent and intimidating. He seemed to threaten her like the big powerful yeti had done when he gazed malevolently across the clearing, or squatted in brooding silence above her among the reeds on the island's ridge.

'What is it, darling?' Dorelia said impatiently. 'You can speak to Sean, and you can tell me at the same time. We want to know everything, so does Daddy and everyone else.' Her mother gestured behind her.

Iona still didn't speak. Her eyes swept the room in desperation. She hesitated and her glance swung back across the throng. For the first time she realized that Uncle Robert was there, half hidden in the deep shadows. He stood looking anxiously down at her, his white hair and deeply lined face framed in the candlelight.

Iona's eyes locked on to his. If there was anyone who could help her, it was him. Helpless and confused, she stared at Cabot in frantic silent appeal. Cabot didn't respond. He continued to look down at her with his grave, unfathomable gaze. Iona's heart sank and tears brimmed over her eyes. In anguish she started to turn away.

'Dorelia –'

Iona's head jerked back. Uncle Robert had stepped forward. He had addressed her mother but what he said embraced everyone else in the room.

'For Iona this whole business started with me,' Cabot continued. 'I think it might be a good idea if she and I had a word together alone.'

Iona stared at her godfather again. His voice was its usual mild drawl – 'the accent, I fear, my dear,' as he'd so often said to her, 'of a Yankee sailor out of Nantucket' – but his tone was clear and commanding. Iona's mother glanced at him, puzzled. She looked back uncertainly at her daughter. Then she stood up.

'Very well, Robert,' she said. She took Sean Ryan's hand and walked out. A moment later everyone else had left too. Behind the closed door Iona could hear the murmur of conversation in the hall of the inn, but she and Cabot were alone.

'Snow –'

Cabot grunted. Ignoring Iona he had crossed the floor and was peering out of the window. '*Istasa-na-mi*. "The eternal wedding gown of the crests". That's what the Nepalese call it. Been falling ever since you came down from the ridge. You know that, I'm sure –' Cabot paused. 'Perhaps you've learnt another word for it.'

He glanced back at her. He was as tall and remote and daunting as he'd been the first time Iona remembered seeing him. But the smile on his face, gentle and quizzical, was as warm as it had been then.

Iona walked forward to join him. Side by side they looked out into the dark. Beyond the thick glass of the windowpanes the snow was drifting down in a dense canopy of whiteness that had already mantled the ground and covered the scuffed prints outside.

'The people name the snow *anuit*,' Iona said.

'*Anuit?*' Cabot frowned. 'Translate for me, young lady.'

'It's the same word they use for the down breast feathers of the young eagles. The feathers keep the birds warm. When the down goes, the birds are ready to fly. The snow keeps the valley warm. When it melts, the valley moves towards harvest.'

'You call them the people. Are they what we would call the yeti?'

Iona nodded.

'And that's where you've been, with them?'

'Yes.'

'What are they like?'

Iona hesitated. She thought of Manu, Kekua, Churinga and Tana, of the two old patriarchs, their mates, and the clans. There was no way in which she could describe them.

'I thought they were monsters at first,' she answered. 'But they're not. They're people like us, except they're different, that's all. They found me, well, Manu found me – he's one of them. They looked after me. They helped me to come back.'

Iona stopped. Cabot scratched his nose and frowned. 'But you didn't want to tell your mother about them?'

Iona raised her head. Uncle Robert was so tall that she had to strain her neck to see his face. He was still staring out into the darkness. He was her last hope, her only hope. If she could convince him, he might be able to stop the others. It was the most important thing she had ever done. She reached out and took his hand.

'Uncle Robert, you remember when we found those flowers?'

'The orchids?' Cabot nodded. '*Orchidaceae*, as I recall.'

'You said we shouldn't tell anyone we'd found them. The place had to stay a secret. If people knew and came, the flowers would be lost.'

Cabot chuckled. His remark had been partly a joke – the site where they'd come across *tridentulata* was so remote that there was no chance of anyone else finding it too. But Iona was right – there was enough truth in his words for him to stand by them.

'It's the same with the yeti,' Iona went on. 'People, I mean people like us, are getting closer to them all the time. They're already in danger. If people get into the valley the yeti will be destroyed. Someone like Mummy's friend, Sean, he'd be the worst of all –'

She paused and took a deep breath. 'I'd sooner die than have Sean go there. I'll tell you about them, and about what happened to me.'

When she had finished Cabot looked down at his goddaughter. Iona was gazing up at him, her cheeks pale but her eyes unwavering. The expression on her face was the most resolute he had ever seen on anyone, man, woman or child. She looked implacable. For several moments Cabot was silent.

He had sensed the girl had been through an extraordinary experience, but never anything quite so extraordinary as she had just described to him. He tried to take it in. For four months Iona had lived among creatures the world believed were mythical. If the story had come from anyone else and in any other circumstances, Cabot would have dismissed it as a fantasy.

It was not a fantasy. Cabot knew his godchild. Iona was too direct and straightforward to have invented it. From the words she'd used in the yeti's language to her description of the valley's topography, everything she'd said, every detail and every incident, rang true. Cabot also knew the circumstances she was talking about. No European child could have survived alone for four months in the Himalayas. She would have needed nurture and support, shelter and food.

In the Helambu there was no one to give it – no one except, if they existed, the yeti. The crazed Welshman had assured him they did, and shown him their tracks to prove it. The scarlet-eyed Hughes was right.

'This one you call Manu,' Cabot said eventually, 'the one who helped you to leave the valley and find us. How did he even know we were here?'

A shadow crossed Iona's face. Her account had stopped at cloud-time, and she hadn't spoken of the events at the pass. Her eyes clouded and her mouth tightened in distress.

'A man came into the valley with the oduna –'

'Oduna?' Cabot interrupted her. 'What are they?'

'The yeti call them that,' Iona replied. 'The oduna were once yeti themselves, but they were driven out of the valley and had children with the villagers. Now they are scavengers. Some of them follow the man with the rifle.'

'What happened?'

Iona's face became even more troubled. 'There was a terrible fight. Manu fought with Wengen. Kekua saved him and killed Wengen, but the man shot her. Afterwards the man was killed by Manu's leopard, Babilla. The oduna scattered and fled –' Iona's voice was husky and her eyes tormented.

'I knew the man and the oduna must have been searching for me. As long as I stayed in the valley, other people would search for me too. I told Manu I had to leave and he understood. He said that if I followed the man's tracks I would come to where you were. That's what I did.'

Cabot looked back into the darkness beyond the window.

If he had needed convincing, what the child had just told him would have done so once and for all. Geraint Hughes, his story about the tracks and the wild creatures in the valley, his claim about his friends – everything fell into place now.

Cabot squeezed the girl's hand. 'Look,' he said. 'The snow's still falling.'

Iona peered into the darkness.

Uncle Robert was right. It wasn't a blizzard. The wind was too light for that, but the snow was floating down in a great shining tapestry of white flakes that even as she watched began to build up in a thick layer on the windowsill.

'Do you think anyone could follow tracks beneath that?' Cabot asked.

Iona shook her head.

'Nor do I. So the valley's effectively cut off until the spring. And that leaves us a nice space of time in which to spin a few tales and tell a few lies.'

Iona glanced up at him, bewildered.

'For heaven's sake, young lady.' Cabot gave her his quizzical smile. 'I'm a scientist and, if you'll forgive me, you're a child. We both deal in truth, which means we should both be experts on the other side of the coin – fibs. Here –'

Cabot reached down. He caught Iona round the waist and lifted her up until she was resting on his hip.

'We're about to invent some fine ones,' Cabot went on. 'A mountain tribe for a start. A human but very boring one. A faction of the Gurkhali nation no one's ever been interested in and, God willing, no one ever will be. A nomadic group who found you, looked after you, and returned you to civilization before winter set in. They lived in the valley once, but no longer. They've headed on towards Tibet. How about that?'

Iona looked at her godfather wide-eyed. 'That's what you're going to say?'

He nodded.

'Nothing about the yeti?' she asked hesitantly.

'Of course not,' Cabot answered crisply. 'The yeti don't exist. If they did, they'd be monsters. And we all know monsters don't exist.'

'But what about the man who came looking for me with the oduna?'

Cabot wrinkled his eyes in a rueful smile. 'I'm afraid I organized that.'

'You?' Iona gasped.

'Yes, young lady. It seems to have been a mistake, but I wasn't to know that. His name was Hughes, although he told me he was known as the Snowman, and he was half-crazy with what I guess was mountain sickness. He said he knew you were with the yeti, he convinced me he was telling the truth, and he said he could bring you back. As that was all I wanted, I offered him anything he asked for to do it.'

'But he's dead,' Iona said. 'Babilla's killed him.'

'I think we can handle that,' Cabot replied. 'I'm a New England Yankee, young lady. We're as sharp as a maple knife, but even the smartest Yankee sometimes buys a jar of snake-oil. That's what Hughes sold me. I bought his story, then he took the money and ran. Or at least that's what I'm going to tell the rest of them here.'

'Will they really believe that?'

'The Snowman's vanished. The tracks are buried. The valley's cut off until the spring. Above all, you're back safe. That's all that matters. They'll believe it.'

Iona was silent. The two clans, she thought, would also be safe – safe at least until the spring. With the snow falling ever more thickly in the darkness outside, spring seemed a world away.

Iona threw her arms round Cabot's neck, rested her cheek against his bristly chin, and wept. Cabot let her tears stream down his face for a few moments, then he pushed her gently away.

'Compose yourself, young lady,' he said gruffly but kindly. 'We've work to do and lies to tell. Lies are always more convincing if delivered with confidence and dry eyes.'

Iona wiped her face. Cabot smiled at her and she smiled back. Then, as he lowered her to the floor, she said, 'Wait, Uncle Robert.'

She felt for her survival pouch, opened it and pulled out the object Manu had given her. She hadn't had time to examine it before. Looking at it now, it appeared to be a piece of bone. It was the only thing she'd brought back from the valley, and she wanted her godfather to have it.

'Manu gave it to me when I left,' she said. 'I think it's a piece of bone. It's not much, I'm afraid, but I'd like you to have it as a present from me.'

Cabot looked at what the child had handed him. It wasn't a piece of bone. It was the tooth of a large meat-eating animal, a carnivore. Cabot wasn't a palaeontologist but he'd studied fossils long enough to know that this one belonged to a member of the sabre-toothed tiger family. Sabre-toothed tigers had been extinct for thousands of years. Their incisor teeth were occasionally found buried in fossil sites. The finds were always pitted and eroded by the immense passage of time.

This particular tooth gleamed bright and smooth and yellow. Cabot's first impression was that it might have come from an animal which had died yesterday. He fumbled for his glasses and studied it more closely. Scored with what he guessed was some sharpened stone implement was the outline of a leopard.

The creature's shape was unmistakable, but the style of the carving was unfamiliar to Cabot. It reminded him of the rock art of the San hunter-gatherers of the Kalahari, or the animals painted on the walls of the Lascaux caves. But the lines of the leopard here were both simpler and more sinuous, more abstract and yet more vivid.

Cabot stared at it for a long time. Then he peered over his spectacles at Iona. 'Do you know where your friend Manu got this?'

She nodded. 'He was given it by his mother, Burra. Burra was one of the ranging's greatest hunters. She told him that whoever had this would always hunt with success and safety.'

Cabot turned and gazed back into the darkness.

The storm had passed. Another would press in soon behind it and the air would fill again with the downward spiral of the silting snowflakes, but for the moment the sky was clear. Under the moon's glow lay great drifts of whiteness. Spider-thin spindrifts of ice were etched on the inn's coarse glass panes and light-shafts fell from a billion stars.

A yak coughed in the stables. A trail of smoke and sparks from a dung fire were plucked up into the branches of the trees. An old man, a Tibetan employed to gather wood, ventured out into the circle of candlelight cast from the inn's windows. He muttered, gathered his cloak round him against the cold, and retreated. There was enough fuel to last until morning.

Amid snows like this, on a starry night like this, the Magi had ridden up to a stable in Bethlehem. There in a manger the modern world had been born. And it wasn't remotely important that Bethlehem that night might have been sweltering in the summer heat of a Palestinian summer, or that seasons, rituals and feasts might have been adapted and altered to fit the political requirements of the centuries that followed.

It didn't even matter if Bethlehem itself hadn't existed.

On Cabot's hand, cupped in the hollow of his palm, was the carving of a leopard scored on the fang of a sabre-toothed tiger. Whatever had been born in Bethlehem, he was holding something infinitely older, something that had been valued and trusted as a talisman long before Christ, Buddha and Mohammed, that had been passed from hand to hand in an unbroken line from the dawn of human time. Older than Mecca and the Cross, older than the Pyramids and the temples of the Indus valley, it was still venerated today by the creatures who'd given it to the child.

'Thank you, young lady,' Cabot said. 'It was a fine gift. I'm glad to have held it for a few moments. But it was given to you and I'm going to return it to you.'

He reached for Iona's hand, placed the tooth on her palm and pressed her fingers down over it. He paused.

'Beware of the old,' he said. 'They care only for themselves. For them time's at an end. Their interests are entirely selfish and they don't mind if they damage the rest of us. But when I'm old, and that means a hell of a lot older than I am now, when I'm beyond doing damage, come and visit me. Tell me about Manu. Tell me about the people. Tell me where we, the human race, come from. Promise?'

Iona looked at him, frowning. She didn't really understand what he was saying, but she nodded. 'I promise.'

'Fine.' Cabot let go of her hand.

During the past four months a great deal had happened outside the world of the valley that would change Iona's life profoundly. The child knew nothing about her parents' divorce and Cabot wondered briefly if he should break the news to her now. He decided against it – he would leave that to Dorelia. For the moment Iona had gone through enough although, Cabot suspected, over the years ahead there would be many broken pieces he would be called on to glue together again.

Before they rejoined Dorelia he wanted an answer to the one question which had bewildered him that morning on the ridge when he found Iona missing, and which had haunted him ever since.

'Why did you walk out into the storm that night?' Cabot asked her.

Iona didn't reply. She stood silently, her face puckered and grave. Then she flushed and smiled.

'I thought there were monsters in the tent,' she said. 'But monsters don't really exist, do they?' She looked anxiously at Cabot.

Cabot stared back at her for a long time without replying. Then he shook his head firmly and decisively.

'Only if you're afraid,' he answered. 'And you're certainly not afraid, young lady. If you ever were, you'll never be frightened again. You've got a Yankee's word for that –'

He gave the child another of his rare comforting smiles. Then he reached down and took her hand. 'Let's go through and set them all straight. No yeti, no monsters, no Snowman, not even a Manu or a Kekua.' He squeezed her fingers. 'Never forget the cast-iron rule of the poker players who worked the frontier saloons. "Doesn't matter what story we tell about the cards we're dealt, as long as we all tell the same story." OK, young lady?'

Iona squeezed his hand back. She smiled at him and nodded. Together they walked through into the inn.

55

'Mr Simpson!' Iona ran across the grass and threw her arms round his chest.

She shouldn't have done it, she knew that. She was too old now. Only four months had passed, but the months might have been years and the time had changed her out of all recognition, changed her both physically and mentally from a child into a woman. A young woman, maybe, a very young woman, but still a woman.

Women didn't hug their employees, least of all a man old enough to be their grandfather. Iona didn't care. She saw the old gardener standing by one of the arches in the yew hedge and happiness welled uncontrollably over her. That was why she was holding and shaking him now.

'God bless us, child, what's come over ye –'

Embarrassed and confused but his face scarlet with pleasure, Mr Simpson managed to struggle out of her embrace.

'Let's have a look at ye.' He stepped back and studied her. 'Ye've grown, that's for sure. Shot up like the raspberry canes in spring. Ye're brown as a nut too. That'll be the effect of the foreign sun, nae doubt.'

'Anything else?' Iona demanded.

Simpson narrowed his eyes. 'A wee bit more body to ye, child, but that's nae bad thing. Ye always were as thin as my caley rake. Apart from that –' He paused and shook his head. 'Nothing. Ye're still a bonny lass, Iona. Or Miss Iona as I'm thinking it's proper it should be now.'

'"Miss" Iona,' she mocked him. 'Do I really look like "Miss" Iona?'

Simpson chuckled but didn't answer.

'If you ever call me that again,' Iona went on. 'I'm going to get another gardener. And I don't ever want another gardener. Understand?'

Simpson wrinkled his nose and grunted.

She took his hand as she used to do in the past. She'd held it then because there were strange wild places in Mainwarden's grounds, and the strong firm clasp of the old man was a rope that anchored her in safety. Now she held on to him out of pleasure and familiarity. They went through the arch in the yew hedge and headed down the avenue of pleached fruit trees that led towards the walled garden.

Simpson plucked out his red-and-white-checked handkerchief and coughed. 'I'm sorry your ma and da have chosen to go their ain separate ways,' he said gruffly as they walked.

Iona didn't reply. She simply nodded in acceptance of the regret in the old man's voice. There was disapproval in his words too, but she had expected that. She knew it was something he had to say and now it was said, it was done. She let the observation hang in the air until its weight dissolved in the clear morning air.

'But as the matter was put to me, it will not affect Mainwarden,' the gardener added.

She nodded. 'Daddy inherited Mainwarden. Mummy made it what it is. Now Daddy's taken over my uncle's house in Scotland, and Mummy wants to go back to New York. So they've given Mainwarden to me.'

Iona still wasn't sure she understood what had happened. Her mother had tried to explain it to her on the flight back to London. Sensitivity wasn't one of Dorelia Howard's natural graces, and what she told Iona had come out bluntly, almost brutally. While Iona had been 'away' she and Iona's father had decided to part. Although of course Iona wouldn't have known, they had been thinking about it for most of the past year.

They were leaving each other with immense regret, but they knew it was best for both of them and not least for Iona. Dorelia was keeping the house in the Boltons, but from now on she'd be living mainly in New York with Sean. During Iona's time in the valley, too, her Uncle Harry had died, and Iona's father had taken over Harry's estate in Scotland.

It meant Mainwarden was left empty. Her parents had considered selling it, but knowing how much the house meant to Iona and on the advice of Charles Lefanu, who said there would be considerable advantages, Mainwarden had been made over to her.

'So there it is,' Dorelia Howard finished brightly and thankfully. 'Of course, you'll still really be living with me and now Sean, of course. But you can visit Daddy in Scotland whenever you want. And you'll have a house of your own. Frankly I find Mainwarden cold and draughty, but I know how much you love it and now it's yours. All the staff have been told and they seem happy enough. I hope you're happy too. Isn't it exciting?'

Iona didn't answer. Outside the aircraft's porthole window the clouds were milky-white and veined with storm shadows. They had looked exactly the same on the morning she climbed out of the valley. Above the clouds the peaks of the Himalayas soared towards the setting sun.

'Now, then –' Mr Simpson paused at the end of the walled garden.

He and Iona had inspected the autumn vegetables. They'd toured the glasshouses and seen the late fruit – the grapes and peaches and nectarines – ripening on their branches. They'd looked at the compost heaps being prepared for the spring manuring. They'd picked bunches of white and fiery gold chrysanthemums from the houseplant cutting beds.

'Is there anything else you'd like to see, miss?'

'Yes,' she answered. 'A new gardener.'

Iona was holding the flowers in her arms. She smiled mischievously at him. Mr Simpson's face reddened and he swallowed.

'Apart from that – Iona.'

'The gorilla house,' she said.

Mr Simpson glanced at her. He opened his mouth but something in Iona's face made him close it again without speaking. Instead, parting the brambles as he walked, he led the way along the winding overgrown path until they reached the pavilion. Outside the door he fumbled in his pocket and pulled out the key.

He was about to put the key in the lock when Iona stopped him. 'Give it to me, please, Mr Simpson,' she said. 'I want to go in alone.'

'Alone?' There was a look of surprise on the gardener's face. 'Ye want to be alone with the monsters again? I'd have thought ye'd have had enough of them when ye were here before. Will ye no be afeared?'

Iona shook her head. 'I won't be frightened, I promise you,' she smiled. 'And they're not really monsters. I think they're more like friends. Wasn't that what you called them?'

Reluctantly Simpson handed her the key. 'I'll be waiting for ye outside,' he said. 'There's a few wee jobs I can be getting on with nearby until you're through.'

'No, Mr Simpson,' Iona said. 'Don't wait for me. I know you've more important things to do in the garden. I'll come back to the house and give you the key when I'm ready –'

She opened the door and paused, then took a deep breath and added, 'Tomorrow I'd like another key cut just for me. Then we'll both have keys. As I'll probably be coming here quite often, I'd also like the path mowed and cleared.'

Iona felt her heart thumping. It was the first instruction she'd given to anyone in her life. It was also, she realized, her first decision as the new mistress of Mainwarden.

For what seemed an endless time Simpson stared down at her. His face was as gnarled and cracked and hard as ancient leather, and his flint-grey Border eyes, haloed now with rings of age, were unfathomable. Suddenly and unexpectedly, he smiled.

'I can't say as I approve,' he said. 'This is no place for a lassie to be coming and going without company. But the choice is the laird's and I like a laird as knows her ain mind. I'll do what ye say, miss.'

Simpson turned. As he began to trudge away, Iona called him back. 'You called me "miss" again, Mr Simpson,' she said.

The old gardener turned back. He studied her again. 'A laird's a laird however ye wrap it,' he said. 'But for ye, I'll cut the key and mow the path. It'll be just as ye wish – Iona.'

Iona went into the pavilion.

She was about to close the door when she heard a mewing outside – she had forgotten about Misty. As Iona let the cat in, Misty coiled herself round her legs and purred. She padded forward and inspected the great silent shapes of the mounted gorillas before selecting the place she had always chosen before. The cat sprang on to the silver-backed male, climbed up its body and lay down on its shoulders. For a moment she inspected Iona through her single unwinking blue eye, then she settled down to sleep. Iona lowered herself to the floor and crossed her legs.

Her glance swept across the gorillas. They weren't monsters, they were people, and she could name them all now with her own names, private names that no one else would ever know. Her eyes rested on the small juvenile – it was a female. Whoever had skinned and stuffed her had given her bright alert eyes and an eager, forward-leaning stance. She might have been setting out into the grounds on her first gathering expedition.

Iona frowned. Then she decided. From now on the little female was to be called Tumba, as Churinga had named the infant Iona had guided and pulled from the yeti's heaving womb. She thought of the baby's first cries, of the relief on Churinga's drawn and exhausted face in the shadows of the shelter, and she whispered the name again. Tumba. Iona smiled. Afterwards she began naming the others.

Above her Misty slept as still and calm as the leopard, Babilla, on the bank above the river.

KALA

Nicholas Luard

'If you're looking for a blockbuster, try *Kala* . . . It's brimming with adventure, love and excitement'
Me Magazine

1882. The Kalahari desert, the Okovango delta, the veldt of Southern Africa.

Kala, the beautiful mute descendent of Cleopatra, carries a huge diamond, the key to a mystery as old as the African night.

Sweeping through time and across continents, the author and explorer Nicholas Luard has written a masterpiece of adventure and beauty.

'A fascinating feat of storytelling'
New York Times Review of Books

'An epic power struggle . . . fascinating'
Toronto Star

GONDAR

Nicholas Luard

'Exotic, imaginative and gorgeously readable . . . *Gondar* is an exceptionally well-told and ingeniously constructed adventure story'
Sunday Times

GONDAR – a magical kingdom perched atop a hill in Abyssinia, in the mountains they call the Mountains of the Moon. To this awesome landscape comes Jamie Oran, a young Scottish explorer – evicted from his home during the Highland Clearances – who is intent on finding the source of the Nile.

Jamie is destined to meet the exquisite Ozoro Rachel, Gondar's exiled yet rightful queen. Their love will be played out against an epic conflict in the most exotic, romantic place in the world – GONDAR.

'I defy any reader to skip a single page of *Gondar*'
Gary Jennings, author of *Aztec*